2009

Preliminary Overview of the Economies
of Latin America and the Caribbean

UNITED NATIONS

Alicia Bárcena
Executive Secretary

Antonio Prado
Deputy Executive Secretary

Osvaldo Kacef
Chief of the Economic Development Division

Susana Malchik
Officer-in-Charge
Documents and Publications Division

The *Preliminary Overview of the Economies of Latin America and the Caribbean* is an annual publication prepared by the Economic Development Division of the Economic Commission for Latin America and the Caribbean (ECLAC). This 2009 edition was prepared under the supervision of Osvaldo Kacef, Chief of the Division; Jürgen Weller was responsible for its overall coordination.

In the preparation of this edition, the Economic Development Division was assisted by the Statistics and Economic Projections Division, the ECLAC subregional headquarters in Mexico and Trinidad and Tobago and the Commission's country offices in Bogota, Brasilia, Buenos Aires, Montevideo and Washington, D.C.

The regional analyses were prepared by the following experts (in the order in which the subjects are presented): Osvaldo Kacef, who was assisted by Rafael López Monti (introduction), Juan Pablo Jiménez (fiscal policy), Rodrigo Cárcamo (exchange-rate policy), Omar Bello (monetary policy), Sandra Manuelito (economic activity and investment and domestic prices), Jürgen Weller (employment and wages), Luis Felipe Jiménez and Sarah Mueller (external sector). The tables were produced by Claudio Aravena, Andrea Podestá and Claudia Roethlisberger, together with Ricardo Zapata, Sergio Saldaña, Myriam Urzúa and Asha Kambon.

The country notes are based on studies conducted by the following experts: Dillon Alleyne (Guyana and Jamaica), Omar Bello (Plurinational State of Bolivia), Fernando Cantú (Ecuador), Rodrigo Cárcamo (Bolivarian Republic of Venezuela), Stefan Edwards (Suriname), Álvaro Fuentes (Uruguay), Randolph Gilbert (Haiti), Michael Hendrickson (Bahamas and Belize), Daniel Heymann and Adrián Ramos (Argentina), Luis Felipe Jiménez (Chile), Beverly Lugay (Eastern Caribbean Currency Union), Roberto Machado (Trinidad and Tobago), Sandra Manuelito (Peru), Jorge Mattar and Indira Romero (Mexico), Juan Carlos Moreno (Panama), Sarah Mueller (Paraguay), Carlos Mussi (Brazil), Ramón Padilla (Costa Rica and Nicaragua), Igor Paunovic (Cuba and Honduras), Willard Phillips (Barbados), Juan Carlos Ramírez, Olga Lucía Acosta and María Alejandra Botiva (Colombia), Juan Carlos Rivas (Guatemala) and Francisco Villareal (Dominican Republic and El Salvador). Claudia Roethlisberger coordinated the notes on the Caribbean countries; the economic projections were produced by Claudio Aravena, Fernando Cantú and Sandra Manuelito, and Alejandra Acevedo, Vianka Aliaga, Leandro Cabello, Jazmín Chiu, Hans Fricke, Rafael López Monti and Karen Martínez were responsible for the processing and presentation of the statistical data and graphical presentations.

Notes
In this publication, the term "country" is used to refer to territorial entities, whether these are States as understood by international law and practice or simply territories for which statistical data are maintained on a separate and independent basis.
The word "dollars" means United States dollars, unless otherwise specified.
The following symbols have been used in the tables shown in the *Preliminary Overview*: Three dots (…) indicate that data are not available or are not separately reported. A dash (-) indicates that the amount is nil or negligible. A point is used to indicate decimals.

United Nations Publication
ISBN: 978-92-1-323388-7
ISSN printed version: 1014-7810   ISSN online version: 1684-1387
LC/G.2424-P
Sales No.: E.09.II.G.149
Copyright © United Nations, December 2009. All rights reserved
Printed in Santiago, Chile

Contents

	Page
Summary	9
Regional panorama	11

Chapter I
Introduction	13
A. The international context	14
B. Recent trends in the Latin American and Caribbean economies	17
1. Channels of transmission of the crisis	18
2. The social effects of the crisis	20
C. Macroeconomic policy	21
1. Fiscal policy	22
2. Monetary and exchange-rate policy	22
D. The recovery of the economies of Latin America and the Caribbean in the second half of 2009	24
E. Prospects, risks and challenges facing the region	26
1. Anticipated developments in the economies of Latin America and the Caribbean in 2010	26
2. Risks resulting from the external scenario	28
3. Challenges beyond the short term	29

Chapter II
Economic policy	31
A. Fiscal policy	31
B. Exchange-rate policy	39
C. Monetary policy	43
1. Bank loans and deposits	47

Chapter III
Domestic performance	49
A. Economic activity and investment	49
B. Domestic prices	55
C. Employment and wages	56

Chapter IV

The external sector 61

   A. Balance-of-payments current account 61

      1. Goods and services balance 62

      2. International prices and terms of trade 65

      3. The income and transfers balance 66

   B. The capital and financial account 66

South America 71

   Argentina 73

   Bolivarian Republic of Venezuela 76

   Brazil 78

   Chile 81

   Colombia 83

   Ecuador 85

   Paraguay 87

   Peru 89

   Plurinational State of Bolivia 91

   Uruguay 93

Mexico and Central America 95

   Costa Rica 97

   El Salvador 99

   Guatemala 101

   Honduras 103

   Mexico 105

   Nicaragua 108

   Panama 110

The Caribbean 113

   Bahamas 115

   Barbados 117

   Belize 119

   Cuba 121

   Dominican Republic 123

   Guyana 125

   Haiti 127

   Jamaica 129

   Suriname 131

   Trinidad and Tobago 133

   Eastern Caribbean Currency Union 135

Statistical annex 137

ECLAC publications 163

Tables

Regional panorama

Table I.1   Annual variations in world growth 17

Table II.1   Latin America and the Caribbean: central government fiscal indicators 33

Table II.2   Latin America and the Caribbean: variation in fiscal revenues, 2008-2009 34

Table II.3   Latin America (selected countries): evolution of private bank lending 48

Table II.4   Latin America (selected countries): evolution of public bank lending 48

Table III.1   Latin America and the Caribbean (selected countries): employment, participation and
              unemployment rates, by gender and national total, first three quarters of 2009
              compared with first three quarters of 2008 58
Table IV.1   Latin America and the Caribbean: variation in exports and imports, by volume and value 64

South America

Argentina: main economic indicators 74
Bolivarian Republic of Venezuela: main economic indicators 77
Brazil: main economic indicators 79
Chile: main economic indicators 82
Colombia: main economic indicators 84
Ecuador: main economic indicators 86
Paraguay: main economic indicators 88
Peru: main economic indicators 90
Plurinational State of Bolivia: main economic indicators 92
Uruguay: main economic indicators 94

Mexico and Central America

Costa Rica: main economic indicators 98
El Salvador: main economic indicators 100
Guatemala: main economic indicators 102
Honduras: main economic indicators 104
Mexico: main economic indicators 106
Nicaragua: main economic indicators 109
Panama: main economic indicators 111

The Caribbean

Bahamas: main economic indicators 116
Barbados: main economic indicators 118
Belize: main economic indicators 120
Cuba: main economic indicators 122
Dominican Republic: main economic indicators 124
Guyana: main economic indicators 126
Haiti: main economic indicators 128
Jamaica: main economic indicators 130
Suriname: main economic indicators 132
Trinidad and Tobago: main economic indicators 134
Eastern Caribbean Currency Union: main economic indicators 136

Statistical annex

Table A-1   Latin America and the Caribbean: main economic indicators 139
Table A-2   Latin America and the Caribbean: gross domestic product 140
Table A-3   Latin America and the Caribbean: per capita gross domestic product 141
Table A-4   Latin America and the Caribbean: gross fixed capital formation 142
Table A-5a   Latin America and the Caribbean: financing of gross domestic investment 142
Table A-5b   Latin America and the Caribbean: gross domestic investment, national income and saving 142
Table A-6   Latin America and the Caribbean: balance of payments 143
Table A-7a   Latin America and the Caribbean: exports of goods, f.o.b. 146
Table A-7b   Latin America and the Caribbean: imports of goods, f.o.b. 146
Table A-8   Latin America and the Caribbean: terms of trade for goods f.o.b./f.o.b. 147
Table A-9   Latin America and the Caribbean: net resource transfer 148
Table A-10   Latin America and the Caribbean: net foreign direct investment 149
Table A-11   Latin America and the Caribbean: total gross external debt 150
Table A-12   Latin America and the Caribbean: gross international reserves 151
Table A-13   Latin America and the Caribbean: stock exchange indices 152

Table A-14   Latin America and the Caribbean: overall real effective exchange rates 152
Table A-15   Latin America and the Caribbean: participation rate 153
Table A-16   Latin America and the Caribbean: open urban unemployment 154
Table A-17   Latin America and the Caribbean: employment rate 155
Table A-18   Latin America and the Caribbean: trends in real average wages 156
Table A-19   Latin America and the Caribbean: monetary indicators 157
Table A-20   Latin America and the Caribbean: representative lending rates... 158
Table A-21   Latin America and the Caribbean: consumer prices 159
Table A-22   Latin America and the Caribbean: central government balance 160
Table A-23   Latin America and the Caribbean: revenue and expenditures of the central government 161
Table A-24   Latin America and the Caribbean: public debt 162

Figures

Regional panorama

Figure I.1   Latin America and the Caribbean: growth rates, 2009..   13
Figure I.2   Seasonally adjusted index of industrial output, by region   15
Figure I.3   Variation in trade volume (average volume of imports plus exports), by region   15
Figure I.4   Growth in GDP and the components of demand..   16
Figure I.5   Latin America and the Caribbean: variation in per capita GDP, current account
               balance and overall balance...   17
Figure I.6   Variation in goods exports, f.o.b., by volume and value, 2009   18
Figure I.7   Latin America and the Caribbean: year-on-year variation in international
               tourist arrivals, 2009...   18
Figure I.8   Latin America and the Caribbean: year-on-year variation in remittances
               from migrant workers, seasonally adjusted..   19
Figure I.9   Brazil, Chile and Peru: private bank lending   19
Figure I.10   Latin America (selected countries): bank lending to the private sector, 2008   19
Figure I.11   Latin America and the Caribbean: breakdown of total supply and demand   20
Figure I.12   Latin America: variation in nominal wages, inflation and real wages   20
Figure I.13   Latin America: revenue, primary spending and primary balance   22
Figure I.14   Latin America (selected countries): variation in public expenditure, nine months
               of 2008 compared with nine months of 2009...   22
Figure I.15   Latin America (selected countries): variation in public and private bank lending
               between December 2008 and September 2009   24
Figure I.16   Latin America (selected countries): leading indicators   24
Figure I.17   Latin America: terms of trade   25
Figure I.18   Employment status of Latin American citizens in the United States and Spain   25
Figure I.19   Latin America (selected countries): seasonally adjusted monthly unemployment rates...............   26
Figure I.20   Stock market indicators: Dow Jones and emerging markets..   26
Figure I.21   Latin America and the Caribbean: growth rates, 2010..   27
Figure I.22   Interbank interest rates   28
Figure I.23   Bank lending to the private sector...   29
Figure II.1   Latin America: variation in fiscal revenues and expenditures, 2008-2009   32
Figure II.2   Latin America and the Caribbean: central government revenues, 1990-2009   32
Figure II.3   Latin America (6 countries): real tax receipts of central government, not
               including social security...   36
Figure II.4   Latin America (4 countries): evolution of government transfers in real terms   37
Figure II.5   Latin America and the Caribbean: central government expenditures, 1990-2009.......................   37
Figure II.6   Latin America and the Caribbean (18 countries): growth in public debt of the central
               government, 1991-2009..   38
Figure II.7   Extraregional real effective exchange rate   39
Figure II.8   Latin America (selected countries): nominal exchange rates in relation to the dollar   40
Figure II.9   Latin America (selected countries): exchange-rate intervention...   40
Figure II.10   Latin America and the Caribbean (selected countries): total real effective exchange rates..........   43

Figure II.11   Latin America (selected countries): effective, core and target range inflation 44

Figure II.12   Latin America and the Caribbean (selected countries): interbank rate 45

Figure II.13   Latin America and the Caribbean (selected countries): nominal monetary policy
                 benchmark rate of interest 46

Figure II.14   Latin America and the Caribbean (selected countries): real monetary policy
                 benchmark rate of interest 47

Figure III.1   Latin America and the Caribbean: change in gross domestic product, 2008-2009 50

Figure III.2   Latin America and the Caribbean: per capita gross domestic product, 2004-2009 50

Figure III.3   Latin America and the Caribbean: per capita gross domestic product,
                 by country, 2004 and 2009 50

Figure III.4   Latin America: annual change in gross domestic product and in components of
                 aggregate demand, 1991-2009 51

Figure III.5   Latin America: year-on-year variation in quarterly gross domestic product, 1998-2009 51

Figure III.6   Latin America: gross fixed capital formation, 2009 53

Figure III.7   Latin America: gross fixed capital formation in construction and in machinery
                 and equipment, 1990-2009 54

Figure III.8   Latin America: financing of investment, 1990-2009 54

Figure III.9   Latin America: annual change in gross domestic investment, gross disposable
                 national income and domestic savings 54

Figure III.10   Latin America: twelve-month changes in industrial production index, January 1995
                 to September 2009 54

Figure III.11   Latin America and the Caribbean: cumulative twelve-month inflation rates,
                 2008 and 2009 55

Figure III.12   Latin America and the Caribbean: twelve-month inflation rate 56

Figure III.13   Latin America: contribution to cumulative twelve-month inflation rates 56

Figure III.14   Latin America: consumer price index and core inflation index, twelve-month variation 56

Figure III.15   Latin America (7 countries): year-on-year change in formal employment 57

Figure IV.1   Latin America and the Caribbean: structure of the current account, 2003-2009 62

Figure IV.2   Latin America (19 countries): current account, 2008-2009 62

Figure IV.3   The English-speaking Caribbean and Suriname (13 countries): current acount, 2008-2009 62

Figure IV.4   Year-on-year variation in imports from Latin America and the Caribbean, by destination 63

Figure IV.5   Latin America and the Caribbean (19 countries): variation in exports and imports, by
                 volume and unit price, 2009 63

Figure IV.6   Latin America and the Caribbean (27 countries): year-on-year variation in international
                 tourist arrivals, first semester 2009 64

Figure IV.7   Latin America and the Caribbean: price indices of commodities and manufactured goods 65

Figure IV.8   Latin America (19 countries): estimated variation in terms of trade, 2008-2010 65

Figure IV.9   Latin America and the Caribbean (8 countries): year-on-year variation in remittances
                 from emigrants 66

Figure IV.10   Latin America and the Caribbean: Emerging Market Bond Index Global (EMBIG) and
                 EMBIG Latin America 67

Figure IV.11   Latin America (selected countries): changes in the EMBIG of countries with relatively
                 low and intermediate risk 67

Figure IV.12   Latin America and the Caribbean (selected countries): EMBIG of countries with
                 higher risk ratings 68

Figure IV.13   Latin America and the Caribbean: EMBIG and external bond issues 68

Figure IV.14   Latin America: structure of the balance-of-payments financial account 69

Figure IV.15   Latin America and the Caribbean: variation in gross international reserves, 2008-2009 69

South America

Argentina: GDP, inflation and unemployment 73

Bolivarian Republic of Venezuela: GDP, inflation and unemployment 76

Brazil: GDP, inflation and unemployment 78

Chile: GDP, inflation and unemployment 81

Colombia: GDP, inflation and unemployment 83

Ecuador: GDP, inflation and unemployment 85
Paraguay: GDP and inflation 87
Peru: GDP, inflation and unemployment 89
Plurinational State of Bolivia: GDP and inflation 91
Uruguay: GDP, inflation and unemployment 93

Mexico and Central America

Costa Rica: GDP and inflation 97
El Salvador: growth and inflation 99
Guatemala: Monthly Index of Economic Activity (MIEA) and inflation 101
Mexico: GDP, inflation and unemployment 105
Nicaragua: GDP and inflation 108
Panama: GDP and inflation 110

The Caribbean

Dominican Republic: GDP and inflation 129
Jamaica: GDP, inflation and unemployment 129
Trinidad and Tobago: GDP, inflation and unemployment 133

Boxes

Box I.1   Social measures in Latin America and the Caribbean   21
Box I.2   Monetary policy objectives in Latin America   23
Box I.3   Estimating potential GDP   27
Box II.1   Fiscal policy responses to the international crisis   34
Box II.2   Sustainability of public debt in the English-speaking Caribbean   38
Box II.3   Latin America: measures adopted to moderate capital inflows   41
Box II.4   Monetary policy measures taken in the region in response to the international financial crisis   45
Box III.1   Main consequences of the disasters in Latin America and the Caribbean   52
Box III.2   Job creation measures in the crisis environment   59

Summary

After six years of uninterrupted growth, the GDP of Latin America and the Caribbean is expected to fall by 1.8% and per capita GDP by close to 2.9% in 2009. The international crisis hit the region hard at the end of 2008 and in early 2009, taking a toll on all of its countries. However, a recovery began to take shape in the second quarter and became more widespread in the second half of the year.

The break in economic growth cut into labour demand, and the unemployment rate is therefore expected to rise to about 8.3% for the region overall, and new jobs created will be of poorer quality.

The effects of the crisis were channelled through the real sector of the economies, damaging what had been the main engines of regional growth. Exports plunged, while the contraction of economic activity worldwide, together with the drop in international trade flows, lowered commodity prices, which hurt the region's terms of trade. At the same time, income from remittances and tourism fell, with Mexico and countries of Central America and the Caribbean suffering the most, and foreign direct investment plummeted by 37%.

Domestic activity also declined in some countries as a result of the tighter credit conditions in the private banking sector which stepped-up public sector lending failed to offset.

This convergence of factors, combined with deteriorating expectations, triggered a slump in private consumption and investment. In fact, public sector consumption was the only component of demand that grew during the first semester, thanks to the countercyclical policies implemented by many of the countries in the region, which accelerated the recovery in the second half of the year.

The positive stimulus of fiscal policy action was one of the distinctive features of economic management in 2009. The region's primary balance fell from a surplus equivalent to 1.4% of GDP in 2008 to an estimated primary deficit of 1% of GDP in 2009. Fiscal revenues have been substantially curtailed, owing to lower levels of activity and falling commodity prices. Also, up to the third quarter of 2009, current expenditures increased significantly, as did capital expenditures, though to a lesser extent.

The region's central banks lowered monetary policy rates and adopted measures aimed at ensuring liquidity in financial markets. In many cases, public-sector banks played a strategic countercyclical role by offsetting the tight credit stance of private banks. In order to defend the real level of the exchange rate to some extent and to sustain domestic liquidity, many central banks intervened in the exchange market, which in some cases enabled them to replenish international reserves.

During the second half of the year, positive signs began to emerge in the economies of the region. Manufacturing and exports picked up, while renewed global activity and expanding international trade volumes spurred demand for commodities, raising prices and improving terms of trade.

The fiscal stimulus packages introduced to boost domestic demand, together with the factors mentioned above and the gradual return to normalcy in the financial markets, often with help from central banks, created the conditions for the resumption of economic activity and the improvement of labour-market indicators. In addition, renewed access to international credit for some countries and the recovery of the stock markets furthered the process. This allowed the private sector to restructure its assets and helped normalize lending which, together with improved labour market indicators and recovery of private-sector confidence, should boost domestic demand.

Growth is projected at 4.1% for 2010 and is expected to be somewhat higher in the countries of South America than in the rest of the region, given their larger domestic markets in some cases, greater export-market diversification and closer trade ties with China. On the other hand, growth is expected to be slower in some of the more open economies that have a less diversified portfolio of trading partners and a heavier dependence on manufacturing. The same can be said of the Caribbean economies, some of which are facing complex financial and exchange-rate situations.

However, it remains to be seen whether or not the developed economies will be able to sustain growth once the copious stimulus packages implemented by the United States and Europe are withdrawn. This, together with increasing unemployment and the still-volatile international financial market, raises questions about the strength of the recovery that began in 2009.

The emergence from this crisis has been quicker than was expected, largely thanks to the ramparts that the countries of the region had built through sounder macroeconomic policy management. Upturns in several of the factors that drove demand in the years prior to the crisis, added in many cases to strong impetus from public policies, should enable a rapid recovery in the context of substantial idle capacity. But how can that recovery be transformed into a process of sustained growth beyond 2010?

In the short term, the countries of the region responded to the crisis to the best of their capacities —in the process revealing major differences among them. But the objective of regaining sustained growth poses fresh and more complex challenges. Accordingly, the Latin American and Caribbean countries now face the fundamental task of generating and expanding policy space. To do this, they must increase resources, create instruments and strengthen institutions, particularly those involved in coordination.

Regional panorama

Chapter I

Introduction

After six years of economic growth, the GDP of the Latin American and Caribbean region will shrink by an estimated 1.8% in 2009, which translates into a contraction of around 2.9% in per capita GDP. The impact of the international crisis was felt heavily in late 2008 and early 2009, albeit in different ways, in all the countries of the region. A recovery began to take shape in the second quarter, however, and became more widespread in the second half of the year. The heaviest contractions in economic activity occurred in Mexico and some of the Central American and Caribbean countries. Generally speaking, positive growth rates are projected for South America although, in all cases, they fall far short of the rates posted between 2004 and 2008.

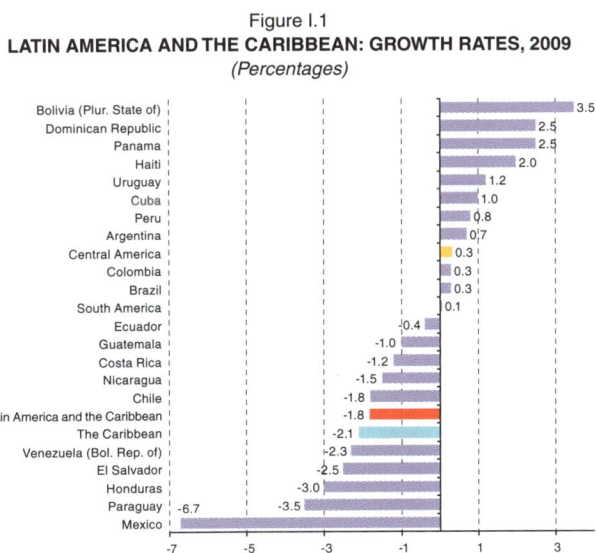

Figure I.1
LATIN AMERICA AND THE CARIBBEAN: GROWTH RATES, 2009
(Percentages)

Country	Rate
Bolivia (Plur. State of)	3.5
Dominican Republic	2.5
Panama	2.5
Haiti	2.0
Uruguay	1.2
Cuba	1.0
Peru	0.8
Argentina	0.7
Central America	0.3
Colombia	0.3
Brazil	0.3
South America	0.1
Ecuador	-0.4
Guatemala	-1.0
Costa Rica	-1.2
Nicaragua	-1.5
Chile	-1.8
Latin America and the Caribbean	-1.8
The Caribbean	-2.1
Venezuela (Bol. Rep. of)	-2.3
El Salvador	-2.5
Honduras	-3.0
Paraguay	-3.5
Mexico	-6.7

Source: Economic Commission for Latin America and the Caribbean (ECLAC), on the basis of official figures.

The economic slowdown, predictably, cut into labour demand and the unemployment rate is expected to rise to around 8.3% for the region overall and new jobs created are likely to be of poorer quality. The inflation rate dropped sharply from 8.3% in 2008 to around 4.5% in 2009, as a result of falling international prices for some of the commodities included in household consumption baskets, in addition to the effect of currency appreciation and the impact of slacker activity levels on demand.

The emergence of some positive signals in the second half of 2009 has supported a gradual shift in economic prospects and lent weight to the hypothesis that the worst of the crisis may be over, even though financial markets continue to exhibit some volatility and the situation of the global economy is not risk-free.[1] Beyond the short term,

---

[1] For example, the events that occurred in the real-estate and financial markets of Dubai (United Arab Emirates) in late 2009 and their immediate repercussions on other markets, given the high levels of exposure of a number of European banks.

however, a number of questions arise as to whether this rapid recovery will develop into sustained growth at the world level and in Latin America and the Caribbean.

Given the magnitude of the crisis, it reached every part of the world and the Latin American and Caribbean region was no exception. Yet it is increasingly evident that this crisis differs from those the region has experienced in the past. Not only because the epicentre of the crisis lay in the developed countries, although this plays no small part in accounting for recent economic trends, but, above all, because of the juncture at which the crisis broke out in the region and how the region was affected.

First, the combination of highly favourable external conditions and more prudent management of macroeconomic policy has enabled the region to reduce its outstanding debt and to renegotiate it on advantageous terms, while also building up international reserves. The Latin American economies thus went into the crisis with unprecedented liquidity and solvency, at least by comparison with their position during previous episodes since the 1980s, because, unlike on those occasions, the countries' financial systems have not deteriorated and there has been no flight from local currency, which has helped to maintain calm in the region's currency markets.[2] As discussed in detail in *Economic Survey of Latin America and the Caribbean 2008-2009* (ECLAC, 2009a), a number of Caribbean countries are carrying hefty external debts and facing rather more complex exchange-rate situations.[3]

Also unlike the situation during previous crises, the broadened macroeconomic policy space in many of the region's countries gave them substantial capacity for anti-crisis policymaking. In general, as will be discussed later, the public policy space is greater in some South American countries. The improved net financial position also afforded renewed access to international financial markets fairly promptly, which further boosted capacity to implement public policies. As a result, even though the downturn in real variables was very sharp, the recovery looks fairly solid.

Although poverty levels in the region remained high, despite the gains made in recent years, and the impact of the crisis on social variables was predictably negative, the deterioration was not as great as had initially been projected, owing to a number of factors. On the one hand, the drop in activity levels and its impact on the labour market were both smaller than expected, so the unemployment rate did not rise as much as the initial contraction led analysts to fear it would. On the other, international commodity prices, combined with currency appreciation, helped to significantly lower the rate of inflation and limit the erosion of real income, thereby at least partially offsetting the downturn in labour indicators.

The rise in social spending in the last few years and the increase in the number and effectiveness of social programmes played an important role in containing the social costs of the crisis. Learning the lessons from previous crises, the countries have sought to maintain —and even expand— the coverage of these programmes, even in the context of a gradually tightening fiscal space.

This chapter looks at the hallmarks of the current situation and considers the scenarios the region will face in 2010 and beyond. Section B below briefly examines the current international conditions. Section C reviews the main features of recent economic performance and examines the channels through which the crisis affected the economies of the region and its impacts on labour and social indicators. Section D analyses the macroeconomic policies implemented as the crisis deepened in late 2008 and section E lays out the evidence available on the signs of recovery in the region's economies, especially as of the second half of 2009. The last section discusses the short-term outlook and the risks that could threaten the fledging recovery and the main challenges for Latin America and the Caribbean beyond the crisis.

A. The international context

The global economy is recovering from the deepest recession the world has seen in the last 60 years. The international financial crisis, which originated in the United States and other developed countries, spread rapidly to the rest of the world's economies, and its effects were soon being felt in the real sector. From mid-2008 to the first quarter of 2009, industrial activity worldwide fell by 11.6% and in the developed countries by 16.4%. International trade volumes meanwhile shrank by 19%. Given that the impact of the crisis was still strong in the first semester of 2009, world GDP is projected to fall by 2.2% over the year.

---

[2]   There were some stress in the region's foreign-exchange markets in the last quarter of 2008 which resulted in heavy currency depreciations in some countries. This episode was quickly neutralized, however, and had no major repercussions.

[3]   See box I.2 in *Economic Survey of Latin America and the Caribbean 2008-2009* (ECLAC, 2009a).

Nevertheless economic activity and international trade started to show some signs of recovery in the middle of the year. The rapid recuperation from the worst moment of the crisis was largely the result of the expansionary monetary policy response coordinated by the world's main central banks, which was subsequently replicated by monetary authorities in the developing world. Copious amounts of liquidity were injected into the markets, and these, together with the fiscal stimulus packages that governments implemented, have been driving the incipient recovery now under way. Also, the relatively strong performance of the developing Asian economies, especially China, prevented an even greater slump in global demand. Initial fears of a long drawn-out depression thus dissipated, and the first signs of a synchronized emergence from the recession began to appear in the second quarter of 2009.

Manufacturing activity has been picking up in general in the different regions of the world since the middle of the year (see figure I.2). In this regard, the industrial output of the developing Asian economies not only contracted less than that of other regions, it was also the first to pick up again at the beginning of 2009.

Figure I.2
SEASONALLY ADJUSTED INDEX OF INDUSTRIAL OUTPUT, BY REGION [a]
(Percentages)

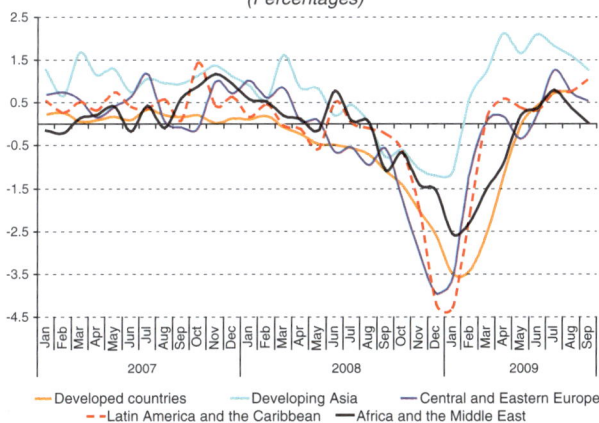

— Developed countries — Developing Asia — Central and Eastern Europe
- - Latin America and the Caribbean — Africa and the Middle East

Source: Economic Commission for Latin America and the Caribbean (ECLAC), on the basis of data from Centraal Planbureau (CPB), Netherlands Bureau for Economic Policy Analysis.
[a] Three-month moving averages compared with the previous quarter.

The volume of international trade began to grow again towards the second half of the year (see figure I.3), largely driven by activity in the developing Asian economies. Their openness to foreign trade and their external orientation meant that most of them were hit hard by the decline in world trade, but, as is analysed below, this did not have a significant impact on economic activity levels thanks to the expansionary policies implemented by the authorities in those countries.

The world's larger economies began to show signs of recovery as of the second half of 2009. In the United States, seasonally adjusted and annualized GDP grew by

2.8% in the third quarter of the year compared with the previous quarter, after falling for four consecutive quarters since mid-2008 and dropping by 5.4% and 6.4% in the last quarter of 2008 and the first quarter of 2009, respectively. All the components of demand posted positive growth in the third quarter of 2009, with the rise in imports and exports heralding the recovery of world trade. At the same time, household consumption, a key indicator in the United States economy (see figure I.4a), began to climb again thanks to growing consumer confidence and increased spending on durables, such as cars and household appliances.

Figure I.3
VARIATION IN TRADE VOLUME (AVERAGE VOLUME OF IMPORTS PLUS EXPORTS), BY REGION [a]
(Percentages)

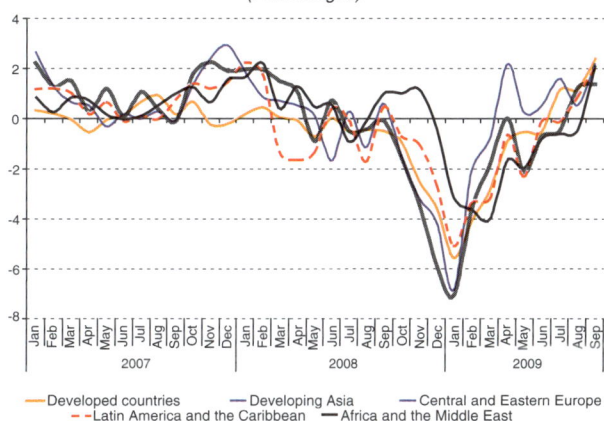

— Developed countries — Developing Asia — Central and Eastern Europe
- - Latin America and the Caribbean — Africa and the Middle East

Source: Economic Commission for Latin America and the Caribbean (ECLAC), on the basis of data from Centraal Planbureau (CPB), Netherlands Bureau for Economic Policy Analysis.
[a] Three-month moving averages compared with the previous quarter.

It should be noted that public-sector consumption is the only component of demand that continued to grow in three of the four quarters of the United States recession, a clear reflection of the fiscal effort put into counteracting the effects of the crisis. The United States economy is projected to grow at the same rate in the fourth quarter as it did in the third, closing 2009 with a downslide of 2.5%. Inventory shedding is down and its negative influence waning. The need to replenish stocks is expected to help push GDP growth in the United States up to around 2.0% in 2010. However, rising unemployment, which has already hit double-digit levels (10.2%), and the difficulties still affecting the financial markets at a time when both the public- and private-sectors are heavily burdened with debt, are warning signs of the possible future course of the United States economy.

The economies of the euro 16 area also began to recover in the third quarter of 2009, after five quarters of negative growth, thanks to the significant countercyclical role played by public consumption (see figure I.4b). After shrinking by 4.0% in 2009, aggregate GDP for the area is expected to recover slowly and gradually, growing by less than 1% in 2010.

Figure I.4
GROWTH IN GDP AND THE COMPONENTS OF DEMAND [a]
(Percentages)

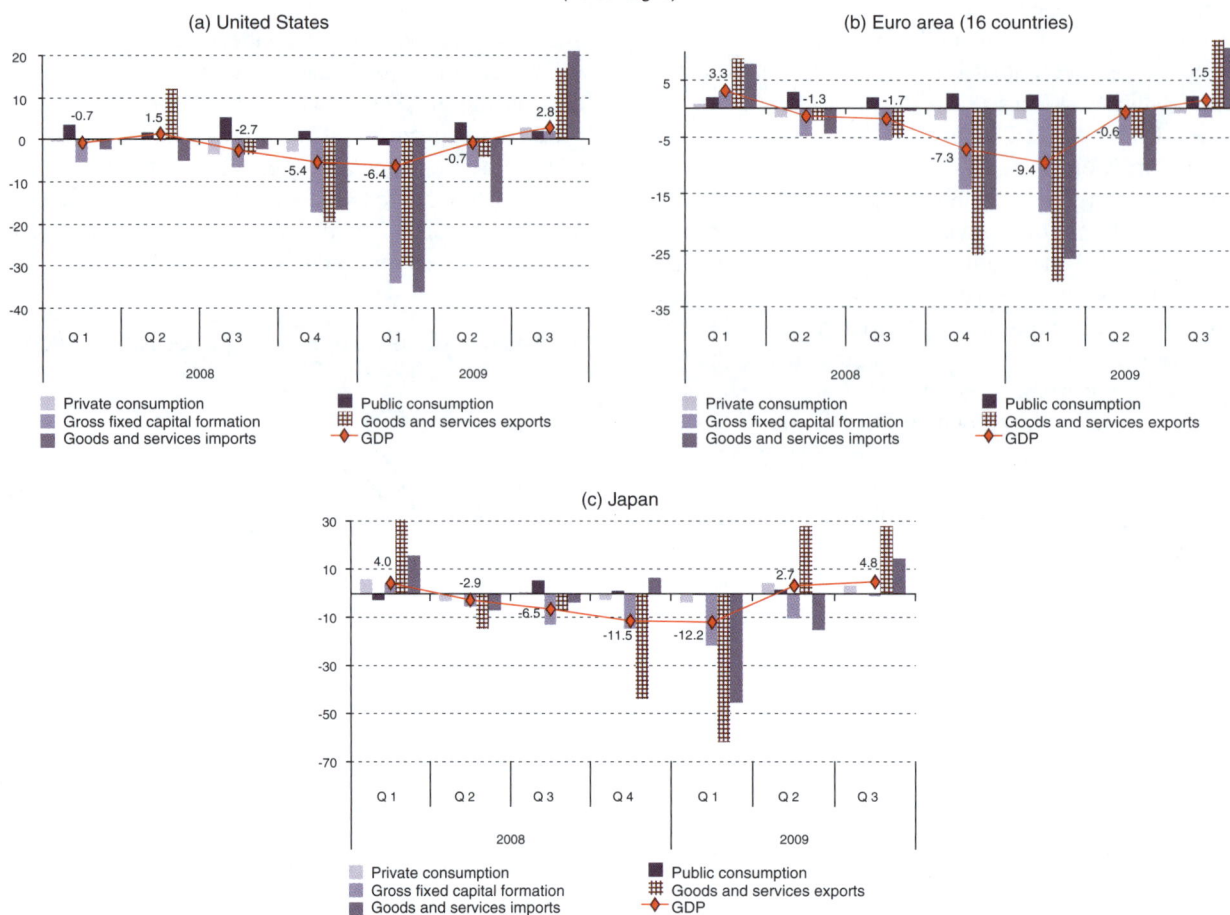

(a) United States

(b) Euro area (16 countries)

(c) Japan

Private consumption
Gross fixed capital formation
Goods and services imports

Public consumption
Goods and services exports
GDP

Source: Economic Commission for Latin America and the Caribbean (ECLAC), on the basis of official figures.
[a] Seasonally adjusted figures. Annualized variation from the previous quarter.

The Japanese economy came out of recession in the second quarter of 2009 after two quarters of drops of over 10% in annualized GDP in relation to the previous quarter (see figure I.4c). After this sharp contraction, the economy grew again at an annualized rate of 2.7% in the second quarter of the year (compared with the previous quarter) and by an even more robust 4.8% in the third quarter. This recovery was driven by strong export growth and the fiscal stimulus package implemented by the Japanese authorities, as well as by the rise in transfers to the private sector which encouraged household consumption, albeit at the cost of further debilitating an already weak fiscal position. Despite the recovery recorded in the second semester, the heavy contraction of the economy at the beginning of 2009 (-12.2% annualized in relation to the previous quarter) means that GDP growth for 2009 overall is expected to be -5.9%. GDP growth for 2010 is projected at 1.1%.

As noted earlier, the developing Asian economies were the first to reverse the negative effects of the crisis, and some countries, such as China, India and Indonesia, suffered slowdowns but never actually went into recession. This superior performance was largely achieved through the use of major fiscal and monetary stimuli.

The Chinese economy was back on its path of robust growth towards the second quarter of 2009 thanks to the expansionary policies deployed on both the fiscal and monetary fronts. The government took advantage of the enormous fiscal space it had built up (after years of surpluses in public accounts and thanks to its position as the net creditor of the rest of the world) to launch an ambitious public programme that included an increase in infrastructure spending, tax cuts and the introduction of a new social security system. Also, unlike in other financial markets, lending in China soared, especially credit financing for infrastructure projects. These two factors fuelled domestic demand and contributed to a recovery in imports, which in turn stimulated regional and global trade.

Table I.1
ANNUAL VARIATIONS IN WORLD GROWTH
(Percentages)

	2003	2004	2005	2006	2007	2008	2009 [a]	2010 [b]
World	2.7	4.1	3.5	3.9	3.8	1.7	-2.2	2.5
Developed countries	1.8	3.0	2.5	2.7	2.5	0.4	-3.6	1.4
United States	2.5	3.6	3.1	2.7	2.1	0.4	-2.5	2.0
Euro area (16 countries)	0.8	2.1	1.7	3.0	2.7	0.6	-4.0	0.7
Rest of Europe (11+3)	2.4	3.5	2.7	3.6	3.1	1.1	-4.1	0.7
Japan	1.4	2.7	1.9	2.0	2.3	-0.7	-5.9	1.1
Developing countries	5.2	7.4	6.6	7.3	7.5	5.2	1.6	5.3
Africa	5.5	9.2	5.5	6.2	6.1	6.0	1.9	4.3
Latin America and the Caribbean	2.2	6.1	5.0	5.8	5.8	4.1	-1.8	4.1
China	10.0	10.1	10.4	11.6	13.0	9.0	8.4	8.7
India	6.9	7.9	9.2	9.8	9.3	7.3	5.9	6.5
Recently industrialized countries	3.1	6.0	4.8	5.6	5.7	1.5	-2.4	3.6
Rest of Asia	6.1	6.8	6.3	5.9	5.8	4.4	-0.1	3.8
Transition economies	7.5	8.0	6.7	8.3	8.7	5.7	-5.9	1.9
Developing countries (excluding China and India)	3.9	6.6	5.4	5.9	5.8	3.9	-0.9	4.0

Source: Economic Commission for Latin America and the Caribbean (ECLAC), on the basis of official figures.
[a] Estimates.
[b] Projections.

B. Recent trends in the Latin American and Caribbean economies

As noted in the introduction, in order to understand why the impact of this crisis on Latin America and the Caribbean was different from that of previous ones, it is important to understand the situation in which the region found itself when the crisis struck. First of all, the global economic crisis brought to a sudden end the longest and most intense phase of economic growth that the region had seen in a very long while. A similar period of steady per capita GDP growth of over 3% per year (as recorded in 2004-2008) had not been seen for 40 years, since the boom that lasted from the end of the 1960s to the oil shock at the beginning of the 1970s, during which the region posted comparable growth rates for seven consecutive years.

As shown in figure I.5, steady growth was accompanied by quantitative and qualitative improvements in macroeconomic fundamentals, making 2004-2008 a period of expansion unprecedented in the region's recent history. On the one hand, the region enjoyed a current account surplus (largely generated by improvement in the terms of trade, especially in South America) as well as increasing remittance flows from migrant workers (mainly in Mexico and, above all, Central America). Meanwhile in public accounts, ever-larger primary surpluses were being posted, and the region's overall deficit was drastically reduced (even turning into a surplus in 2006/2007).

Figure I.5
LATIN AMERICA AND THE CARIBBEAN: VARIATION IN PER CAPITA GDP, CURRENT ACCOUNT BALANCE AND OVERALL BALANCE
(Percentages of GDP)

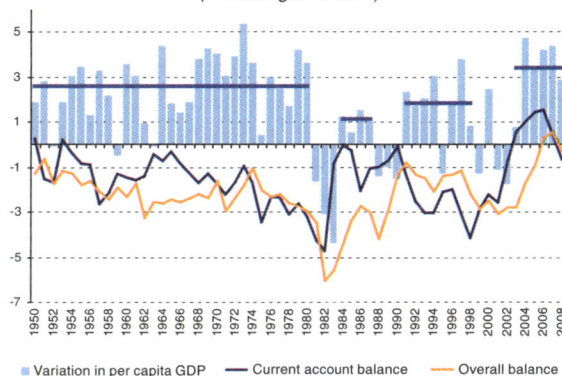

■ Variation in per capita GDP ── Current account balance ── Overall balance

Source: Economic Commission for Latin America and the Caribbean (ECLAC), on the basis of official figures.

At a time of abundant liquidity in international financial markets, the current account surplus allowed countries to reduce their external debt burdens and to renegotiate more advantageous terms, as well as to accumulate reserves.[4] Greater fiscal slack, meanwhile, made it possible to slash public debt.

---

[4] As noted earlier, the situation is rather different in some Caribbean economies.

Therefore, although the crisis imposed heavy constraints on macroeconomic policy as it plunged the economies back into deficit positions on their external and public accounts, their favourable situation in terms of financial stocks (more assets, fewer and better liabilities) meant that, unlike in previous crises, in 2009, they did not have to contend with

problems in the domestic financial systems, runs against domestic currencies or difficulties meeting their external obligations. This explains why this time around, with a few exceptions which will be discussed later, the strongest effects of the crisis were channelled not through the financial sector but through the real economy.

1.   Channels of transmission of the crisis

As noted above, the repercussions of the crisis on Latin America and the Caribbean were channelled through the real sector, damaging what had been in recent times one of the main engines of regional growth.

Exports plummeted as of the second semester of 2008, both in volume and value terms. Even though the fall has slowed in the second half of 2009, Latin American export volumes are projected to fall by slightly over 9.5% by the end of the year. Mexico's exports have suffered the most, and will slide by about 14% in real terms. Drops of about 5% and 6.5% in export volumes are estimated for Central America and South America, respectively.

The slowdown in economic activity worldwide, together with the drop in international trade flows, had a negative impact on commodity prices, which hurt the region's terms of trade. Prices had soared in the first half of 2008, but the crisis hit the international goods markets hard, especially after the collapse of Lehman Brothers in September that year. Although the downtrend in international commodity prices bottomed out at the beginning of 2009, average price levels for the year are far lower than in 2008, which suggests that the terms of trade for the region as a whole worsened by an estimated 6.1%. This has implications mainly for South America, and for the oil and hydrocarbon and metal producers in particular, as well as, albeit to a lesser extent, for countries that specialize in food production. The terms of trade of Central America, which imports those commodities, on the other hand, can be expected to improve. This will only partially offset the worsening of the terms experienced in previous years, however.

Tourism, which is of major importance to the economies of the Caribbean and Central America, declined sharply in the first part of 2009 as shown in figure I.7. The contraction was particularly notable in Mexico in the second quarter of the year due to the outbreak of influenza A (H1N1). Overall, tourism is expected to fall by 5%-10% in 2009, even though the latest available data reveal a slight upturn.

Figure I.6
VARIATION IN GOODS EXPORTS, F.O.B., BY VOLUME AND VALUE, 2009
(Percentages)

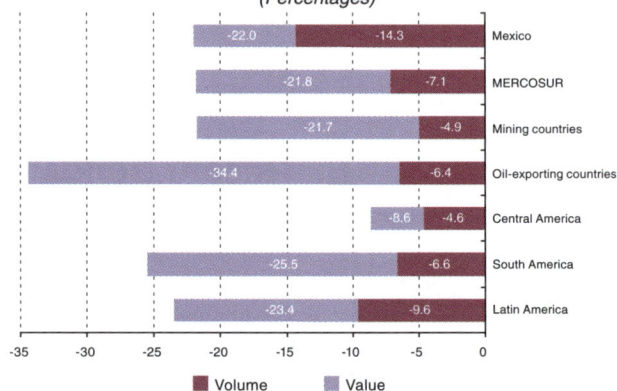

Source: Economic Commission for Latin America and the Caribbean (ECLAC), on the basis of official figures.

Figure I.7
LATIN AMERICA AND THE CARIBBEAN: YEAR-ON-YEAR VARIATION IN INTERNATIONAL TOURIST ARRIVALS, 2009
(Percentages)

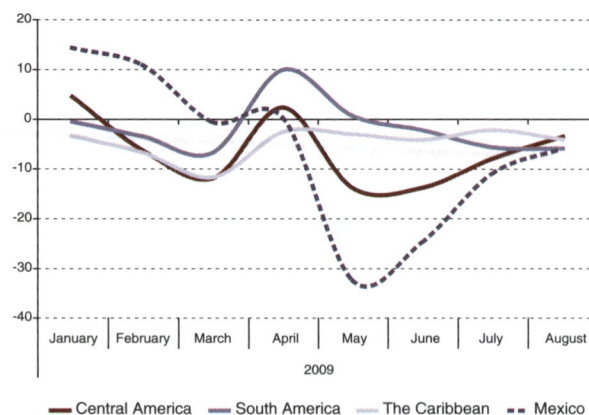

Source: Economic Commission for Latin America and the Caribbean (ECLAC), on the basis of the World Tourism Organization (UNWTO).

Given that the main destinations of most Latin American and Caribbean emigrants are the United States and Spain, two of the countries worst hit by the crisis, it is not surprising that remittances to the region have plummeted. The latest available data suggest that this trend might be being reversed, but even then, annual falls of close to 10% in remittances have been recorded in some Central American countries, such as El Salvador and Guatemala, and even larger drops in countries such as Colombia, Ecuador, Jamaica and Mexico. Smaller declines have been estimated for the Dominican Republic and Nicaragua.

Meanwhile, foreign direct investment (FDI) in the region as a whole is expected to fall by 37%, by far the largest drop for at least 30 years. Between 1999 and 2003, FDI flows fell by about 47%, but then the drop was concentrated in only two countries (Argentina and Brazil), while this time around, the downturn is spread across the region, although diminished flows to Brazil account for a significant proportion of the total decline.

Although, generally speaking, the impacts of the international crisis were felt mainly through the channel of the real economy, in some cases there were impacts on financial systems that may have had significant repercussions on activity levels. Although the turbulences in the region were mostly related to trade rather than reversals of capital inflows, there were three major exceptions: Brazil, Chile and Peru, whose financial systems were more exposed than those of the rest of the region in late 2008.[5]

As shown in figure I.9, the manifestation of this situation in these countries' financial systems was a major contraction in private bank credit in real terms. The public banks then played an active role in many countries as part of countercyclical strategy although, with the exception of Brazil (where public banks account for a large proportion of total credit), the capacity to offset the contraction in private bank credit was fairly small.

This factor been crucial in explaining the relative weakness of the Chilean economy between late 2008 and the third quarter of 2009, despite its sound macroeconomic fundamentals and the active intervention of the State through countercyclical policies. The evidence shown in figure I.10 regarding the magnitude of credit to the private sector as a proportion of GDP speaks for itself as regards the impact on activity levels of shrinking private bank lending in the Chilean economy, compared with the Brazilian and Peruvian economies and, in general, the rest of the region.

---

[5] See ECLAC (2009a), in which box I.1 gives an analysis of the consequences of the shocks experienced by the region after the crisis deepened in late 2008. Figure I.4 of that publication shows the net external position of the financial systems of the Latin American countries and discusses certain aggregates in developed countries and emerging economies. These data are based on information from the Bank for International Settlements.

Figure I.8
LATIN AMERICA AND THE CARIBBEAN: YEAR-ON-YEAR VARIATION IN REMITTANCES FROM MIGRANT WORKERS, SEASONALLY ADJUSTED [a]
(Percentages)

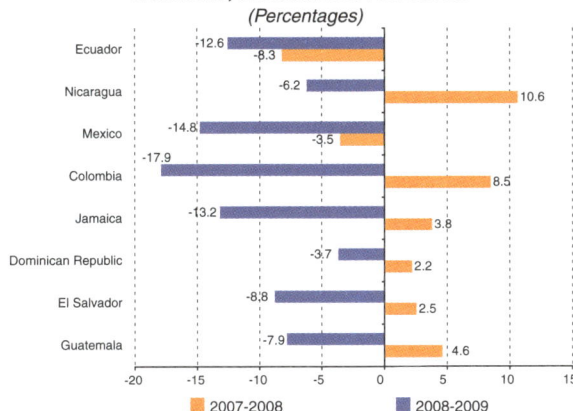

Source: Economic Commission for Latin America and the Caribbean (ECLAC), on the basis of official figures.
[a] Projections for 2009.

Figure I.9
BRAZIL, CHILE AND PERU: PRIVATE BANK LENDING
(Index: first quarter 2008=100)

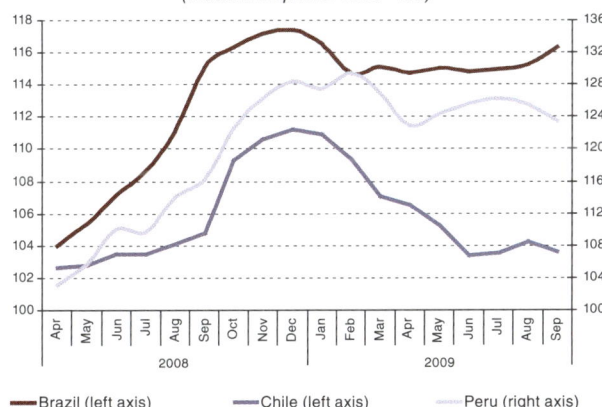

Source: Economic Commission for Latin America and the Caribbean (ECLAC), on the basis of official figures.

Figure I.10
LATIN AMERICA (SELECTED COUNTRIES): BANK LENDING TO THE PRIVATE SECTOR, 2008
(Percentages of GDP)

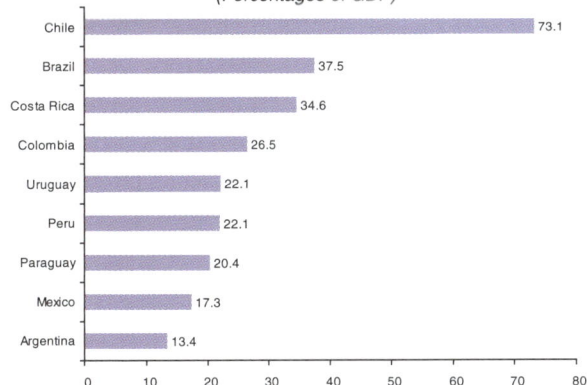

Source: Economic Commission for Latin America and the Caribbean (ECLAC), on the basis of official figures.

Generally-speaking, the expectations of consumers and businesspeople alike worsened towards the end of 2008 and at the beginning of 2009, which translated into lower levels of both private consumption and investment. In fact, as shown in figure I.11, public consumption was the only type of consumption to increase in the first part of the year when many countries in the region had at least some room to implement countercyclical policies that partially offset the negative performance posted by the other components of domestic demand and helped speed up the recovery in the second part of the year as discussed below.[6]

Figure I.11
LATIN AMERICA AND THE CARIBBEAN: BREAKDOWN OF TOTAL SUPPLY AND DEMAND
(Percentages)

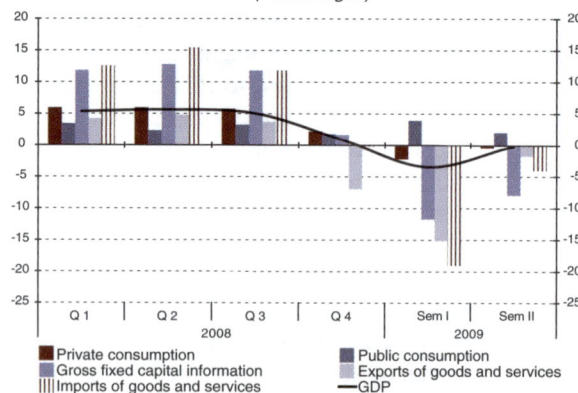

■ Private consumption   ■ Public consumption
■ Gross fixed capital information   □ Exports of goods and services
||||Imports of goods and services   —GDP

Source: Economic Commission for Latin America and the Caribbean (ECLAC), on the basis of official figures.

2.   The social effects of the crisis

The sudden slowdown in economic growth had a negative impact on the labour market: the employment rate fell for the first time in six years, as shown in section III.C. Unemployment rose by almost one percentage point from 7.4% to 8.3%. The slack labour supply, as indicated by the participation rate, averted a larger rise in unemployment.[7] Governments implemented a series of measures (see box I.1) whose impact is impossible to gauge on the basis of the information available to date, but which probably helped stem the rise in unemployment.

The improvements under way in recent years in job quality, however, stopped as the creation of wage jobs in the private sector and of formal employment in general slowed considerably.

On the other hand, the crisis contributed to the lowering of regional inflation from 8.3% in 2008 to 4.5% in 2009. This was the result of the dual impact of the global recession and the decline in trade on food and energy prices, on the one hand, and of the widening of the gap between observed and potential GDP brought about by the regionwide drop in demand, on the other (see box I.3).

Lower inflation staved off a fall in real wages, which partly explains why the negative impact on poverty was more moderate than initially projected.[8]

The smaller-than-expected increase in poverty can also be attributed to the social spending policies implemented

by most of the countries of the region, especially to those deployed by the larger countries that have a more tightly woven institutional fabric, which enables them to implement strategies that, by being more targeted, tend to be more effective during crises than the general subsidies on consumption of certain goods and services. As shown in box I.1, general subsidies tend to be the instruments most commonly used in some Central American and Caribbean countries whose institutional framework is weaker.

Figure I.12
LATIN AMERICA: VARIATION IN NOMINAL WAGES, INFLATION AND REAL WAGES [a]
(Percentages)

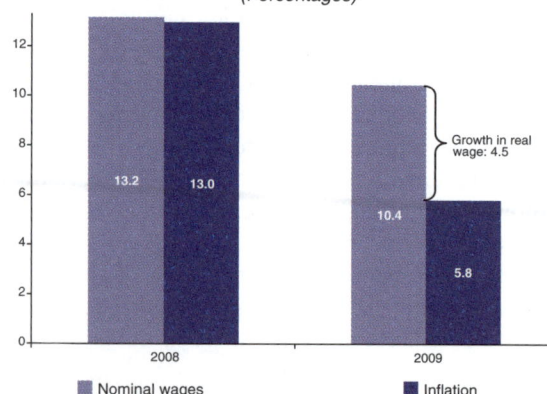

■ Nominal wages   ■ Inflation

Source: Economic Commission for Latin America and the Caribbean (ECLAC), on the basis of official figures.
[a] Simple average (10 countries).

---

[6]   As no disaggregated data are available on investment, no distinctions could be made between public investment which, as noted below, increased over the year, and private investment, which contracted sharply and whose weight is far greater, masking the compensatory effect of public investment.

---

[7]   The projected rise in the unemployment rate is smaller than mid-year forecasts. For example, in ECLAC/ILO (2009), it is estimated that unemployment could come close to 9% for the year overall.

[8]   As noted in *Social Panorama of Latin America* (ECLAC, 2009c).

Box I.1
SOCIAL MEASURES IN LATIN AMERICA AND THE CARIBBEAN

The Latin American and Caribbean countries have announced social measures that may be classified under consumption subsidies, on the one hand, and support for poor families, on the other. The consumption subsides consist of subsidies for fuel, food and other items, transport and electric power. Support for poor families has encompassed mainly help with housing, health care and education for vulnerable groups. Of the 33 countries and 2 dependent territories in the region, 27 have information on these measures (9 of 11 in South America, 8 of 9 in Central America and 10 of 15 in the Caribbean).

Regionwide, a total of 45 measures were registered. Of the 33 countries and 2 dependent territories, 24 have announced measures to support poor families and 18 to subsidize consumption. Accordingly, the portfolio leans slightly towards support for poor families (57%).

A breakdown of the measures by subregion, however, shows a major difference in portfolio composition. In South America and Mexico, three quarters of the measures announced involve support for poor families, while in Central America and the Caribbean countries the distribution is fairly balanced, with half of the measures announced corresponding to consumption subsidies and the other half to family support.

Apart from the different ways in which the crisis may have affected the different subregions, these divergences may also have to do with disparities in institutional capabilities for carrying out social policies. Targeted policies tend to be more effective during crises, since they reach those who need them directly, but they make greater demands on institutions. By contrast, consumption subsidies are relatively simpler to implement, but less effective because they are spread across the entire population and may even be regressive insofar as their benefits may accrue excessively to those who consume most.

COMPOSITION OF PORTFOLIO OF SOCIAL PROGRAMMES IN SOUTH AMERICA AND MEXICO, CENTRAL AMERICA AND THE CARIBBEAN
(Percentages)

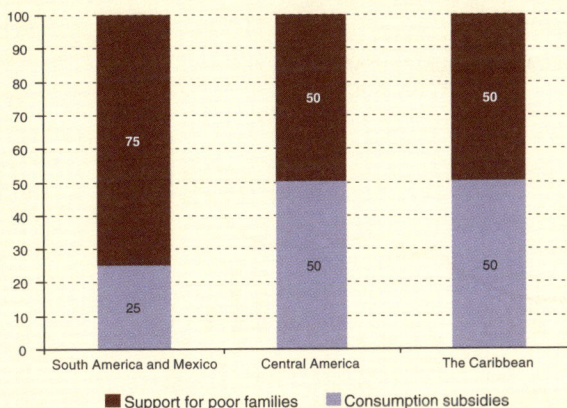

■ Support for poor families   ■ Consumption subsidies

Source: Economic Commission for Latin America and the Caribbean (ECLAC), *The reactions of the Governments of the Americas to the international crisis: an overview of policy measures up to 30 September 2009* (LC/L.3025/Rev.5), Santiago, Chile, October 2009.

C. Macroeconomic policy

Many countries in the region had some room to implement countercyclical policies that not only allowed them to at least partially offset the negative evolution of most of the components of domestic demand, but also to speed up the recovery process, which took hold in some countries as of the second quarter and in nearly all by the third quarter of 2009.

One characteristic feature of the crisis has been the capacity shown (by some countries more than others) to implement macroeconomic and sectoral policies to mitigate the negative effects of the crisis on economic activity and employment. To different extents, according to the type of problem faced and, above all, according to each country's capacity (in not only financial, but also institutional terms) to put into practice public policies, the governments of the region have introduced a wide array of initiatives which can broadly be grouped into the following categories: fiscal measures; monetary, financial and exchange measures; and social and employment measures.

1.   Fiscal policy

The positive stimulus of fiscal policy action was one of the distinctive features of economic management in 2009. The region's primary balance fell from a surplus equivalent to 1.4% of GDP in 2008 to an estimated deficit of 1% of GDP in 2009. This drop of more than two percentage points, which is a measure of the size of the fiscal stimulus, reflects both the decline in public revenues and the increase in public expenditures (including both current and capital expenditures), as shown in figure I.13.

Figure I.13
LATIN AMERICA: REVENUE, PRIMARY SPENDING AND PRIMARY BALANCE
(Simple average, percentages of GDP)

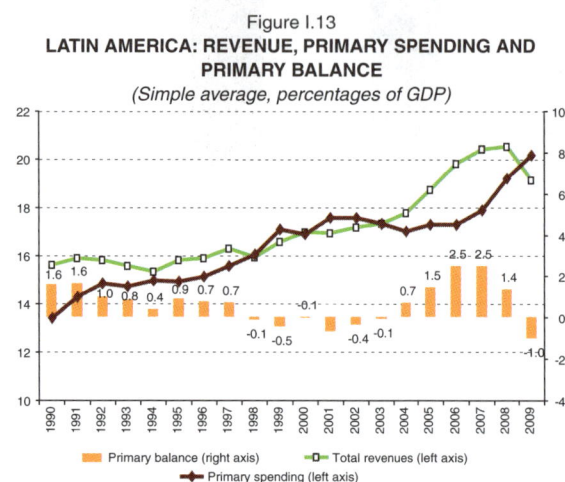

Source: Economic Commission for Latin America and the Caribbean (ECLAC), on the basis of official figures.

Revenues, which are examined in detail in the corresponding chapter, have been conditioned by economic growth (which in turn has determined tax receipts) and by the fall in the prices of the commodities that the region exports and that in some countries account for a high proportion of public income.

In addition to these factors, in many cases, policy measures taken in association with anti-crisis strategies to stimulate domestic demand have reduced tax receipts. Income tax rebates and other tax benefits for both companies and private individuals are among the most widely used instruments, having been introduced in 12 of the 19 countries of Latin America.

The governments in the region also announced fairly ambitious spending plans. As far as their implementation is concerned, in most of the countries for which information on actual spending is available for up to the third quarter of the year, current expenditures (which can generally be stepped up more quickly) increased significantly in the first half of the year, while capital expenditures (which are usually slower to materialize) did so to a lesser extent. The drop in commodity prices reduced the fiscal space available in some of the countries that are highly specialized in commodities, however, which prevented them from implementing countercyclical measures.[9] This occurred in the Bolivarian Republic of Venezuela, where the drop in fiscal revenues compelled the authorities to take steps to contain public spending, which gave fiscal policy a procyclical start.

Figure I.14
LATIN AMERICA (SELECTED COUNTRIES): VARIATION IN PUBLIC EXPENDITURE, NINE MONTHS OF 2008 COMPARED WITH NINE MONTHS OF 2009
(Percentages of GDP)

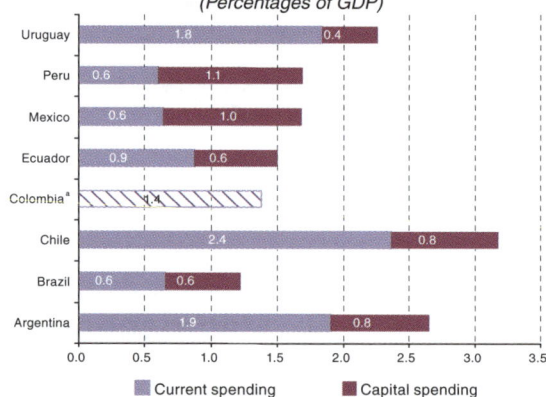

Source: Economic Commission for Latin America and the Caribbean (ECLAC), on the basis of official figures.
a Variation in total spending.

2.   Monetary and exchange-rate policy

As soon as the crisis broke out, the central banks of the region prioritized a series of wide-ranging measures aimed at guaranteeing either recovery or the liquidity of local financial markets, or both. The widespread fall in inflation freed up monetary policy both in countries that run inflation-targeting schemes and those that use other targets, such as certain monetary aggregates.

As discussed in chapter II, the substantial lowering of monetary policy rates by most of the region's monetary authorities occurred most quickly in the countries with inflation-targeting schemes. In many cases, however, although interest rates plummeted, inflation rates fell even faster, cancelling out in real terms the effect pursued by policy action.

---

9   See chapter II.A.

Box I.2
MONETARY POLICY OBJECTIVES IN LATIN AMERICA

The principal mandate of central banks in countries that run inflation-targeting schemes is to keep prices rises under control. In such a system the credibility of the monetary authority is crucial because it is expected to act to ensure that inflation targets are met. However, goods prices are not the only macroeconomic variable that fluctuates in an economy. Variations in real exchange rate and in GDP can, at particular times, also cause concern for central banks. For example, in their monetary policy and inflation reports, the central banks of those countries have noted that the reduction in monetary policy reference rates since the first semester of 2009 has also been intended to help revive domestic demand amid slack economic activity. Sharp fluctuations in the nominal exchange rate, which are also passed through to the real exchange rate, have also prompted central banks to intervene in the foreign-exchange markets.[a] In Chile, for example, in response to the nominal appreciation of the peso in 2009, the central bank announced and implemented a series of interventions aimed at strengthening the international reserve position.

All this goes to show that, under certain circumstances, monetary authorities may respond to variables other than price movements. In order to evaluate these observations empirically, a modified Taylor rule was estimated using autoregressive vectors and including the cyclical components of GDP and the real exchange rate for Brazil, Chile, Colombia, Mexico and Peru.[b] As will be recalled, the dependent variable for this rule is the monetary policy reference rate. In other words, the idea is to estimate how a central bank will respond to deviations from trend in these variables.

The following equation was estimated:

$$(1) \quad TRPM_t = \beta_0 + \beta_1 i_t^E + \beta_2 (\delta_t - \delta_t^{Obj}) + \beta_3*(PIB_t - PIB_t^{Ten}) + \beta_4*(TCR_t - TCR_t^{Ten}) + \varepsilon_\tau$$

where i^E is the equilibrium rate of interest, $\delta_t - \delta_t^{Obj}$ represents the deviation of effective inflation from target inflation, $PIB_t - PIB_t^{Ten}$ is the deviation of effective GDP from trend, estimated using a Hodrick-Prescott filter, and $TCR_t - TCR_t^{Ten}$ is the deviation of the real exchange rate, whose trend was estimated using the aforementioned methodology for quarterly data, given that these countries have an inflation-targeting scheme.

Preliminary results show that central banks react to variables other than deviations from the inflation target. The figure below shows response impulse functions for Chile and Colombia. The response variable is the monetary policy reference rate, while the impulses are provided by standard deviations in inflation, GDP and the real exchange rate. The longitude of the response graphed in the figure is 10 periods. In the case of Chile, the monetary policy reference rate reacts basically to changes in the deviation of inflation and output and, to a lesser extent, to real exchange rate variations. In Colombia, the monetary policy reference rate reacts to all three variables. This evidence is consistent with that found in other regions, in Asia for example, for countries that maintain an inflation-targeting system.

RESPONSE IMPULSE FUNCTIONS
Response to Cholesky one standard deviation

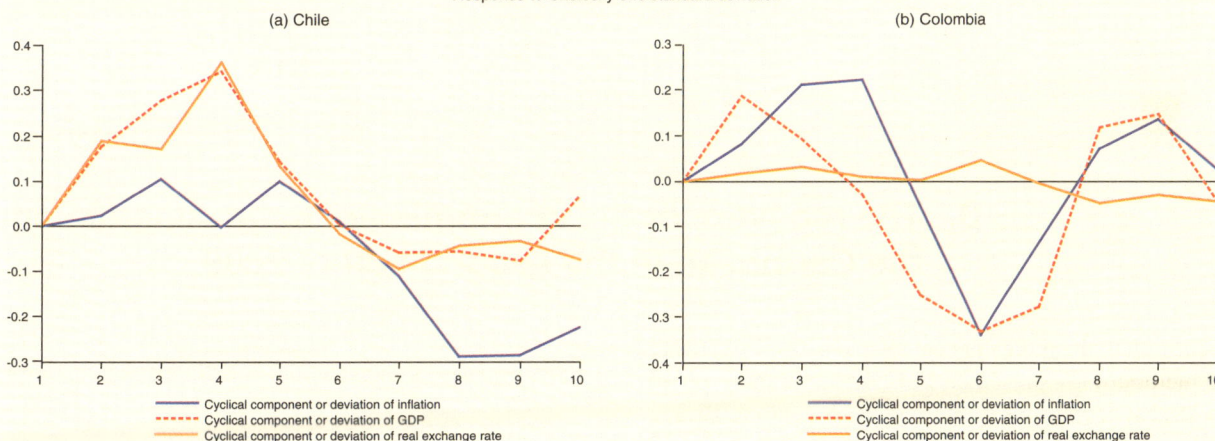

(a) Chile

(b) Colombia

Cyclical component or deviation of inflation
Cyclical component or deviation of GDP
Cyclical component or deviation of real exchange rate

Source: Economic Commission for Latin America and the Caribbean (ECLAC), on the basis of J.B. Taylor, "Discretion versus policy rules in practice", *Carnegie – Rochester Conference Series on Public Policy*, N° 39, 1993; y F. Neumann y S. Yi Kim S., "What do they target? A profile of Asian central banks", *Macro Asian Economics*, HSBC Global Research, 2009.
[a] See section on exchange-rate policy in this publication.
[b] Since the study is at a preliminary stage, only the results for Chile and Colombia are presented.

Also, the central banks' efforts to inject more liquidity into the financial system failed to translate into an increase in credit in the private banking sector (see figure I.15). As noted earlier, in response to this situation, many governments of the region had the public banking sector play a role in their countercyclical strategies and stepped up public lending to compensate, in some cases partially, in others totally, the tighter stances of private banks. Naturally, the impact of this instrument depends on the magnitude of the official banking sector in the financial system. Hence, it has been very significant in Brazil, where public bank lending represents around 35% of total credit.

Figure I.15

LATIN AMERICA (SELECTED COUNTRIES): VARIATION IN PUBLIC AND PRIVATE BANK LENDING BETWEEN DECEMBER 2008 AND SEPTEMBER 2009

(*Percentages*)

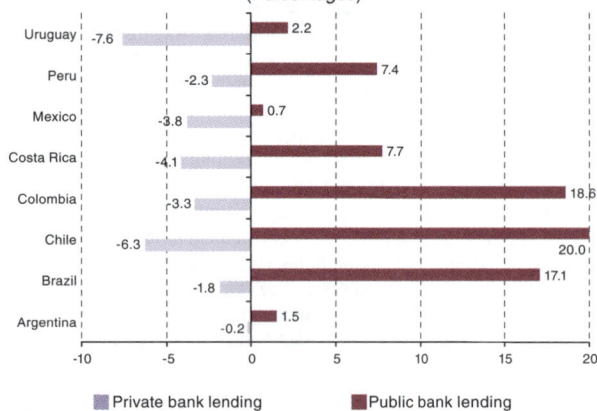

■ Private bank lending   ■ Public bank lending

Source: Economic Commission for Latin America and the Caribbean (ECLAC), on the basis of official figures.

As far as exchange rates are concerned, once the strain experienced at the end of 2008 (which in some cases lasted into the beginning of 2009) was over, the general trend in South America was a return to the appreciation of local currencies under way prior to the crisis. The search for higher returns during a time of abundant liquidity in the international market, together with the relatively robust performance of many of the region's economies, resulted in large inflows of capital that pushed down the exchange rate in most of South America. The notable exception has been Mexico, where the exchange rate is 22% higher in real terms than it was before September 2008 when the international crisis unfolded.

In order to defend the real exchange rate to some extent and to sustain domestic liquidity levels, many central banks intervened in the exchange market, which in some cases enabled them to restore international reserve levels to those seen prior to the last quarter of 2008.[10] One notable example is Brazil, where international reserves rose by 19% to over US$ 37 billion and the real exchange rate fell by 26% between December 2008 and October 2009.

The changes observed in the countries' international reserves over 2009 are particularly interesting. The increase recorded by Brazil was larger than that posted by Latin America and the Caribbean as a whole. The situation varied across the region, with the increases in reserves in some countries managing to offset the losses observed at the end of 2008, while in others, such as Argentina and Mexico, the increments were minimal in terms of their impact on the total regional rise. It should be noted that in some cases, especially in the smaller economies, such as those of the Caribbean, the expansion of reserves was mainly the result of the recent allocation of Special Drawing Rights by the International Monetary Fund.

D. The recovery of the economies of Latin America and the Caribbean in the second half of 2009

According to the indicators calculated by ECLAC using the methodology presented in ECLAC (2009a), six of the largest economies of the region, Argentina, Brazil, Chile, Colombia, Mexico and Peru, which together account for about 90% of regional GDP, were on the road to economic recovery in the third quarter of 2009 (see figure I.16).[11]

Figure I.16

LATIN AMERICA (SELECTED COUNTRIES): LEADING INDICATORS

(*Probability of recovery*)

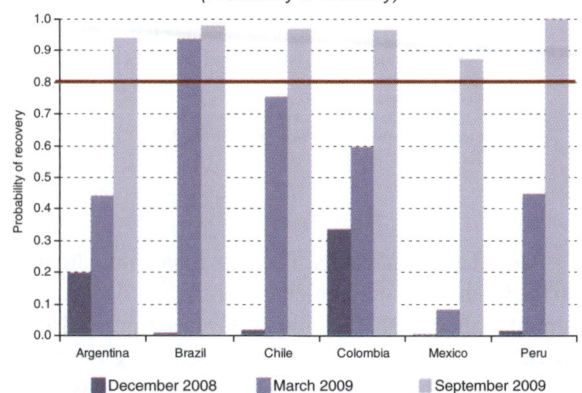

■ December 2008   ■ March 2009   ■ September 2009

Source: Economic Commission for Latin America and the Caribbean (ECLAC), on the basis of official figures.

---

[10] The collapse of Lehman Brothers produced some stress in the financial and exchange markets of the region, which led central banks, among other things, to step in to prevent an even greater depreciation of local currencies than that seen in the last quarter of 2008. This sapped about US$ 50 billion of the region's international reserves, approximately 10% of total holdings.

[11] See Cantú, Acevedo and Bello (2009).

Expectations that the downturn witnessed in economic activity between the fourth quarter of 2008 and the second quarter of 2009 will be reversed are in keeping with the improvements detected in the analysis of the latest information on most of the variables for the real economy referred to in section C.

Export volumes began to expand again as of the third quarter of 2009 (see figure I.3), as shown in chapter IV.A, while the increase in global economic activity and international trade is having a positive effect on demand for commodities and has been pushing up commodity prices since the second quarter of 2009. This is, in turn, reversing the worsening of the region's terms of trade, which are expected to improve by 3.8% in 2010 for the region as a whole, and by even more in the hydrocarbon- and metal-exporting countries of South America and in Mexico. The terms of trade of Central America, in contrast, are projected to worsen.

Figure I.17
LATIN AMERICA: TERMS OF TRADE
(Index 2000=100)

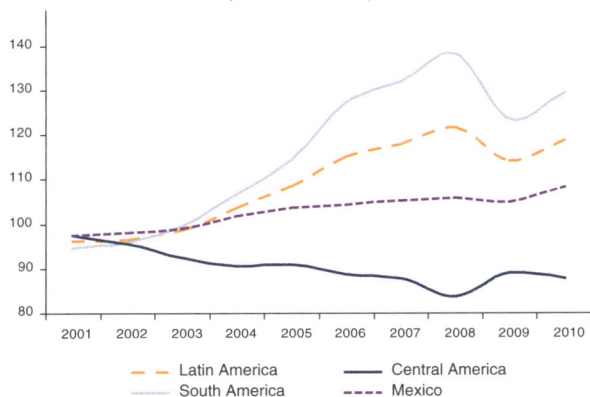

Source: Economic Commission for Latin America and the Caribbean (ECLAC), on the basis of official figures.

Remittance flows, which were one of the other engines of growth in 2003-2008, are beginning to pick up again. Moreover, the onset of economic recovery in the United States and Spain, the two main destinations for Latin American and Caribbean emigrants, adds weight to expectations of a recovery in foreign-exchange inflows to the region in the form of remittances. Indicators for the Latin American labour markets meanwhile show that both the downturn in employment and the rise in unemployment halted in the third quarter of the year.[12]

As noted in the preceding section, domestic demand is continuing to receive fiscal stimulus in the second half of 2009 which, along with the factors referenced earlier and as a result of a gradual return to normalcy in financial markets,

in many cases with the additional support of official banks, is leading to a recovery —at fairly rapid rates, in some cases— which is reflected in the gradual improvement in labour-market indicators for the region (see figure I.19).

Figure I.18
EMPLOYMENT STATUS OF LATIN AMERICAN CITIZENS IN THE UNITED STATES AND SPAIN
(Thousands of persons)

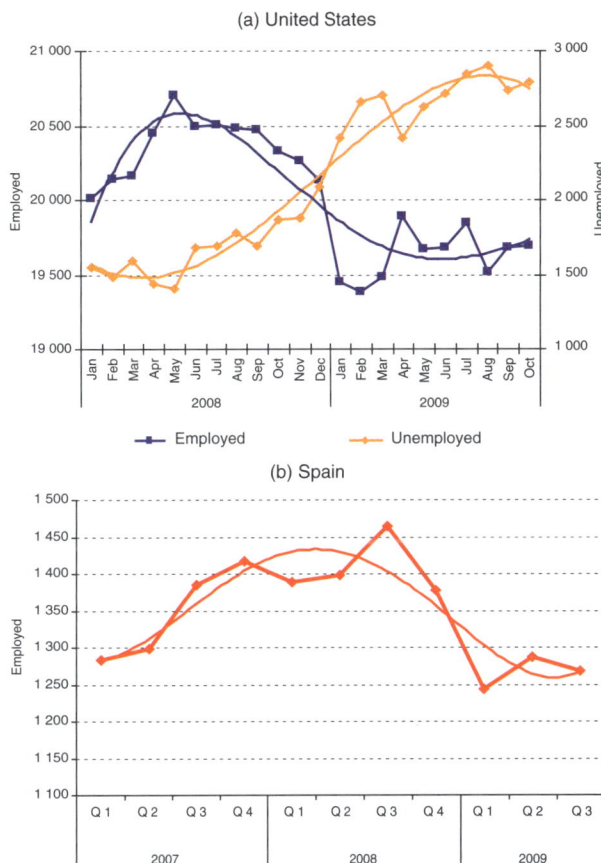

(a) United States

(b) Spain

Source: Economic Commission for Latin America and the Caribbean (ECLAC), on the basis of official figures.

At the same time, the increased tolerance for risk in a context of high liquidity in international financial markets —along with a positive perception of prospects for several of the economies in the region— is resulting, as noted in the previous section, in a number of countries regaining access to international credit. This is having a positive effect on stock markets, which are returning to levels seen prior to the worsening of the crisis. In turn, the private sector should be able to restructure assets and lending activity should return to normal which, together with the gradual improvement in labour market indicators and the renewed confidence within the private sector, as indicated by surveys of business and consumer expectations, should sustain a recovery in domestic demand for both consumer and capital goods.

---

[12] See Ratha, Mohapatra and Silwal (2009).

Figure I.19
**LATIN AMERICA (SELECTED COUNTRIES): SEASONALLY
ADJUSTED MONTHLY UNEMPLOYMENT RATES**
(Percentages)

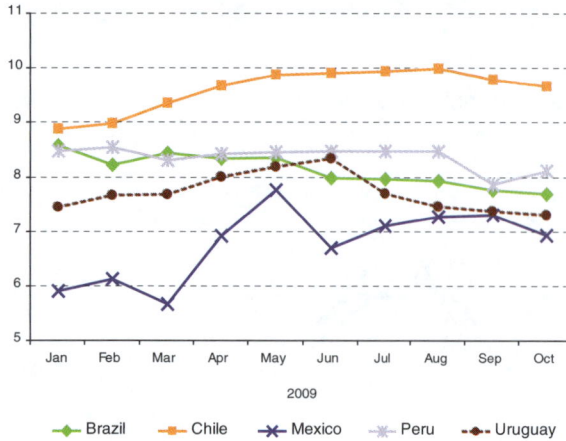

Figure I.20
**STOCK MARKET INDICATORS: DOW JONES AND
EMERGING MARKETS**
(Index 2000=100)

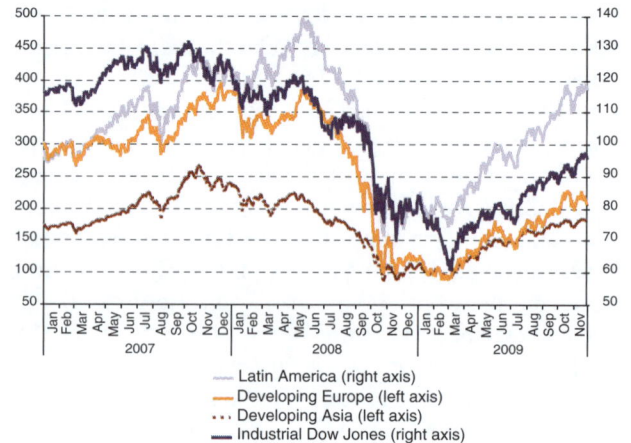

—◆— Brazil   —■— Chile   —✕— Mexico   —✳— Peru   —●— Uruguay

Source: Economic Commission for Latin America and the Caribbean (ECLAC), on
the basis of official figures.

Latin America (right axis)
Developing Europe (left axis)
Developing Asia (left axis)
Industrial Dow Jones (right axis)

Source: Economic Commission for Latin America and the Caribbean (ECLAC), on
the basis of figures from Bloomberg.

E. Prospects, risks and challenges facing the region

1. Anticipated developments in the economies of Latin America and the Caribbean in 2010

Given the speed of the recovery that became evident in the second quarter of 2009, in 2010 the region could return to growth rates that, in some cases, will come close to matching those seen prior to the crisis. While this is the most likely scenario, it is not without risks. Moreover, there is considerable scepticism as to whether this recovery will lead to sustained growth.

The projected growth rate for 2010 is 4.1%, with expectations of stronger growth in South America than in the other subregions, given the larger size of the domestic markets in some of the countries (particularly Brazil and, to a lesser extent, Argentina and Colombia), the diversification of export markets, and the greater role played by Asia, China, in particular, as export markets for a number of countries (Argentina, Brazil, Chile and Peru). By contrast, slower growth is expected in more open economies that have a less diversified portfolio of trading partners and are more heavily reliant on manufacturing trade, such as Mexico and the Central American economies.

The Caribbean economies may be similarly placed and many face additional difficulties arising from a complex financial and exchange-rate situation.

In this context of increased growth and higher prices for a number of commodities in which the region specializes, there is reason to expect a rise in public revenues and, to the extent that private sector demand increases, a gradual decline in government consumption throughout the year.[13] However, in countries that specialize more heavily in natural-resource-intensive processed goods, higher fiscal revenues will boost the governments' capacities to inject impetus into domestic activity. Capital expenditures, responding more slowly, will continue to increase as a result of various projects initiated in 2009. This should not prevent an improvement in the fiscal balance, however.

---

[13] Some countries have already begun, in 2009, to reduce current spending, while others, such as Mexico, have announced fiscal reform programmes that would involve a major increase in tax collections.

Figure I.21
LATIN AMERICA AND THE CARIBBEAN: GROWTH RATES, 2010
(Percentages)

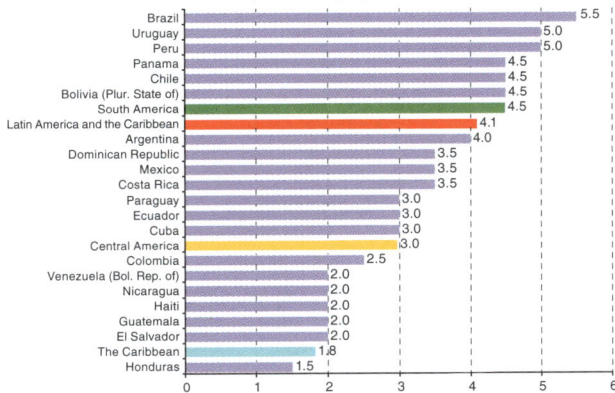

Brazil	5.5
Uruguay	5.0
Peru	5.0
Panama	4.5
Chile	4.5
Bolivia (Plur. State of)	4.5
South America	4.5
Latin America and the Caribbean	4.1
Argentina	4.0
Dominican Republic	3.5
Mexico	3.5
Costa Rica	3.5
Paraguay	3.0
Ecuador	3.0
Cuba	3.0
Central America	3.0
Colombia	2.5
Venezuela (Bol. Rep. of)	2.0
Nicaragua	2.0
Haiti	2.0
Guatemala	2.0
El Salvador	2.0
The Caribbean	1.8
Honduras	1.5

Source: Economic Commission for Latin America and the Caribbean (ECLAC), on the basis of official figures.

To the extent that growth takes hold and approaches potential growth rates, inflation could begin to edge up, which could lead to a tightening of monetary policy, perhaps towards the end of the year. Here, however, central banks will again face the choice between maintaining price stability and limiting currency appreciation, in an environment in which exchange rates will very probably be subject to downward pressure (currency appreciation) owing to a surplus of hard currency resulting from abundant international market liquidity.

While there is reason to expect a deterioration in the balance-of-payments current account compared to 2009, mostly as a result of an upturn in imports, the availability of external financing, together with increased FDI inflows, will probably suffice not only to cover this larger deficit, but even to continue restoring international reserve levels.

Economic growth should help to increase rates (and, probably, the quality) of employment, although it will likely mean a corresponding increase in the participation rate, which will partially offset the impact on unemployment. All in all, it is estimated that unemployment could fall to around 8%, settling mid-way between pre- and post-crisis levels. This, in turn, would have a positive effect on poverty indicators.

Box I.3
ESTIMATING POTENTIAL GDP

An economy's growth potential —how much it would grow if production resources were fully employed— is an important concept for economic analysis and, in particular, for economic policymaking. This growth potential is not something that can be observed however, but must be estimated.

This box offers a brief explanation of the estimation of Latin America's potential growth for the period 1980-2020,[a] measured by means of the production function methodology, whose main advantage is that it is built on a sound theoretical model that is lacking in other, purely statistical, methodologies. Production function methodology calls for the estimates of total factor productivity (TFP), on the one hand, and the valuation of the factors of production (employment and capital) at full potential, on the other.

TFP is obtained from the difference between the variation rates of GDP, employment and capital stock (with this last variable adjusted using an installed capacity use index).

The capital stock of the different types of production activity under way in the economy is estimated from 1950 onwards using the following formula:

$$K_{t,j}^p = \sum_{t=0}^{T_j} I_{j,t-t} R_{j,t} E_{j,t}$$

where $I_{j,t-t}$ is the investment of t age expressed at constant prices, $R_{j,t}$ is the retirement function, which determines the proportion of investment made t periods ago that is currently surviving and $E_{j,t}$ represents the age-efficiency profile, which tracks the production efficiency loss of assets as they age.

In order to achieve the largest possible geographical and time coverage, the analysis used only two types of production asset: machinery and equipment and construction,[b] which are assumed to have average useful lives of 20 and 50 years, respectively.[c]

The capital services flow is obtained from the effect of variations in installed capacity use over the business cycle. Since this is a particularly hard variable to measure, variations in installed capacity use are approximated using energy consumption series.

Potential employment is measured by discounting the trend unemployment rate, estimated using a Hodrick-Prescott filter, from the economically active population published by the International Labour Organization (ILO).

The results shown in the figure show that Latin America's growth potential has increased steadily in the last two decades, from rates of just over 2% in the early 1990s to over 4% in the last few years. The steady rise over time is mainly the result of increases in productivity and capital. Accordingly, rising investment rates accounted for the jump in growth potential from 2004 to 2008 and drove actual growth above potential. This trend went unbroken until 2009, when GDP growth fell well below potential. Effective growth could return to above-potential rates in 2010, however.

Box I.3 (concluded)

LATIN AMERICA: POTENTIAL OUTPUT GROWTH
(Percentages)

—— Potential GDP   —●— Effective GDP

Source: C. Aravena, "Estimación del crecimiento potencial de América Latina", Santiago, Chile, Economic Commission for Latin America and the Caribbean (ECLAC),
2009, unpublished.
[a] The growth potential of Latin America was calculated on the basis of growth registered by Argentina, the Bolivarian Republic of Venezuela, Brazil, Chile, Colombia, Ecuador,
Mexico, Paraguay, Peru, the Plurinational State of Bolivia and Uruguay.
[b] Based on official fixed gross capital formation figures from each country.
[c] A sensitivity analysis conducted for different average lifespans and rate of efficiency losses showed variation of less than 10% in capital variation at the extremes.

2.   Risks resulting from the external scenario

Beyond the problems that persist in some economies of Eastern Europe, it remains to be seen whether the developed economies will be able to grow as they phase out the substantial stimulus initiatives associated with the countercyclical policies implemented in the United States and Europe. Added to the increase in unemployment and the still volatile international financial market, this raises questions about the strength of the recovery that began in 2009.

As mentioned earlier, expansionary monetary policy, led by the world's principal central banks, with the emerging economies following suit, led to historically low interbank interest rates (see figure I.22). This greater liquidity, however, was not reflected in increased credit to the private sector, which has been slowing in much of the world, and even declining in year-on-year terms in the United States and the euro area.[14]

The credit squeeze is the result of a combination of factors limiting both supply and demand, associated with declining economic activity and the loss of wealth experienced by economic agents most notably towards the end of 2008. Since then, banking institutions have been

focusing on shoring up their balance sheets and reducing their exposure, and are maintaining greater liquidity in order to deal with potential problems. Added to the banks' more conservative stance is the reduced solvency of many businesses whose balance sheets —and, thus, their eligibility for credit— were damaged by the crisis.

Figure I.22
INTERBANK INTEREST RATES [a]
(Percentages)

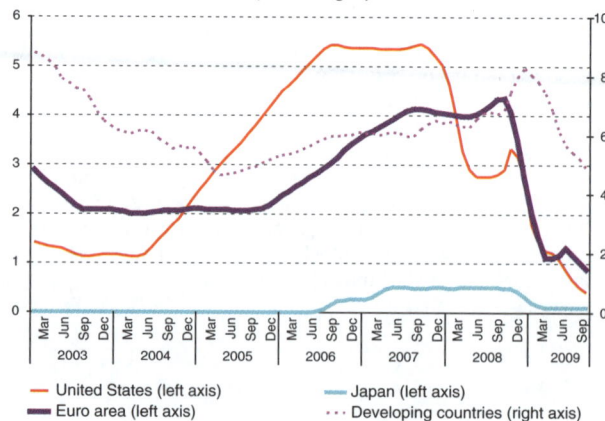

—— United States (left axis)   —— Japan (left axis)
—— Euro area (left axis)   ····· Developing countries (right axis)

Source: Economic Commission for Latin America and the Caribbean (ECLAC), on
the basis of official figures and International Monetary Fund (IMF).
[a] Three-month moving average.

---

[14]   The Latin American and Caribbean region has been no exception
to these trends, as noted in section D.2.

The challenge facing the global economy is how to leverage credit to speed up the recovery, particularly with regard to financing consumption and SMEs, at a time when the public sectors of many developed countries will have greater need for financing to cover the massive deficits built up by their fiscal stimulus measures.

This situation creates a tension between the need to maintain the policy stimulus if private sector demand is slow to pick up, and the increasing problem this creates in terms of availability of credit for businesses and consumers, as well as the burden of financing the enormous deficits accumulated in some countries. All of this must be considered against a backdrop of continued limitations in supply due to uncertainty and the bias toward liquidity that are still evident in financial markets.

The other major risk is that concern over the need to progressively close fiscal gaps will take precedence over other policy objectives, and that this will lead to a premature withdrawal of fiscal and monetary stimulus measures that, at least thus far, have been the principal

factors buttressing demand, and the main (in some cases the only) engine driving the global economic recovery.

Figure I.23
BANK LENDING TO THE PRIVATE SECTOR [a]
(Percentages)

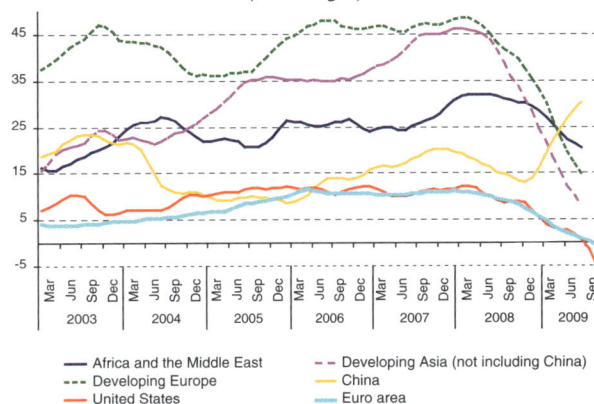

Legend:
- Africa and the Middle East
- Developing Europe
- United States
- Developing Asia (not including China)
- China
- Euro area

Source: Economic Commission for Latin America and the Caribbean (ECLAC), on the basis of official figures and International Monetary Fund (IMF).
[a] Year-on-year growth, three-month moving average.

3.   Challenges beyond the short term

It is highly probable that the crisis will lead to profound changes that will produce a less growth-friendly international environment than the conditions the region experienced between 2003 and 2008. One factor is that the post-crisis world is likely to see slower overall growth, given the drop in aggregate demand in the developed countries, counterbalanced in part by rising overall demand in the developing countries.

As a result, the emerging economies may be expected to play a stronger role in world growth, but within the framework of a slowdown in trade flows. The drop in demand for imports among developed economies will mean that emerging economies will have fewer opportunities to place their products in those markets, which will exacerbate competition and encourage the adoption of domestic-market-oriented strategies, at least in the larger economies. At the same time, this shows up the need to redefine patterns of production and trade specialization and encourage innovation, the building-in of knowledge and product diversification, on the one hand, and to build up a highly diversified portfolio of destination markets, with many in Asia, on the other.

The global financial crisis has also highlighted the need to reform the international financial architecture and, in particular, the regulatory and oversight systems, in order

to ensure greater international financial stability. Though it is clear that the reform impetus is weakening as the global economy recovers, it may be expected that a new, more transparent banking model will be developed, with less incentive for risk-taking and lower levels of leveraging. This could lead to a reduction in international financial flows and, therefore, a partial reversal of the pattern of financial integration seen prior to the crisis.

Although it is not yet clear how these factors will affect interest rates in general, there is a risk they will rise, given projections of steadily mounting public debt in some developed countries and the lack of any tax or fiscal reform that might lead to lower demand for resources on the part of the public sector in those countries. Nevertheless, this situation could change, insofar as awareness increases of the risks to growth, fiscal reforms are put in place and saving rates begin to rise.

Be this as it may, resource flows from the most demanding segments of the international capital markets to higher-risk countries are very likely to decrease, given the greater caution prevailing in the wake of the financial crisis and the possibility of regulatory changes that could limit risk-taking. This could deepen the differences among developing countries in terms of access to the international capital markets, which would oblige less well-endowed or more macroeconomically vulnerable countries to rely more heavily on financing from multilateral agencies or on more expensive, less advantageous financing.

The question then arises as to how the region can make further inroads in a world characterized, on the one hand, by lower growth rates in the developed countries and developing countries playing a larger role in global growth, and, on the other, financial systems that are subject to stricter regulations and oversight, with less dynamic credit markets and higher interest rates? How, moreover, is this to be accomplished in a way that allows for sustained growth at rates that will make it possible to meet social needs, while at the same time providing for more equitable distribution of the benefits of that growth?

The recovery from the crisis seems to have been quicker than expected, largely thanks to the domestic strengths built up by the countries of the region as a result of sounder macroeconomic policies. Upturns in several of the factors that drove demand in the years prior to the crisis, added in

many cases to strong impetus from public policies, should enable a rapid recovery in the context of substantial idle capacity. But how can that recovery be transformed into a process of sustained growth beyond 2010?

Answering these questions satisfactorily is well beyond the scope and ability of this publication, which confines itself to offering a brief discussion of the role of public policies in this connection. Aside from differences from country to country, the Latin American and Caribbean economies have certain features in common that underscore the importance of State involvement. In the short term, the countries of the region acted to offset the effects of the crisis to the best of their capacities —in the process revealing major differences in terms of this capacity. But the objective of regaining a sustained growth path poses fresh and more complex challenges. For this reason, the Latin American and Caribbean countries face the unavoidable task of generating and expanding the policy space, for which they must (with few exceptions) increase the resources available for financing policies, create instruments and strengthen their institutions, particularly those involved in coordinating different policy areas.

Chapter II

Economic policy

A. Fiscal policy

As noted in previous publications by ECLAC, in the period from 2003 to 2008 the particular combination of external conditions, macro environment and macroeconomic policy management helped to broaden the fiscal space available to most of the countries of the region.[1] During this period, most of the countries were able to reduce their external vulnerability and lower their public debt burdens, thanks to favourable international conditions and improved macroeconomic policy design and management.

In 2009 a number of factors were involved in shaping the fiscal position in Latin America and the Caribbean. First, slackening economic activity, which impacted heavily on fiscal revenues. Second, prices for natural resources, which dropped from the values seen in mid-2008 to figures close to those recorded in 2004-2005, cutting into the fiscal income of the exporting economies. Third, the implementation of measures to lessen the impact of the crisis by propping up aggregate demand and offsetting the damage to the most vulnerable sectors, which pushed up public spending. These combined effects led to a deterioration in the public accounts in the countries of the region (with the exception of some Caribbean countries, including Barbados, Dominica, the Dominican Republic, Grenada, Guyana, Saint Kitts and Nevis and Saint Lucia). In order to compensate for the fall in revenues and finance the counter-crisis measures, the countries that operate fiscal rules limiting either their structural balances (Chile) or spending and borrowing (Argentina, Brazil and Peru) relaxed the respective targets for 2009.

Latin America's central governments recorded a primary fiscal deficit of 1.0% of GDP, as a simple average, at the close of 2009, compared with a surplus of 1.4% of GDP in 2008. The overall balance (including public debt servicing payments) was in deficit by 2.8% of GDP, compared to a deficit of 0.3% in 2008. The deterioration in the average fiscal balance in the region reflects the position of the fiscal accounts more or less across the board. In 2009, of the 19 Latin American countries

---

[1]   The policy space available to governments for pursuing their objectives is a function of three factors: the volume of fiscal resources available, the number of independent instruments for meeting their proposed objectives and the competency of the policies competing for the use of resources and instruments. Macroeconomic shocks affect the fiscal space not only because they affect resources, but also because they determine the extent and intensity of competition among policies. For a more detailed account of fiscal space, see ECLAC (2008) and Fanelli and Jiménez (2009).

shown in table II.1, only six posted a primary surplus (31% of the total), which stands in sharp contrast to the position in 2008, when 13 countries (68% of the total) ran a primary surplus.

In the Caribbean, the combination of falling revenues and rising expenditures led to a worsening of the subregion's fiscal deficit, which rose slightly from 2% of GDP in fiscal year 2007-2008 (simple average) to an estimated 2.3% of GDP in 2008-2009, as shown in table II.1. Jamaica's estimated fiscal deficit of 11% of GDP was a record high for Latin America and the Caribbean and comparable to the deficit of 13% of GDP recorded in the United States. Trinidad and Tobago experienced a major fiscal adjustment of over 13 percentage points of GDP, from a surplus of 7.8% of GDP in fiscal year 2007-2008 to a deficit of 5.3% in fiscal year 2008-2009. The increase of over 10 percentage points of GDP in the fiscal surplus of Saint Kitts and Nevis reflected a 120% rise in grants received in the second quarter of 2009, compared with the year-earlier period.

The generalized deterioration in the public accounts reflected the combination of differing performances in the countries of the region, as shown in figure II.1, whose two axes depict the evolution of fiscal revenues and expenditures in 2008-2009 in percentages of GDP. Most of the countries show lower revenues and higher spending (upper left quadrant). Only four countries registered increases in both spending and revenues (Argentina, Colombia, Paraguay and Uruguay) and another four have seen both income and spending fall (the Bolivarian Republic of Venezuela, the Dominican Republic, Ecuador and the Plurinational State of Bolivia). Coincidentally, three of these last four rely heavily on natural resources for their fiscal revenues. As might be expected, the empty quadrant corresponds to higher income and lower spending.

Figure II.1
LATIN AMERICA: VARIATION IN FISCAL REVENUES AND EXPENDITURES, 2008-2009
(Percentages of GDP)

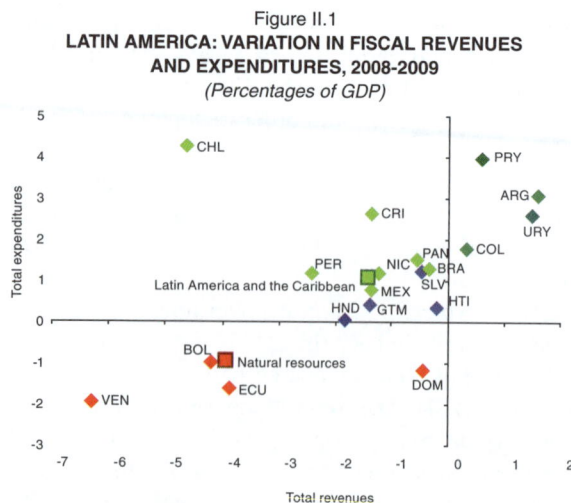

Source: Economic Commission for Latin America and the Caribbean (ECLAC), on the basis of official figures.

The leitmotiv of public accounts in 2009 has been the decline in fiscal revenues, which are expected to have dropped by 1.4 percentage points of GDP. This is the first such fall relative to GDP since 1998 and places them at a similar level to that of 2005.

Figure II.2
LATIN AMERICA AND THE CARIBBEAN: CENTRAL GOVERNMENT REVENUES, 1990-2009
(Percentages of GDP)

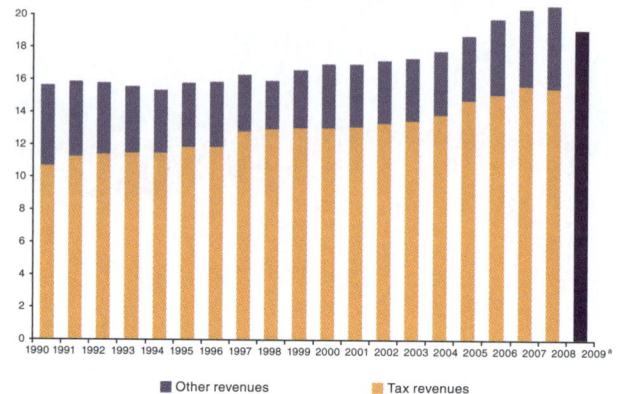

Source: Economic Commission for Latin America and the Caribbean (ECLAC), on the basis of official figures.
[a] Estimate.

Fiscal income slumped in almost all the countries of the region (15 of 19), in some cases by over six GDP percentage points, owing to a range of factors including the fall in the prices and volumes of commodity exports, slackening economic activity and, in some countries, countercyclical tax measures.

The sharp drop in fiscal resources shows how highly exposed public revenues were to the crisis. It will be recalled that the rise in public resources in 2002-2008 was heavily driven by exploitation of natural resources. This sector provides over 30% of fiscal resources in the Bolivarian Republic of Venezuela, Ecuador, Mexico and the Plurinational State of Bolivia, and between 14% and 18% in Argentina, Chile, Colombia and Peru. Accordingly, much of the drop in income in 2009 was a function of the great significance of natural resources —whose prices plummeted— as a financing source in many of the region's countries.[2] Hence, the exposure of fiscal systems to the crisis was differentiated chiefly by the type of resources sustaining each country's public revenues. Countries whose public revenues depend on resources from primary goods may therefore be distinguished from those without large endowments of natural resources, whose tax income relies basically on activity in the domestic economy.

---

2   For a detailed analysis of the differentiated impact of the crisis on fiscal income, see Gómez Sabaini and Jiménez (2009).

Table II.1
LATIN AMERICA AND THE CARIBBEAN: CENTRAL GOVERNMENT FISCAL INDICATORS [a]
(Percentages of GDP, at current prices)

| | Primary balance | | | | | Overall balance | | | | | Public debt [b] | | | | | | | | | |
| | | | | | | | | | | | Central government | | | | | Non-financial public sector | | | | |
	2005	2006	2007	2008	2009 [c]	2005	2006	2007	2008	2009 [d]	2005	2006	2007	2008	2009	2005	2006	2007	2008	2009
Latin America and the Caribbean	**2.2**	**1.8**	**2.1**	**1.5**	**-0.1**	**-1.1**	**-1.3**	**-0.6**	**-1.2**	**-2.6**	**60.2**	**53.6**	**47.2**	**45.7**	**48.0**	...	...	...	...	...
Latin America [c]	**1.5**	**2.5**	**2.5**	**1.4**	**-1.0**	**-1.0**	**0.3**	**0.5**	**-0.3**	**-2.8**	**42.7**	**35.7**	**29.9**	**27.9**	**28.3**	**47.6**	**40.4**	**33.4**	**31.4**	**31.7**
The Caribbean [c]	**3.7**	**1.2**	**1.8**	**2.3**	**1.3**	**-1.0**	**-3.5**	**-2.1**	**-2.0**	**-2.3**	**85.8**	**79.7**	**72.6**	**71.8**	**79.3**	...	...	...	...	...
Argentina	2.3	2.7	2.7	2.8	1.4	0.4	1.0	0.6	0.7	-0.8	72.8	63.6	55.7	48.3	52.1	87.6	76.3	66.7	56.9	60.8
Bolivia (Plurinational State of) [e]	0.4	5.3	3.5	0.8	-1.4	-2.3	3.5	2.3	0.0	-3.2	75.6	49.8	37.1	33.8	34.7	78.3	52.6	40.0	36.7	34.3
Brazil	2.5	2.1	2.3	2.5	0.9	-3.6	-2.9	-1.9	-1.3	-2.9	30.9	31.0	31.4	25.2	29.6	38.5	47.0	46.2	39.9	44.0
Chile	5.4	8.4	9.4	5.8	-3.1	4.6	7.7	8.8	5.3	-3.6	7.3	5.3	4.1	5.2	4.0	13.0	10.6	9.1	12.1	9.4
Colombia	-1.2	0.1	1.0	0.9	-0.6	-4.1	-3.5	-2.7	-2.3	-3.7	39.6	37.6	32.9	33.5	35.0	50.8	47.5	43.7	42.9	43.1
Costa Rica	2.0	2.7	3.7	2.4	-1.5	-2.1	-1.1	0.6	0.2	-3.8	37.5	33.3	27.6	24.9	24.8	42.9	38.4	31.9	29.9	29.8
Ecuador [f]	2.9	5.4	4.0	-0.2	-3.1	0.7	3.3	2.1	-1.5	-3.8	35.9	29.4	27.5	23.7	21.2	38.6	32.0	30.0	25.8	23.2
El Salvador	1.1	2.0	2.2	1.7	0.8	-1.0	-0.4	-0.2	-0.6	-2.3	37.6	37.5	34.5	33.4	33.8	39.7	39.7	36.6	35.7	36.2
Guatemala	-0.3	-0.6	0.0	-0.3	-1.9	-1.7	-1.9	-1.4	-1.6	-3.4	20.8	21.7	21.4	20.2	20.8	21.5	21.9	21.6	20.5	21.1
Haiti	0.5	0.8	-1.2	-0.9	-1.4	-0.5	0.0	-1.6	-1.2	-1.7	44.1	35.6	32.2	37.6	36.5	47.5	38.1	34.5	39.6	38.4
Honduras	-1.1	-0.1	-2.3	-1.7	-3.6	-2.2	-1.1	-2.9	-2.3	-4.2	44.7	28.7	17.3	16.6	16.8	44.8	30.0	18.2	18.3	18.3
Mexico [g]	1.9	2.1	1.9	1.6	0.1	-0.1	0.1	0.0	-0.1	-2.1	20.3	20.7	21.2	24.7	27.1	23.0	22.7	23.0	27.2	34.5
Nicaragua	0.1	1.8	1.9	0.0	-2.1	-1.8	0.0	0.4	-1.2	-3.5	92.6	68.7	42.4	38.2	34.6	92.8	69.1	43.3	39.3	35.6
Panama	0.5	4.4	4.7	3.4	1.3	-3.9	0.2	1.2	0.3	-1.8	65.1	60.3	53.2	44.6	43.0	66.2	61.0	53.7	45.2	44.3
Paraguay	2.0	1.5	1.8	3.3	0.0	0.8	0.5	1.0	2.6	-0.7	31.4	23.8	16.9	15.3	16.0	32.8	24.8	19.9	18.3	18.6
Peru	1.1	3.2	3.5	3.6	-0.1	-0.7	1.5	1.8	2.2	-1.4	36.9	30.1	26.2	24.4	22.3	38.2	31.3	27.2	24.8	22.6
Dominican Republic	0.7	0.3	1.4	-1.6	-1.4	-0.6	-1.1	0.1	-3.2	-3.0	22.0	20.4	18.4	20.0	23.4	...	...	19.0	20.8	24.1
Uruguay	2.7	3.2	2.1	1.7	0.6	-1.6	-1.0	-1.6	-1.0	-2.1	64.2	57.2	48.2	46.2	48.3	67.4	60.4	51.4	49.4	51.6
Venezuela (Bolivarian Republic of)	4.6	2.1	4.5	0.1	-4.1	1.6	0.0	3.0	-1.2	-5.5	32.7	23.9	19.3	14.0	13.3	32.7	23.9	19.3	14.0	13.3
The Caribbean [h]																				
Antigua and Barbuda	21.8	-4.3	-3.1	-3.6	-4.5	18.0	-7.8	-6.4	-6.7	-7.1	...	94.6	82.0	82.6	90.2	...	...	...	...	...
Bahamas	0.2	0.9	0.2	0.6	-2.7	-2.6	-1.5	-2.4	-2.0	-3.0	32.9	32.8	35.1	36.6	...	...	...	...	...	...
Barbados [f]	0.6	3.1	2.8	-0.5	0.1	-4.3	-2.0	-1.8	-5.9	-3.2	82.0	79.0	84.0	88.0	101.7	41.8	42.6	44.7	47.9	...
Belize	3.5	2.8	4.3	4.1	1.6	-3.4	-4.2	0.0	0.3	1.2	79.5	75.1	71.4	82.7	86.8	99.0	95.0	101.0	103.0	116.0
Dominica	5.8	5.4	4.0	4.2	4.2	2.6	1.4	1.0	0.8	2.2	95.9	92.6	82.0	74.1	72.3	82.1	76.8	72.9	84.0	88.0
Grenada	5.6	-4.5	-4.6	-4.2	-3.6	3.7	-6.4	-6.6	-6.1	-5.8	...	112.4	107.5	100.0	95.8	...	...	...	...	...
Guyana	-9.1	-9.3	-4.6	-5.1	-4.0	-13.5	-13.1	-7.5	-7.9	-6.5	...	155.3	98.8	103.7	115.2	...	...	...	...	...
Jamaica	11.1	8.8	8.1	5.6	3.0	-3.5	-5.3	-4.7	-7.4	-11.0	...	117.8	110.9	109.9	118.5	...	...	...	...	...
Saint Kitts and Nevis	4.0	6.0	6.0	8.9	19.7	-4.1	-2.4	-2.4	0.4	10.9	...	112.0	109.4	100.7	105.2	...	...	...	...	...
Saint Vincent and the Grenadines	-1.3	-0.7	-0.6	2.1	0.7	-4.2	-3.9	-3.6	-1.3	-3.0	70.6	66.3	56.1	54.1	57.8	...	...	...	...	...
Saint Lucia	-3.5	-3.0	0.9	2.9	5.5	-6.5	-6.1	-2.1	-0.2	1.3	55.8	56.8	61.7	60.7	63.2	...	...	...	...	...
Suriname	1.7	1.7	5.7	5.8	0.8	-0.8	-0.6	7.1	2.3	-1.0	38.9	24.9	28.5	25.2	25.7	...	...	...	...	...
Trinidad and Tobago	7.5	8.3	3.7	9.7	-3.3	5.0	6.3	1.8	7.8	-5.3	20.1	16.8	16.8	14.5	19.0	...	...	...	...	...

Source: Economic Commission for Latin America and the Caribbean (ECLAC), on the basis of official figures.

[a] Includes social security.
[b] At 31 December each year, using the average exchange rate for external debt. The figures for 2009 correspond to balances at June that year.
[c] Simple averages.
[d] Official targets as cited in 2010 budgets.
[e] General government.
[f] Non-financial public sector.
[g] Public sector.
[h] Fiscal years.

Within the first group, the most exposed countries were the Bolivarian Republic of Venezuela, Ecuador, Mexico and the Plurinational State of Bolivia, which may be considered highly specialized in natural resources. Their combined fiscal income fell by 3.9 percentage points of GDP.[3] Another group is formed by countries which have an intermediate level of natural resources specialization (Argentina, Chile, Colombia and Peru). Their average fiscal income fell by 1.3 GDP percentage points.

By contrast, the countries of the region that do not specialize in natural resources experienced a combined negative variation of 0.5 GDP points. Here, fiscal income is highly sensitive to changes in output, as shown by the GDP elasticities of fiscal aggregates, which are generally above 1. This is basically because tax receipts rise more than proportionately to output during expansionary cycles, since the upturn in the formal economy drives a more than proportionate increase in imports and in related taxes. Conversely, during recession the tax take falls faster than output because of the reversal of these same mechanisms, as well as a significant rise in tax evasion.

As discussed in box II.1, the countries of the region have adopted a range of measures in response to the crisis. Most of these measures consisted of different forms of public spending hikes, but some countries (such as Brazil and Chile) also created tax incentives, which had repercussions on receipts.

The various tax cuts implemented in Brazil since 2008, at an estimated fiscal cost of 0.8% of GDP, include: deferment of tax payments, tax breaks on purchases of automobiles, accelerated reimbursement of tax credits, reduction of financial transactions tax and lower rates for personal income tax. In Chile, the tax measures carried an annual cost of around 0.8% of GDP and included the elimination of stamp tax on loans extended in 2009, the temporary reduction of first category monthly provisional payments, early corporate tax refunds, and tax incentives and subsidies to encourage worker retention and training.

Table II.2
LATIN AMERICA AND THE CARIBBEAN: VARIATION IN FISCAL REVENUES, 2008-2009
(Percentages of GDP)

	Variation 2008-2009	Share in average variation
Countries highly specialized in commodities	-3.9	-0.8
Countries somewhat specialized in commodities	-1.3	-0.3
Countries not specialized in commodities	-0.5	-0.3
Total	-1.4	-1.4

Source: Economic Commission for Latin America and the Caribbean (ECLAC), on the basis of official figures.

Box II.1
FISCAL POLICY RESPONSES TO THE INTERNATIONAL CRISIS

Countries responded to the crisis with a broad range of measures that sought mainly to strengthen aggregate demand and offset the regressive social effects on the more vulnerable sectors of either the crisis itself or the adjustment measures it may have triggered.

The fiscal measures adopted vary widely, given the different capacities each country has to manage and execute them, and depending on the availability of resources. The measures announced may be grouped into two categories of instruments: (i) measures involving tax systems and (ii) measures involving fiscal spending.[a]

The following table provides a schematic view of the wide range of government measures. On the income side, these run the gamut from changes to the income tax structure, through adjustments to the tax base (deductions, exemptions or accelerated depreciation systems) or to nominal tax rates, to reform of taxes on goods and services (VAT, specific taxes or tariffs). On

the spending side, the measures sought mainly to boost investment in infrastructure, housing, programmes to support small- and medium-sized enterprises (SMEs) and small farmers, or financed variety of social programmes.

However, falling fiscal revenue, tight credit conditions and limited capacity in some countries to execute investment projects have delayed implementation of many of these measures. Some initiatives that have been or are being implemented are discussed below.

Tax measures:

Although tax cuts or expanded tax benefits were not as common as spending measures in the Latin American and Caribbean countries, some specific cases are worthy of note. Brazil temporarily lowered the industrialized products tax (IPI), which is levied on vehicles, electrical appliances and construction materials, cut the rate of tax on financial transactions and introduced lower personal income tax rates

(of 7.5% and 22.5%) for those earning up to US$ 875 per month.

As part of its fiscal stimulus plan, Chile temporarily reduced monthly income tax withholdings, eliminated stamp duty on loans extended during 2009 and broadened tax incentives for some sectors.

Uruguay implemented a bonus in the form of a waiver of the economic activities income tax (IRAE), for up to 120% of the value of investments made in 2009, under the law on investments, which especially benefits projects that create new jobs.

Several countries, such as Chile and Peru, implemented mechanisms for early tax rebates and accelerated tax reimbursements for companies and exporters.

Fiscal spending measures:

This type of measure seeks mainly to stabilize aggregate demand and mitigate the effects of the crisis on the most vulnerable sectors. However, these policies need to be implemented in a timely manner in order to have a real effect.

---

[3]   In Ecuador, although non-oil revenues rose on the back of receipts from income tax, VAT and other taxes, the drop of just over 40% in oil income (owing to the fall in oil prices) led to a contraction of over 10% in the central government's total income.

Box II.1 (concluded)

LATIN AMERICA (19 COUNTRIES): MAIN FISCAL MEASURES ANNOUNCED IN RESPONSE TO THE CRISIS [a]

	Argentina	Bolivia (Plurinational State of)	Brazil	Chile	Colombia	Costa Rica	Ecuador	El Salvador	Guatemala	Haiti	Honduras	Mexico	Nicaragua	Panama	Paraguay	Peru	Dominican Rep.	Uruguay	Venezuela (Bolivarian Republic of)
Tax system																			
Corporate income tax (cuts/depreciation)			X	T	X	T	X		X			T	X			X	X	T	
Personal income tax (cuts)	X		X	T	X		X		X	X		T	X	X			X		
Foreign trade taxes	X	X	T				X					X	T		T		X	X	
Taxes on goods and services			T			X	X					X						X	X
Social contributions	X											T							
Other			X	T	X				T			X			T		X	X	
Public spending																			
Infrastructure investment	X	X	X	X	X	X	X		X		X	X	X		X	X	X	X	
Housing	X	X	X	T	X	X	X	X	X		X	X	X		X	X	X	X	
Support for SMEs or agricultural producers			X	X	X	X	X	X	X	X	X	X	X		X	X	X	X	X
Support for strategic sectors	T	X	X	X	X				X		X	X				X		X	
Direct transfers to families	T	X		T	X			X			X	X			X				
Other social programmes	X		X	X	X		X		X	X	X	X	X	X	X	X	X	X	
Other spending			X	X										X					

Source: Economic Commission for Latin America and the Caribbean (ECLAC).

[a] T= Temporary measures

The Government of Argentina sought to sustain public investment, increasing the national public sector's real direct investment by an annualized 82.4% during the first half of 2009, with a sharp rise in investment going to infrastructure and energy.

Chile also adopted a number of spending-side countercyclical measures, including its fiscal stimulus plan (PEF), which provided for a US$ 700-million increase in public investment in urban and rural roads, housing, public health, educational facilities and irrigation works, a plan to stimulate lending, job creation and training schemes, as well as other measures aimed at strengthening social protection. By June 2009, 58.7% of the resources allocated to investments under PEF had been executed.

In Mexico, the National Agreement on Family Economy and Employment (ANFEFE) was set up in January 2009. Like the countercyclical measures contained in the Growth and Employment Stimulus Programme (PICE), ANFEFE was aimed at hastening recovery from the negative impacts of the crisis. Also, in response to the epidemiological emergency, 6 billion pesos were deposited in the trust fund of the health protection system, and 27 billion pesos were allocated to the sectors worst affected (such as the swine industry, hotels, aviation, restaurants and leisure activities).

Peru implemented a two-year economic stimulus plan for 2009-2010 worth some 3.6% of GDP, which focuses on infrastructure projects

and measures to jumpstart economic activity and address social protection issues.

Many countries sought ways to strengthen social programmes, including financial assistance for the most vulnerable; for example, the Plurinational State of Bolivia introduced the Juancito Pinto grant for school children, the Juana Azurduy grant for expectant mothers and the "Dignity Income" programme for those over 60 years of age. Chile offered two one-off payments for low-income families, each of approximately US$ 70 per dependant, which benefited about 1.5 million people. Costa Rica extended the period of social security unemployment benefits, subsidized transport and food and raised pensions under the non-contributory scheme by 15%.

Other fiscal measures:

Several countries, such as Brazil, Chile, Colombia, Panama and Peru, lowered their primary surplus targets. For example, Brazil's budgetary guidelines Act of 2007 set the primary surplus target for the consolidated public sector at 4.25% of GDP for 2009. The 2008 budgetary guidelines act adjusted the 2009 target downwards, to 3.8% of GDP. Later, the target was further reduced to 2.5% of GDP in response to the crisis.

Colombia also adjusted its deficit target for the consolidated public sector, from 1.5% of GDP at the beginning of the year to 2.6% of GDP in the latest revision.

Chile, whose structural balance rule initially specified a surplus of 1% of GDP,

lowered the target to 0.5% early in 2009, then reduced it again to 0%, where it will remain for 2010. Peru modified its fiscal responsibility and transparency law to allow increased public spending. Panama's fiscal social responsibility law, which went into force in January, capped the fiscal deficit at 1% of GDP, then raised that ceiling to 2.5% of GDP in June.

To compensate for the fall in transfers to subnational governments (occasioned by the decline in central governments' tax revenues), some countries, including Peru, implemented compensatory transfer mechanisms, while others eased restrictions on subnational governments. For example, Argentina's fiscal responsibility law, which had imposed spending and borrowing caps on provincial governments, was reformed so as to lift its core restrictions during fiscal years 2009 and 2010.[b] Brazil provided partial relief to the finances of subnational governments by allowing subnational governments to renegotiate their debts owed to social security.

Lastly, to support investment financing through increased lending, Brazil poured capital into the National Economic and Social Development Bank (BNDES) amounting to three percentage points of GDP over a two-year period. Chile also injected fresh capital into government agencies such as the Chilean Development Corporation (CORFO) and Banco Estado, to support lending to SMEs and microenterprises, and into the State-owned copper company (CODELCO).

Source: Economic Commission for Latin America and the Caribbean (ECLAC), *The reactions of the Governments of the Americas to the international crisis: an overview of policy measures up to 30 September 2009* (LC/L.3025/Rev.5), Santiago, Chile, 30 October 2009.

[a] This distinction is important because the use of different fiscal policy instruments does not produce the same outcomes. See study on the potential outcomes of different fiscal policy instruments in Gómez Sabaini and Jiménez (2009).

[b] Under this reform, provincial primary spending growth can outstrip GDP growth, governments can run deficits, the provinces can finance current spending by selling fixed assets and budget entries, such as capital expenditures, can be reallocated to current expenditures.

The evolution of tax resources in some of the countries of the region in 2009 shows the largest fall in receipts occurring in the second quarter, with the drop easing in the third quarter. Among the countries for which information is available, Chile stood out in both quarters, with a real negative variation of as much as 30%. Year-on-year variation in tax revenue was still negative in the third quarter, but significantly less so than in the second quarter, pointing to an upturn in receipts.

Figure II.3

LATIN AMERICA (6 COUNTRIES): REAL TAX RECEIPTS OF CENTRAL GOVERNMENT, NOT INCLUDING SOCIAL SECURITY

(Year-on-year quarterly variation, in percentages)

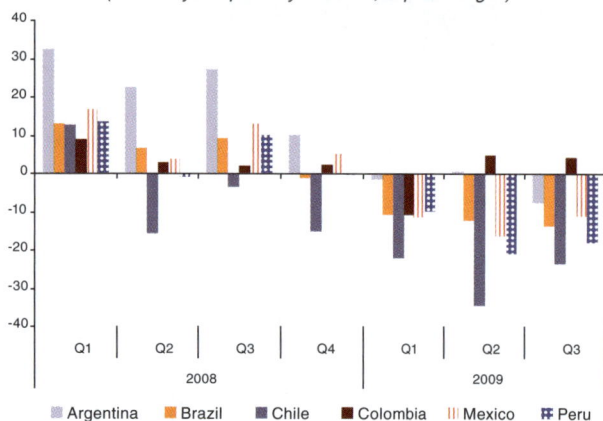

Source: Economic Commission for Latin America and the Caribbean (ECLAC), on the basis of official figures.

In the case of Argentina, the slight real decrease in tax revenue is caused by a rise in revenues from payment instalment schemes, which compensate the downturn in income tax receipts to a certain extent (by 5% in real terms up to September). This, in turn, was associated with changes in income tax regulations and in social security contributions, which affected the receipts from personal income tax and reduced revenues from tax withholdings and prepayments by wage-earners and independent workers. The smaller tax collection also reflected the option of reduced tax advances for certain firms, a decrease in the amounts corresponding to income tax returns and a fall in imports, which affected customs receipts. Resources from export duties dropped 21% in real terms, owing to the fall in exports in dollars and tariff reductions on some products. In the case of Brazil, slackening economic activity, especially in manufacturing, combined with the tax cuts mentioned earlier, generated a reduction in nominal federal receipts. The largest drops occurred in corporate income tax (IRPJ), the industrial products tax (IPI), and the contributions to the financing of the social security system (COFINS and the social integration programme

PIS/PASAEP). Over 93% of the year-on-year fall in total tax revenues is accounted for by these three items. In Chile, the slump in tax receipts was due mainly to the 42% drop in income tax revenues, which reflected a fall of 83% in real terms in tax payments by private mining (because of the lower copper price) and a drop of 18% in income tax receipts from other taxpayers (as a result of the temporary reduction in monthly provisional payments under the fiscal stimulus plan and slackening economic activity). Receipts of value added tax (VAT) fell by a cumulative 15.8% up to September, mainly owing to a decline in consumption and a rise in rebates. In Mexico, non-oil tax receipts dropped by 12.8% in real terms in January-September, owing to falls in takings from VAT (down 19.5%), income tax (down 12.0%) and flat-rate business tax (IETU) (down 7.5%). Colombia is the only country to show an increase in tax revenues in the second and third quarters of 2009, on the back of a rise in income tax which was basically due to income from withholding tax, especially the higher payments projected from the mining sector, mainly ECOPETROL.

The deterioration in central government fiscal revenue directly affects the finances of lower levels of government in the more decentralized countries in the region, because the income structure of the subnational governments is based essentially on transfers from central government. Transfers make up over 7% of GDP in Argentina, Mexico and the Plurinational State of Bolivia, and around 5% of GDP in Colombia and Ecuador, and represent 80% of the total income of subnational governments in Ecuador and Mexico. Given the importance of transfers in financing the operations of subnational governments and their sensitivity to national tax receipts, it is important to monitor their evolution during times of crisis such as this. As shown in figure II.4, transfers slowed heavily since the first quarter of 2009 and fell outright in the third in Argentina, Brazil, Peru and the Plurinational State of Bolivia. Peru made a transfer to local government in July 2009 as a one-off support package, to offset the impact of the previous fall. Accordingly, transfers rose by 12% in real terms, otherwise they would have dropped by 17%.

As for expenditures, since the end of 2008, in line with growing consensus about the countercyclical role of fiscal policy in times like these, the countries have made many announcements involving mostly greater expenditures (whether current or capital expenditures).[4] However, not all of these announcements were implemented in 2009, for a number of reasons. First, the combination of reduced

---

[4]   See box II.1 for a detailed list of the fiscal measures announced in response to the crisis.

fiscal revenues and tightened credit at the beginning of the year reduced the fiscal space needed to implement the announced expenditure increases. An example of this is Guatemala's National Emergency Economic Recovery Programme, which was announced in 2009 but has seen limited results because of funding shortfalls. Several countries of the region have had problems executing their expenditures, which has stymied many of the announced public investment programmes.

Figure II.4
LATIN AMERICA (4 COUNTRIES): EVOLUTION OF GOVERNMENT TRANSFERS IN REAL TERMS
(Year-on-year quarterly variation, in percentages)

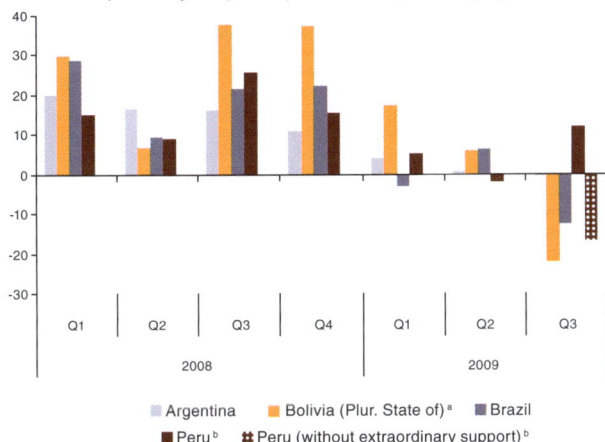

Argentina Bolivia (Plur. State of) [a] Brazil
Peru [b] Peru (without extraordinary support) [b]

Source: Economic Commission for Latin America and the Caribbean (ECLAC), on the basis of official figures.
[a] Includes the benefit known as "dignity income".
[b] Does not include fees or royalties, or ordinary resources from transfers of items beginning in 2009.

Figure II.5
LATIN AMERICA AND THE CARIBBEAN: CENTRAL GOVERNMENT EXPENDITURES, 1990-2009
(Percentages of GDP)

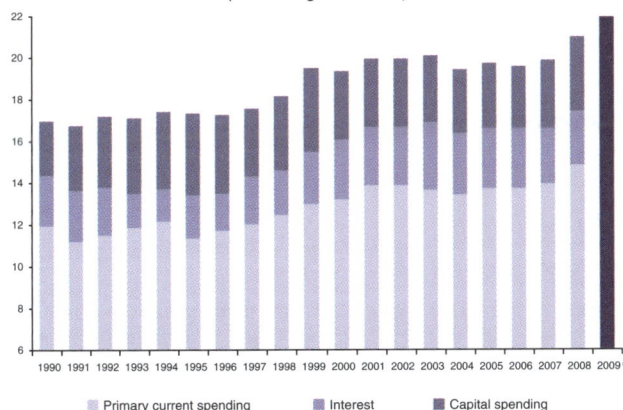

Primary current spending Interest Capital spending

Source: Economic Commission for Latin America and the Caribbean (ECLAC), on the basis of official figures.
[a] Estimate.

The evolution of expenditures over the year is related to the capacity of the governments to deploy countercyclical policies. The countries can be broken down into three groups: those that increased spending, those that kept it relatively constant and those that reduced it.

Chile is the most notable in the first group. Its countercyclical strategy consisted of a fiscal stimulus plan equivalent to 2.8% of GDP, the main measures of which were public investment, home-buying subsidies, loans to SMEs and microenterprises and grants for lower-income families. Costa Rica is also in this first group, with higher outlays mainly in the form of current expenditures resulting from policy action such as expanded unemployment coverage, food and transport subsidies and a rise in pensions. Argentina's higher expenditures reflected expansions in social security benefits and coverage, transfers for financing welfare funds in the provinces, public wage hikes and the implementation of infrastructure, housing and energy programmes.

The second group includes the countries of Central America, many of which announced significant measures (for example, Guatemala and El Salvador), though implementation had to be postponed because of falling revenue and a lack of financing. The authorities of these countries expect the effects of these measures to begin to be seen in 2010.

The third group encompasses the countries that are highly specialized in natural resources and the Dominican Republic, whose public expenditures have contracted. In the case of the Bolivarian Republic of Venezuela, spending was most reduced in the area of capital expenditures, which reflects the drop in capital transfers and a cutback in fixed-asset acquisitions. As for current spending, public sector wages were increased below the rate of inflation, representing a drop in wage outlays in real terms. In Ecuador capital spending tumbled in 2009 from the extraordinary level recorded in 2008, but remained quite high compared with 2007.

As figure II.6 shows, after several years of successive reductions, the ratio of public debt to GDP edged up in 2009. Up to June 2009, public debt had increased as a percentage of GDP in most of the countries of the region, which was reflected in an increase in the indebtedness of the region as a whole.

Several factors that had helped to reduce the debt-to-GDP ratio in 2002-2008 reversed their trends in 2009. The drop in primary balances and in the level of economic activity were the main factors affecting variations in public debt stock.

Figure II.6

LATIN AMERICA AND THE CARIBBEAN (18 COUNTRIES): GROWTH IN PUBLIC DEBT OF THE CENTRAL GOVERNMENT, 1991-2009

(Percentages of GDP)

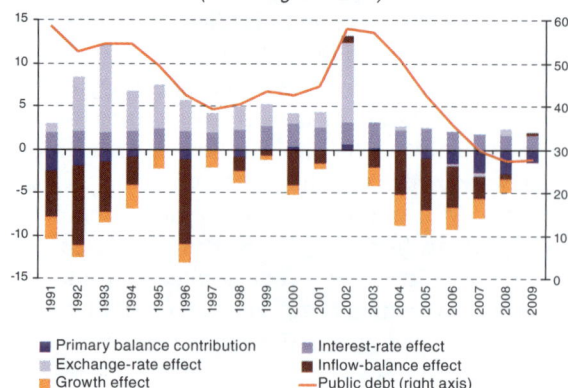

- ■ Primary balance contribution
- ■ Interest-rate effect
- ■ Exchange-rate effect
- ■ Inflow-balance effect
- ■ Growth effect
- — Public debt (right axis)

Source: Economic Commission for Latin America and the Caribbean (ECLAC), on the basis of official figures.

As can be seen in table II.1, the averages mask some very diverse situations among the countries: Chile's debt-to-GDP ratio is 4%, whereas Guyana's and Jamaica's are over 115%. Thus, average levels of indebtedness differ greatly between the countries of Latin America (28% of GDP) and the Caribbean (79% of GDP).

As ECLAC (2009a) has indicated, the public debt of most of the English-speaking Caribbean countries has exceeded levels that could in any way be defined as sustainable, and the situation only worsened in 2009 (see box II.2). In table II.1 it can be observed that, except for Bahamas, Suriname, and Trinidad and Tobago, at the close of 2009 this subregion showed levels of public debt that ranged from 60% of GDP in Saint Lucia and Saint Vincent and the Grenadines, to almost 120% in Jamaica.

Box II.2

SUSTAINABILITY OF PUBLIC DEBT IN THE ENGLISH-SPEAKING CARIBBEAN

The high level of public indebtedness of most English-speaking Caribbean countries raises questions about future debt sustainability. Machado (2008) calculates the primary balance needed to stabilize the ratio between public debt and GDP. This primary balance correlates positively with the real interest rates of both debt types (external and domestic) and with the rate of depreciation, whereas it correlates negatively to the GDP growth rate.

The first table shows the figures used to calculate the primary balance needed to stabilize the ratio of public debt to GDP in four English-speaking Caribbean countries in fiscal year 2009-2010. Shown are the implicit interest rates on internal and external debt in 2006, the debt burden at the close of the most recent fiscal year, inflation rates for 2007 and the average annual GDP growth rate for 2002-2007. For Guyana and Jamaica, the nominal rates of

depreciation recorded in 2007 (1.2% and 6.2%, respectively) are used.

The second table shows the primary balance in fiscal year 2008-2009, the primary balance needed for the ratio between public debt and GDP to remain constant in fiscal year 2009-2010 and the primary balance needed to reduce the level of public debt to 40% of GDP in 20 years.

THE CARIBBEAN (FOUR COUNTRIES): FIGURES USED TO ANALYSE THE SUSTAINABILITY OF PUBLIC DEBT

(Percentages)

	Ratio of external debt to GDP, 2009	Ratio of domestic debt to GDP, 2009	Interest rate on external debt [a]	Interest rate on domestic debt [a]	Inflation rate in 2007 (close of year)	Average annual GDP growth rate, 2002-2007 [b]
Barbados	29.1	72.6	6.9	5.0	4.0	3.0
Belize	74.6	12.2	6.6	9.3	4.1	4.6
Guyana	78.0	37.2	1.8	3.8	4.2 [c]	1.7
Jamaica	51.6	66.9	7.2	5.7	5.8 [c]	1.8

Source: Economic Commission for Latin America and the Caribbean (ECLAC), on the basis of official figures.
[a] Interest paid in fiscal year 2006-2007 on the debt burden at the close of the previous fiscal year.
[b] In dollars at constant 2000 prices.
[c] Corresponds to 2006.

THE CARIBBEAN (FOUR COUNTRIES): ANALYSIS OF PUBLIC DEBT SUSTAINABILITY

(Percentages of GDP)

	Primary balance observed, 2008-2009	Primary balance needed to maintain constant the ratio of public debt to GDP in 2009-2010	Primary balance needed to reduce the level of public debt to 40% of GDP in 20 years
Barbados	0.1	-1.5	3.1
Belize	1.6	-1.5	2.3
Guyana	-4.0	-2.9	3.8
Jamaica	3.0	1.7	3.9

Source: Economic Commission for Latin America and the Caribbean (ECLAC), on the basis of official figures.

According to these calculations, Barbados, Belize, Guyana and Jamaica would have to post primary surpluses of between 2.3% and 3.9% of GDP over the next 20 years in order to reduce their current public debt to 40% of GDP, a level considered to be sustainable. Based on their primary balances and public debt at

the close of fiscal year 2008-2009, next year, Barbados would have to make a fiscal adjustment of 3% of GDP, whereas for Belize and Jamaica the adjustments would need to be in lesser amounts, 0.7% and 0.9% of GDP, respectively. Guyana's fiscal undertaking would have to be immense as it would need to convert a primary deficit of

4% of GDP into a primary surplus of 3.8% of GDP. In every case, it is important to bear in mind the marked recessionary effects of such fiscal adjustments, as well as their economic and social costs, which would be magnified if the current recessionary climate and economic slowdown resulting from the international crisis were to continue.

Source: R. Machado, "The sustainability of public debt", *Un gasto que valga. Los fondos públicos en Centroamérica y República Dominicana*, R. Machado (ed.), Washington, D.C., Inter-American Development, Bank (IDB), 2008.

Although the region is better placed, in fiscal terms, to face the crisis than it has been in times past, the greatest need for State intervention comes just as the gap between fiscal revenues and growing demand for public expenditures is being stretched wider. This means that significant challenges lie ahead if the capacity of the public sectors is to be increased, both to respond to critical episodes and to meet the many existing demands.

The state of affairs in the Caribbean countries merits separate mention. The virtual insolvency of the public sectors in these countries is of great concern, because debt servicing saps large amounts of funds from the public treasury. In Jamaica, these payments reached a record 14% of GDP in fiscal year 2008-2009. Furthermore, the weight of public debt, which is fed by chronic fiscal deficits, significantly limits the design and implementation of fiscal policy and, in many cases, jeopardizes the sustainability of the subregion's macroeconomic regimes.

Lastly, it should be stressed that each country's potential to implement a countercyclical public measure has less to do with the need for the measure than with its ability to fund it, which requires an assessment of the fiscal space attained.

These different capacities seem to have two faces: first, in those countries that specialize in natural resources they are a function of the response to the increase in public revenues driven in many cases by higher export prices. Second, particularly in countries which exhibit high poverty levels and experience terms of trade losses, once again a debate has arisen regarding the consequences of the crisis and the need to address them with countercyclical policies shows up the inadequacy of public sectors to respond to the needs of the population, not only because of institutional deficiencies (a clear sign of this is a limited capacity to execute policies), but also because of very low tax burdens.

B. Exchange-rate policy

As can be seen in figure II.7, in 2009 the extraregional real effective exchange rate of Latin America and the Caribbean (which excludes trade among the countries in the region) appreciated slightly compared with 2008. Although the regional average was almost unchanged in 2009, some important differences were observed among the countries of the region. Between December 2008 and October 2009, the currencies of the countries of South America experienced real appreciation (with a few exceptions), while Mexico, Central America and the Caribbean experienced effective depreciation.

The international financial crisis that emerged in the third quarter of 2008 triggered rapid nominal depreciation (in relation to the dollar) of the currencies of those countries that had the highest levels of exchange-rate flexibility, monetary policy regimes with explicit inflation targets and the greatest access to international capital markets, such as Brazil, Chile, Colombia and Mexico. The currencies of other countries in South America that depend heavily on commodities prices or that have close relations with Brazil, such as Paraguay and Uruguay, also depreciated (see figure II.8). During this period, the dollar appreciated in relation to other currencies as international investors sought liquid assets they perceived as low-risk, such as United States treasury bonds. In Central America and the Caribbean, other than the sharp depreciation of Jamaican

currency, the only currency that showed notable depreciation as a result of the economic crisis was the Guatemalan quetzal, which fell because of lower export prices and a considerable decline in remittances from emigrants.

Figure II.7
EXTRAREGIONAL REAL EFFECTIVE EXCHANGE RATE
(Base, January 1990-December 1999=100)

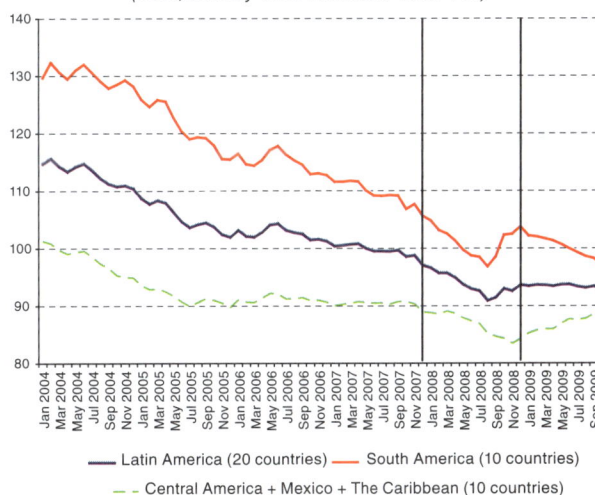

Legend: Latin America (20 countries) — South America (10 countries) — Central America + Mexico + The Caribbean (10 countries)

Source: Economic Commission for Latin America and the Caribbean (ECLAC), on the basis of official figures.

Figure II.8
LATIN AMERICA (SELECTED COUNTRIES): NOMINAL EXCHANGE RATES IN RELATION TO THE DOLLAR
(Base index, July 2008=100)

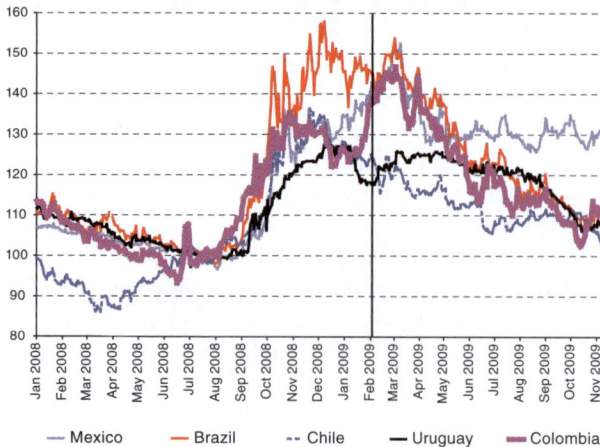

Source: Economic Commission for Latin America and the Caribbean (ECLAC), on the basis of official figures.

Currencies continued to depreciate nominally until March 2009. At that time, a number of factors converged to cause those currencies that had depreciated most to begin appreciating, a trend that would extend through the remainder of the year. With the United States facing low interest rates, a large fiscal deficit and ballooning public debt, and with expectations among the international capital markets improving as some indicators suggested that the worst of the crisis had passed for several countries (including many emerging countries), the demand for dollar-denominated assets fell. This was accompanied by investors showing an increased appetite for risk, which boosted demand for assets denominated in the currencies of several countries in the region. Also, the prices of some commodities, such as oil, some metals (copper, for instance) and of exports produced by countries in South America began to rise from the lows they had touched as a result of the international crisis. All of these factors increased investor interest in the assets of emerging countries, such as Brazil, and stimulated the nominal appreciation of their currencies during the period. Specifically, between March 2009 and November 2009: the Brazilian real appreciated by 25.4% in relation to the dollar; the Colombian peso, by 20%; the Uruguayan peso, by 13.5%; and the Chilean peso, by 11.9%. Thus, these currencies regained the trend of appreciation, as in 2007 and 2008, prior to the crisis.

For its part, the Mexican peso appreciated nominally by 9.3% during the period, on account of the appreciation that occurred between March and April, as shown in figure II.8. From then onwards and through November 2009, the Mexican peso hovered 30% above the level it held prior to the international crisis, owing partly to investor expectations about the short-term outlook for the economy.

Between March 2009 and November 2009, nominal exchange rates in Central America and the Caribbean registered few changes or minor depreciations: -2.7% in Guatemala, -1.5% in Costa Rica and -1.1% in the Dominican Republic. These countries, unlike those in South America, saw a decline in the inflows of international currencies owing to the drop in exports and shrinking remittances from emigrants.

In parallel with what was happening internationally —depreciation followed by appreciation of currencies of many countries in South America and Mexico— the central banks of those countries disaccumulated reserves or at least made no significant accumulations of reserves (between June 2008 and March 2009). As of March 2009 and through September 2009, they resumed their accumulations. This can be seen in figure II.9, which shows the exchange-rate interventions of Brazil, Colombia and Uruguay, three of the four countries whose currencies registered the highest nominal appreciations, as of March 2009. Brazil's accumulations were particularly strong, having acquired US$ 31.276 billion between April 2009 and October 2009. This pattern was repeated in other countries, such as Argentina, Mexico, Paraguay and Peru. There were some exceptions to this pattern in South America, however: the Plurinational State of Bolivia accumulated reserves in both periods, after having fixed its exchange rate; and the Bolivarian Republic of Venezuela saw a significant decrease in its international reserves owing in part to the central bank's transfer of reserves to the National Development Fund (FONDEN), to be used for a number of the Fund's projects.

Figure II.9
LATIN AMERICA (SELECTED COUNTRIES): EXCHANGE-RATE INTERVENTION
(Millions of dollars)

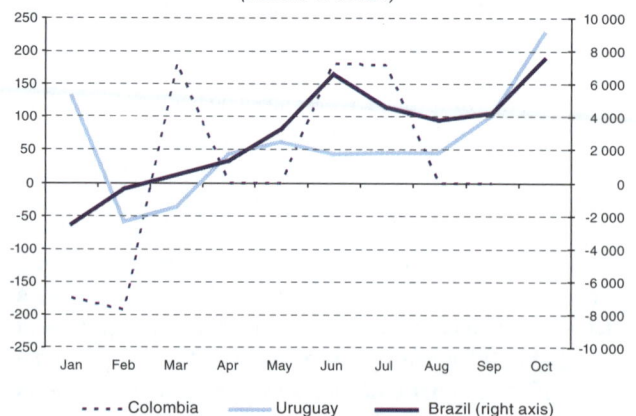

Source: Economic Commission for Latin America and the Caribbean (ECLAC), on the basis of official figures.

As was pointed out in the *Economic Survey of Latin America and the Caribbean 2008-2009*, since the international economic crisis began in the third quarter of 2008, the countries of the region with the freedom to do so, implemented a monetary policy that sought to reduce the impact the crisis on GDP in a context of decreasing inflation. Specifically, this policy called for significant reductions of interest rates and, in several cases, increases in monetary aggregates; in other cases, such as in Brazil, it meant taking additional measures to inject liquidity into the private sector, in both domestic and international currencies. This approach to monetary policy was maintained throughout 2009.[5]

Despite the significant lowering of the monetary policy rates and the Brazilian central bank's intervention as a purchaser in the exchange market, as has already been mentioned, the real appreciated by 25.4% in relation to the dollar between March 2009 and November 2009. In response to this, on 20 October 2009, Brazilian authorities decided to impose a tax on investment capital inflows (direct foreign investment was exempted). Later, on 19 November 2009, a 1.5% tax was imposed on American Depositary Receipts (ADR) of Brazilian companies listed on the New York Stock Exchange, in order to increase the effect the tax had on the market value of the real (see box II.3).

Box II.3
LATIN AMERICA: MEASURES ADOPTED TO MODERATE CAPITAL INFLOWS

In March 2009, the currencies of many countries of the region began to appreciate against the dollar, resuming a trend that had been in place until the international crisis began. In particular, capital flows into those countries, among which Brazil, Chile and Colombia stand out, were an important element behind the appreciation of their currencies. Since the first quarter of 2009, given the high levels of international liquidity, low interest rates in industrialized countries such as the United States (and the prospects that they will remain low in the near future), the limited growth of their economies and the fundamental variables of emerging countries, financial flows to emerging economies have been strong.

As occurs in other parts of the world, in the Latin American countries whose currencies have been appreciating steadily, authorities have, by and large, adopted the policy of accumulating international reserves to prevent excessive currency volatility or to counteract significant fluctuations driven by expectations that do not necessarily correlate with changes in the fundamental variables of the economy. As the sections in this document that deal with exchange rates and capital flows have shown, this practice has enabled the countries of the region to build sizeable reserves.

There have been, however, instances in which the countries of the region have turned to instruments other than intervention in the foreign-exchange market to achieve these aims. At times, they have used tools such as legal reserve requirements, taxes on incoming capital and restrictions imposed on sales to foreigners of some assets that are denominated in national currency to influence capital flows and their impact on exchange rates.

Some of these recently implemented alternative instruments are examined below:

Chile imposed reserve requirements on capital entering from abroad during the 1990s, as a control mechanism, in response to a surge in inflows at the start of the decade (Cowan and De Gregorio, 2005). In June 1991, a non-yield-bearing reserve requirement, initially set at 20%, was applied to capital inflows for periods that varied according to investment type. As Cowan and De Gregorio (2005) indicate, in 1992 and 1995, the reserve requirement also applied to international currency and currency obtained through offerings of American depository receipts (ADR), and the reserve requirement was raised to 30% of capital flows for a fixed 12-month term, regardless of an instrument's maturity or nature. In June 1998, in response to the crisis that year, the reserve requirement was lowered to 10%, and in September, to 0% (Forbes, 2002). The central bank did away with the requirement completely in April 2001 (see [online] http://www.bcentral.cl/prensa/comunicados-consejo/pdf/16042001.pdf). It should be noted that the free trade agreement between Chile and the United States allows Chile to impose restrictions on capital inflows and outflows for periods of up to one year without these becoming susceptible to dispute (DIRECON, 2009).

Since June 2005, Argentina has required a deposit, in dollars, against international currency inflows, equal to 30% of the dollar value of the total operation. Through November 2009, this obligatory deposit was being applied, with some exceptions, to a variety of types of inflows: financial debts of the financial and non-financial private sectors; initial stock offerings by resident companies that are not offered through initial public offerings or publically traded in self-regulating markets (insofar as these are not equity-related funds); portfolio investments by non-residents leading to ownership of local currency and financial assets and liabilities of the financial and non-financial private sectors, as well as acquisition of secondary-market warrants for securities issued by the public sector and initial subscriptions to bonds issued by the central bank; international currency that enters the local exchange-rate market from sales of external assets by private sector residents, in amounts exceeding US$ 2 million per calendar month; and funds entering the local foreign exchange market for the purpose of subscribing to initial offerings of debt instruments, bonds or certificates of participation issued by the fiduciary of a trust.[b] International debts assumed and refinanced by residents are subject to a minimum 365-day term and may not be cancelled before the term expires.

From May 2007 to October 2008, Colombia required that foreign investors make a non-yield-bearing deposit for foreign portfolio investments in stocks and that foreign direct investment remain

---

Box II.3 (concluded)

in the country for minimum of two years. The required deposit, originally set at 40% of the total to be invested, was raised to 50% on 30 May 2008 (see Bulletin No. 19 of Banco de la República de Colombia). These requirements were lifted as part of the policy to counteract the effects of the international crisis, specifically in the case of new inflows for the purchase of stocks and bonds that are convertible into common stock, as well as investment in mutual funds consisting exclusively of stocks or convertible bonds. However, the deposit requirement continued to be imposed on other foreign portfolio inflows, especially investments in fixed-income assets.

The Central Reserve Bank of Peru, in addition to making direct interventions in the foreign exchange market, uses adjustments to dollar reserve requirements as a tool for managing internal liquidity in foreign currency (Rossini, Quispe and Gondo, 2008). The upsurge of capital inflows in early 2008 caused the bank to adopt other measures to limit capital

inflows, in addition to its heavy intervention in the exchange market and increases to its reserve requirements for both nuevos soles and dollars (in order to reduce the need for sterilization).[c] For a time, the bank stopped issuing certificates of deposit, replacing them first with auctions of non-transferable deposits and, later, with certificates of deposit with restricted negotiability. These could only be acquired by domestic financial entities, thus restricting their role to that of liquidity control instruments and disallowing their conversion into attractive investment assets for foreign investors. Negotiation of these instruments was limited to those who had participated in the placement auction. According to the central bank's January 2008 inflation report, on 5 February 2008 non-residents owned 30% of the certificates of deposit. Another measure taken at that time was to impose a commission on transfers of ownership of certificates of deposit to non-residents. It should be noted that, as of the signing of its free trade agreement with the United States, Peru is restricted when it comes

to imposing discriminatory measures on United States investments.

The most recent example is Brazil; on 20 October 2009 a 2% tax went into effect on capital inflows to be used to purchase stocks and bonds, though foreign direct investment was exempted. One month later, in order to make the capital inflows tax more effective, Brazil decided to levy a 1.5% tax on ADRs of Brazilian companies listed on the New York Stock Exchange. During the previous period, when the real was appreciating significantly in nominal terms, Brazil had imposed a 1.5% tax on foreign investment in fixed-income assets. This tax was subsequently eliminated in October 2008 with the onset of the international crisis.

Interest in instruments such as the ones mentioned, for the purpose of (potentially) modifying capital inflows, is not limited to policymakers in Latin America, but extends to the other emerging markets as well, as exemplified by Taiwan Province of China's decision to prohibit term deposits by non-residents.

Source: Economic Commission for Latin America and the Caribbean (ECLAC), on the basis of K. Cowan and J. De Gregorio, "International borrowing, capital controls and the exchange rate: lessons from Chile", *Working document*, No. 322, Santiago, Chile, Banco Central de Chile, May 2005; K.J. Forbes, "One cost of the Chilean capital controls: increased financial constraints for smaller traded firms", *MIT Sloan Working Paper*, No. 4273-02, December 2002; Dirección General de Relaciones Económicas Internacionales de Chile (DIRECON), *Chile: 20 años de negociaciones comerciales*, Santiago, Chile, Foreign Ministry, November 2009; Banco Central de la República Argentina, Communiqué, No. 49561, 19 November 2009; R. Rossini, Z. Quispe and R. Gondo, "Macroeconomic implications of capital inflows: Peru 1991–2007", *Financial Globalisation and Emerging Market Capital Flows*, BIS Papers, No. 44, December 2008.
[a] Especially, if these movements cause the exchange rate to reach levels that raise concerns about possible currency misalignment.
[b] Among the exceptions are loans in foreign currency issued by local financial entities, foreign direct investment, investments by non-residents for the purchase of real estate and financial borrowing from the international non-financial private sector if the term of debt is not less than two years and is for the purpose of investment in non-financial assets (see Banco Central de la República Argentina, Communiqué No. 49561).
[c] In 2008, marginal reserve requirements for deposits of non-residents reached 120%.

In Central America, Mexico and Jamaica, remittances from emigrants began to fall off in the fourth quarter of 2008, a downturn that became even sharper in the first two quarters of 2009, as is covered in the section of this document that addresses the external sector. As remittances play an important role in the external sectors of the countries of the region (especially the smaller ones), their decline was a factor in the depreciation of several of the currencies of the region.

Regarding the total effective exchange rate, between December 2008 and October 2009, the currencies of only five countries in the region showed effective appreciation: Brazil, by 26.2%; the Bolivarian Republic of Venezuela, by 13.3%; Colombia, by 10.2%; Uruguay, by 9.1%; and Chile, by 8.5%. As is discussed in the section of this document that deals with inflation, the overall inflation rate started dropping abruptly when the international financial crisis began. It is important to note that the Bolivarian Republic of Venezuela has maintained a fixed and unchanged exchange rate since March 2005, in a context of high inflation. This has caused the real effective exchange rate to appreciate sharply, though still less than its real appreciation in relation to the dollar given the real appreciation of the currencies of its trading partners in the region.

In addition to the Central American countries, Ecuador, the Plurinational State of Bolivia and Paraguay also registered depreciation of their effective exchange rates during the period. In the case of the Plurinational State of Bolivia and Paraguay, the depreciation stems mostly from the significant appreciation of the currencies of their trading partner since March 2009 (especially the Brazilian real), which improved their relative competitiveness. In Ecuador's case, the weakness of its legal currency (the dollar), beginning in the second quarter of 2009 (especially in relation to trading partners such as Colombia), led to its effective depreciation.

As a result of currency depreciation in 2008 and the subsequent appreciation experienced by several countries in South America, in October 2009, the real effective exchange rates for the region were as they appear in figure II.10, where they are presented in relation to 20-year historical averages.[6] Two important points should be emphasized: first, the real effective exchange rate of the currency of the Bolivarian Republic of Venezuela was, in October 2009, 50.7% below (appreciation) its 20-year historical average, the lowest level for the past 30 years. Secondly, one can observe how the process of nominal appreciation of the currencies of Brazil, Chile, Colombia and Uruguay led to, in a short time, significant reductions in the exchange rates of those countries. However, in the case of the latter two countries, exchange rates were not far off their historical averages.

Figure II.10
LATIN AMERICA AND THE CARIBBEAN (SELECTED COUNTRIES): TOTAL REAL EFFECTIVE EXCHANGE RATES
(Rates in December 2008 and October 2009, compared to averages for 1990-2009)

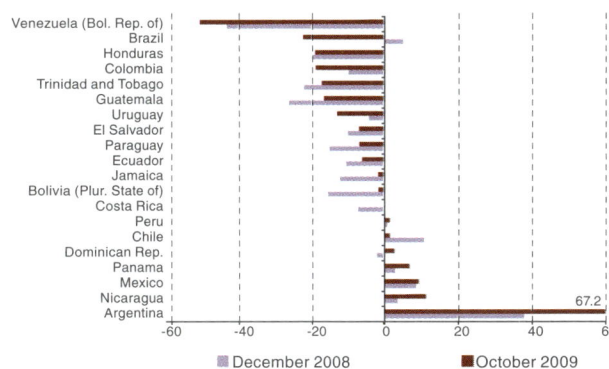

Source: Economic Commission for Latin America and the Caribbean (ECLAC).

C. Monetary policy

In 2009, with the exception of Mexico, the countries of the region that run inflation-targeting schemes —Brazil, Chile, Colombia, Paraguay and Peru— recorded inflation below or within the target range set by their central banks. Though this stands in contrast to the pattern of inflation seen in 2008 (see figure II.11), it also differs from the three years prior to 2008, inasmuch as inflation is actually below the target range in quite a few of the countries. In 2009, the central banks of these countries did not raise their inflation target ranges, their interpretation being that the inflationary surge had been associated with the effect of external turmoil on international commodity and oil markets driving up the prices of those goods, especially between the third quarter of 2007 and the second quarter of 2008.

Monetary policy began to be loosened in September 2008. In response to international financial shocks the central banks began to take a number of measures, including the opening of special lines of credit to inject liquidity into national financial systems, both in national currency and in dollars (see box II.4). Reflecting the prevailing uncertainty and liquidity squeeze, the interbank rate rose in the fourth quarter of 2008, especially in Uruguay (see figure II.12a and b). The central banks followed these infusions of liquidity with cuts in monetary policy benchmark rates, which passed through to a greater or lesser degree to the interest rate structures in the economies. The interbank rate was no exception, as the two rates are closely related under normal conditions of liquidity within the financial sector. Another indicator that liquidity problems seemed to have been solved in a number of the region's countries in 2009 was that as of the second quarter some central banks began to accumulate international reserves, a shift from what had occurred in the fourth quarter of 2008 and first quarter of 2009.[7]

---

[6] More specifically, during the period 1990-2009.

[7] See the section on exchange-rate policy for more details.

Figure II.11
LATIN AMERICA (SELECTED COUNTRIES): EFFECTIVE, CORE AND TARGET RANGE INFLATION
(Percentages)

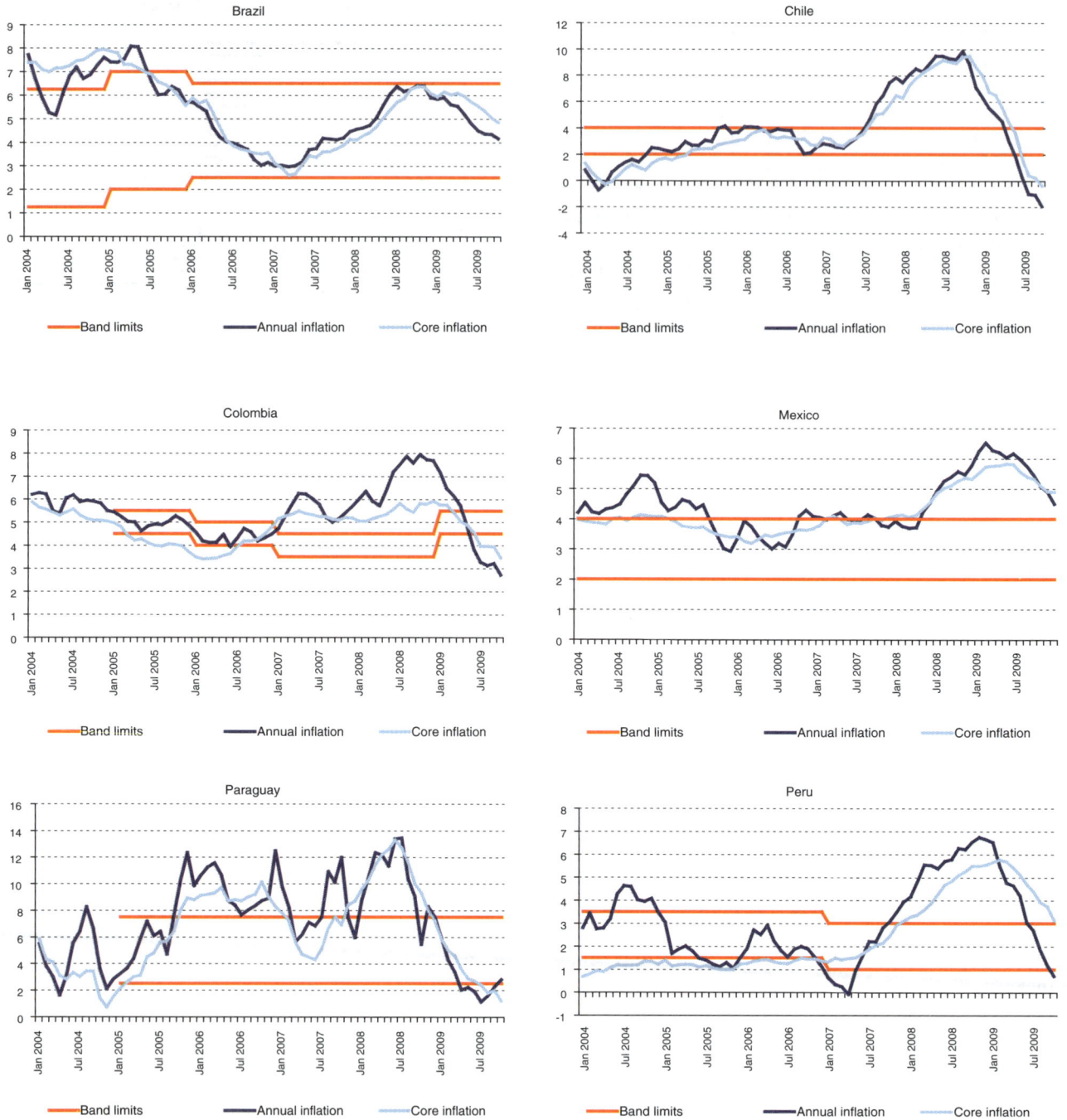

Brazil

Chile

Colombia

Mexico

Paraguay

Peru

Source: Economic Commission for Latin America and the Caribbean (ECLAC), on the basis of official figures.

Box II.4

MONETARY POLICY MEASURES TAKEN IN THE REGION IN RESPONSE TO THE INTERNATIONAL FINANCIAL CRISIS

Monetary policy began to be loosened in September 2008. In response to international financial shocks the central banks began to take a number of measures, including the opening of special lines of credit to inject liquidity into national financial systems, both in national currency and in dollars (see table).[a]

In addition to adjusting monetary policy reference rates, central banks also modified legal reserve requirements and took steps to inject liquidity into the financial system and guarantee its stability. Regarding the first of these measures, monetary authorities of 12 Latin American and Caribbean countries lowered their cash reserve requirements in both domestic and international currency, in order to increase the secondary expansion potential of the money supply. The reserve requirement was also lowered for foreign-currency deposits, in the case of the Plurinational State of Bolivia, to below the requirement for deposits in bolivianos, thus encouraging holdings in domestic currency.

Twenty-seven countries in the region implemented a variety of measures aimed at increasing liquidity in the financial system, including the early repurchasing of bonds issued by central banks or the net redemption of securities (which, in practice, means reducing the balance of outstanding bonds issued by the central bank), increasing lines of credit with the financial system or securing loans against the credit portfolios of institutions, expanding repurchasing operations and injecting liquidity through debt repurchases. Some of the measures taken represented innovative ways of supplying liquidity to the financial system. For example, the central bank of Uruguay offered banks the possibility of swapping tax rebate certificates for cash, and the central bank of Colombia replaced liquidity absorption operations with a more liquid instrument: interest-bearing deposits.

Lastly, other examples of measures taken can be seen in Argentina, where tighter regulation was imposed on international transfers, prohibiting operations with countries that do not facilitate access to information, in order to avoid deposits in banks outside of Argentina;[b] or in Brazil, which expanded the central bank's power to intervene in troubled financial institutions. El Salvador, Barbados, Guyana and Trinidad and Tobago proposed measures to improve regulation and supervision of the financial system.

LATIN AMERICA AND THE CARIBBEAN: MONETARY POLICY MEASURES

	AR	BO	BR	CL	CO	CR	CU	EC	SV	GT	HT	HN	MX	NI	PA	PY	PE	DO	UY	VE	BS	BB	BZ	GY	JM	SR	TT	AI	AG	DM	GD	MS	KN	LC	VC	CA	US
Monetary and financial policy																																					
Change in banking reserve	X	X	X	X	X				X	X		X			X	X	X								X												
Injection of liquidity in national currency	X	X	X	X	X	X				X		X	X	X	X	X	X	X	X			X			X		X	X	X	X	X	X		X	X	X	X
Changes in benchmark interest rate			X	X	X	X		X				X	X			X	X	X	X			X			X		X									X	X
Other measures	X		X						X	X		X			X	X				X	X	X	X		X	X	X										X

[a] See ECLAC (2009) for a descriptions of the measures taken by each country.
[b] This measure was taken jointly by the Federal Public Revenue Administration (AFIP), the central bank of the Republic of Argentina (BCRA) and the National Securities Commission (CNV).

Figure II.12

LATIN AMERICA AND THE CARIBBEAN (SELECTED COUNTRIES): INTERBANK RATE
(Percentages)

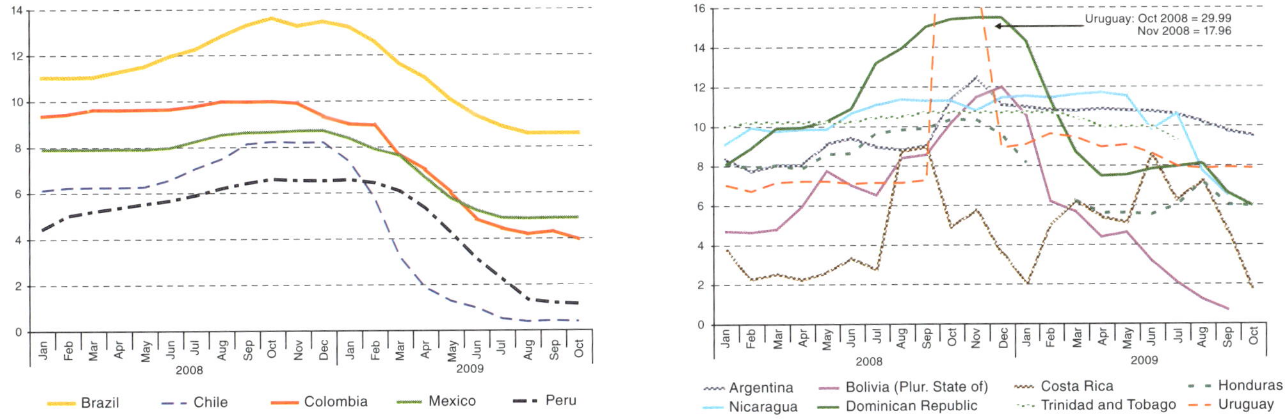

Source: Economic Commission for Latin America and the Caribbean (ECLAC), on the basis of official figures.

The main measure taken by the central banks in 2009 was to maintain their expansionary stance by lowering reference rates, once clear signs had emerged that inflationary pressures were easing.[8] The first central banks to lower benchmark rates were those that run inflation-targeting schemes (see figure II.13a). The Bank of Mexico began lowering its rate in January, the same month inflation began to slow in that country. In Brazil, Chile and Colombia, whose year-on-year inflation rates began to subside in November 2008, monetary authorities started to lower their monetary policy rates upon receipt of the December inflation rate. The Central Reserve Bank of Peru lowered its rate in February, after inflation dropped for three months in a row. The central bank of Uruguay lowered its interest rate in April, while the central bank of Trinidad and Tobago did so after four consecutive months of decreasing inflation. The central bank of Jamaica lowered its rate for the first time in July, after seven consecutive months of falling year-on-year inflation.

Figure II.13
LATIN AMERICA AND THE CARIBBEAN (SELECTED COUNTRIES): NOMINAL MONETARY POLICY BENCHMARK RATE OF INTEREST
(Percentages)

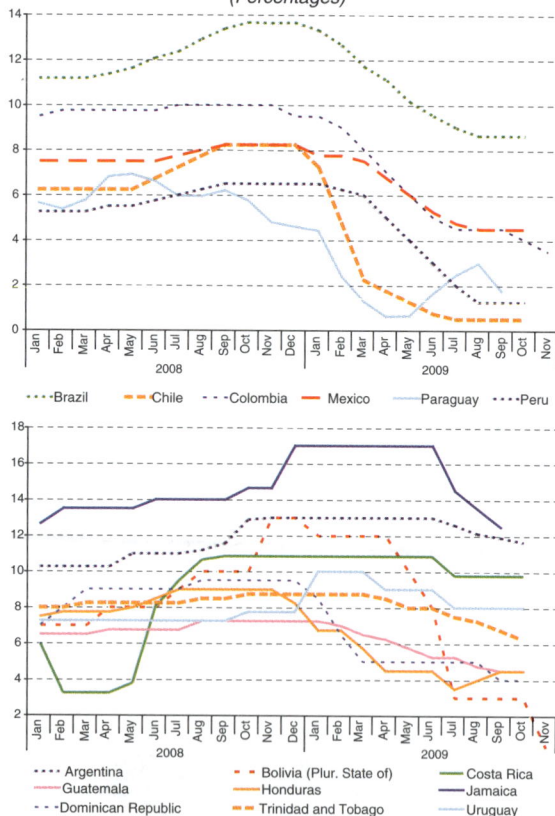

Source: Economic Commission for Latin America and the Caribbean (ECLAC), on the basis of official figures.

[8] The central banks of Honduras and Paraguay were the only ones to break the downward trend of benchmark rates: rate cuts ran from September 2008 to July 2009 in Honduras and from October 2008 to April 2009 in Paraguay.

In most cases, monetary policy benchmark rates were adjusted several times during the year, amid expectations of disinflation owing to slack economic conditions, which gave monetary authorities greater leeway to leverage demand-stimulus policies. The central bank of Colombia lowered its rate nine times; the central banks of Chile, Guatemala, Mexico and Peru did so seven times; Trinidad and Tobago, six; Honduras, five; the Dominican Republic and Jamaica, four; and Costa Rica and Uruguay, twice and once, respectively. Overall, the cuts were similar in magnitude in all the countries. In absolute terms, the largest rate reductions took place in the Plurinational State of Bolivia (1,000 basis points), Chile (775 basis points), the Dominican Republic (550 basis points), Colombia (550 basis points), Peru (525 basis points) and Brazil (501 basis points), while the smallest were recorded in Uruguay (25 basis points), Argentina and Costa Rica (109 basis points each). These three countries also showed the smallest relative variation in reference rates, measured as the ratio between recent highs and lows (80%, 92% and 90%, respectively). The countries with the largest relative variation were Chile, where the rate dropped to a low that represented 6% of its maximum value; Peru, at 19%; the Plurinational State of Bolivia, 23%; Colombia, 35%; and the Dominican Republic, 42%.[9] In Brazil, Chile, Colombia and Peru, the nominal rates at the end of November were the lowest recorded since those countries adopted an inflation-targeting system, and in Mexico the lowest since August 2003. Despite these efforts, because of the sharp fall in inflation, some central banks showed increases in their reference rates in real terms (see figure II.14).

The effect of these lowered rates on average bank lending rates varied among countries. In Colombia, the Dominican Republic, Mexico and Uruguay, the reduction of the monetary policy benchmark rate led to an even greater absolute drop in bank lending rates, whereas in Chile, Costa Rica, Peru, the Plurinational State of Bolivia, and Trinidad and Tobago the bank lending rate came down by less. In Brazil, the reductions in the two rates were similar. Proportionally speaking, however, lending rates dropped less than monetary policy benchmark rates (lending rates remain high compared with the reference rates in the region overall). In October 2009, the ratio between the average lending rate and the benchmark rate ranged from 1.9 in Uruguay to 23.3 in Chile. In Peru, the ratio was 12.4, though the ratio of the average preferential

[9] The central bank of Jamaica lowered its reference rate by 450 basis points and the ratio of the rates at their lowest and highest points was 74%. The Bank of Mexico cut its benchmark rate by 3.75 percentage points, and the respective ratio was 55%. In the case of the central bank of Guatemala, these figures were 2.75 percentage points and 62%, respectively, and in the case of the monetary authority of Trinidad and Tobago, 2.50 percentage points and 71%, respectively.

Figure II.14
LATIN AMERICA AND THE CARIBBEAN (SELECTED COUNTRIES): REAL MONETARY POLICY
BENCHMARK RATE OF INTEREST
(Percentages)

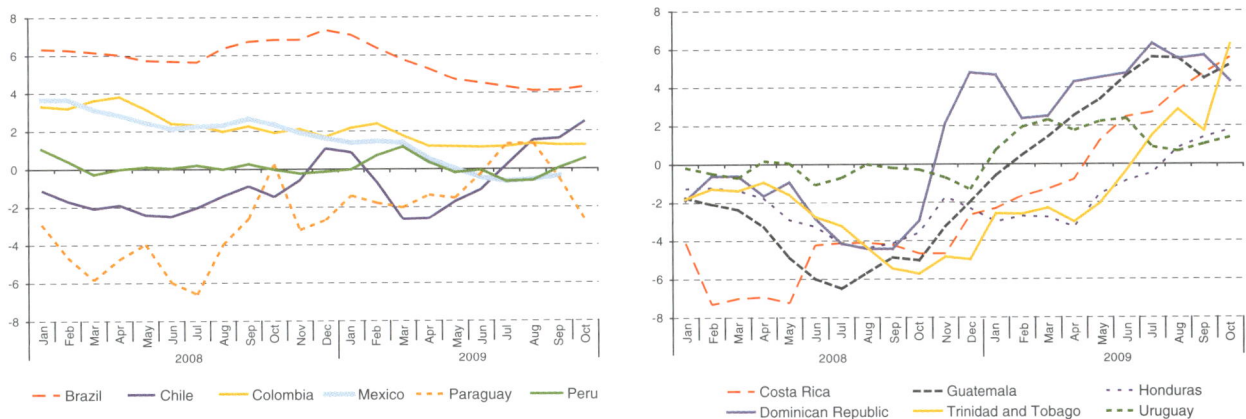

Source: Economic Commission for Latin America and the Caribbean (ECLAC), on the basis of official figures.

lending rate to the monetary policy benchmark rate was 1.2. The spread between bank lending and deposit rates did not fall below the 2008 fourth-quarter spread until the third quarter of 2009, with the exception of Chile, Costa Rica, Honduras and the Plurinational State of Bolivia.

In some countries, the liquidity generated by net redemption of securities by the central bank is not necessarily channelled into the private sector, but has also gone to finance the public sector. This is the case in the Plurinational State of Bolivia, where the treasury increased its domestic-currency bond issues by 39.3% between October 2008 and October 2009. This increase in bond issues is equivalent to 49.3% of the drop in the central bank's open market operations. To September, Paraguay saw a 39% year-on-year drop in the balance of monetary regulation instruments, which has been partially offset by the issuance of treasury bonds.

1.   Bank loans and deposits

In 2009, the rate of growth of private lending, as may be expected following the economic downturn, slowed in all of the countries (including Chile, Colombia, Honduras, Mexico and Uruguay), as compared with the four previous years (see figure II.3). Consumer and commercial credit fell off the most. Figure II.4 shows the evolution of lending by public banks, which increased considerably, except in Uruguay, showing that some of the region's governments have tried to use public banks to compensate for sluggish private lending. A further sign of slump in lending is the increase in non-performing loans as a percentage of total loans. In year-on-year terms, for September 2009, this indicator was up in Argentina from 2.8% to 3.7%; the Bolivarian Republic of Venezuela, from 2% to 2.6%; in Brazil, from 2.8% to 4.4%; in Chile, from 0.9% to 1.3%; in Colombia, from 4.1% to 4.5%; in Mexico, from 2.8% to 3.5%; and in Peru, from 1.2% to 1.6%. In contrast, in the Plurinational State of Bolivia, the rate dropped from 5% to 4.2%. However, the banking systems of the aforementioned countries have sufficient loan-loss provisions.

One fact worthy of note is that this weak phase of the economic cycle, generated by the international financial turmoil, brought no major bank failures in Latin America. The only exception was when, in November, the Superintendency of Banks and Financial Institutions of the Bolivarian Republic of Venezuela intervened in four banks that accounted 7.1% of total private bank deposits. Meanwhile, in the Caribbean the financial system felt the impacts of the international crisis. In January 2009, Trinidad and Tobago intervened in the CLICO Investment Bank and two of its subsidiary insurance companies. The bank held 11% of the country's financial assets, and the insurance companies 50% of all insurance policies. Between February and April, the governments of Bahamas, Barbados, Belize, Guyana, Suriname, as well as authorities in the Eastern Caribbean Currency Union (ECCU), assumed control of CLICO subsidiaries. The Stanford Bank was also intervened in 2009, in Antigua and Barbuda. As a result of these developments, financial services in the Caribbean countries recorded a downturn in 2009.

Table II.3
LATIN AMERICA (SELECTED COUNTRIES): EVOLUTION OF PRIVATE BANK LENDING
(Percentage annual variation)

Country	Period	Industrial		Commercial		Mortgage		Consumer		Rural		Total	
		2008	2009	2008	2009	2008	2009	2008	2009	2008	2009	2008	2009
Brazil	September to September	33.80	-4.17	29.29	-4.37	34.01	25.55	21.32	6.38	18.06	-4.90	26.84	1.11
Chile	September to September	...	...	-2.68	-3.86	22.49	18.28	3.33	-0.91	...	...	1.20	-1.10
Colombia	September to September	....	...	11.23	0.25	3.69	0.22	7.27	-3.25	...	...	8.88	-1.12
Costa Rica	September to September	23.10	4.76	1.58	-6.03	22.49	18.28	32.51	-4.03	5.49	10.86	17.63	7.79
Honduras	September to September	-3.40	0.01	3.91	-34.44	...	...	13.66	-10.97	-0.89	11.93	20.83	-0.36
Mexico	June to June	...	...	16.74	2.20	12.08	3.81	10.82	-19.02	...	...	14.32	-3.26
Paraguay	September to September	...	...	50.85	17.44	...	...	74.16	17.68	41.84	14.06	40.21	32.51
Peru	September to September	13.32	-2.20	28.34	0.77	12.88	22.43	35.68	-3.14	4.84	5.91	24.21	6.24
Uruguay	September to September	14.05	-20.98	37.28	-8.92	...	...	49.87	13.97	25.08	-23.82	26.23	-11.37

Source: Economic Commission for Latin America and the Caribbean (ECLAC), on the basis of official figures.

Table II.4
LATIN AMERICA (SELECTED COUNTRIES): EVOLUTION OF PUBLIC BANK LENDING
(Percentage annual variation)

Country	Period	Industrial		Commercial		Mortgage		Consumer		Rural		Total	
		2008	2009	2008	2009	2008	2009	2008	2009	2008	2009	2008	2009
Brazil	September to September	30.56	22.23	25.74	20.10	25.90	40.76	26.18	37.58	12.59	7.71	26.00	33.00
Chile	September to September	...	...	-3.60	33.62	12.72	9.33	5.31	10.38	...	...	3.81	20.67
Colombia	September to September	...	...	30.21	32.40	-0.17	-2.16	9.78	30.19	...	...	19.97	36.19
Costa Rica	September to September	-10.60	8.53	21.79	11.27	17.57	7.72	16.08	3.20	15.08	11.23	15.40	5.82
Honduras	September to September	...	...	...	...	...	...	...	...	...	...	...	...
Mexico	June to June	...	...	-14.27	11.11	71.60	59.67	16.11	15.67			-13.28	27.56
Paraguay	September to September	13.32	-2.20	-19.16	77.30	...	...	28.34	9.34	-11.74	21.93	-2.14	35.18
Peru	September to September	...	...	-3.29	7.60	-17.78	3.15	...	-9.01	...	...	10.65	10.19
Uruguay	September to September	50.11	-28.13	4.78	56.54	...	...	85.67	-22.96	35.04	39.00	63.82	-2.18

Source: Economic Commission for Latin America and the Caribbean (ECLAC), on the basis of official figures.

No major changes are expected on the monetary front in the near future, barring the occurrence of external turmoil that could alter current macroeconomic conditions and unless further changes are made to reference rates, such as the decision in late November by Colombia's central bank to reduce its rate from 4% to 3.5% in order to offset shrinking trade with the Bolivarian Republic of Venezuela.

Chapter III

Domestic performance

A. Economic activity and investment

For Latin America and the Caribbean, GDP is expected to decline by 1.8% in 2009, which represents a drop of 2.9% in per capita GDP for the region. These figures reflect the impact of the international economic and financial crisis, which the countries of the region began to feel with increasing intensity in the last quarter of 2008. Economic activity declined most sharply in Mexico, owing to its closer proximity to, and greater dependence on, the United States economy and the impact of the influenza A (H1N1) outbreak in the second quarter of the year, and in the English- and Dutch-speaking Caribbean, which experienced a 2.1% downturn in GDP owing to the effects of the crisis on tourism and on external demand for commodities. Meanwhile South America and Central America will post a rise of 0.2% in GDP.[1] Economic performance varied considerably across the region, and despite the negative average variation for the region as a whole, GDP in a significant number of countries increased in 2009.[2]

The steepest rises in GDP were in the Plurinational State of Bolivia (3.5%), the Dominican Republic (2.5%), Panama (2.5%) and Haiti (2%), while the sharpest declines were in Mexico (-6.7%) Paraguay (-3.5%), Honduras (-3%), El Salvador (-2.5%) and the Bolivarian Republic of Venezuela (-2.3%). In the remaining countries, the variation in GDP was between -1.5% and 1.2%.

Despite declining, per capita GDP in 2009 exceeded that of 2007. The sole exception was Mexico, where the 7.7% drop brought this indicator down to levels last seen in 2004.

---

[1] Includes Costa Rica, Cuba, the Dominican Republic, El Salvador, Guatemala, Haiti, Honduras, Nicaragua and Panama.
[2] The simple average rate of change in GDP is -0.4%, while the median is 0.0%.

With the exception of El Salvador, Guatemala, Haiti, Mexico, Nicaragua and Paraguay, per capita GDP in 2009 was between 15% and 50% higher than in 2004 —the year in which regional economic activity began to gain greater momentum.

Figure III.1
LATIN AMERICA AND THE CARIBBEAN: CHANGE IN GROSS DOMESTIC PRODUCT, 2008-2009
(Percentages, in dollars at constant 2000 prices)

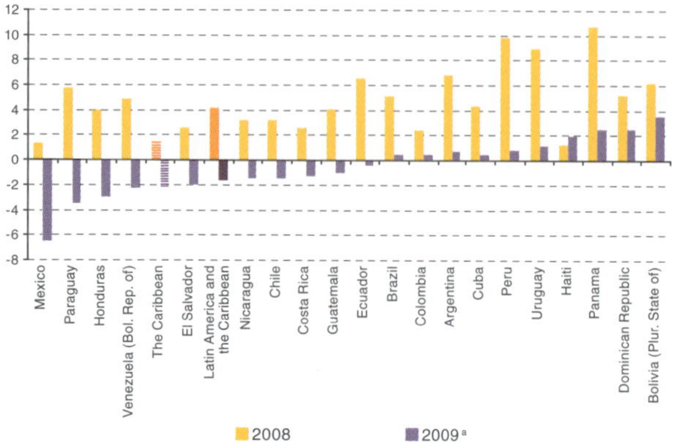

Source: Economic Commission for Latin America and the Caribbean (ECLAC), on the basis of official figures.
a Estimate.

Figure III.2
LATIN AMERICA AND THE CARIBBEAN: PER CAPITA GROSS DOMESTIC PRODUCT, 2004-2009
(2000=100, in dollars at constant 2000 prices)

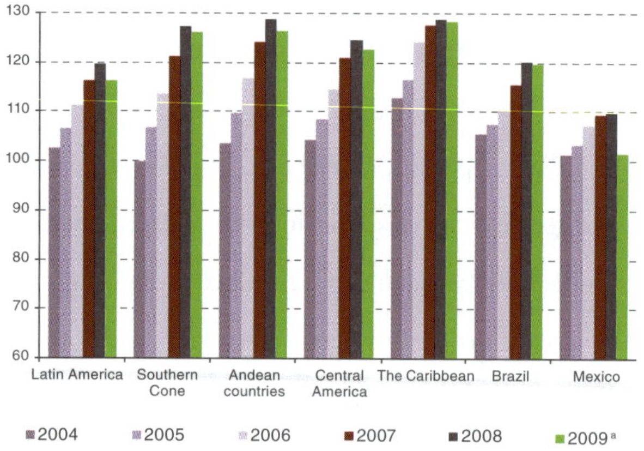

Source: Economic Commission for Latin America and the Caribbean (ECLAC), on the basis of official figures.
a Estimate.

The effects of the abrupt change in international economic conditions during the final months of 2008 were felt more acutely by the economies of Latin America and the Caribbean in 2009. Up to the third quarter of 2008, the economic performance of the region as a whole had

been notably robust, having been driven by strong external demand and rising domestic demand, which pushed up both consumption and investment. This, bolstered by the appreciation of national currencies with respect to the United States dollar, had led to a marked rise in the volume of imported goods and considerable accumulation of inventories.

Figure III.3
LATIN AMERICA AND THE CARIBBEAN: PER CAPITA GROSS DOMESTIC PRODUCT, BY COUNTRY, 2004 AND 2009
(2000=100, in dollars at constant 2000 prices)

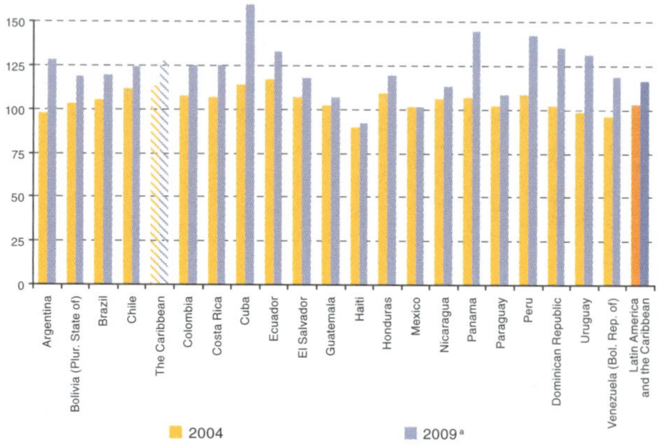

Source: Economic Commission for Latin America and the Caribbean (ECLAC), on the basis of official figures.
a Estimate.

In the fourth quarter of 2008, this scenario changed noticeably. There was an acute drop in external demand, the volumes and prices of the region's exports plummeted, and restrictions on supply and higher interest rates made accessing credit increasingly difficult. All of this occurred in an environment of heightened uncertainty about the fallout of the crisis in the international financial system, the capacity of developed economies to recover, the impact of the crisis on emerging economies, and changes in the price of commodities and exchange rates.

Expectations among economic agents worsened, and, in an environment of increased uncertainty and tighter credit, this led to a major decline in total spending. Fears of unemployment and the sharp drop in remittances from emigrants lowered household consumption, which provoked a downturn in retail sales in many of the region's countries. Gross fixed capital formation plummeted as investment projects were halted and investment in machinery and equipment plunged as a result of the rise in unused installed capacity and the higher cost of imports caused by the depreciation of a number of the region's national currencies in the fourth quarter of 2008 and the first quarter of 2009.[3] As a result, the volume of imported goods contracted sharply.

The analysis of the effect of the current economic crisis on regional macroeconomic aggregates reveals certain similarities with what occurred during the crises of 1995 and 1999. In those years, domestic demand contracted sharply, with investment being the most severely affected component. While the crises of 1995 and 1999, like the present one, were triggered by external factors, their strong impact on the region's economies was due primarily to domestic imbalances that proved to be unsustainable. Moreover, these crises originated in emerging economies, and in that period, demand in the developed economies continued to grow, particularly in the United States, where GDP grew at an average annual rate of 3.8% between 1993 and 2000. In both periods, regional economies, suffered balance-of-payments crises, and their inability to continue financing external imbalances led to contractions of domestic demand and currency devaluations. In this context, the rising volume of goods exports was the main component of aggregate demand, and the factor that allowed the region's economies to start their economic recovery.

A number of factors differentiate the present crisis from previous ones. The current one originated in the developed countries, at a time when the countries of the region generally did not have significant external imbalances. However, the sharp contraction of external demand meant that the countries with greater trade openness and less diverse export markets were the hardest hit. The external turmoil, which was aggravated by uncertainty surrounding the future course of the international economy, caused the volume of goods and services exports, as well as commodity prices, to plummet (thus reducing the export-based revenues of agents in both the public and private sectors), and economic agents adjusted their spending and production levels accordingly. Import volumes also shrank considerably, in fact, more than export volumes, so net exports contributed positively to economic growth. Domestic demand fell over the year, but not as much as expected considering the sharp decline in imports, owing to the major reductions in inventories. Public consumption was the only component, at the

regional level, that continued to grow. Although this aggregate had also been a positive factor in previous crises, its impact on the region was even greater this time because a number of countries had managed to boost their savings as a result of the increased revenues obtained from commodity exports.

Figure III.4
LATIN AMERICA: ANNUAL CHANGE IN GROSS DOMESTIC PRODUCT AND IN COMPONENTS OF AGGREGATE DEMAND, 1991-2009
(Percentages, in dollars at constant 2000 prices)

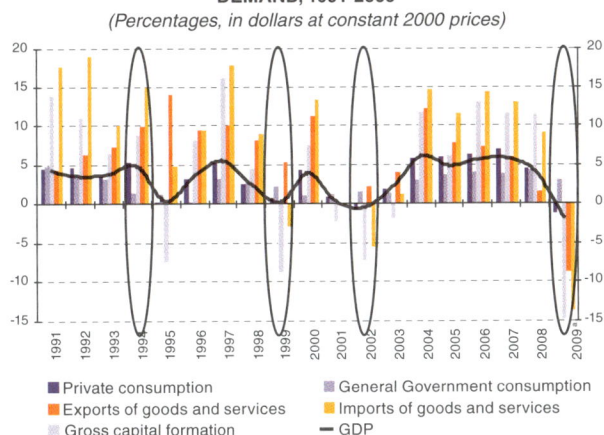

■ Private consumption   ■ General Government consumption
■ Exports of goods and services   ■ Imports of goods and services
■ Gross capital formation   — GDP

Source: Economic Commission for Latin America and the Caribbean (ECLAC), on the basis of official figures.
[a] Estimate.

Figure III.5
LATIN AMERICA: YEAR-ON-YEAR VARIATION IN QUARTERLY GROSS DOMESTIC PRODUCT, 1998-2009
(Percentages, in dollars at constant 2000 prices)

——— Estimate

Source: Economic Commission for Latin America and the Caribbean (ECLAC), on the basis of official figures.

---

[3]   Imports of capital goods fell sharply in most of the countries during 2009. In September of that year, as compared to September 2008, the value of such imports declined by 35% in Argentina, 25.6% in Peru, 23.4% in Mexico, 14% in Brazil and 6.4% in the Bolivarian Republic of Venezuela.

Box III.1
MAIN CONSEQUENCES OF THE DISASTERS IN LATIN AMERICA AND THE CARIBBEAN

In 2009, large-scale disasters caused damages and losses in the region totalling over US$ 10 billion, more than the average losses incurred in 2000-2008 (US$ 8.6 billion). The seriousness of the disasters in Latin America and the Caribbean particularly impacted tourism and agriculture. Tourism suffered mainly as a result of the influenza A (H1N1) outbreak in Mexico, but the worst damage in the agricultural sector was caused by floods in north-eastern Brazil and in El Salvador. This is worrying inasmuch as natural disasters have been

identified as one of the factors that will adversely affect agriculture in the future and they are expected to increase in terms of frequency and intensity as a result of climate change.

The year 2009 was exceptional in terms of major health disasters in the region. In addition to influenza A (H1N1), several countries suffered outbreaks of dengue fever, which spread most aggressively in the Plurinational State of Bolivia.

As can be seen in the following table, climatic disasters are both the most

common type (accounting for nearly 80% of all disasters) and the most damaging as far as the region's population is concerned (accounting for 55% of deaths and 78% of number of people affected). In economic terms, however, 90% of disaster-associated costs in 2009 were attributable to health disasters, mainly as a result of the influenza A (H1N1) outbreak and the ensuing downturn in economic activity in Mexico, where the costs incurred were equivalent to 1% of GDP.

LATIN AMERICA AND THE CARIBBEAN: PRELIMINARY OVERVIEW OF THE IMPACT OF DISASTERS, 2009 [a]

Type	Disasters		Deaths		Population affected		Economic impact	
	Number	Percentage	Persons	Percentage	Persons	Percentage	Millions of dollars	Percentage
Climatic	37	79	642	55	2 375 532	78	1 088	11
Geological	8	17	378	32	239 748	8	200	2
Health	2	4	144	12	415 925	14	9 008	87
Total	47	100	1 164	100	3 031 205	100	10 297	100

Source: Economic Commission for Latin America and the Caribbean (ECLAC), on the basis of data from ReliefWeb and from EM-DAT.
[a] Preliminary data up to 20 November 2009.

In addition to the outbreak of influenza A (H1N1), excess humidity, hurricanes and storms, followed in importance by strong seismic activity in Central America, incurred high costs in the northern part of the region. South America was marked by floods in north-eastern Brazil, which affected nearly two million people and caused damage to vast livestock-raising and crop-growing areas, and by dengue

fever in the Plurinational State of Bolivia. The spread of this disease was worsened by inadequate solid waste management and increasingly heavy rains in the affected area.

Although in absolute terms, Brazil and Mexico were hit the hardest by disasters in 2009, El Salvador was the country most severely affected in the region in relative terms. In absolute terms,

Mexico accounted for 90% of the costs, while Brazil accounted for 60% of the population affected by disasters in Latin America. Both Mexico and El Salvador suffered costs equivalent to 1% of GDP, but El Salvador also had the highest percentage of affected population in the region (3.6%), owing primarily to the powerful earthquake of May 2009 and the serious flooding in November.

LATIN AMERICA AND THE CARIBBEAN: PRINCIPAL DISASTERS, 2009

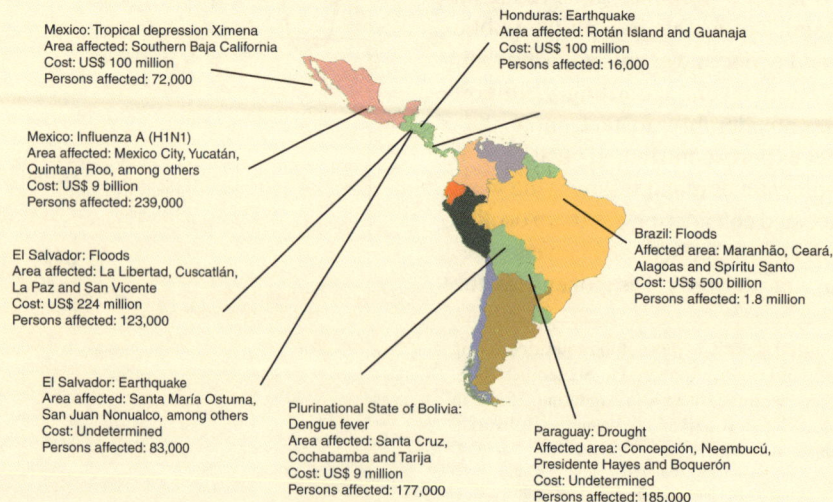

Source: Economic Commission for Latin America and the Caribbean (ECLAC).

After posting quarterly year-on-year growth rates of 5% or more between the first quarter of 2004 and the third quarter of 2008, regional GDP rose by only 1.2% in the last quarter of 2008 and then declined by about 2.5%, on average, in the first three quarters of 2009.

As of the second quarter of 2009, and to an even greater extent in the third quarter, the region's economies began to show signs of recovery in relation to the figures posted in the first half of the year, although at varying paces. This recovery was driven by several factors: the stimulus programmes and economic initiatives implemented by authorities; the reduction in benchmark interest rates; the rise in real wages in most of the countries brought about by the sharp drop in inflation; and the increase in financial sector activity (particularly lending, which had come to a halt in the fourth quarter of 2008), generated by expectations regarding the future of the international economy and by the recovery of industrial activity (albeit from a low starting point and because the inventory shedding process came to an end) That was spurred by both domestic and external demand. Activity in the construction and trade sectors also picked up, consumer confidence indicators improved, and export volumes began to rise. In most countries, however, the increased economic activity in the second half of 2009 has not been sufficient to offset the negative results seen in the first half of the year.

Figure III.6
LATIN AMERICA: GROSS FIXED CAPITAL FORMATION, 2009 [a]
(Dollars at constant 2000 prices)

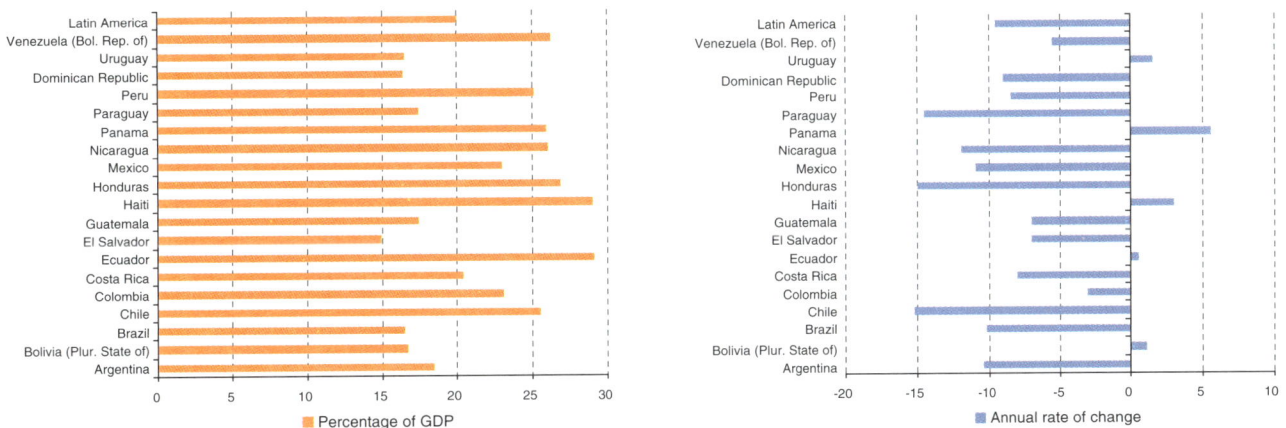

Source: Economic Commission for Latin America and the Caribbean (ECLAC), on the basis of official figures.
[a] Estimate.

In regional terms, domestic demand in 2009 shrank by 4.0%, private consumption by 1.3%, and investment by 15.5%. The sizeable decline in investment reflects the downturns seen in investment in all the countries; the decline in private consumption largely reflects the sharp drop in this type of consumption in Mexico. Gross fixed capital formation fell by 9.8% because investment in machinery and equipment and construction activity plummeted despite increased public investment on the part of both general government and public enterprises in a number of countries (Brazil, Colombia and Peru). Gross fixed capital formation in constant dollars (expressed as a percentage of GDP) thus fell from 21.9% in 2008 to 20.1% in 2009. The countries registering the steepest declines in gross fixed capital formation were Brazil, Chile, Honduras, Nicaragua, Mexico and Paraguay. The contraction in domestic demand, meanwhile, resulted in an appreciable drop in the volume of imported goods and services (-11.5%). Goods and services export volumes also fell (-8.4%) owing not only to the slump in goods imports, but also to the decrease in the volume of service exports, particularly those connected with tourism. As mentioned earlier, government consumption was the only component that grew in 2009, rising by 3%.

In current dollars, regional gross domestic investment in the region declined from 23.0% of GDP in 2008 to 19.5% of GDP in 2008. Regional domestic savings also fell, from 22.3% of GDP in 2008 to 19.1% of GDP in 2009. Income account deficits were smaller, but the disposable gross national income of the countries of the region shrank by 3.3% owing to the severe loss of earnings generated by the worsening of the terms of trade and decreases in net current transfers.

Figure III.7
LATIN AMERICA: GROSS FIXED CAPITAL FORMATION IN CONSTRUCTION AND IN MACHINERY AND EQUIPMENT, 1990-2009
(Annual percentage variation, in dollars at constant 2000 prices)

Construction   Machinery and equipment

Source: Economic Commission for Latin America and the Caribbean (ECLAC), on the basis of official figures.
a Estimate.

Figure III.8
LATIN AMERICA: FINANCING OF INVESTMENT, 1990-2009
(Percentages of GDP, in current dollars)

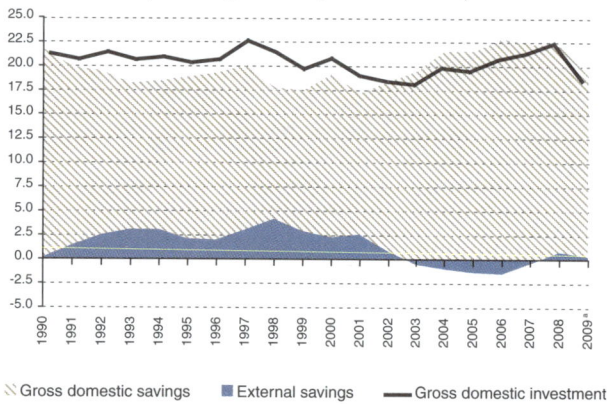

Gross domestic savings   External savings   Gross domestic investment

Source: Economic Commission for Latin America and the Caribbean (ECLAC), on the basis of official figures.
a Estimate.

The variations in aggregate supply and demand reflected the changes in activity levels in the different sectors. Agricultural activity diminished slightly in the region overall, with the situation varying from country to country. Agricultural activity declined in Argentina, Costa Rica, Paraguay and Uruguay but expanded in Cuba, the Dominican Republic, El Salvador, Haiti, Peru and the Plurinational State of Bolivia, as well as in several countries of the English-speaking Caribbean. The performance of the mining sector was also mixed, with output falling in Chile and the Dominican Republic, as well as in most of the English-speaking Caribbean, but rising in Belize, Suriname and Trinidad and Tobago.

Oil production in the Bolivarian Republic of Venezuela, Ecuador and Mexico fell, while the mining sectors of Argentina, Colombia, Peru, and the Plurinational State of Bolivia posted growth. Manufacturing was the worst-hit and suffered declines in all the countries. The production of capital goods and durable consumer goods and specific segments, such as the textile and maquila industries, experienced the sharpest downturns. In comparison with production in the same period in 2008, automobile production in the first 10 months of 2009 contracted by 40.3% in Argentina, 35% in Mexico and 10.3% in Brazil.

Figure III.9
LATIN AMERICA: ANNUAL CHANGE IN GROSS DOMESTIC INVESTMENT, GROSS DISPOSABLE NATIONAL INCOME AND DOMESTIC SAVINGS
(Percentages, in dollars at constant 2000 prices)

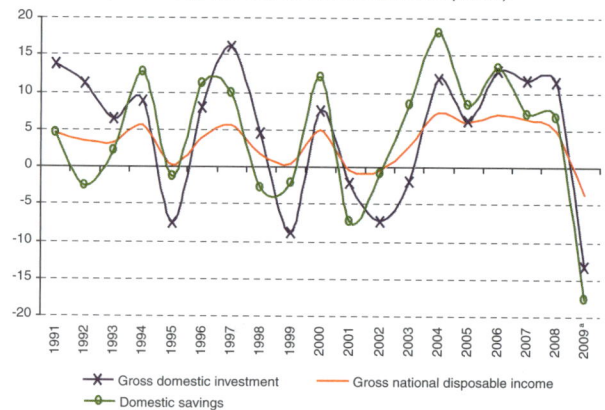

Gross domestic investment   Gross national disposable income
Domestic savings

Source: Economic Commission for Latin America and the Caribbean (ECLAC), on the basis of official figures.
a Estimate.

Figure III.10
LATIN AMERICA: TWELVE-MONTH CHANGES IN INDUSTRIAL PRODUCTION INDEX, JANUARY 1995 TO SEPTEMBER 2009
(Percentages)

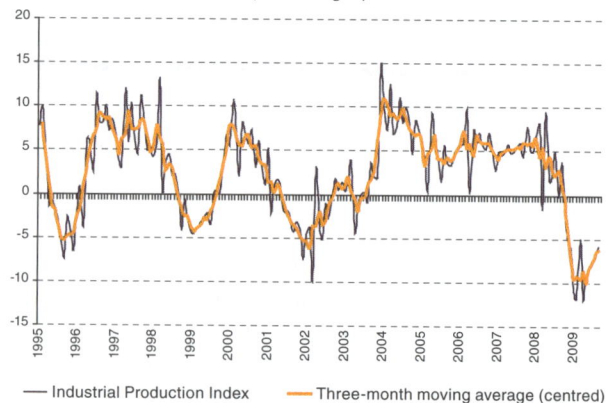

Industrial Production Index   Three-month moving average (centred)

Source: Economic Commission for Latin America and the Caribbean (ECLAC), on the basis of official figures.

Activity in the construction sector declined in all countries except Ecuador, Panama, Peru and the Plurinational State of Bolivia. Trade also fell, owing in large part to the strong contraction in Mexico and the lower levels of activity recorded in the hotels and restaurants segment as a result of the drop in tourism.[4] Activity in the government and personal services sector increased on account of the rise in public spending.

B. Domestic prices

Inflation in Latin America and the Caribbean was lower in 2009 than in 2008, and, for 2009 as a whole, the weighted average for the region is projected to drop from 8.3% (its 2008 level) to around 4.5%. The simple average of inflation in the region fell from 9.3% in 2008 to 3.6% for the 12 months ending October 2009. All of the countries had lower inflation in 2009 than in the previous year. In 2009, as in 2008, the Bolivarian Republic of Venezuela had the highest inflation in the region and was the only country to post double-digit inflation.

Figure III.11
LATIN AMERICA AND THE CARIBBEAN: CUMULATIVE TWELVE-MONTH INFLATION RATES, 2008 AND 2009 [a]
(Percentages)

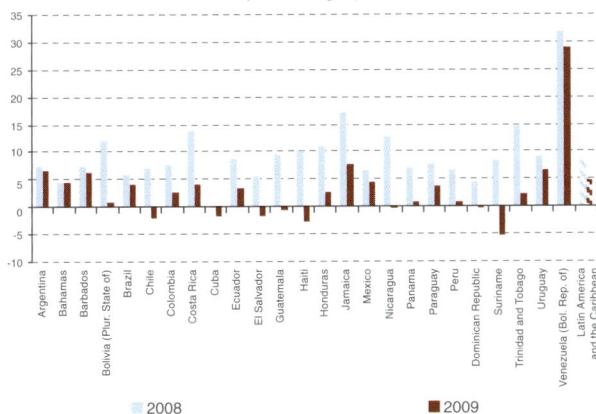

■ 2008   ■ 2009

Source: Economic Commission for Latin America and the Caribbean (ECLAC), on the basis of official figures.
[a] The 2008 rate is for the period from December 2007 to December 2008, while the 2009 rate is from October 2008 to October 2009.

There are two main reasons for the high inflation in the Bolivarian Republic of Venezuela, which has persisted despite price controls on a large group of consumer goods and services. First, there is the limited availability of foreign currency at the official exchange rate which meant that a large proportion of the imported goods on the domestic market were brought in and valued at the parallel-market exchange rate. Second, structural limitations on domestic supply, stemming from the surge in domestic demand between 2003 and 2008, led to shortages of certain products of mass consumption in the domestic market.

Beginning in October 2008, inflation fell sharply across the region thanks to the marked decline in international prices for foods (cereals, oils and oilseeds) and fuel (natural gas, gasoline and other oil derivatives). International food prices have a huge influence on inflation in the region because of the relatively large weight of food and beverages in the basket of goods on which Latin American and Caribbean countries' national consumer price indices are based. Similarly, the drop in international prices for oil and fuel brought down domestic transportation and energy prices. Domestic demand also shrank significantly, as national economies felt the effects of the international crisis. International price declines were transmitted to domestic prices, at first moderately, as a result of the national currency depreciations of late 2008 and early 2009, and then more sharply as those currencies appreciated in the second half of 2009. Currency appreciations also cushioned the effect of rising international fuel prices. These prices, although they remained far below their October 2008 levels, rose throughout 2009, and by year's end were well above the levels at which they had started the year.

Inflation fell steadily in the South American countries and Mexico in 2009 and even more steeply in the Central American countries, which had experienced the highest inflation rates in 2008.

A number of the region's countries (Chile, the Dominican Republic, El Salvador, Guatemala, Haiti and Nicaragua) even experienced deflation as a result of: lower domestic demand; the influence of international prices on domestic

---

[4] According to statistics from the World Tourism Organisation, cumulative figures for January-August 2009, compared to the same period of 2008, show that tourist arrivals fell by 5.1% in the Caribbean and 6.9% in Central America but increased by 3.6% in South America.

prices; changes in the prices of certain key products; and the high baseline for measuring changes in inflation (given that inflation had been accelerating up to October 2008).

Except in Argentina, the Bolivarian Republic of Venezuela and Paraguay, wholesale price indices have also decreased significantly as a result of the fall in prices for energy products and raw materials. As a simple average for the region, wholesale prices fell by 0.2%, after increasing by 8.1% in 2008.

Figure III.12
LATIN AMERICA AND THE CARIBBEAN: TWELVE-MONTH INFLATION RATE
(Percentages)

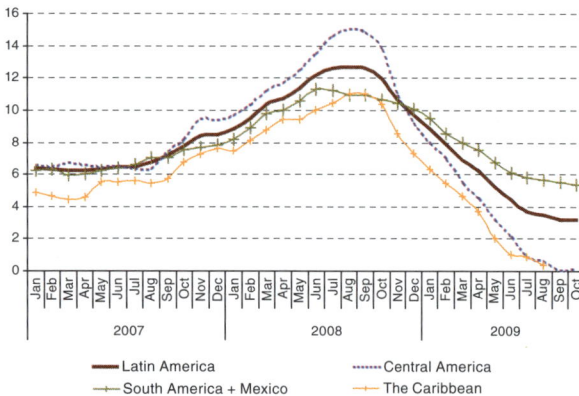

Source: Economic Commission for Latin America and the Caribbean (ECLAC), on the basis of official figures.

Core inflation began to come down in the first few months of 2009. This reflected the fact that reductions in food and energy prices were being passed on to other areas —principally the service sectors where price formation mechanisms are indexed to the aggregate inflation of the preceding months. As in 2008, this was most noticeable in the prices of basic services and in health and education services. An additional factor was the contraction in domestic demand, which limited the transmission of 2008 inflation to non-tradables.

Figure III.13
LATIN AMERICA: CONTRIBUTION TO CUMULATIVE TWELVE-MONTH INFLATION RATES
(Percentages)

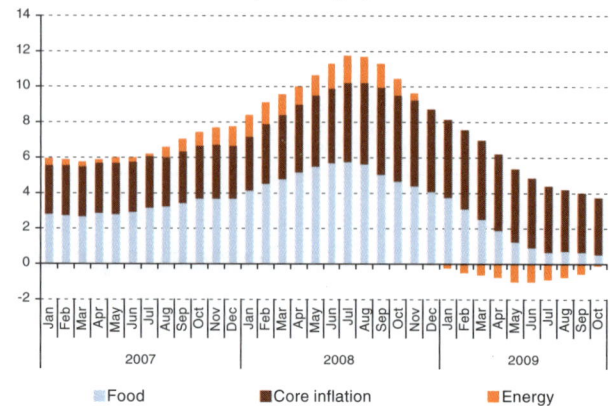

Source: Economic Commission for Latin America and the Caribbean (ECLAC), on the basis of official figures.

Figure III.14
LATIN AMERICA: CONSUMER PRICE INDEX AND CORE INFLATION INDEX, TWELVE-MONTH VARIATION
(Percentages)

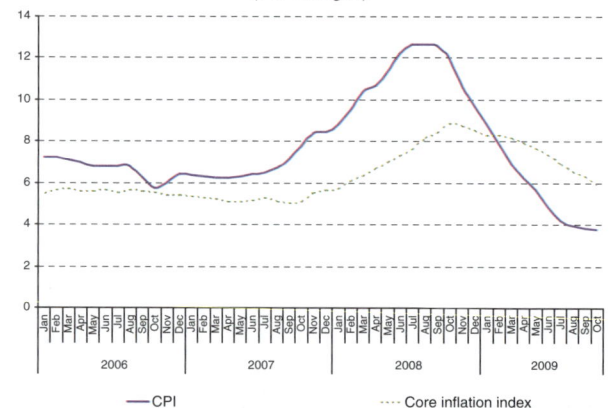

Source: Economic Commission for Latin America and the Caribbean (ECLAC), on the basis of official figures.

C. Employment and wages

The end of the five-year phase of relatively robust economic growth had repercussions in the labour market in 2009. The employment rate declined by 0.6 percentage points, which led to an increase of nearly one percentage point in the unemployment rate (from 7.4% to 8.3%). The rise in unemployment would have been even greater had the participation rate not remained stable.

In addition to affecting employment numbers, the decline in growth interrupted the upward trend in job quality seen in preceding years. Demand for labour diminished sharply. In many countries, this was reflected in a reduction of private-sector wage employment, as well as weaker job creation in the formal sector. These factors were partially offset by growth in own-account (informal) employment and in public-sector employment. At the same time, real wages rose in most countries, primarily because of the drop in inflation.

The decline in the employment rate was fairly widespread, occurring in 12 of the 16 countries for which information is available, and amounting to as much as one percentage point or more in some cases (Barbados, Chile, Costa Rica, the Dominican Republic Ecuador, Jamaica and Mexico). This lower employment rate does not equate to a reduction in the absolute number of employed persons, since the absence of a social protection network obliges many people to work under far-from-ideal conditions. For the year as a whole, the number of urban employed increased by 1.0%.

The slowdown in the region's economies dampened labour demand, resulting in a sharp decrease in the creation of wage jobs, most notably in the private sector. In some countries, such as the Bolivarian Republic of Venezuela, the Dominican Republic Costa Rica, Mexico and Panama, the number of private-sector wage earners actually dropped in absolute terms. Meanwhile, a number of countries, including the Bolivarian Republic of Venezuela, Brazil, the Dominican Republic and Costa Rica, saw significant increases in public-sector employment, as a result of either specific development strategies or temporary countercyclical measures. As a simple average of eight countries, private-sector wage employment dropped by 0.5%, while public-sector employment increased by 3.0%. Another category that partially compensated for low labour demand in the private sector was own-account work, which expanded in a number of countries, at a simple average rate of 3.4% for those eight countries.

The weakness of labour demand in the private sector was also reflected in a marked slowdown in formal employment (see figure III.15). This process began in Mexico, where it also peaked in terms of absolute numbers. However, in most of the countries for which information is available, formal employment increased, on average, in comparison with the previous year.[5] In some countries, such as Argentina and Costa Rica, the increase in public-sector employment softened the impact of the reduction in formal private-sector jobs, while in others, such as Brazil and Uruguay, formal employment in the private sector also expanded, in part, perhaps, as a result of the formalization of previously existing jobs.

Figure III.15
LATIN AMERICA (7 COUNTRIES): YEAR-ON-YEAR CHANGE IN FORMAL EMPLOYMENT [a]

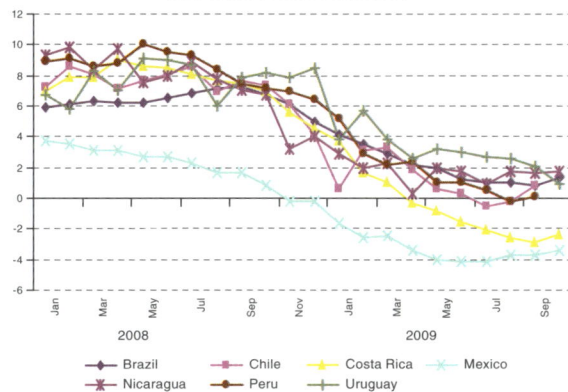

Source: Economic Commission for Latin America and the Caribbean (ECLAC), on the basis of official figures.

[a] Data on Brazil are for wage-earners who pay into the social security system (workers with *carteira assinada*); data on Chile, Costa Rica, Mexico, Nicaragua and Uruguay are for those who contribute to social protection systems (limited to private employees in the cases of Mexico and Nicaragua); and data on Peru are for employees of companies with 10 or more workers.

Of the main economic sectors, manufacturing and construction were the worst-hit in employment terms. The 13 countries for which information is available show that, on average, manufacturing jobs declined by 0.7 percentage points as a proportion of total employment, and jobs in construction by 0.3 percentage points. On the other hand, trade, financial services and business, as well as social, community and personal services, increased their share in total employment by between 0.2 and 0.4 percentage points. The situation in the agricultural sector varied. The sector apparently served as an employer of last resort in some countries (the Bolivarian Republic of Venezuela, Colombia, the Dominican Republic, Honduras and Panama), especially for a segment of the rural population, which led to an increase in employment in the sector as a proportion of all employment. The long-term downward trend in the sector's contribution to total employment, however, continued in other countries (Chile, Costa Rica, Mexico, Trinidad and Tobago and Uruguay).

Worsening labour conditions in a number of countries were reflected in underemployment in per-hour terms, which rose in Argentina, Chile, Ecuador, Honduras and Mexico, while remaining largely unchanged in Brazil and Peru and declining in Colombia and Uruguay.

In terms of both employment and unemployment, the economic slowdown in 2009 had a greater impact on men than on women. In most of the countries, the employment rate for women declined less sharply than for men, and in six countries it even increased (see table III.1).[6]

---

[5] Figure III.15 shows only those countries that publish monthly information. Argentina, which publishes quarterly data, also suffered a major slowdown in the creation of formal jobs, with year-on-year growth rates falling from 6.7% and 5.0% in the third and fourth quarters of 2008, respectively, to 1.7% in the first quarter of 2009 and -2.0% in the second quarter.

[6] Among those countries for which information is available, only Colombia and Uruguay showed an increase in employment among men.

Table III.1

LATIN AMERICA AND THE CARIBBEAN (SELECTED COUNTRIES): EMPLOYMENT, PARTICIPATION AND UNEMPLOYMENT RATES, BY GENDER AND NATIONAL TOTAL, FIRST THREE QUARTERS OF 2009 COMPARED WITH FIRST THREE QUARTERS OF 2008 [a]

(Percentages)

	Employment rate		Participation rate		Unemployment rate	
	Men	Women	Men	Women	Men	Women
Brazil	-0.8	+0.1	-0.5	+0.1	+0.5	-0.1
Chile	-2.4	-0.2	-0.6	+0.4	+2.6	+1.3
Colombia	+1.2	+1.5	+1.8	+2.3	+0.6	+0.9
Costa Rica	-2.7	-1.2	-1.0	+0.4	+2.4	+3.7
Ecuador	-2.4	-2.2	-1.3	-1.2	+1.7	+2.1
Jamaica	-2.8	-1.0	-1.9	-1.4	+1.4	-0.4
Mexico	-2.6	-0.6	-1.3	0.0	+1.7	+1.4
Panama	-1.2	+0.4	-0.6	+1.1	+0.7	+1.4
Peru	-1.7	+0.5	-1.5	+0.2	+0.4	-0.5
Dominican Republic	-0.5	-3.9	0.1	-4.2	+0.9	-0.4
Uruguay	+1.1	+1.0	+1.1	+0.8	-0.1	-0.6
Venezuela (Bolivarian Republic of)	-0.2	+0.7	0.0	+1.0	+0.2	+0.5

Source: Economic Commission for Latin America and the Caribbean (ECLAC), on the basis of official figures.

[a] Data on Brazil are for six metropolitan areas. For Ecuador, data are based on national figures for urban areas. Figures for Peru are for metropolitan Lima. Data on Costa Rica are for July, on Panama for August and on the Dominican Republic for April.

The only countries in which the change in the employment rate was worse for women than for men were the Dominican Republic —where tourism and the free zones (two areas with significant numbers of women workers) contracted noticeably— and Uruguay, where employment remained high for both men and women.

There are two possible reasons for the increase in employment among women. In some cases, the characteristic trend in men's and women's employment rates has also been observed in formal employment. In Chile, for example, the average for the first three quarters showed that the number of male employees contributing to the pension system fell by 0.8%, while the number of female employees rose by 4.2%. In others, the increase in female employment appears to be linked to own-account employment, such as jobs in commerce, where entry barriers are low and jobs are of poor quality.

The decline in regional output may have had a larger impact on male than female employment because of the structure of the labour market: men represent a larger proportion of wage earners in the areas most affected by the economic downturn (industry and, particularly, construction) than they do in the services sector.[7]

---

[7]   In Chile, for example, between the third quarter of 2008 and the third quarter of 2009, the number of unemployed men rose by 31%, while the number of unemployed women rose by 17%. The manufacturing and construction industries accounted for 43% of the rise in unemployment among men and for 7% of the increase among women, while 31% of the increase in women's unemployment was linked to job seeking by women who had recently entered the labour market –a factor that was responsible for only 12% of the rise in unemployment among men.

The regional participation rate remained stable, although there were major differences by country and gender. Of the 15 countries for which information is available, labour participation for the year as a whole increased in five, including Argentina, the Bolivarian Republic of Venezuela and Colombia, while it declined in nine, including Brazil, the Dominican Republic, Ecuador, Jamaica and Peru. In Mexico, it remained unchanged.

At the regional level, the participation rate for men fell sharply, while the participation rate for women continued its long-term upward trend. Thus, although some of the increase in the participation rate for women was due to temporary factors (entry in the labour market to replace income lost because another member of the household was unemployed), it also seems to reflect the growing phenomenon of increased integration of women in the labour market. Thus, eight of the twelve countries for which information is available showed a rise in the participation rate for women (see figure III.1).

Changes in the participation rate varied between age groups. In 2009, there was a decline in the number of young people and older adults who joined the labour market. In the Bolivarian Republic of Venezuela, Brazil, Chile, Costa Rica, Mexico and Peru, the participation rate of people aged between 24 and 29 fell by between 0.7 and 2.4 percentage points, and except in Brazil and Chile, the participation rate for older adults also decreased. On the other hand, in the intermediate age brackets, labour participation increased. The reduction in the participation rate among young people has a positive side inasmuch as more young people are staying in the education system for longer. In fact, in Mexico, the number of students, as a percentage of the entire population in their age bracket, increased between the third quarter of 2008 and the same period a year later (from 52.1% to 54.4% among 14- to 19-year-olds, and from 8.8% to 10.0% in the 20-29 age bracket). The proportion of people otherwise economically inactive thus declined.

Rising unemployment was a widespread phenomenon in 2009, with only Peru and Uruguay showing a (slight) decline (see table A-17). In Uruguay, this coincided with an increase in the employment rate. In many countries, such as Barbados, Chile, Costa Rica and Mexico, the unemployment rate increased by more than one percentage point.

While the change in employment rates was generally more favourable –or less unfavourable– to women than to men, the unemployment situation affected both, reflecting the aforementioned increase in women's participation in the labour market. In four of twelve countries, unemployment among women rose more than among men. In three countries, however, unemployment rose less for women, while in five countries it actually declined. Nonetheless, rates for participation, employment and unemployment still show large and persistent gender gaps.

At the regional level, the rise in the unemployment rate, from 7.4% to 8.3%, represents an increase of 2.3 million urban unemployed, bringing the number to 18.2 million.

In a context of falling inflation, real wages in the formal sector in the large majority of the countries remained stable or rose (see table A-19). One reason for this was the increase in nominal wages introduced to offset the real losses caused by high inflation in 2008.[8] Nevertheless, year-on-year growth of nominal wages declined in 2009, reflecting the worsening labour market conditions. In some countries, such as Brazil and Uruguay, increases in the minimum wage also contributed to the improvement in wages. As a result of these changes, the median increase

in real average wages in the formal sectors of eleven countries was 4.4%, with the weighted average of the increase being 2.2%. In many countries, this improvement in wages helped prevent a drop in household purchasing power and, thus, in private consumption as well.

Third-quarter data from a number of the region's countries show signs of an incipient revival in the labour markets. Significant job creation occurred, for example, in Brazil and Chile in the third quarter (0.9% and 0.7%, respectively, over the second quarter on a seasonally adjusted basis). In addition, Brazil's unemployment rate in October of 2009 was back down to its October 2008 rate. Even in Mexico, the country most severely hit by the crisis and where the impact on the labour market was felt earlier and stronger and lasted longer, the employment rate recovered 0.5 percentage points in the third quarter on a seasonally adjusted basis (compared with the previous quarter). The Uruguayan labour market has been least affected by the worsening macroeconomic environment. Employment there has continued to rise on average throughout the year, as has formal employment, while unemployment and underemployment have declined slightly. In addition, average real wages in Uruguay have continued the recovery begun in 2005, and are reaching the levels seen before the crisis at the start of the decade.

In comparison, formal employment continued on a downward path in Costa Rica in the third quarter of 2009, both on a year-on-year basis and with respect to the immediately preceding quarter. In the Bolivarian Republic of Venezuela, Ecuador and Jamaica, employment fell significantly in the third quarter compared with the preceding quarter and, as in Argentina, the unemployment rate rose on a seasonally adjusted basis from its second-quarter level, indicating that, in these countries, the labour market it not yet recovering.

Box III.2
JOB CREATION MEASURES IN THE CRISIS ENVIRONMENT

One of the priority goals of governments in Latin America and the Caribbean as the macroeconomic climate worsened was to protect jobs. Various types of measures were taken for this purpose.

A number of countries implemented countercyclical policies whose immediate objective was neither to create nor protect jobs, but which nonetheless played an important role in doing so. In addition to introducing many high-impact policies, examined in other sections of this work, governments took steps to improve access to credit for micro-small and medium-

sized enterprises, which, although main job creators, tend to encounter greater financial problems when the macroeconomic situation is perceived to be risky. Increased public investment, which formed part of a number of national packages implemented to counteract the effects of the crisis, has also played a major role in protecting employment.

In addition, many countries put in place specific employment policy instruments. In some cases, this involved activating existing mechanisms; in others, it was a matter of establishing new programmes.

Some of the most noteworthy initiatives are described below:
• Measures were taken to protect existing jobs that were at risk of being eliminated as a result of the difficulties that firms faced. In Argentina, Chile, Mexico and Uruguay, for example, programmes were designed to prevent layoffs by reducing the number of hours worked in order to lower labour costs, or by establishing training programmes. To compensate for the decline in workers' incomes, wage subsidies or training subsidies were provided,

---

[8]   In 2008, the median change in real wages in the formal sector was -0.5%.

Box III.2 (concluded)

using unemployment-insurance or public funds.

- Chile increased the subsidy for hiring young people from low-income households given that the difficulty this segment has in entering the labour market is accentuated during economic crises.

- Few of the region's countries have unemployment insurance, and a number of those that do, such as Brazil, Ecuador and Uruguay, have expanded access to unemployment benefits and, under certain circumstances, extended their duration.

- Training has been used not only to increase workers' likelihood of remaining employed, but also to improve their job options. Peru has launched a job-retraining programme for those who are laid off, and the Bahamas has established a programme to train a significant portion of the unemployed population. Colombia has expanded its national apprenticeship service to create 250,000 additional trainee positions (most of these to be added in 2009) and to prepare more people for future integration in the labour market.

- Although not directly related to the job market, conditional transfer programmes that encourage students to remain in the education system longer support the goals of labour policies. These programmes originally targeted primary schooling, but more and more countries (such as Costa Rica) are using them to encourage students to complete secondary school.

- A number of countries, including Chile, Mexico and Peru, have strengthened emergency job programmes that finance labour-intensive public works projects designed to maintain or build socially useful infrastructure. One notable case is Chile, which has established labour market indicator thresholds so that financing for this type of activity is automatically triggered and provided. In some cases, such as the Construyendo Perú ("Building Peru") programme, an effort is made to link these temporary jobs with training designed to improve workers' opportunities for future integration in the labour market.

Source: Economic Commission for Latin America and the Caribbean (ECLAC), on the basis of official information from the countries of the International Labour Organization (ILO).

Chapter IV

The external sector

A. Balance-of-payments current account

In 2009, the balance-of-payments current account is expected to close with a slight deficit, equivalent to 0.5% of GDP, compared with 0.6% of GDP in 2008. This narrowing of the deficit was primarily the result of slackening domestic demand, which led to a sharp contraction in imports (-24.4%) in excess of the drop in exports (-23.6%). An increase in the trade surplus is also projected, from 0.3% of GDP in 2008 to 0.4% in 2009, while the current transfers surplus is forecast to narrow from 1.6% to 1.4% of GDP. The deficit on the income balance is expected to edge down from 2.6% to 2.3% of GDP.

As can be seen in figure IV.2, the current account improved in Central America and in the mineral-exporting countries (Chile and Peru), but worsened in South America and the oil-exporting countries (the Bolivarian Republic of Venezuela, Colombia, Ecuador and the Plurinational State of Bolivia).

In the English-speaking Caribbean countries and Suriname, the current account surplus will dip from 5% of GDP in 2008 to 4.4% in 2009. The current account balance of this group of countries largely reflects the sizeable trade surplus of Trinidad and Tobago. Excluding that country, the subregion has not run a current account surplus in recent years. Its deficit peaked at over 16.9% of GDP in 2008, falling to around 8.7% of GDP in 2009. The large external gaps common to all of the countries of the English-speaking Caribbean except Trinidad and Tobago is especially worrisome, given that nearly all involve some combination of public-sector over-indebtedness, insufficient international reserves and sustained exchange-rate appreciation in the framework of fixed or quasi-fixed exchange-rate regimes.

Figure IV.1
LATIN AMERICA AND THE CARIBBEAN: STRUCTURE OF THE CURRENT ACCOUNT, 2003-2009 [a]
(Percentages of GDP)

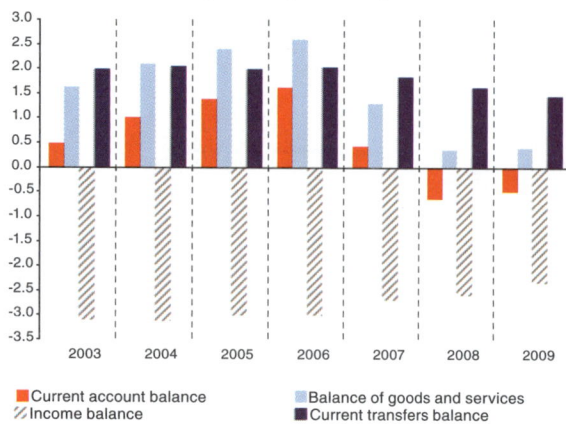

Figure IV.2
LATIN AMERICA (19 COUNTRIES): CURRENT ACCOUNT, 2008-2009 [a]
(Percentages of GDP)

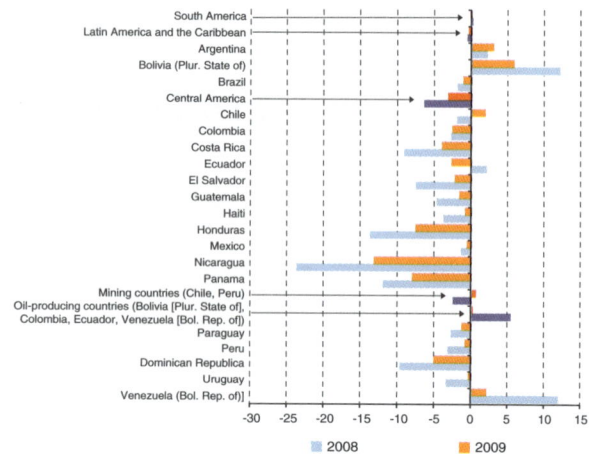

Source: Economic Commission for Latin America and the Caribbean (ECLAC), on the basis of official figures.
[a] Preliminary data. Does not include Cuba.

Source: Economic Commission for Latin America and the Caribbean (ECLAC), on the basis of official figures.
[a] Preliminary data.

Figure IV.3
THE ENGLISH-SPEAKING CARIBBEAN AND SURINAME (13 COUNTRIES): CURRENT ACOUNT, 2008-2009 [a]
(Percentages of GDP)

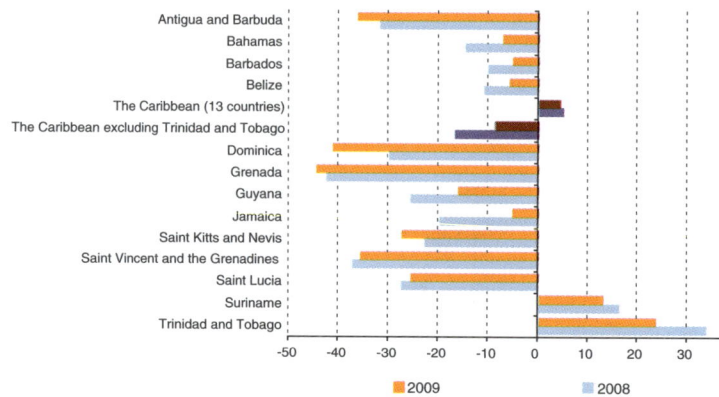

Source: Economic Commission for Latin America and the Caribbean (ECLAC), on the basis of official figures.
[a] Preliminary data.

1.   Goods and services balance

International trade was one of the main channels through which the international crisis was transmitted to the region. Globally, merchandise trade volumes dropped by 7.1% during the first half of 2009, and this was reflected in the region's trade.

External demand dropped. As shown in figure IV.4, imports to the United States, the European Union and China from Latin America and the Caribbean first slowed, then fell outright with respect to the preceding year. These falls bottomed out in the second quarter of 2009, and import figures have stabilized somewhat since then. For Latin America overall, the reduction in exports in 2009 is projected at around 23.4% in current terms, or 9.6% in constant terms.

Imports are expected to post a steeper decline: 24.4% in current terms and 16.3% in constant terms. This heavy drop is primarily the result of slowing consumption and investment at the national level. The contraction in imports, associated with lower domestic demand amid the financial crisis, is largely responsible for the improvement in the current account balance.

As can be clearly seen in figure IV.5, both exports and imports fell steeply practically across the board. A breakdown of price and volume variations in exports shows that in commodity-exporting countries the sharper contraction took place in unit values, whereas in countries that export manufactures volumes fell more heavily. In the case of imports, unit values fell less in countries whose imports have a higher manufacturing component, since these prices are normally less sensitive to short-term market conditions, making declines in volume the dominant effect there.

Figure IV.4
YEAR-ON-YEAR VARIATION IN IMPORTS FROM LATIN AMERICA AND THE CARIBBEAN, BY DESTINATION [a]
(Three-month moving average, percentages)

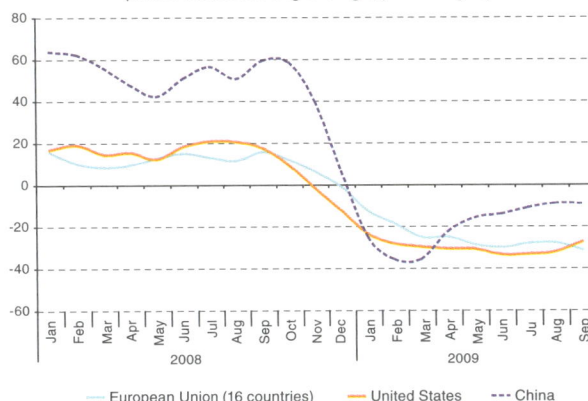

European Union (16 countries) — United States --- China

Source: Economic Commission for Latin America and the Caribbean (ECLAC), on the basis of figures from Bloomberg, the Statistical Office of the European Communities (EUROSTAT) and the United States International Trade Commission.

[a] Data on the European Union (16 countries) and China do not include imports from the Caribbean.

Figure IV.5
LATIN AMERICA AND THE CARIBBEAN (19 COUNTRIES): VARIATION IN EXPORTS AND IMPORTS, BY VOLUME AND UNIT PRICE, 2009 [a]
(Percentages)

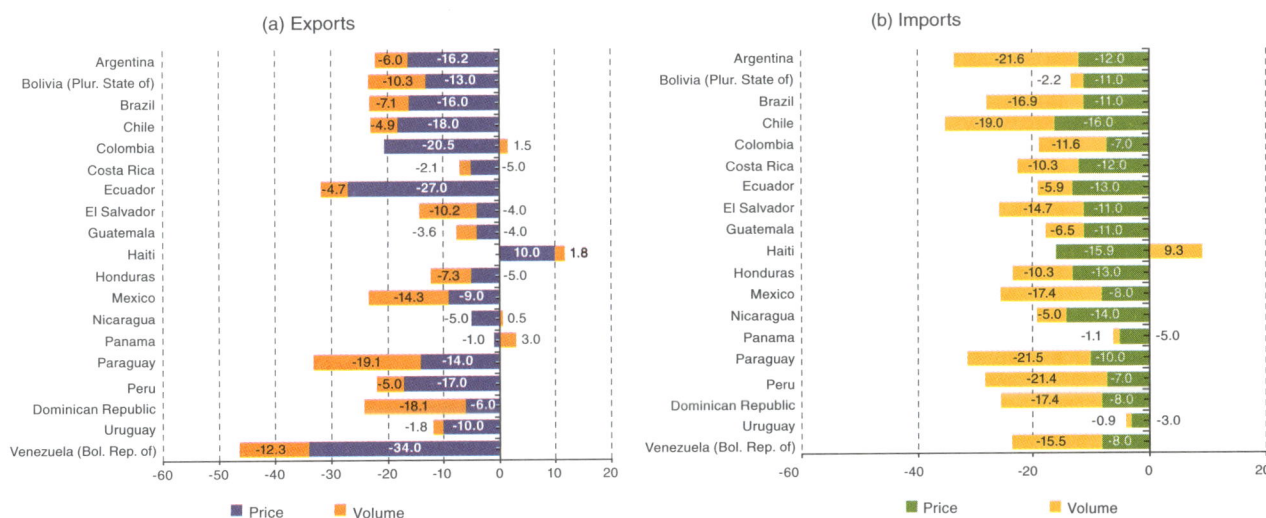

(a) Exports — Price / Volume

(b) Imports — Price / Volume

Source: Economic Commission for Latin America and the Caribbean (ECLAC), on the basis of official figures.
[a] Preliminary data.

It is also useful to analyse separately the results of the different Latin American subregions and country groups. In the case of exports, a number of different trade performance patterns may be identified. As table IV.1 shows, Mexico experienced the greatest contraction in exports in constant terms, owing to its economy's close link to the United States market, which absorbed around 80% of Mexican exports in 2008. The oil-producing countries and the four countries making up MERCOSUR also saw exports decline heavily (by 6.4% and 7.1%, respectively, in constant terms).

Table IV.1
LATIN AMERICA AND THE CARIBBEAN: VARIATION IN EXPORTS AND IMPORTS, BY VOLUME AND VALUE [a]
(Percentages)

	Exports		Imports	
	Year-on-year variation		Year-on-year variation	
	Current values	Constant values	Current values	Constant values
Latin America	-23.4	-9.6	-24.4	-16.3
South America	-25.5	-6.6	-25.9	-16.8
The Caribbean	-30.7	...	-29.3	...
Central America	-8.6	-4.6	-18.5	-9.7
MERCOSUR	-21.8	-7.1	-27.8	-18.0
Mexico	-22.0	-14.3	-24.0	-17.4
Mining countries	-21.7	-4.9	-30.3	-19.7
Oil-producing countries	-34.4	-6.4	-19.6	-12.2

Source: Economic Commission for Latin America and the Caribbean (ECLAC), on the basis of official figures.
[a] Figures for the subregions and country groups are weighted averages based on the value of exports and imports of the countries in each group. Data are preliminary.

Although the Central American countries (Costa Rica, El Salvador, Guatemala, Haiti, Honduras, Nicaragua, Panama and the Dominican Republic) have strong links with the United States market (the destination for 44% of their exports), their exports slowed by only 4.6%, less than the regional average.

In the case of the English-speaking Caribbean countries and Suriname, the international crisis had a different impact. Although the value of these countries' exports slid by around 30.7%, the sharp drop in international food and energy prices —along with the contraction in domestic economic activity, especially during the first half of the year— contributed to a drop of 29.3% in the import bill.

The crisis also affected trade in services. The drop-off in merchandise trade hurt related services, such as transportation, freight and insurance. There was also a downturn in tourism services, which are important for this subregion, especially for the countries of the English-speaking Caribbean and Central America, where tourist spending is a major source of revenue. In 2008, this spending generated revenue equivalent to 17.3% of GDP in the English-speaking Caribbean: here, the countries most reliant on tourism are Saint Lucia, Antigua and Barbuda, and the Bahamas, where this revenue amounted to 31.5%, 29.6% and 28.6%, respectively, of GDP. Tourism also plays an important role in Central America, where tourist spending in 2008 was equivalent to 5.5% of GDP on average and accounted for even more in Panama (9.6% of GDP) and the Dominican Republic (9.2% of GDP).

Figure IV.6 shows the variation in international tourist arrivals during the first six months of 2009, signalling major declines, primarily in the English-speaking Caribbean countries. By contrast, some countries, including Colombia, Nicaragua and Uruguay, saw an increase in tourist arrivals. The most recent data indicate that this downturn has, in some cases, shown signs of easing. The influenza A(H1N1) pandemic has also damaged tourism, as seen clearly in the case of Mexico, where tourist arrivals were down 32% and 25%, respectively, in May and June 2009.

Figure IV.6
LATIN AMERICA AND THE CARIBBEAN (27 COUNTRIES): YEAR-ON-YEAR VARIATION IN INTERNATIONAL TOURIST ARRIVALS, FIRST SEMESTER 2009
(Percentages)

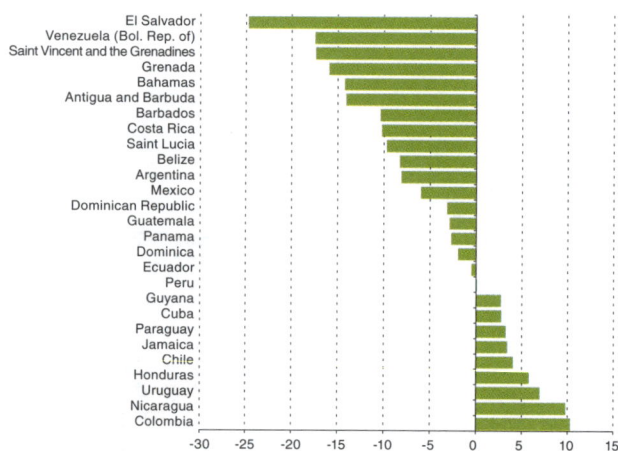

Source: Economic Commission for Latin America and the Caribbean (ECLAC), on the basis of figures from the World Tourism Organization.

The trends cited here are reflected in the services trade balance, for which a deficit equivalent to 0.7% of GDP —the same as for the previous year— is projected for the region as a whole. The worst affected part of the region will be the English-speaking Caribbean, which is forecast to run a sharply smaller services surplus (down from 6.2% of GDP in 2008 to 3.6% in 2009).

2.   International prices and terms of trade

The slide in commodity prices in the latter months of 2008 came to a halt early in 2009. Beginning in the second quarter of 2009, the main aggregate price indices began to edge back up month to month. Between January and October 2009, prices for food grew by a cumulative 9.5%, those for minerals and metals, 35.1%, and those for oil by, 57.5%. And, although these three indices remained below their 2008 averages at the end of 2009, they were still above the average for the 2000s, as shown in figure IV.7. The manufacturing price index, which is much less volatile than the commodity price index, followed a similar pattern, declining after a peak in July 2008, and beginning to climb back up again in the second quarter of 2009.

Price volatility in recent years had led to considerable variations in Latin America's terms of trade. For 2009, a drop on the order of 6.1% is projected for the region as a whole, following a rise of 3.1% in 2008. Terms-of-trade developments depended on the type of products traded by the countries, worsening by a significant 23.4% for commodity-exporting (particularly oil-exporting) nations, but improving by 6.4% in the Central American countries, most of which are net commodity importers. Assuming that prices continue to rise slightly for commodities and manufactured goods, terms of trade will see an upturn in 2010. For Latin America overall the gain is projected at 4.0%, with 4.7% for South America, 7.5% for mining countries, 11.0% for oil-producing countries and 3.4% for Mexico. Terms of trade are expected to slip by 1.6% for Central America and to remain unchanged in MERCOSUR.

Figure IV.7
LATIN AMERICA AND THE CARIBBEAN: PRICE INDICES OF COMMODITIES AND MANUFACTURED GOODS
(2000=100)

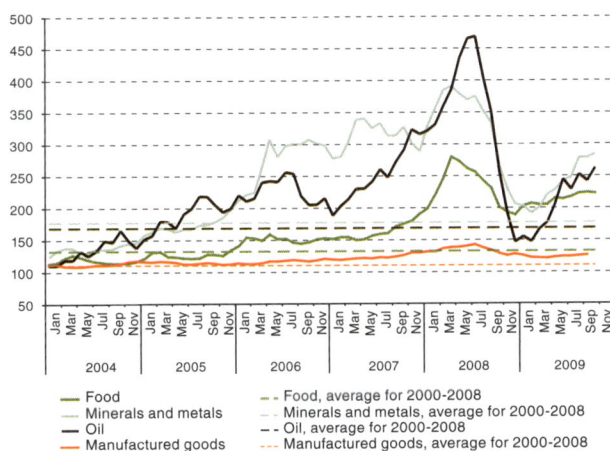

- Food
- -- Food, average for 2000-2008
- Minerals and metals
- -- Minerals and metals, average for 2000-2008
- Oil
- -- Oil, average for 2000-2008
- Manufactured goods
- --- Manufactured goods, average for 2000-2008

Source: Economic Commission for Latin America and the Caribbean (ECLAC), based on figures from the United Nations Conference on Trade and Development (UNCTAD) and from Netherlands Bureau for Economic Analysis (CBP).

Figure IV.8
LATIN AMERICA (19 COUNTRIES): ESTIMATED VARIATION IN TERMS OF TRADE, 2008-2010 [a]
(Percentages)

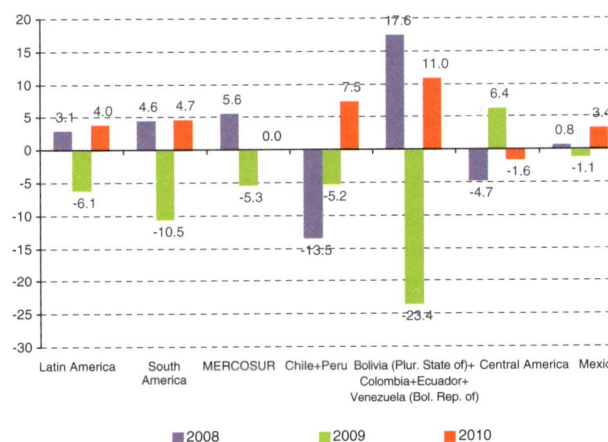

- ■ 2008
- ■ 2009
- ■ 2010

Source: Economic Commission for Latin America and the Caribbean (ECLAC), on the basis of official figures.
[a] Preliminary data. Figures for 2010 are projections.

3.   The income and transfers balance

The deficit on the factor income account, which includes employee remuneration, profits and accrued interest, will decline by approximately US$ 13.214 billion to 2.3% of GDP, as compared with 2.6% in 2008. This reduction may be attributed principally to smaller outflows of profits from the region. Brazil, Chile, Colombia and Mexico record the largest net outflows in absolute terms, though all four saw a significant drop in these outflows (down 21.6%, 16.2%, 18.7% and 17.6%, respectively). The English-speaking Caribbean as a whole, on the other hand, registered larger net outflows. Higher repatriation of earnings in Trinidad and Tobago (up from nearly US$ 900 million in 2008 to some US$ 1.5 billion in 2009) accounts for the sharp deterioration in the subregion's income balance.

Current transfers, composed primarily of remittances from workers residing abroad, dropped in 2009 in contrast to the uptrend in evidence hitherto. Remittances are an extremely important source of foreign exchange for a number of countries, such as Guyana (24.0% of GDP), Honduras (19.7%), Haiti (18.0%), El Salvador (17.2%) and Jamaica (15.8%). Figure IV.9 shows the decline in remittances beginning in the second half of 2008.

The principal —though not the only— factor in the fall in remittances in 2009 was the international financial crisis and its impact on the jobs of emigrants from the region living in the United States and Europe. Inasmuch as various indicators show some improvement in the countries hit by the crisis, data from the third quarter and partial data from the fourth suggest that the downtrend in remittances may be slowing, although they are unlikely to regain their pre-2008 strength in the short term.

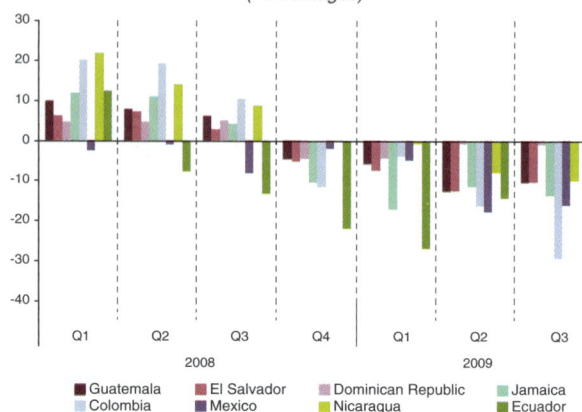

Figure IV.9
LATIN AMERICA AND THE CARIBBEAN (8 COUNTRIES): YEAR-ON-YEAR VARIATION IN REMITTANCES FROM EMIGRANTS
(Percentages)

Source: Economic Commission for Latin America and the Caribbean (ECLAC), on the basis of official figures.

The recovery in the United States and Spain (the two countries with the highest numbers of immigrants from Latin America and the Caribbean) is expected to be slow.

The tightening of immigration policy in the United States and in Europe, as well as the natural decline in remittances as emigrants become more settled in their new countries of residence, also reduce the likelihood that remittances will regain former levels in the near future.

Against this background, the region's current transfers surplus is projected to fall from 1.6% of GDP in 2008 to 1.4% in 2009. All the subregions will experience this decline, with the two worst affected being the English-speaking Caribbean and Central America, in the latter case from the equivalent 7.3% of GDP in 2008 to 6.7% in 2009.

B.   The capital and financial account

The external financial environment faced by the region in 2009 was marked by the fallout from the global financial crisis that broke out in late 2008 and the gradual return to normalcy in the international financial markets that began early in the second quarter of the year.

As uncertainty rose and spread across world markets in the wake of the Lehman Brothers bankruptcy in September 2008, in the Latin American and Caribbean region, as in the emerging countries in general, risk premiums and capital outflows spiked and banks found their external credit lines suspended. Until then the region had enjoyed ready and uninterrupted access to international capital markets, but now demand for fresh issues of external bonds dried up altogether. This combination of factors sapped international reserves and pushed up exchange rates.

This bleak state of affairs began to turn around in the first quarter of 2009, thanks to programmes to bail out financial systems in a number of developed countries, the creation of special liquidity lines for Brazil and Mexico by the United States, and the introduction of new lines of credit by the International Monetary Fund (IMF) and regional multilateral credit institutions. Meanwhile, a number of the region's central banks increased or created special credit lines to provide banks with domestic- and foreign-currency liquidity and many fiscal authorities put in motion countercyclical programmes. These efforts helped to boost expectations, and financial market agents became more confident that authorities in the developed countries would act to stave off any other financial-institution bankruptcy that could have systemic repercussions. A number of the region's countries adopted fiscal and monetary measures to cushion their economies from the real effects of the crisis.

Colombia and Mexico also signed agreements with IMF for new, flexible, low-conditionality credit facilities. Costa Rica, El Salvador, Guatemala and the Dominican Republic sought precautionary standby agreements with the Fund, involving no conditionalities unless funds were transferred. Other countries in the region, such as Dominica, Grenada, Haiti, Nicaragua, and Saint Vincent and the Grenadines already had financial support agreements in place as part of programmes to reduce poverty or to deal with natural disasters and external financial turbulence, and these underwent their normal phases of disbursement. The Latin American Reserve Fund approved a programme of credits to shore up Ecuador's balance of payments.

This set of factors helped to gradually bring down the region's risk premiums over the course of the year. As figure IV.10 shows, premiums nearly tripled at the peak of the crisis, but began to decline during the first quarter of 2009. Thus, by late 2009, risk premiums for emerging countries and for Latin America and the Caribbean were below their average levels for the three years preceding the crisis.

This gradual normalization of foreign financing conditions differed markedly from one country to another, however. For one group of countries —including Brazil, Chile, Colombia, Mexico and Panama— whose risk ratings have been relatively low over the last decade, the spike seen at the peak of the crisis eased in January 2009 and a steady improvement began to take hold in April, with larger drops in risk ratings leading to levels that actually fell below pre-crisis figures (see figure IV.11). The ratings for Uruguay and El Salvador also came down sufficiently to place them within this group of better-performing countries.

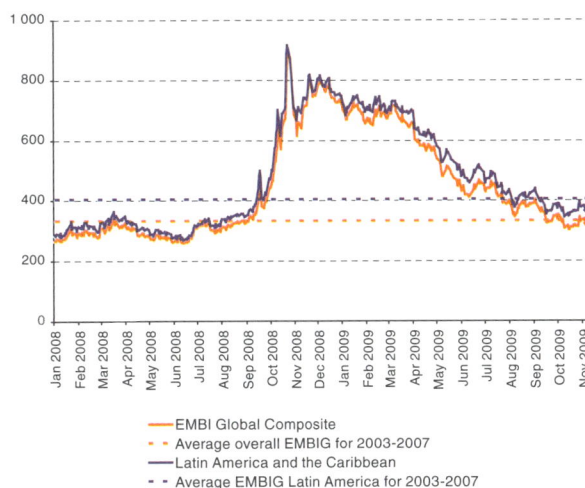

Figure IV.10
LATIN AMERICA AND THE CARIBBEAN: EMERGING MARKET BOND INDEX GLOBAL (EMBIG) AND EMBIG LATIN AMERICA
(Basis points)

Source: Economic Commission for Latin America and the Caribbean (ECLAC), on the basis of figures from JP Morgan.

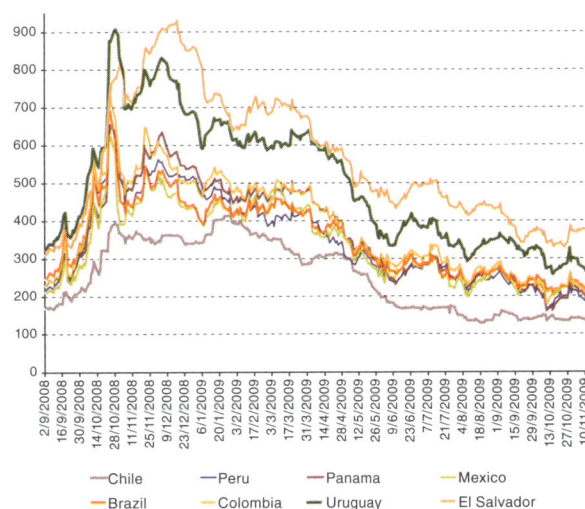

Figure IV.11
LATIN AMERICA (SELECTED COUNTRIES): CHANGES IN THE EMBIG OF COUNTRIES WITH RELATIVELY LOW AND INTERMEDIATE RISK
(Basis points)

Source: Economic Commission for Latin America and the Caribbean (ECLAC), on the basis of figures from JP Morgan.

A second group of countries which have shown higher risk premiums over the last decade —Argentina, Belize, Jamaica, the Bolivarian Republic of Venezuela and the Dominican Republic— also saw a surge in ratings. Here, however, risk premiums were much slower to recede. Of this group, only Argentina, which has signalled its intention to reach a new agreement with its creditors, and the Dominican Republic regained risk levels comparable to pre-crisis figures by the end of the year (see figure IV.12). In the case of the other countries, the expectation of continued external borrowing needs and increased bond issues have kept risk perception high. In Ecuador, where premiums rose sharply above those of other countries, the impact of the global crisis was aggravated by judicial rulings that suspended the servicing of a portion of external debt. As it became clear which foreign debts would be affected, risk premiums eased somewhat, albeit still within very high ranges.

Figure IV.12

LATIN AMERICA AND THE CARIBBEAN (SELECTED COUNTRIES): EMBIG OF COUNTRIES WITH HIGHER RISK RATINGS

(Basis points)

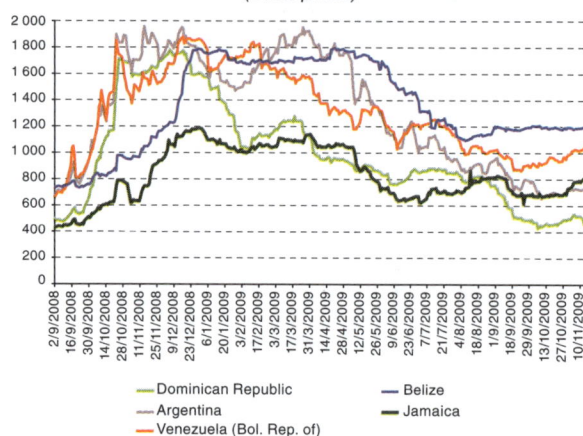

Source: Economic Commission for Latin America and the Caribbean (ECLAC), on the basis of figures from JP Morgan.

As global uncertainty abated, the region regained access to international financial markets. In fact, at the end of 2009, none of the new agreements between IMF and countries of the region had resulted in disbursements, reflecting the return of external borrowing conditions to a more normal footing. Around November 2009, a total of US$ 61 billion in sovereign and corporate bonds had been issued by the region on international markets: more than either the total for 2008 (US$ 19 billion) or the average for 2006 and 2007 (US$ 42 billion annually). The surge in corporate bond issues had a strong hand in this high total figure (see figure IV.13).

The lessening of global uncertainty, along with a renewed appetite for risk and positive growth expectations for the region in 2010, as well as the allocation of almost US$ 21 billion in fresh allocations of special drawing rights (SDRs) by IMF, helped to maintain financial inflows into the region, though at lower levels than in 2008 (see figure IV.14). Those same factors contributed to reducing outward investment by the region's residents and keeping foreign investment in the region from falling more than it did, with the result that net FDI dropped 31%, less than had been expected at the start of the crisis. Thus, net FDI amounted to 1.6% of GDP, representing a second consecutive year of decline. These figures, accompanied by a slight current account deficit, resulted in a balance-of-payments surplus for the region and a build-up of US$ 30 billion —equivalent to 0.8% of Latin America's GDP— in international reserves.

Figure IV.13

LATIN AMERICA AND THE CARIBBEAN: EMBIG AND EXTERNAL BOND ISSUES

(Basis points and millions of dollars)

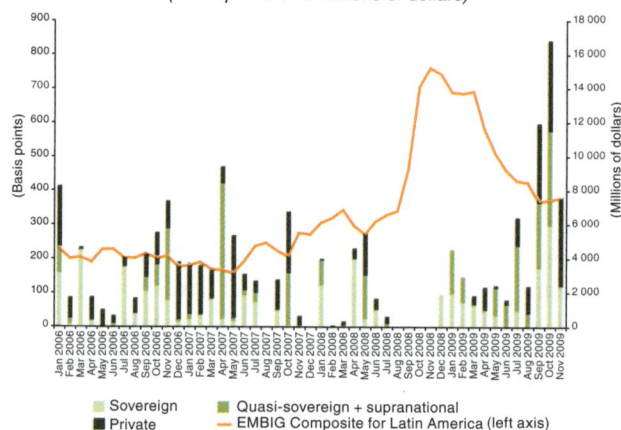

Source: Economic Commission for Latin America and the Caribbean (ECLAC), on the basis of figures from JP Morgan.

Total reserves reached US$ 540 billion, thereby fully regaining the record high reached just before the global financial crisis broke out. The new SDRs accounted for a significant part of this, however. Without these allocations, 12 countries would have shown declines in their international reserves, not five (as was the case), and the reductions would have been larger. The overall figure largely reflects a jump of nearly US$ 37 billion in Brazil's reserves, as well as major declines in Mexico and the Bolivarian Republic of Venezuela. Figure IV.15 shows the variations in reserves in the different countries and the extent to these reflected SDR allocations.

Figure IV.14
LATIN AMERICA: STRUCTURE OF THE BALANCE-OF-PAYMENTS FINANCIAL ACCOUNT [a]
(Percentages of GDP)

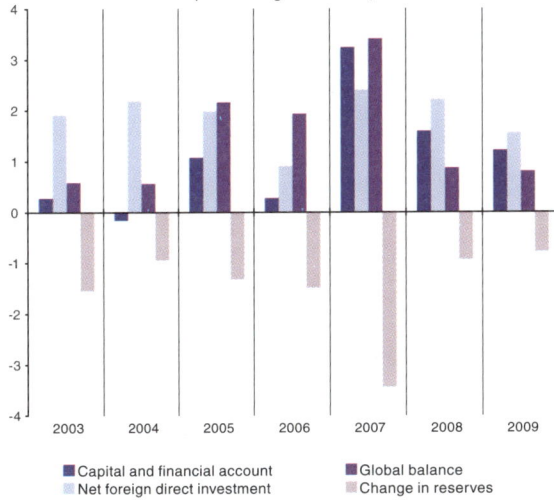

- Capital and financial account
- Net foreign direct investment
- Global balance
- Change in reserves

Source: Economic Commission for Latin America and the Caribbean (ECLAC), on the basis of official figures.
[a] A negative variation implies an accumulation of reserves.

Figure IV.15
LATIN AMERICA AND THE CARIBBEAN: VARIATION IN GROSS INTERNATIONAL RESERVES, 2008-2009
(Percentages)

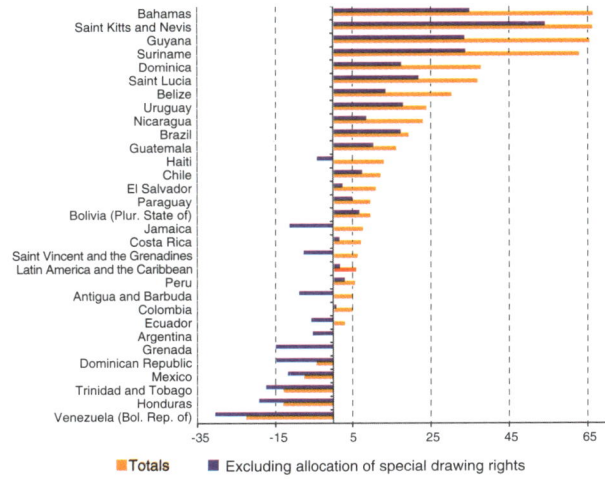

Bahamas
Saint Kitts and Nevis
Guyana
Suriname
Dominica
Saint Lucia
Belize
Uruguay
Nicaragua
Brazil
Guatemala
Haiti
Chile
El Salvador
Paraguay
Bolivia (Plur. State of)
Jamaica
Costa Rica
Saint Vincent and the Grenadines
Latin America and the Caribbean
Peru
Antigua and Barbuda
Colombia
Ecuador
Argentina
Grenada
Dominican Republic
Mexico
Trinidad and Tobago
Honduras
Venezuela (Bol. Rep. of)

- Totals
- Excluding allocation of special drawing rights

Source: Economic Commission for Latin America and the Caribbean (ECLAC), on the basis of official figures and figures from the International Monetary Fund (IMF).

South America

Argentina

Following six years of robust growth, the Argentine economy experienced a sharp slowdown in 2009, and the growth rate for the year as a whole is expected to stand at 0.7%. Notwithstanding a strong outflow of private capital throughout the year and despite the economic and political uncertainties which, at times, impacted on financial markets, macroeconomic policymakers were able to control the foreign-exchange market and liquidity levels thanks to the substantial trade surplus (resulting from a sharper reduction in imports than in exports) and the availability of previously accumulated reserves. Thus, no severe financial tensions were generated and, in keeping with international trends, the demand for local securities recovered appreciably by the end of the period.

The central bank's foreign-currency transactions resulted in a slight variation in international reserves, and the exchange rate against the dollar increased by approximately 10% between the end of 2008 and mid-November 2009. This represented a significant nominal and real depreciation of the Argentine peso in relation to the currencies of some of the country's main trading partners (such as Brazil and the European Union), which had gained value against the dollar. The fall in tax collections, together with the substantial increase in government spending, lowered the national public sector primary surplus, while some provincial governments experienced financing constraints. Both official and private statistics attest to a reduction in the rate of inflation, which had a positive impact on poverty and indigence rates, although discrepancies in the different measurements of price levels and other variables cast doubts as to the extent of the actual improvement in these social indicators.

International conditions resulted in a deterioration in the terms of trade, although these remained at historically high levels. At the same time, agriculture, which had been buoyant in the preceding years, was hit by a severe drought and by diminished expectations in the sector. The decline in domestic and external demand observed since the end of 2008 dampened industrial output even though the consumption of non-durables (in terms of volumes) remained strong. Construction was also down slightly.

Investment in production equipment for durable goods fell significantly, albeit from a high starting position.

In response to the economic recession, policymakers put in place various instruments. The government bolstered public investment and mobilized the resources transferred to the public sector (following the reform of the pension system in 2008) in order to direct credit towards durable

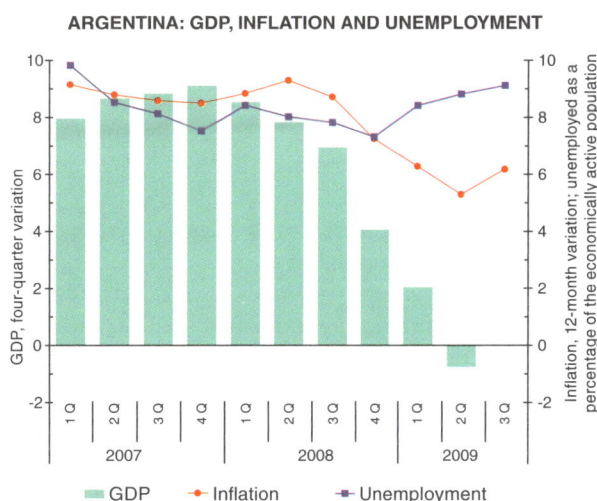

ARGENTINA: GDP, INFLATION AND UNEMPLOYMENT

Source: Economic Commission for Latin America and the Caribbean (ECLAC), on the basis of official figures.

goods production and the construction sector in particular. Companies willing to retain their staff were offered assistance to enable them to meet their wage obligations. Import controls were instituted in order to channel demand towards locally produced goods. Income taxes for wage-earners were lowered, and a moratorium was granted on the payment of social security and tax obligations and on the declaration of undeclared assets. Towards the end of the year, provision was made for unemployed and unregistered workers to receive a monthly allowance for each of their children.

With access to foreign credit subject to tight restrictions, the government's financial policy was geared towards enhancing expectations regarding its compliance with its debt servicing obligations and regularizing outstanding debt owed to the Paris Club and to the bondholders that had not taken part in the 2005 restructuring operation. In addition, IMF was approached with a view to reinstating economic monitoring mechanisms.

In the latter part of 2009, there were signs of an upturn in activity which could spell an incipient recovery. Notwithstanding the remaining uncertainties, the improvement in the international and regional macroeconomic climate strengthened expectations of a rally in external demand and more promising conditions on credit markets. There were no strong disturbances in the country's financial or foreign-exchange markets. Industrial activity actually picked up, thanks in part to the robust growth of the Brazilian economy. Favourable weather conditions suggested that crop volumes, in particular soya output, would rebound.

Fiscal performance in 2009 was influenced by economic policy measures and by macroeconomic developments, and their effects on tax bases. Revenues from national taxes rose slightly as a percentage of GDP, largely on account of the higher contributions to social security resulting from the unification of the pension system under the State pay-as-you-go scheme. Conversely, the proceeds of taxes on foreign trade decreased substantially. The drop in imports also had an impact on value added tax (VAT), but receipts from consumption-based taxes remained stable. Public expenditure expanded significantly more than GDP, reflecting increases in wages, social security benefits and capital expenditures. Transfers to the private sector (consisting largely of energy, transport and food subsidies) held firm at approximately 4% of GDP.

The national government primary surplus is estimated to have shrunk by 1.5 percentage points to 1.4% of GDP; provincial States, for their part, have recorded a primary deficit of close to 0.2% of GDP. In the course of the year, large amounts were disbursed in the form of capital and interest payments on the public debt, which diminished by US$ 5 billion in the first half of the year.

ARGENTINA: MAIN ECONOMIC INDICATORS

	2007	2008	2009 [a]
	Annual percentage growth rates		
Gross domestic product	8.7	6.8	0.7
Per capita gross domestic product	7.6	5.7	-0.3
Consumer prices	8.5	7.2	6.5 [b]
Average real wage [c]	9.1	8.8	11.6 [d]
Money (M1)	26.8	11.1	6.6 [e]
Real effective exchange rate [f]	1.9	3.1	5.3 [g]
Terms of trade	3.7	13.3	-4.8
	Annual average percentages		
Urban unemployment rate	8.5	7.9	8.8 [d]
National public administration overall balance/GDP	0.6	0.7	-0.8
Nominal deposit rate	7.9	11.1	12.1 [h]
Nominal lending rate	11.1	19.5	21.3 [i]
	Millions of dollars		
Exports of goods and services	66 356	82 110	66 373
Imports of goods and services	53 352	67 536	49 079
Current account balance	7 412	7 034	8 816
Capital and financial account balance [j]	4 188	-10 724	-8 323
Overall balance	11 600	-3 690	493

Source: Economic Commission for Latin America and the Caribbean (ECLAC), on the basis of official figures.
[a] Preliminary estimates.
[b] Twelve-month variation to October 2009.
[c] Manufacturing sector. Registered workers in the private sector.
[d] Estimate based on data from January to September.
[e] Twelve-month variation to September 2009.
[f] A negative rate indicates an appreciation of the currency in real terms.
[g] Year-on-year average variation, January to October.
[h] Average from January to October, annualized.
[i] Average from January to July, annualized.
[j] Includes errors and omissions.

The yields on public bonds came down from the high levels reached at the end of 2008. Nevertheless, access by the public sector to international credit markets remained limited.

In 2009, the monetary aggregates expanded more slowly, and liquidity ratios therefore showed a moderate reduction. Monetary policy was directed towards limiting fluctuations in the financial and exchange-rate variables through operations involving both external and internal assets. The demand for bank deposits fell towards the middle of the year but subsequently picked up. Following a spike in the latter part of 2008, interest rates declined, settling, however, at higher levels than in previous years (11% for fixed-term deposits in October). In a small financial system, where the preference for liquidity and the demand for foreign exchange play an important part, credit volumes remained limited. The stock exchange rebounded, especially in the second half of the period.

Reported data on the variations in real GDP show dissimilar trends between the goods-producing sectors (which recorded a year-on-year decline of just over 5.5% in the first half) and the services sector (which expanded by 4 %). In the case of the former, the slide in agricultural output led the downturn. The grain harvest dropped from over 90 million tons to just over 60 million in 2008-2009, the lowest level in the decade. The decline in agriculture was reflected in lower demand for agricultural equipment and utility vehicles. The drop in industrial activity was due mainly to a downturn in the capital goods and consumer durables sectors. Automobile production fell by approximately 20% year-on-year in the first ten months of 2009, although it remained at historically high levels. As the year drew to a close, signs of a recovery were evident from a rally in domestic demand and the renewed buoyancy of the Brazilian market, factors that were also beginning to shape the performance of other manufacturing branches.

In October, the consumer price index (CPI) of Greater Buenos Aires was reported to show a 6.5% year-on-year increase, while the general wage index (which covers public and private, registered and informal workers) rose by 16% over the 12 months up to September. The demand for labour mirrored the slowdown in economic activity. Data for the third quarter revealed a slight decrease in year-on-year employment figures, with the jobless rate at 9.1% (1.3 percentage points higher than a year earlier). Employment fell in manufacturing and construction. Official figures point to appreciable reductions in the poverty and indigence rates (down to approximately 14% and 4%, respectively), although other sources indicate no improvement or even a rise in these rates.

The external sector witnessed sharp reductions in imports as well as exports. As a result, the already considerable trade surplus expanded, mirroring the deficit on the capital and financial accounts. In the first three quarters of 2009, private financial foreign-exchange transactions totalled US$ 13 billion in net outflows, with a peak of US$ 5.8 billion in the second quarter and a sharp slowdown (to US$ 2.3 billion) in the third. Interventions by the central bank, which bought or sold foreign exchange as circumstances dictated, enabled it to maintain the level of international reserves, which stood at approximately US$ 47 billion in mid-November, slightly higher than at the end of 2008. This position was further enhanced by an allocation of US$ 2.65 billion in special drawing rights. The central bank also concluded currency swap agreements with its counterpart institutions in China and Brazil.

Export prices plunged 18% in the first ten months of the year, offsetting in part the sharp increases recorded in 2008. Export volumes fell by 10% during this period. Export values were substantially lower than a year earlier, particularly in the case of primary products (down 47%, reflecting lower prices as well as reduced volumes) and fuels (down 30%, despite an increase in volumes) and slightly less so in the case of both agricultural or industrial manufactures. Imports were down by 33% over the first 10 months (-7% in prices), with significant decreases being recorded in capital, intermediate and consumer goods.

Bolivarian Republic of Venezuela

According to projections, GDP in the Bolivarian Republic of Venezuela contracted by 2.3% in 2009 mainly as a result of the economic impact of lower international oil prices. The country continued to have the highest inflation rate in Latin America, as well as a fiscal deficit, and access to foreign currency at the official exchange rate became more restricted.

Public finances deteriorated significantly between 2008 and 2009, largely because of the drop registered in public revenue. This led to an expansion of aggregate demand, although the effect was less pronounced than in previous years. In the first quarter of 2009, the public sector (narrowly defined) had an overall deficit equivalent to 0.9% of annual GDP. The sector's revenue declined by the equivalent of 3.8% of GDP, year-on-year, while outlays (including lending) fell by a mere 1.6%. Projections based on available data indicate that the overall deficit of the public sector (narrowly defined) will be equivalent to about 4.0% of GDP for all of 2009.

The worsening fiscal situation was due largely to lower petroleum revenue, the elimination of the financial transaction tax and declining income tax receipts, especially from petroleum. Capital expenditures (including those related to the National Development Fund projects) shrank, reflecting the reduction in capital transfers and, to a lesser extent, cutbacks in the acquisition of fixed assets.

To bring down the deficit, the government raised the value added tax rate from 9% to 12% in March 2009 and increased public sector wages by less than inflation. In the future, changes may be expected in the accounts of the State enterprise sector following the nationalizations decreed in 2009, most notably, the nationalization of goods manufacturers and service providers involved in upstream gas and petroleum activities, in May; of the Banco de Venezuela and of steel-sector companies involved in iron production, in July; and of two coffee roasting plants, in November.

The public debt balance increased, along with the deficit, in 2009. In June, the foreign debt stood at US$ 29.894 billion and the domestic debt at 43.950 billion bolivares. If the US$ 4.99 billion in international sovereign bonds maturing in 2019 and 2024 that were issued on 28 September 2009 are included, total public debt at the official exchange rate of 2.15 bolivares fuertes per

United States dollar, is equivalent to 14% of GDP. The State-owned oil company, Petróleos de Venezuela S.A. (PDVSA), also issued debt in 2009.

Year-on-year inflation in the Bolivarian Republic of Venezuela, as measured by the national consumer price index, reached 26.7% in October 2009, while cumulative inflation for the first ten months of the year was 20.7%. In part, this reflects the impact of the decreased availability of hard currency at the official exchange rate of BsF 2.15 per United States dollar in 2009, which led the private sector to meet its needs for importing goods by purchasing dollars on the parallel market, at a significantly higher exchange rate. The amount of foreign currency that the Foreign Exchange Administration Commission (CADIVI) authorized for sale at the official exchange rate decreased by 49.9% between the second quarter of 2008 and the same period in 2009. The effective real exchange rate appreciated by an average of 26% in the first nine months

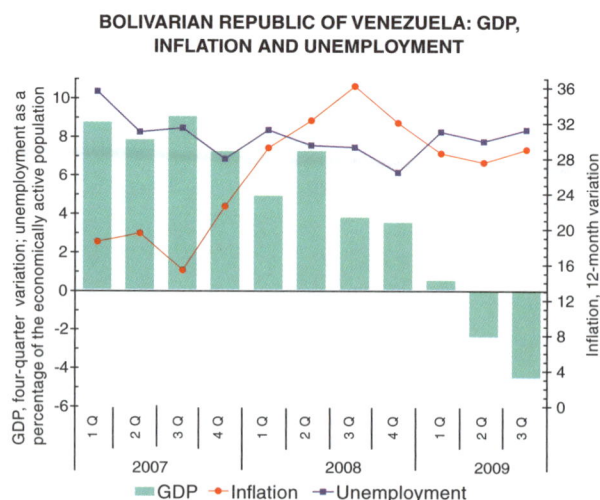

BOLIVARIAN REPUBLIC OF VENEZUELA: GDP, INFLATION AND UNEMPLOYMENT

Source: Economic Commission for Latin America and the Caribbean (ECLAC), on the basis of official figures.

of 2009, mainly as a result of the confluence of high inflation and a fixed exchange-rate regime.

High inflation was caused not only by the passthrough effect of the rising bolivar price of imports but also by the strong expansion of monetary aggregates in 2009. Broad money (M3) expanded as of the first quarter of 2009, reaching a 33.4% year-on-year rate in the third quarter. Although greater liquidity was accompanied by increased term deposits in commercial banks in 2009, lending remained flat, reflecting the lack of economic growth in the country during the year.

In the banking sector, the critical situation in terms of finances and assets at Banco Industrial de Venezuela led to government intervention in May 2009 (although it continued to conduct financial intermediation activities). In November, the government also took over Bolívar Banco, Banco Confederado, Banco Canarias de Venezuela and Banpro. The latter two, which, between them, held the savings of 750,000 depositors, were subsequently liquidated.

GDP is estimated to have fallen by 2.3% in 2009. The hardest-hit sectors were manufacturing, petroleum and commerce. Growth in the communications, construction and government services sectors was insufficient to counteract the economic slowdown. In terms of overall demand, the contractions in private consumption, investment and exports were only partially offset by government consumption. In the fourth quarter, drought and the inability of supply to keep up with demand, led to problems with the electricity and water supply.

According to the Organization of Petroleum Exporting Countries (OPEC), petroleum output in the Bolivarian Republic of Venezuela fell by 100,000 barrels per day between the fourth quarter of 2008 and the third quarter of 2009. The drop in production may be due to the fact that investments by PDVSA in exploration and development have failed to make up for the declining output of the oldest oil wells operated by the company. The fact that the Baker Hughes company points to a sharp reduction in the number of drilling rigs, from 81 in the fourth quarter of 2008 to only 54 in the third quarter of 2009, seems to support this explanation.

As a result of the economic downturn, the unemployment rate rose to 8.1% in October 2009 from 7.2% a year earlier. Average real wages (in the first three quarters of the year) declined, on a year-on-year basis, by 5.5% in the private sector and by 8.2% in the public sector.

The surplus of the balance-of-payments current account plummeted from the equivalent of 13.5% of

GDP in the first nine months of 2008 to 0.7% in the same period in 2009, as falling oil prices slashed the value of petroleum exports by 51.7%. Goods imports decreased by only 13.6%, however, and the merchandise trade balance surplus therefore shrank from 15.9% of GDP terms in the first nine months of 2008 to only 2.8%. The current account is projected to end 2009 with a surplus.

The capital and financial account ran a negative balance (2.8% in GDP terms) for the first nine months of 2009. In the first quarter of the year, aside from the accounting transfer of US$ 12.299 billion of international reserves to the National Development Fund, the other main event was the increase in the liabilities of the public sector (in particular, the US$ 4.0 billion loan from the Bank of China to a joint Chinese-Venezuelan fund) and the decline of assets of the public sector. The balance between outward and inward FDI was negative, with the former exceeding the latter by US$ 4.432 billion, or 1.1% of GDP.

BOLIVARIAN REPUBLIC OF VENEZUELA: MAIN ECONOMIC INDICATORS

	2007	2008	2009 [a]
Annual percentage growth rates			
Gross domestic product	8.2	4.8	-2.3
Per capita gross domestic product	6.3	3.0	-3.9
Consumer prices	22.5	31.9	28.9 [b]
Average real wage	1.2	-4.5	-5.5 [c]
Money (M1)	24.6	26.5	22.2 [b]
Real effective exchange rate [d]	-10.5	-18.6	-25.5 [e]
Terms of trade	9.6	23.4	-28.3
Annual average percentages			
Urban unemployment rate	8.4	7.4	8.0 [f]
Central government overall balance/GDP	3.0	-1.2	-5.5
Nominal deposit rate	10.6	16.0	15.7 [g]
Nominal lending rate	16.7	22.8	21.0 [g]
Millions of dollars			
Exports of goods and services	70 683	97 005	56 746
Imports of goods and services	54 656	59 703	46 344
Current account balance	18 063	37 392	7 986
Capital and financial account balance [h]	-23 805	-28 117	-17 686
Overall balance	-5 742	9 275	-9 700

Source: Economic Commission for Latin America and the Caribbean (ECLAC), on the basis of official figures.
[a] Preliminary estimates.
[b] Twelve-month variation to October 2009.
[c] Estimate based on data from January to September.
[d] A negative rate indicates an appreciation of the currency in real terms.
[e] Year-on-year average variation, January to October.
[f] Estimate based on data from January to October.
[g] Average from January to October, annualized.
[h] Includes errors and omissions.

Brazil

In 2009, the Brazilian economy recovered from the effects of the international financial crisis of 2008. Despite some initial difficulties, the central bank's measures to maintain domestic liquidity and reduce interest rates together with the stimulus provided by the increase of public bank lending, succeeded in increasing credit flows. An expansionary fiscal policy was adopted, with tax cuts for specific sectors and higher spending, which widened the budget deficit. Private consumer spending also bolstered the recovery. Lastly, the fact that Brazil's macroeconomic conditions and prospects remained attractive encouraged capital inflows in the form of both FDI and portfolio investment, which helped to swell international reserves. The policy mix adopted helped to fuel the economic upswing and, after projected GDP growth of 0.3% in 2009, growth expected to approach pre-crisis levels (5.5%) in 2010.

The achievement of higher investment rates and the levels of the exchange and interest rates represent the main macroeconomic challenges for Brazil's economy. In order to boost investment, which had been badly hit by the crisis, the government increased capital spending and investment in infrastructure and energy, and started up an extensive programme of government incentives and subsidies for housing construction. In the final months of the year, there were hints of a revival in private sector investment plans, particularly those funded by public sources such as the National Bank for Economic and Social Development (BNDES).

With regard to monetary policy, a number of measures were adopted in 2009. The central bank reduced deposit requirements and authorized the use of a portion of deposits to buy portfolios from smaller banks and to provide loans to micro- and small enterprises, among other banking instruments. Because of the liquidity problems that surfaced during the early months of the crisis, the central bank authorized the financing of exports through advance exchange contracts, and offered credit lines to refinance the foreign debts of Brazilian firms. Several of these mechanisms were used, but once credit lines were re-established, demand tapered off.

The central bank reduced the basic interest rate in the Special System for Settlement and Custody (SELIC)

to its lowest level in over 20 years (8.75%, equivalent to a real annual rate of less than 5%), given projected inflation of 4.0%. This rate, however, remains far above that of other countries. As the economic recovery proceeds apace, no further cuts in the rate are anticipated for 2009. Maintaining the interest rate differential could prompt the

BRAZIL: GDP, INFLATION AND UNEMPLOYMENT

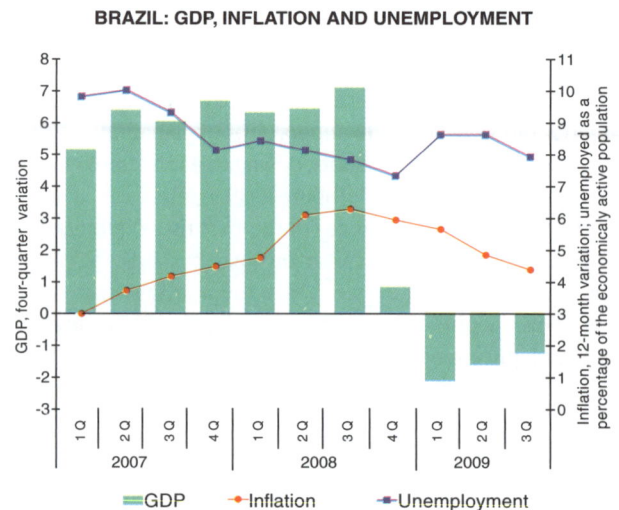

Source: Economic Commission for Latin America and the Caribbean (ECLAC), on the basis of official figures.

revision of investment plans and sharpen the appreciation of the Brazilian real.

In addition to these measures, the government decided to use public banks to expand credit. As of September 2008, total loans represented 38.7% of GDP, and by September 2009 this figure had risen to 45.7%. In June 2008, nearly 34% of all loans (12% of GDP) were concentrated in public banks, but by September 2009 this percentage had increased to 41% (18.5% of GDP). During this same period, lending by private domestic banks, foreign banks and public banks swelled by 7%, 2.4% and 38.8%, respectively

With regard to the exchange rate, the real had regained its pre-crisis value by October 2009, after a nominal devaluation of nearly 50% in the initial weeks of the crisis. This upward movement was spurred by developments in the real sector, including prospects for future production of new oil fields (pre-salt layer) and expectations of increased commodities exports. An additional factor was expectations with respect to financial variables, such as short-term transactions generated by domestic and international interest rate arbitrage. In order to mitigate the impact of these expectations, the authorities levied a 2% tax on foreign-exchange inflows related to the purchase of stock or fixed-yield securities. Taking into account the cumulative change in the wholesale price index between September 2008 and September 2009, the value of the currency rose 9.5% in real terms. According to ECLAC data, the real effective exchange rate dropped 3.4% in the 12 months ending September 2009.

In terms of fiscal policy, one of the principal measures adopted was to temporarily (between March and September 2009) reduce the industrial products tax on automobile sales before, in the final quarter of the year, gradually raising the rate towards its previous levels. This measure was also extended to household electrical appliances and construction inputs. Lower income tax rates were introduced for middle-income families. The federal government and a number of states implemented some additional tax cuts and extended payment deadlines for various taxes.

The lower level of activity, especially in the industrial sector, along with the tax reductions, led to a nominal drop of 1.9% in federal tax receipts between September 2008 and October 2009, in comparison with the same period over 2007-2008. Meanwhile, federal government spending increased by 16.5% (approximately 10% in real terms), owing principally to rises in wages, income transfer programmes and payments of social welfare benefits. Federal government investment rose 12.7%, reaching 20.5 billion reais —slightly over 5% of total primary spending.

As a result, the federal government's primary surplus declined. In order to reach the target of 2.5% of GDP in 2009 (compared with 3.8% of GDP for 2008), the government will have to deduct from its expenditures the

equivalent of nearly all of its investment. The nominal deficit is projected to rise by GDP percentage points, to around 4% of GDP. A primary surplus target of 3.3% of GDP was set for 2010.

The final quarter of 2008 saw a pronounced drop in GDP, which shrank by around 3% with respect to the third quarter. This decline flattened significantly in the first quarter of 2009 (0.9% contraction with respect to the previous quarter), as the downturn in the industrial sector eased (down 4.4% on the fourth quarter of 2008, compared with a contraction of 8.1% between the third and fourth quarters of that year). In the second quarter of 2009, GDP saw an upturn (1.0% on the previous quarter), on the back of the upswing in manufacturing (which gained 2.6% over the first quarter), as firms reduced surplus inventories and consumer and business confidence indices improved. In the third quarter, growth picked up further, inventories reached an acceptable level and business confidence indices rose above their pre-crisis levels. The third quarter also saw the first increase in industrial employment in 2009.

Agricultural production is estimated to have contracted in 2009. Nevertheless, the year's harvest is expected to be the second-largest ever recorded, while it is anticipated that the services sector could show an expansion.

BRAZIL: MAIN ECONOMIC INDICATORS

	2007	2008	2009 [a]
	Annual percentage growth rates		
Gross domestic product	5.7	5.1	0.6
Per capita gross domestic product	4.6	4.1	-0.3
Consumer prices	4.5	5.9	4.2 [b]
Average real wage [c]	1.5	2.1	2.1 [d]
Money (M1)	32.7	-3.5	10.2 [b]
Real effective exchange rate [e]	-7.3	-3.9	7.3 [f]
Terms of trade	2.1	3.6	-5.6
	Annual average percentages		
Urban unemployment rate	9.3	7.9	8.1 [g]
Central government operating balance/GDP	-1.9	-1.3	-2.9
Nominal deposit rate	7.7	7.9	7.0 [h]
Nominal lending rate	34.5	38.8	41.1 [h]
	Millions of dollars		
Exports of goods and services	184 603	228 393	181 499
Imports of goods and services	157 790	220 247	171 399
Current account balance	1 551	-28 192	-18 418
Capital and financial account balance [i]	85 933	31, 161	55 758
Overall balance	87 484	2 969	37 340

Source: Economic Commission for Latin America and the Caribbean (ECLAC), on the basis of official figures.
[a] Preliminary estimates.
[b] Twelve-month variation to October 2009.
[c] Workers covered by social and labour legislation, private sector.
[d] Estimate based on data from January to September.
[e] A negative rate indicates an appreciation of the currency in real terms.
[f] Year-on-year average variation, January to October.
[g] Estimate based on data from January to October.
[h] Average from January to October, annualized.
[i] Includes errors and omissions.

On the demand side, the countercyclical response has been driven by consumption, both private and government. In the first three quarters of 2009, government consumption was 4.3% up on the fourth quarter of 2008, while household consumption rose 2.7%. Goods and services export volumes declined 11.3%, while investment fell 7.8%. The volume of imported goods and services dropped 13.2%. If these rates of decrease continue for the year overall, it is estimated that investment will decline to 16% of GDP.

Between December 2008 and January 2009, the number of jobs in the formal sector fell by 755,000. The unemployment rate increased from 7.6% in September 2008 to 9% in March 2009. The labour market then saw a gradual upturn up to September 2009, with a net increase of 300,000 jobs over September 2008. The employment impacts of the international financial crisis varied by sector: while industry saw a net loss of 280,000 jobs, the number of jobs in commerce and services rose by over 570,000. The unemployment rate was 7.7% in September 2009, comparable to its level in September 2008, with some of the reduction due to a lower participation rate (56.8% in September 2009, as compared with 57.4% 12 months earlier). In August 2009 the wage bill was 3.2% higher than a year earlier, while average income increased 1.9% in the same period.

Inflation, as measured by the consumer price index, declined gradually, from 6.4% in October 2008 (near the ceiling of the target band) to 4.2%, below the target range, in October 2009, while the wholesale price index fell 4.8%.

In the first 10 months of 2009, the current account deficit rose to US$ 14.8 billion (1.26% of GDP), as compared with US$ 28.2 billion in the year-earlier period.

This reflected the combination of a larger trade surplus (US$ 22.6 billion) and a smaller deficit on the income account (US$ 40.1 billion). Net interest payments fell to US$ 7.5 billion, while net remittances of profits and dividends declined to US$ 17.9 billion (as compared to US$ 29.3 billion for the same period in 2008).

The capital and financial account posted a surplus of US$ 52.2 billion. FDI fell to US$ 19.2 billion (US$ 34.8 billion between January and October of 2008), while portfolio investment increased to US$ 39.3 billion (US$ 9.6 billion between January and October of 2008), reflecting the interest of international capital investors in Brazilian assets.

Between January and September of 2009, goods exports slid by 25.9% from the previous year (down 12.5% in volume and 15% in price), reflecting a drop in commodities exports (down 15.3%, with a 4.9% rise in volume and an 18.7% drop in prices), while exports of manufactured and semi-manufactured goods slumped by 32% (down 9.4% in volume and 6.7% in price) and 30.8% (down 26.8% in volume and 23.3% in price), respectively.

Imports of goods tumbled 31% in the same period, owing to drops in imports of intermediate goods (32.3%), fuels (52.5%), capital goods (14.4%), consumer durables (11.4%) and non-durables (4.0%). In volume terms, only durable consumer goods showed an increase (1.9%); all the other categories registered falls.

In November 2009, international reserves stood at US$ 236 billion (equivalent to approximately 22 months of import cover), which represents an increase over the figure for the end of 2008 (US$ 194 billion). In September 2009, total external debt stood at US$ 276 billion, of which US$ 169 billion was medium-term debt and US$ 32 billion was short-term debt.

Chile

In 2009 Chile had to deal with the fallout from the international financial crisis that began in the United States. Thanks to the capacities built up in previous years, the government was able to deploy countercyclical policies which helped to counter external turmoil and gradually bring about conditions conducive to a resumption of growth in 2010.

As a result of the turbulence in the global economy between the fourth quarter of 2008 and the early months of 2009, exports dropped precipitously, in both price and volume terms. Expectations for growth, employment and income deteriorated and private spending in both investment and durable consumer goods fell sharply. Thus, beginning in the second half of 2008, GDP growth fell off steeply, which resulted in a drop in production and inventories and increased unemployment in 2009.

In these conditions the government adopted countercyclical policies which, from mid-2009 onwards, helped to curb losses and, subsequently, fuel a gradual upturn in production, exports and employment.

GDP will have declined by about 1.8% in 2009. Estimates for 2010 put growth at 4.5%, owing to continued demand for exports and an upturn in domestic demand as a result of improved expectations for Chile and the rest of the world.

Fiscal policy was directed towards achieving a structural balance. However, in 2009, owing to the countercyclical measures instituted, together with reduced tax revenues in the wake of the economic slowdown and falling copper prices, government spending increased considerably, as did the effective deficit.

Part of the countercyclical fiscal policy was a fiscal spending plan amounting to some US$ 4 billion, or roughly 2.8% of GDP, that included various subsidies, employment programmes and public investment schemes, as well as credit for small and medium enterprises (SMEs), for all of which the government drew on resources accumulated during previous years. For 2010, public expenditure (total for the consolidated central government) is projected to rise by 4.3%, which represents an easing of expenditure growth. Estimates place the effective deficit for 2009 at 3.6% of GDP, with a figure of 1.1% of GDP for 2010.

Monetary policy continued to be geared towards a target inflation rate of 3% per year on average for the medium term. As of January 2009, given the break in the inflation pattern of the previous year, as well as the liquidity needs triggered by the crisis, the central bank began to steeply lower monetary policy rates. Thus, as of July 2009, the annual rate was 0.5% —a reduction of 775 basis points from the high of 8.25% of September 2008. These cuts in the reference rate were accompanied by a series of measures designed to boost liquidity.

Although the central bank indicated that a low monetary policy rate would be maintained for some time, it began to withdraw quantitative monetary measures towards the end of the year, in response to signs of incipient recovery and with a view to the inflation target.

As a result of these measures, lending rates began to come down in mid-2009 and credit conditions improved. During the second half of the year the pace of lending picked up, although total placements remain below 2008 levels.

As of early 2009, with the gradual return to normalcy in accessing international financial markets, along

CHILE: GDP, INFLATION AND UNEMPLOYMENT

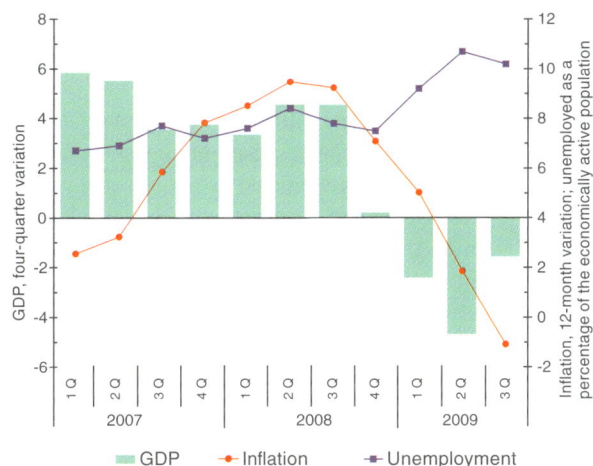

Source: Economic Commission for Latin America and the Caribbean (ECLAC), on the basis of official figures.

with reduced risk perceptions, the previous trend of currency appreciation resumed —a pattern that had been interrupted, in late 2008, by the sharp exchange rate rises that accompanied the onset of the crisis. In response, the monetary authority has limited itself thus far to issuing statements, but has not ruled out the possibility of taking measures at some point.

In the first three quarters of 2009, domestic demand contracted by between 8% and 9% on an annualized basis. Private consumption declined, as a result of worsening expectations. Gross fixed investment dropped by 19%; accordingly, inventory accumulation has slowed since the start of the crisis, and this has persisted during the year. The strongest impetus came from government spending, which grew by 6% to 8%. Exports, which were badly hit at first, rallied towards the end of the year but still registered a downturn of between 4% and 6% in annualized terms. Amid falling domestic demand, imports of goods and services contracted by 20%. In the first 9 months of the year, GDP fell by an annualized rate of 1.6% compared to 2008. Seasonally adjusted figures, however, show the contraction of the four previous consecutive quarters being interrupted in the third quarter, with an annualized growth rate of 1.1%.

In terms of the sectoral effects, it is estimated that, for the year as a whole, the fishing industry experienced the most severe contraction, owing to the crisis in the salmon industry caused by the outbreak of infectious anaemia in fish stocks. The manufacturing and construction industries also contracted sharply as a result of slacker domestic demand. By contrast, the electricity, gas and water sectors showed the greatest expansion, after overcoming energy supply constraints that had affected their performance.

There was a steady increase in the unemployment rate, reaching a maximum of 10.8% between June and August of 2009. Subsequently, owing to a slight increase in job creation and a tapering off of growth in the labour supply, the unemployment rate fell back to 9.7% between August and October.

Amid low demand and falling international prices for some products, the cumulative 12-month inflation rate to October was -1.9% and is estimated to come in at between 0% and -1% for December. Core inflation was also low or nil in 2009. In 2010, inflation is expected to turn moderately positive again, in line with central bank policy.

Nominal wages reflected the effects of indexation mechanisms and the impact of the crisis on the labour market. Thus, the general hourly wage index fell from

CHILE: MAIN ECONOMIC INDICATORS

	2007	2008	2009 [a]
Annual percentage growth rates			
Gross domestic product	4.7	3.2	-1.8
Per capita gross domestic product	3.6	2.1	-2.8
Consumer prices	7.8	7.1	-1.9 [b]
Average real wage [c]	2.8	-0.2	4.8 [d]
Money (M1)	18.1	6.8	20.1 [e]
Real effective exchange rate [f]	1.6	-0.8	7.0 [g]
Terms of trade	3.4	-13.0	-2.4
Annual average percentages			
Urban unemployment rate	7.1	7.8	9.8 [d]
Central government overall balance/GDP	8.8	5.3	-3.6
Nominal deposit rate	5.9	7.8	2.7 [h]
Nominal lending rate	13.6	15.2	13.4 [i]
Millions of dollars			
Exports of goods and services	76 618	77 210	60 829
Imports of goods and services	53 957	69 010	48 719
Current account balance	7 189	-3 440	2 908
Capital and financial account balance [j]	-10 403	9 884	1 047
Overall balance	-3 214	6 444	3 955

Source: Economic Commission for Latin America and the Caribbean (ECLAC), on the basis of official figures.
[a] Preliminary estimates.
[b] Twelve-month variation to October 2009.
[c] General hourly wage index.
[d] Estimate based on data from January to October.
[e] Twelve-month variation to November 2009.
[f] A negative rate indicates an appreciation of the currency in real terms.
[g] Year-on-year average variation, January to October.
[h] Average from January to September, annualized.
[i] Average from January to October, annualized.
[j] Includes errors and omissions.

an annualized 9% in 2008 to 6% in 2009. Given the drop in inflation, real wages, which had contracted slightly in 2008, rose 4% on average in 2009.

In 2009 the balance-of-payments current account, which ran a deficit in 2008, showed a surplus equivalent to 1.9% of GDP. This reflected a drop in the overall value of imports, with volumes contracting in response to slackening domestic demand for durable and capital goods and fuel prices down on 2008. The value of exports also declined, owing to falling prices, but export volumes were less affected. In overall terms, the balance-of-payments current account showed a surplus equivalent to 2% of GDP. International reserves increased for the second consecutive year, partly owing to holdings of Special Drawing Rights recently allocated to Chile. The capital and financial account reflected the continuity in FDI flows, the resumption of corporate bond issues abroad, renewed foreign lending to Chilean banks and their continued access, thanks to Chile's low country risk rating, to resources in the international financial market.

Colombia

The Colombian economy is expected to grow by close to 0.3% in 2009. The repercussions of the international financial crisis on trade and the loss of confidence among economic agents were reflected in a contraction in economic activity in the first half-year. In the second half, the trade restrictions imposed by the Bolivarian Republic of Venezuela hampered the recovery, and exports fell heavily throughout the year. Inflation abated in 2009, permitting a relaxation of the monetary policy stance, and is not expected to exceed 3.0% by the end of the year. In 2010, the inflation rate should come in between 3.0% and 4.0%. The government's main strategy for countering the crisis has been to bring forward expenditure execution, and this has contributed to a degree of buoyancy in some sectors. The economy is expected to pick up in 2010, with growth of around 2.5%, attributable mainly to an upturn in private consumption.

In the fiscal sphere, the government applied a countercyclical policy aimed at reactivating the economy. This strategy rested upon four main pillars: prioritizing public infrastructure expenditure, guaranteeing external financing, facilitating the domestic financing of production and protecting employment. With tax revenue falling sharply (close to 1.1 percentage points of GDP short of the target), the central government deficit projection widened to 4.0% of GDP and will be financed for the most part by domestic borrowing. The target for the consolidated public-sector deficit was adjusted from 1.5% of GDP at the beginning of the year to 2.6% of GDP. It should be noted that some of the measures applied for dealing with the crisis could continue to increase pressure on public spending.

In terms of monetary policy, the lower inflationary pressure enabled the central bank to relax its stance and help to jumpstart the economy. Between November 2008 and November 2009, the central bank reduced its reference rate by 650 basis points, from 10% to 3.5%. Monetary policy transmission was rapidly reflected in other market rates, which fell sharply, except for the rate for consumer lending, which is perceived as higher-risk. Lending overall continued to slow, owing mainly to the performance of the consumer loan portfolio and, to a lesser extent, to that of the mortgage loan portfolio. In the first semester, the commercial portfolio took the lead and offset the falls in the other two. Towards the third quarter, however, the downtrend was resumed. Paradoxically, in the

second half of the year, non-performing loans, other than housing loans, showed a tendency to diminish. Monetary aggregates contracted over the course of the year with M3 displaying the most stable behaviour.

Exchange-rate policy has been influenced by the high volatility of the exchange rate. In the first quarter, the peso tended to devaluate, but this trend was reversed in the second and third quarters. Between April and

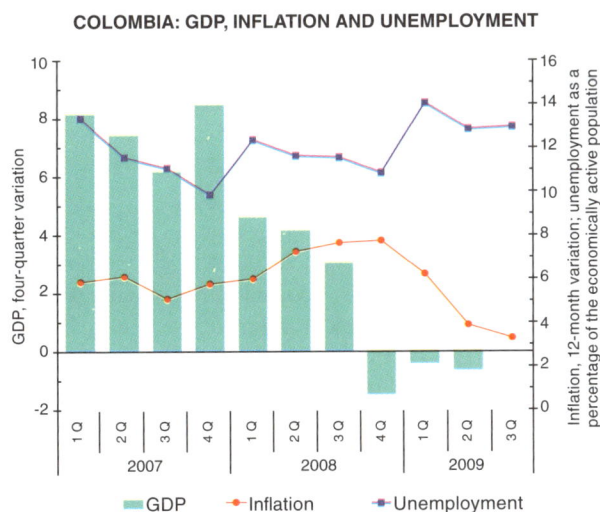

COLOMBIA: GDP, INFLATION AND UNEMPLOYMENT

October, the average nominal rate was down by 19.9%, as a result of which the real effective exchange rate reflected a 10.2% currency appreciation between December 2008 and October 2009. Amid concern at this development and in an effort to generate greater demand for dollars to pay for imports and push up the exchange rate, the government opted not to monetize dollars received from external borrowing and lower to zero the tariff on raw materials produced abroad.

In the first half of 2009, GDP growth slowed by 0.5% compared with the same period of 2008. The manufacturing, commerce and transport sectors, which had led growth in previous years, were hit hardest by the crisis. The agricultural sector has also experienced a downturn. However, the rally in the prices of some primary goods, together with the impetus given to public infrastructure works, revitalized the mining and construction sectors, which grew by 10.6% and 7.7%, respectively. Financial institutions grew by 4.6% during the same period. On the demand side, consumption and investment, which for several years had been the engines of economic growth in Colombia, weakened by 0.3% and 5.5%, respectively. In both cases, the sharpest contraction occurred in the private component. However, this was offset by the major infrastructure projects launched in the country as part of the government's countercyclical strategy. The confidence index showed a recovery starting in May, but deteriorated once again in September and October.

Inflationary pressures, which had been a major concern for the economic authorities in the two preceding years, abated completely in 2009, so that the inflation rate is expected to dip below 3.0% by the end of the year, its lowest point in almost 50 years. Up to October, year-on-year inflation stood at 2.7% (2.0% from December 2008 to October 2009) following a reduction in international prices for food and fuels, a slight increase in demand, the appreciation in the peso and a downward trend in costs. The El Niño phenomenon threatens to spark fresh inflationary pressures in the first half of 2010. The Bank of the Republic is confident, however, that these pressures will be only temporary and has set the inflationary target for that year at between 2.0% and 4.0%.

In the labour market, unemployment has risen, although less than expected. This is due in part to the government's countercyclical policy for boosting infrastructure works. The national unemployment rate increased from 11.3% in 2008 to 11.8% in the 12 months from October 2008 to September 2009, while urban unemployment rose from 11.5% to 12.6%. The higher unemployment is due to the fact that labour supply is growing faster than the employment rate. The increase in supply is attributable to the additional worker effect characteristic of crises in Colombia, in which other family members seek to join the workforce to make

COLOMBIA: MAIN ECONOMIC INDICATORS

	2007	2008	2009 [a]
	Annual percentage growth rates		
Gross domestic product	7.5	2.4	0.3
Per capita gross domestic product	6.0	0.9	-1.1
Consumer prices	5.7	7.7	2.7 [b]
Average real wage [c]	-0.4	-1.9	0.8 [d]
Money (M1)	11.9	8.2	11.4 [e]
Real effective exchange rate [f]	-12.4	-3.1	8.5 [g]
Terms of trade	8.0	11.0	-14.5
	Annual average percentages		
Urban unemployment rate [h]	11.4	11.5	13.0 [i]
National central government overall balance/GDP	-2.7	-2.3	-3.7
Nominal deposit rate	8.0	9.7	6.3 [j]
Nominal lending rate	15.4	17.2	13.6 [k]
	Millions of dollars		
Exports of goods and services	34 213	42 669	35 187
Imports of goods and services	37 416	44 744	37 537
Current account balance	-5 819	-6 857	-6 247
Capital and financial account balance [l]	10 490	9 412	7 396
Overall balance	4 672	2 555	1 149

Source: Economic Commission for Latin America and the Caribbean (ECLAC), on the basis of official figures.
[a] Preliminary estimates.
[b] Twelve-month variation to October 2009.
[c] Manufacturing-sector workers.
[d] Estimate based on data from January to September.
[e] Twelve-month variation to September 2009.
[f] A negative rate indicates an appreciation of the currency in real terms.
[g] Year-on-year average variation, January to October.
[h] Includes hidden unemployment.
[i] Estimate based on data from January to October.
[j] Average from January to November, annualized.
[k] Average from January to October, annualized.
[l] Includes errors and omissions.

up for the income losses. Amid recession, the increase in the employment rate occurs mainly in independent informal activities. The difficult labour situation has once again brought to the fore the structural characteristics of this market, including the high costs of parafiscal measures and the weakness of institutions.

Faltering world demand, exchange-rate appreciation and the trade restrictions imposed by the Bolivarian Republic of Venezuela have significantly depressed the external sector. Lower sales of oil and oil derivatives, ready-made clothing, metals and manufactures in the course of the year resulted in a fall in the value of total exports. In terms of destinations, the steepest decline was recorded in sales to the United States. The contraction in imports in the first nine months of the year was due mainly to lower purchases of vehicles and autoparts, appliances and electrical recording or video-recording equipment and cast iron and steel. Remittances fell significantly in 2009, while foreign direct investment contracted slightly. Flagging investment in the petroleum sector was offset by investment flows towards the mining sector. The current account deficit is expected to stand at approximately 3.0% of GDP, close to the 2008 level.

Ecuador

According to projections, GDP in Ecuador will contract by 0.4% in 2009 —mainly as a result of lower petroleum prices— in contrast with 6.5% growth in 2008. Despite signs of economic recovery in the second half of the year, the fiscal accounts showed a deficit, the balance-of-payments current account balance deteriorated and unemployment rose in 2009. ECLAC expects moderate growth —of close to 3%— in 2010, provided oil prices remain stable and sufficient financing is provided for public-investment projects.

The overall deficit of the non-financial public sector (NFPS) is expected to be about 3.8% by the end of 2009, up from 1.5% in 2008. Although non-petroleum revenue rose in 2009 on the back of higher tax receipts, petroleum revenue has dropped significantly, mainly because of falling prices. Despite significantly lower interest payments, NFPS current expenditures remained nearly unchanged from 2008. Spurred by gross fixed capital formation by the central government and non-financial public enterprises, capital expenditures rose a nominal 9.8%, year-on-year, in the first half of 2009. These expenditures have grown more slowly in the second half of the year, however, so will end 2009 with only a small positive nominal variation with respect to 2008.

A tax reform bill that was sent to the National Assembly in August 2009 proposed to charge value-added tax (VAT) on services imports, modify the formula for calculating the special consumption tax (ICE), impose a minimum corporate income tax rate, tax dividends, raise the foreign exchange outflow tax and introduce tax benefits for the tourism sector. These changes are currently under consideration.

Following the buyback of 91% of outstanding 2012 and 2030 Global Bonds at 35% of their par value, the external public debt decreased from 18.5% of GDP in 2008 to 13.4% in 2009. The outstanding balance on domestic public debt should stand at close to 5.0% of GDP by the end of 2009 —slightly lower than the average balance in 2008.

After the food price shock in 2008, inflation trended downward until September 2009, when it stood at an annual rate of 3.3%. Since then, it has gradually increased and projections indicate that it will end 2009 at a year-on-year rate of 4.0%. Ecuador started the year with a real effective appreciation, mainly because most of the country's trading

partners experienced currency devaluation against the United States dollar. This trend was reversed in the second quarter of the year, however, with a period of real depreciation during the remainder of 2009.

After repeatedly lowering the ceiling for interest rates in 2008, the government froze these limits in 2009. Consequently, interest rates remained nearly unchanged during the year (at about 9.2% for the corporate productive sector and 11.2% for small and medium-sized enterprises). Nevertheless, the ceiling on interest rates for consumer credit was raised slightly to discourage imports. The average deposit rate is projected to be 5.4% in 2009, slightly positive in real terms. Although total assets held by open private banks remained steady in 2009, the proportion of assets held abroad decreased

ECUADOR: GDP, INFLATION AND UNEMPLOYMENT

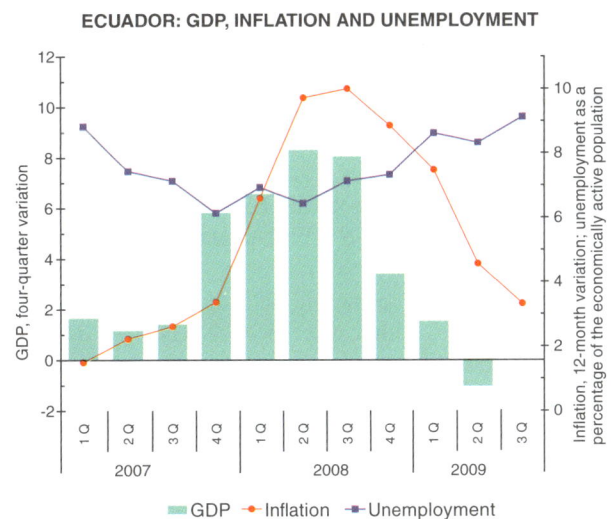

GDP, four-quarter variation

Inflation, 12-month variation; unemployment as a percentage of the economically active population

GDP — Inflation — Unemployment

Source: Economic Commission for Latin America and the Caribbean (ECLAC), on the basis of official figures.

slightly over the year owing to pressure from the government to repatriate capital held abroad. Non-performing loans as a share of the private sector's total outstanding portfolio inched up steadily in 2009.

Freely available international reserves plummeted from US$ 6.477 billion in September 2008 to US$ 2.594 billion in May 2009, as a result of higher spending, lower petroleum revenue and the buyback of bonds. Nevertheless, a US$ 480 million loan from the Latin American Reserve Fund, the receipt of a US$ 1 billion early payment on a petroleum sale to PetroChina, a one-time allocation of US$ 400 million in Special Drawing Rights by the International Monetary Fund, higher petroleum prices and other factors helped reverse this trend, and the amount of freely available international reserves rose to US$ 4.605 billion in October.

Private consumption contracted in 2009, while private investment fell sharply. Whereas activity in manufacturing and commerce declined in 2009, continued activity in the construction sector and the public administration prevented a greater slide in aggregate demand. In the petroleum sector, the aggregate value of petroleum continued to drop as a proportion of output in the Ecuadorian economy in 2009. Crude oil production is expected to be 3.6% lower in 2009 than in 2008, as the 6.7% boost in output by the State-owned company, PETROECUADOR, was insufficient to offset a fall of the approximately 15% in private-sector production. Changes in the distribution of petroleum revenue, which have discouraged private-sector production, and uncertainty over concession contracts have limited private investment in the sector.

In October 2009, the government unveiled a stimulus plan to counter the impact of the international financial crisis, with US$ 2.555 billion to be used to finance housing, municipal works, microlending and infrastructure investment. The plan, which will continue into 2010, is being financed with the central bank's operating profits and the repatriation of international reserves held abroad.

Nationwide urban employment rose gradually from mid-2008, reaching 9.1% in September 2009, and will likely climb even higher by year end. The underemployment rate was also high, and stood at 51.7% in September 2009. The real minimum wage is projected to be 3.7% higher in 2009 than in 2008.

In the external sector, the value of goods exports fell by 31% in 2009, with respect to 2008. The 46% decline in the value of petroleum exports is the main reason for this decline, and is, in turn, explained by the drop in both volume (7%) and, especially, price (42%). The value of non-petroleum exports also declined, albeit less sharply (5%). If not for the strong performance of banana, cocoa and fish exports, the overall drop would have been even steeper. In January 2009, temporary import restrictions

ECUADOR: MAIN ECONOMIC INDICATORS

	2007	2008	2009 [a]
	Annual percentage growth rates		
Gross domestic product	2.5	6.5	-0.4
Per capita gross domestic product	1.4	5.4	-1.4
Consumer prices	3.3	8.8	3.5 [b]
Real minimun wage	3.9	8.5	3.7
Money (M1)	19.4 [c]	27.6	0.6 [d]
Real effective exchange rate [e]	4.2	0.9	-7.5 [f]
Terms of trade	2.8	9.7	-16.1
	Annual average percentages		
Unemployment rate [g]	7.4	6.9	8.6 [h]
Central government overall balance/GDP	2.1	-1.5	-3.8
Nominal deposit rate	5.3	5.5	5.4 [i]
Nominal lending rate	10.1	9.8	9.2 [i]
	Millions of dollars		
Exports of goods and services	16 070	20 460	14 585
Imports of goods and services	15 619	20 730	17 395
Current account balance	1 650	1 120	-1 603
Capital and financial account balance [j]	-264	-172	1 725
Overall balance	1 387	948	122

Source: Economic Commission for Latin America and the Caribbean (ECLAC), on the basis of official figures.
[a] Preliminary estimates.
[b] Twelve-month variation to October 2009.
[c] Eleven-month variation to December 2007.
[d] Twelve-month variation to September 2009.
[e] A negative rate indicates an appreciation of the currency in real terms.
[f] Year-on-year average variation, January to October.
[g] Includes hidden unemployment.
[h] Estimate based on data from January to September.
[i] Average from January to October, annualized.
[j] Includes errors and omissions.

were introduced, as a safeguard to prevent a deterioration of the current account, given that Ecuador cannot use foreign-exchange policy to control the current-account deficit. Import restrictions, along with slumping domestic demand, led to a 20% year-on-year decrease in the value of total imports in 2009. Imports of petroleum and intermediate and consumer goods contracted sharply, while those of capital goods, generally exempt from protection measures, fell less sharply. The country's terms of trade are expected to have deteriorated by 16% by the end of 2009. Consequently, a trade deficit equivalent to 2.1% of GDP is expected —the first deficit in seven years.

Unemployment in the United States and Spain, the main destinations for Ecuadorian emigrants, caused remittances to shrink by some 12% in 2009. Although remittance levels should begin to rise and the debit on the income account will be lower, this reversal will be insufficient to offset the trade deficit; hence, the current account will also run a deficit (of 2.8%) in 2009.

FDI, which had already fallen to very low levels in 2008 (1.8% of GDP), is projected to decrease further in 2009. FDI flows into the agriculture and fishing sectors should rise, while those going to other sectors —in particular, transport and communication, mining and business services— are likely to decline.

Paraguay

The GDP of Paraguay is estimated to have fallen by 3.5% in 2009 as the country experienced one of the sharpest economic slowdowns in Latin America. This contraction was mainly the result of the severe drought that caused major losses in agriculture, the country's most important economic sector. In response to this situation and in order to mitigate the effects of the international financial crisis, the government increased public spending over the course of the year, and the country is consequently expected to record a small fiscal deficit of between 0.7% and 1.2% of GDP. Inflation was lower than in 2008, and, up to November 2009, the 12-month variation in the consumer price index (CPI) was 2.0%. However, with prices for agricultural products rising, the CPI is expected to be slightly higher by year-end. In the external sector, the trade deficit is projected to narrow, and the current account deficit should therefore also diminish. A recovery has been forecast for both the agricultural and the external sectors in 2010, and the economy is expected to grow again at around 3.0%.

For the first time since 2003, the fiscal balance will be negative in 2009, posting an estimated deficit of between 0.7% and 1.2% of GDP. In order to tackle the international financial crisis and the drought, the government adopted an expansionary fiscal policy with investments in road infrastructure works and other labour-intensive projects. Despite the unfavourable economic situation, total tax receipts up to October showed a 6.9% increase over the figure for the same period in 2008. This increase was due mainly to the government's effort to boost non-tax revenues (which rose by 20.3%) in view of the negative expectations regarding income from taxes on goods and services and foreign trade in particular, which in fact declined by 3.7% and 10.4%, respectively. From January to October 2009, total compulsory expenditure rose by 24% as a result of the higher budget execution. Capital expenditure, which accounts for 20% of total expenditure, soared by 65.2%, with investment in physical infrastructure expanding by 71.9%. Public treasury bond auctions were held in May and October 2009, and bids were accepted for 185 billion guaraníes and 389 billion guaraníes, respectively. In addition, the government managed to secure US$ 300 million in financing from multilateral organizations for its economic recovery programme. In October, the external public debt had risen by 6.0% to stand at US$ 2.256 billion or 15.3% of GDP.

With inflation expected to trend downwards, the central bank lowered the interest rates on monetary regulation instruments in 2009 to encourage their net redemption. The amount of outstanding instruments

PARAGUAY: GDP AND INFLATION

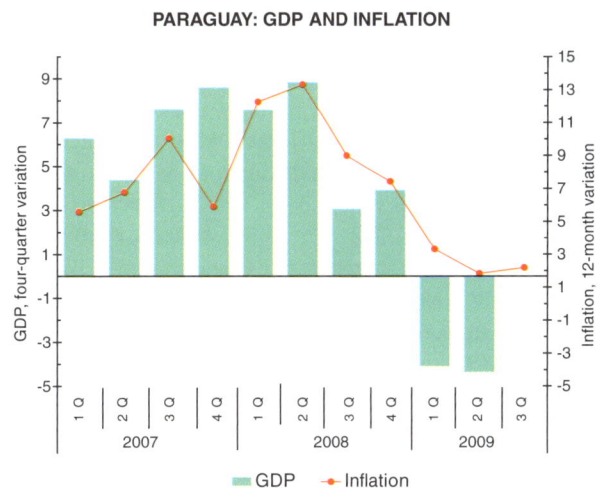

Source: Economic Commission for Latin America and the Caribbean (ECLAC), on the basis of official figures.

in the market thus diminished by 35.5% year-on-year, while the weighted average of their yield up to October 2009 was 2.1%, down from 6.1% in the same period of 2008. This process was interrupted, however, in August and September in response to a spike in inflation. The central bank also applied other measures to inject liquidity into the economy and counteract the negative impacts of the international financial crisis; it reduced national- and foreign-currency legal reserve requirements, and in March it established a line of credit to provide liquidity to local financial institutions. The guaraní continued to lose value against the United States dollar, largely as a result of the poor performance of the external sector and the overall positive movement in the dollar since the start of the crisis. By October, the average nominal exchange rate had fallen by 16.2%. However, the guaraní proved to be more stable in relation to the Argentine peso and the Brazilian real, appreciating by 1.6% against the former and depreciating by only 1.8% against the latter. As a result, the real effective exchange rate reflected a depreciation of 9.9%. The volume of central-bank intervention in the exchange-rate market was significant in 2008, but diminished in 2009. By October 2009, such transactions amounted to a net purchase of US$ 101.6 million. Net international reserves meanwhile totalled US$ 3.594 billion in October, or 24.4% of GDP, compared with 16.2% of GDP for 2008, strengthening the country's position to withstand possible external financial upsets.

Following six years of continuous growth, GDP is expected to contract by 3.5% in 2009. Per capita GDP fell by 5.2% in comparison with 2008, when it increased to a record US$ 1,556. In the second quarter of 2009, agriculture —the mainstay of the Paraguayan economy— recorded the sharpest decline (21.8% year-on-year). This was due in part to weaker external demand, but mostly to the severe drought that ravaged the country. According to estimates of the Ministry of Agriculture and Livestock, cotton production slumped by 61%, soya by 39% and sesame by 23%. Excluding the agricultural sector, the decline in GDP would be barely 0.1%. Other sectors which have also sustained losses were manufacturing and mining (down 7.8%) and construction (down 6.4%). The electricity and water sector and the services sector were the most resilient, recording growth of 4.9% and 2.7%, respectively. In terms of expenditure, much of the fall in GDP was attributable to the decline in domestic demand. Gross fixed capital formation shrank by 17.0%, but was partly offset by the 8.5% growth in government consumption. The year-on-year variation in the consumer price index in November was 2.0%, well below the rate of 8.8% recorded in the previous year. Core inflation, an indicator which excludes the most volatile products in the

PARAGUAY: MAIN ECONOMIC INDICATORS

	2007	2008	2009 [a]
	Annual percentage growth rates		
Gross domestic product	6.8	5.8	-3.5
Per capita gross domestic product	4.8	3.9	-5.2
Consumer prices	6.0	7.5	2.8 [b]
Average real wage	2.4	-0.7	4.3 [c]
Money (M1)	46.1	7.5	7.5 [d]
Real effective exchange rate [e]	-10.4	-12.3	9.9 [f]
Terms of trade	4.8	7.3	-4.4
	Annual average percentages		
Urban unemployment rate	7.2	7.4	...
Central administration overall balance/GDP	1.0	2.6	-0.7
Nominal deposit rate	5.9	6.2	3.3 [g]
Nominal lending rate	14.6	14.6	16.2 [g]
	Millions of dollars		
Exports of goods and services	6 542	8 893	6 473
Imports of goods and services	6 554	9 543	6 853
Current account balance	200	-471	-205
Capital and financial account balance [h]	523	850	1,035
Overall balance	723	379	830

Source: Economic Commission for Latin America and the Caribbean (ECLAC), on the basis of official figures.
[a] Preliminary estimates.
[b] Twelve-month variation to October 2009.
[c] Figure for June.
[d] Twelve-month variation to September 2009.
[e] A negative rate indicates an appreciation of the currency in real terms.
[f] Year-on-year average variation, January to October.
[g] Average from January to September, annualized.
[h] Includes errors and omissions.

basket (fruits and vegetables), showed a 0.1% variation year-on-year, while core inflation X1, which excludes regulated services and fuels as well as fruits and vegetables, rose by 0.9%. Fruit and vegetable prices started to shoot up in May 2009 and by October had soared by 39.6%, as a result of the drought and the losses sustained by the agricultural sector.

The external sector performed poorly in 2009. The volume of agricultural exports shrank as a result of the drought. Export values also decreased owing to the fall in commodity prices in 2008. By September 2009, the terms of trade had worsened by 19.4% year-on-year. External demand contracted, since demand was down also in Paraguay's main trading partners (MERCOSUR countries). Up to October, earnings from merchandise exports declined by 29.9% compared with the same period in 2009. This was counterbalanced, however, by a 29.7% drop in imports, and the trade deficit therefore narrowed by 29.5%. The international financial crisis also had an impact on remittances. Foreign exchange inflows under this heading increased by just 0.4% (in cumulative terms up to September), compared with a 6.6% rise from January to September 2008. A small current account deficit of close to 1.4% of GDP is predicted for the end of the year, compared with 2.8% in 2008.

Peru

In 2009, Peru experienced a sharp slowdown in economic activity in the wake of the international financial crisis. GDP growth fell from 9.8% in 2008 to 0.8% in 2009, owing mainly to a steep drop in external demand, which in turn led to a decline in industrial production, heavy inventory adjustments and significantly less private investment because of lower demand and uncertainty of the outcome of the international economic crisis that held sway in late 2008 and throughout 2009.

Economic activity began to recover in the third quarter of 2009, bolstered by the completion of inventory adjustments, the implementation of a fiscal stimulus package, expansionary monetary policy and the improving expectations of economic agents. This economic recovery is expected to continue into 2010, with GDP growth projected to be between 4.5% and 5%.

As a result of the abrupt slowdown in GDP at the end of 2008, the government announced a major economic stimulus package, with some measures aimed at expanding and accelerating public investment and others targeting specific sectors. However, execution of public investment has fallen short of expectations. Through October 2009, only about half of the public investments that were budgeted had been executed.

As for the central government's fiscal receipts, for the period January-September 2009, current revenues decreased by 17.7% compared with the same period in 2008, because of a downturn in takings from both income tax and non-tax sources. Non-financial expenditures rose by 6.2% reflecting an increase in capital expenditures (70%). For the year as a whole, economic authorities estimate the general government's deficit to be about 2.4%, with a non-financial public sector (NFPS) deficit of the same proportion.

To cover financing needs for 2009 and 2010, the government issued two global bonds; the first, in March 2009 for US$1 billion with a 10-year maturity, and the second, in July, for US$1 billion with a 16-year maturity.

In response to the international financial crisis, the authorities took steps to ensure liquidity in the local financial system, both in national currency and in dollars, in order to stabilize both the money and currency markets. Next, they began to lower the benchmark interest rate; between January and August 2009 the rate came down

from 6.5% to 1.25%, and has since remained unchanged. Consequently, the average local-currency lending rate decreased from 17.2% in December 2008 to 15.1% in October 2009. The average foreign-currency lending rate decreased from 10.1% to 8.9% over the same period.

However, despite the economic situation, lending by the financial system to the private sector continued to grow slowly throughout 2009. Between December 2008 and October 2009, lending in national currency expanded by around 21%, with an increase in mortgage lending in new soles. Lending in dollars remained, through October 2009, at levels similar to those of December 2008. As a result, total lending rose by 6.6% for the period (11.6% with respect to October 2008). With local-currency lending rising faster than foreign-currency lending, the dollarization ratio dropped from 52% in December 2008 to 46% in

PERU: GDP, INFLATION AND UNEMPLOYMENT

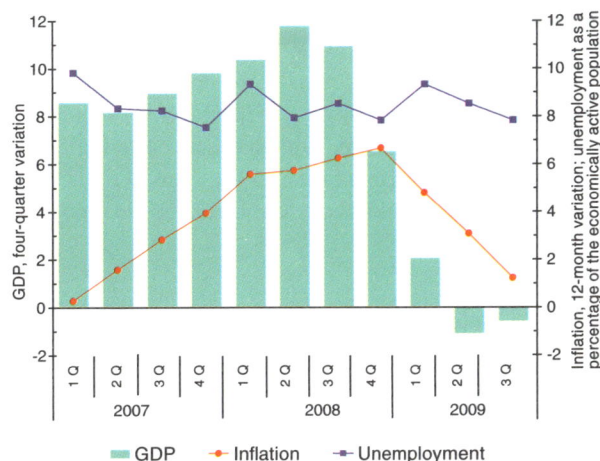

Source: Economic Commission for Latin America and the Caribbean (ECLAC), on the basis of official figures.

October 2009. The percentage of non-performing loans rose from 1.3% to 1.6% between December 2008 and October 2009, with the greatest increase in the portfolio of loans to micro-enterprises.

Between December 2008 and October 2009, the new sol appreciated in nominal terms by 7.8% against the dollar, whereas the real bilateral exchange appreciated less (5.3%). The real effective exchange rate depreciated by 0.5% over the same period.

As for trade policy, in February 2009 the free trade agreement with the United States entered into force, as did the economic complementarity agreement with Chile in March. A free trade agreement was also signed with China.

During the first three quarters of 2009, GDP grew by 0.1% compared with the year-earlier period. This result reflected the contractions in non-primary manufacturing (-9.1%), fishing (-7%) and commerce (-1.2%). The construction sector, by contrast, was the fastest-growing, with 3% growth for the period.

By type of expenditure —and compared with the result for 2008, when domestic demand surged by 12.3%— domestic demand shrank by 3.9% in January-September 2009 because of a drop in gross fixed investment (-9.9%). This was due, to slacker private investment (-14.9%), despite a rise in public investment (21.6%). Aggressive inventory adjustments led to a 22.2% slump in gross domestic investment. Private consumption continued to edge up (2.4%), but did not rise fast enough to offset declining investments. Goods and services export volumes dipped by 3.1%, whereas goods and services import volumes slid by 20.3%.

Throughout 2009, the inflation rate, as measured by the Lima consumer price index, declined significantly, reaching a cumulative 0.04% for the first 10 months of the year (0.7% over 12 months), owing to the drop in international fuel and food prices, which lowered the prices of transport, domestic fuels and electricity.

As for labour indicators, the average unemployment rate for the first 10 months of 2009 was 8.4%, similar to that of 2008. Urban employment in companies with more than 10 employees rose by 1.9% for the period January-August 2009, as compared with the same period in 2008. The average employment rate for the first 10 months of 2009 was 62.3%, and average job-related income was

up on the fourth quarter of 2008. Throughout 2009, the situation gradually improved as compared with the first quarter. To invigorate household demand, in 2009 workers in the formal economy were temporarily allowed to use time-in-service compensation funds and withholdings for twice-yearly bonuses paid to formal wage earners were waived.

Exports of goods slumped by 25.9% during the first three quarters of 2009 (-22.6% in prices and -4.3% in volume), and goods imports declined by 30.8% (-10.3% in prices and -22.9% in volume) in the same period, leading to a trade surplus of US$ 3.58 billion. In the first three quarters of 2009, the average terms of trade fell by 9.5% compared with the average for 2008. Net international reserves stood at US$ 32.92 billion in October 2009, compared with US$ 31.196 billion in December 2008.

PERU: MAIN ECONOMIC INDICATORS

	2007	2008	2009 [a]
	Annual percentage growth rates		
Gross domestic product	8.9	9.8	0.8
Per capita gross domestic product	7.6	8.5	-0.3
Consumer prices	3.9	6.6	0.7 [b]
Average real wage	-1.8	2.2	0.3 [c]
Money (M1)	30.7	16.5	10.0 [b]
Real effective exchange rate [d]	0.2	-3.7	-2.3 [e]
Terms of trade	3.6	-13.3	-10.8
	Annual average percentages		
Urban unemployment rate	8.4	8.4	8.3 [f]
Central government overall balance/GDP	1.8	2.2	-1.4
Nominal deposit rate	3.5	3.3	3.0 [g]
Nominal lending rate	16.5	16.7	16.3 [g]
	Millions of dollars		
Exports of goods and services	31 041	35 166	28 353
Imports of goods and services	23 942	34 005	25 480
Current account balance	1 220	-4 180	-1 224
Capital and financial account balance [h]	8 368	7 292	3 676
Overall balance	9 588	3 112	2 452

Source: Economic Commission for Latin America and the Caribbean (ECLAC), on the basis of official figures.
[a] Preliminary estimates.
[b] Twelve-month variation to October 2009.
[c] Figure for June.
[d] A negative rate indicates an appreciation of the currency in real terms.
[e] Year-on-year average variation, January to October.
[f] Estimate based on data from January to October.
[g] Average from January to October, annualized.
[h] Includes errors and omissions.

Plurinational State of Bolivia

The GDP of the Plurinational State of Bolivia will expand by 3.5% in 2009, which means the growth rate will be 3.2 percentage points lower than in 2008. The urban unemployment rate meanwhile will be 6.8%, 0.1 percentage points higher than in 2008, and inflation will end the year at about 1%, 11 percentage points below the rate recorded in 2008. Both the balance-of-payments current account and the non-financial public sector accounts will close with surpluses, albeit leaner ones than in 2008, mainly thanks to the drop in average hydrocarbon prices during the year. In 2009, the political landscape was dominated by two electoral events: the January 2009 referendum approving the nation's new political constitution; and the presidential and parliamentary elections in December 2009. The new congress is set to debate modifications to a number of laws with a view to adapting legislation to the new constitutional framework.

In keeping with lower inflationary expectations, in the fourth quarter of 2008, the central bank switched policy from issuing bonds in open market operations to redeeming bonds. As a result, between October 2008 and October 2009 the central bank reduced its balance of outstanding government securities by US$ 621.8 million (27.9%). To further expand liquidity, the central bank lowered its repo rate by 10 percentage points from 13% in December 2008 to 3% in October 2009. This liquidity growth was consistent with expansions in total net domestic credit and net domestic credit to the non-financial public sector and with a moderate reduction in net foreign reserves. During the first half of the year these goals were met with ease, especially as regards net internal credit to the non-financial public sector whose reduction came as a result of the accumulation of deposits the sector holds with the central bank. The bank also lowered its benchmark rates, which translated into significantly lower bank lending and deposit rates. From December 2008 to September 2009, bank lending rates dropped from 10.1% to 7.6% and bank deposit rates, from 3.2% to 0.5%. Additionally, in order to stimulate growth in the local currency portfolio, the central bank approved two changes to the reserve requirement. In January, the additional reserve requirement for foreign currency deposits was raised from 7.5% to 30%, and in August the reserve requirement for deposits in local currency was lowered, reflecting the growth in these deposits.

According to available official information, the non-financial public sector had a surplus of approximately 2.8% of GDP in August 2009. In comparison with August 2008, real expenditures were up by 3.5% and revenues were down by 5.3%, mainly because of weaker inflows of customs duties and internal revenue (down by 26.6% and 16.6%, respectively) and because of the 9.5% drop in revenue from the special hydrocarbons tax. The fall-off in

PLURINATIONAL STATE OF BOLIVIA: GDP AND INFLATION

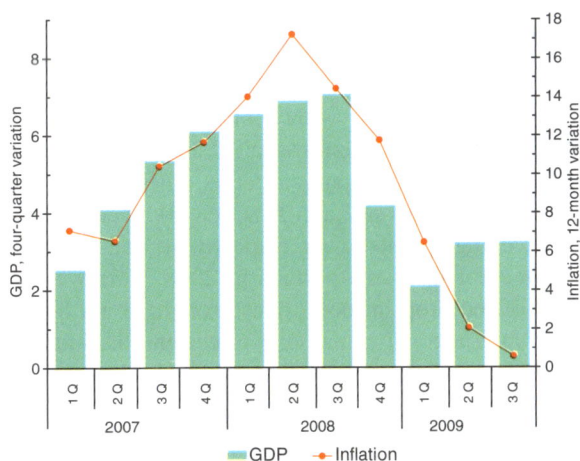

Source: Economic Commission for Latin America and the Caribbean (ECLAC), on the basis of official figures.

customs revenue was mostly tied to the slump in imports, and the decline in hydrocarbon tax revenues reflected the sluggishness in that sector. As regards fiscal spending in 2009, in light of the redefined role of the State, the public sector announced a major investment programme valued at US$ 1.852 billion, a small percentage of which was in execution by September. In the area of social spending, a new benefit called the "Juana Azurduy" grant was instituted, and coverage of the "Juancito Pinto" grant was extended to include students through the eighth grade. The non-financial public sector is expected to close 2009 with a slight surplus, showing a positive balance for public enterprises and a negative balance for the national treasury. The national treasury stepped up its local-currency bond issues by 39.3% between October 2008 and October 2009, in an amount equivalent to 49.3% of the cut-back in the central bank's open market operations. The financial system has been the main buyer of these bonds. The move was the result of a policy decision to improve debt quality, given the low interest rates, and to offer longer maturities; the action also stemmed from the national treasury's need to compensate for shrinking revenue. As a result, domestic public debt of the non-financial public sector increased by 11.4%, while external public debt expanded by 11%, which in turn swelled multilateral debt by 9.8% and bilateral debt by 14.5%.

In the first half of 2009, the GDP of the Plurinational State of Bolivia posted year-on-year growth of 3.2%. The sector that grew the most was metallic and non-metallic minerals, at 14.4%, which mainly had to do with the San Cristóbal mine having operated above capacity for part of the first semester. Although this sector registered the highest growth, its level of activity was actually down in comparison with the same period in 2008, when it grew 63%. The crude oil and natural gas sector contracted by 13.1% because of Brazil's lower demand for gas. On the demand side, GDP growth was driven by gross fixed capital formation and final consumption by public administration, which were up 4.5% and 4.4% and accounted for 0.72 and 0.45 percentage points of GDP growth, respectively. ECLAC estimates that the economy of the Plurinational State of Bolivia will grow by about 3.5% in 2009.

Cumulative inflation was at 0.2% through October 2009, or 0.8% in year-on-year terms. These were some of the lowest rates in Latin America and were 11 and 13 percentage points lower, respectively, than the rates recorded for the same periods in 2008. This was the result of the drop in food prices brought about by the fall in international commodity prices and the increase in domestic supply generated by favourable weather.

PLURINATIONAL STATE OF BOLIVIA: MAIN ECONOMIC INDICATORS

	2007	2008	2009 [a]
Annual percentage growth rates			
Gross domestic product	4.6	6.1	3.5
Per capita gross domestic product	2.7	4.3	1.7
Consumer prices	11.7	11.8	0.8 [b]
Average real wage	-1.3	-1.5	8.2
Money (M1)	58.1	23.2	10.5 [b]
Real effective exchange rate [c]	-1.1	-10.2	-12.6 [d]
Terms of trade	1.6	1.3	-2.2
Annual average percentages			
Urban unemployment rate	7.7	6.7	6.8
General government overall balance/GDP	2.3	-0.0	-3.2
Nominal deposit rate [e]	2.4	3.6	1.7 [f]
Nominal lending rate [e]	8.2	8.9	8.6 [f]
Millions of dollars			
Exports of goods and services	4 958	6 947	5 504
Imports of goods and services	4 143	5 680	5 064
Current account balance	1 591	2 015	1 063
Capital and financial account balance [g]	361	359	-332
Overall balance	1 952	2 374	731

Source: Economic Commission for Latin America and the Caribbean (ECLAC), on the basis of official figures.
[a] Preliminary estimates.
[b] Twelve-month variation to October 2009.
[c] A negative rate indicates an appreciation of the currency in real terms.
[d] Year-on-year average variation, January to October.
[e] Annual average of monthly rates in dollars.
[f] Average from January to October, annualized.
[g] Includes errors and omissions.

In the first half of 2009, the economy of the Plurinational State of Bolivia had a surplus of about US$ 388.3 million in its current account, which was 63.3% less than the US$ 670 million posted in the same period in 2008. Exports were down by US$ 853 million (27.3%) because of the decline in hydrocarbon prices in international markets and because of Brazil's lower demand for gas. Remittances by workers fell by 7.4% and were US$ 39.4 million lower than in the first half of 2008. Real exchange rates through October 2009 depreciated by 12.6% in year-on-year terms. The capital and financial account posted a deficit of US$ 170.2 million which, including errors and omissions, reached US$ 255.7 million. This balance was largely the result of the US$ 255.1 million negative balance on portfolio investment accounts. On the other hand, during the first half of 2009, the net international reserves held by the central bank increased by US$ 233.6 million (3%), and by October 2009 they had reached US$ 859 million, in other words, grown by 11.4%, which represented an increase of US$ 1.062 billion (14.1%) in year-on-year terms.

Uruguay

Uruguay's economy is estimated to have grown by approximately 1% in 2009, primarily due to an increase in private consumption, government consumption and public investment. Private investment, however, declined sharply. Annual inflation is estimated to reach 6% at the end of the year. Meanwhile, growth of 4.5% is being projected for 2010.

The non-financial public sector is expected to end the year with a deficit of 2.6% of GDP. For the rolling year ending September 2009, the sector posted a primary surplus of 0.4% of GDP, which, combined with debt interest payments (2.6% of GDP), resulted in a fiscal deficit of 2.2% of GDP. For that period, real income from the non-financial public sector rose 8%, on account of an increase of 17% in earnings from the Banco de Previsión Social (the bank dealing with social security funds), a rise of 3.3% in central government revenues and a 75% increase in earnings transfers to the treasury from public enterprises.

During the same period, primary outlays from the non-financial public sector grew by 13.7% in real terms, owing to an increase of 9.5% in current expenditures and of 49% in public investment. In terms of current expenditures, September saw a rise of 12.8% in transfers, while pensions grew 7.9% and wages increased 12.3%. The gross-debt-to-GDP ratio of the non-financial public sector as of mid-2009 was about 52%.

Country risk averaged approximately 253 basis points in October, representing a significant drop from the average of 608 registered the previous year, and the 341 basis points recorded in June 2009.

Monetary policy remained focused on ensuring price stability. The Central Bank of Uruguay decided to maintain this contractionary policy. Thus, in March 2009 the Bank set the monetary policy rate at 8%, after having kept it at about 10% since the end of 2008. This decision was based on the fact that although inflation had hovered between 3% and 7%, it was trending downward within a national and international context considered by the authorities to pose inflationary risks.

Towards the end of the second quarter, gross credit in domestic currency increased by 24% in nominal terms (16.3% in real terms) for the rolling year, while gross credit in foreign currency fluctuated within an annual range of 4.2%. After a decline in loans to the private sector in the first quarter of the year, there was a resurgence of loan activity in the second quarter. Despite the international

crisis, default rates have remained at historically low levels (about 1%), with a gradual decrease in defaults in the business sector and a gradual rise in defaults on loans denominated in domestic currency made to households. In June 2009 the default rate was about 2.7%.

In that same month, deposits in foreign currency increased by 21.9%, while those in domestic currency grew by 8.2%. The average interest rate on fixed-term deposits in dollars (the deposit interest rate) fell 55 basis points compared to the same month one year earlier, settling at 0.56%. The lending rate in United States dollars for loans to the non-financial sector was 6.04%.

The nominal exchange rate continued to float. After depreciating steeply in the second half of 2008 —a period during which the international financial crisis worsened— the local currency remained stable in relation to the dollar for the first half of 2009, and the subsequently sharp appreciation failed to entirely reverse the earlier decline. By the end of the year, the Uruguayan peso is expected to have appreciated by about 11% with respect to the dollar.

URUGUAY: GDP, INFLATION AND UNEMPLOYMENT

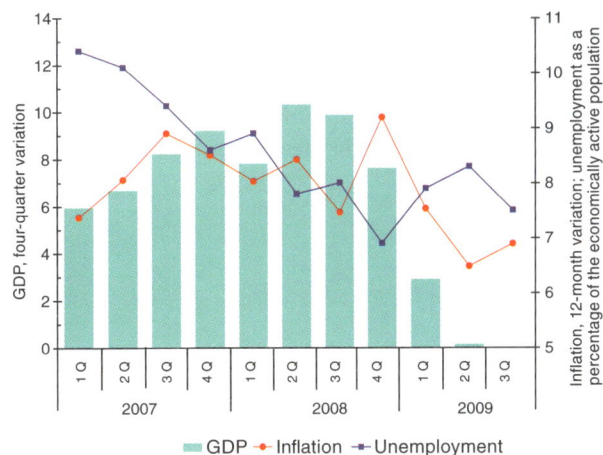

Source: Economic Commission for Latin America and the Caribbean (ECLAC), on the basis of official figures.

The real effective exchange rate, in turn, fell by 5.6% in the 12 months up to October.

In sectoral terms, the GDP growth seen in the first half of 2009 (1.5% compared to the same period in 2008) was led by the transportation, communications, services and construction sectors, while the industrial sector, primary activities and the sector supplying electricity, gas and water contracted. With respect to demand, the first half of the year saw an increase in government final consumption (5.5%), private consumption (0.7%) and exports (1.4%), and a reduction in gross capital formation (-28.3%, due primarily to adjustments in inventories) and in imports (-15.5%). Gross fixed capital formation declined by 4.6% for the period in question as the result of a drop in private investment, which was offset only partly by the increase in public investment.

With inflation at 6.5% for the 12 months ending in October, the year is expected to close with an increase in consumer prices that is within the range set by the central bank. The fall in the international price of commodities, attributable to the effects of the crisis, and the drop in the nominal exchange rate in the second half of the year helped stem the rise in domestic prices. The domestic producer price index (used to estimate wholesale inflation) rose by 8.6% in the first 10 months of 2009.

The employment rate continued to climb, though with fluctuations, throughout the year owing to the uncertainty caused by the international financial crisis. It reached a national level of 58.3% in the first 9 months of 2009 —1.1 percentage points higher than that recorded in the same period of 2008. The activity rate increased one point, to 63.1%. Correspondingly, unemployment declined by 0.3 percentage points in the same period, to an average of 7.6%. The average wage index rose by 7.7% in real terms, on average, between January and September, compared to the same period one year earlier, with similar increases in the private and public sectors. In January-October, the national minimum wage was raised by 12% in real terms compared to one year earlier, to the equivalent of US$ 210 per month.

The sharp drop in imports of goods and services, together with the moderate increase in exports, produced a net positive trade balance in value terms in the first semester

URUGUAY: MAIN ECONOMIC INDICATORS

	2007	2008	2009 [a]
	Annual percentage growth rates		
Gross domestic product	7.6	8.9	1.2
Per capita gross domestic product	7.3	8.6	0.9
Consumer prices	8.5	9.2	6.5 [b]
Average real wage	4.7	3.6	7.3 [c]
Money (M1)	31.8	17.3	7.8 [d]
Real effective exchange rate [e]	-1.0	-8.7	-0.2 [f]
Terms of trade	0.2	6.0	7.1
	Annual average percentages		
Urban unemployment rate	9.6	7.9	7.7 [c]
Central government			
overall balance/GDP	-1.6	-1.0	-2.1
Nominal deposit rate	2.3	3.2	4.1 [g]
Nominal lending rate	10.0	13.1	16.9 [g]
	Millions of dollars		
Exports of goods and services	6 850	9 258	8 385
Imports of goods and services	6 722	10 069	8 171
Current account balance	- 80	-1 119	- 152
Capital and financial account balance [h]	1 091	3 352	1 755
Overall balance	1 010	2 233	1 603

Source: Economic Commission for Latin America and the Caribbean (ECLAC), on the basis of official figures.
[a] Preliminary estimates.
[b] Twelve-month variation to October 2009.
[c] Estimate based on data from January to October.
[d] Twelve-month variation to August 2009.
[e] A negative rate indicates an appreciation of the currency in real terms.
[f] Year-on-year average variation, January to October.
[g] Average from January to October, annualized.
[h] Includes errors and omissions.

that persisted during the remainder of the year. Exports of goods rose in volume terms, driven by the increase in sales of agricultural and agribusiness products. Exports of services declined owing to the impact of the crisis on external demand and despite the fact that there was an increase in the export of tourist services to countries within the region.

The trade account surplus resulted in the balance on the current account being 0.1% of GDP in the first half of the year. This balance, however, is expected to turn negative (-0.5% of GDP) by the end of the year. Thus, during the first semester, the financial account had net revenues of US$ 397 million. As a result of the balance-of-payments surplus, reserve assets in the period up to October exceeded US$ 8 billion —US$ 2 billion more than the previous year.

Mexico and Central America

Costa Rica

In 2009, Costa Rica's economy suffered the effects of the global economic slowdown and, particularly, the recession in the United States. The main channels of transmission were falling external demand and tourist arrivals, as well as weakening flows of foreign direct investment (FDI). As a result, GDP is expected to shrink by about 1.2%, after having grown by 2.6% in 2008. Gross domestic investment and exports declined significantly, though this was partially offset by a moderate increase in consumption. The open unemployment rate rose to 7.8% nationwide. Inflation decreased significantly and is expected to end the year at about 4.5%. The balance-of-payments current account deficit decreased considerably, from 9.2% of GDP in 2008 to 3.3% in 2009, whereas the fiscal deficit rose sharply to 3.8% of GDP.

According to ECLAC estimates, GDP will grow by 3.5% in 2010, driven by recovering external demand. Inflation will remain at about 5%, whereas the current account deficit will be similar to that of 2009. The fiscal deficit, as a percentage of GDP, is also expected to be similar to the previous year's figure. In this context, the new government, which will take office in 2010, is expected to engage in fiscal reform efforts.

The balance of the central government deteriorated significantly, which led to several budget adjustments during the year. The administration also sought temporary authorization from the Legislative Assembly to finance current expenditures by borrowing. Fiscal receipts dropped by 9.5% in real terms, because of the downturn in economic activity and in imports. As a result, income taxes and foreign trade suffered the greatest contractions.

In contrast, central government spending increased by 15.6% in real terms. Current expenditures grew the most, as a result of a higher wage bill and countercyclical policies, which included extending social security coverage to workers laid off from their jobs, subsidizing food and transport and raising pensions. The fiscal deficit was financed mainly through the issuance of domestic debt purchased by institutional investors, which posted an annualized growth rate of 28%. External debt came down from 33% of GDP in 2008 to 30% in 2009, as a result of capital payments. Lines of credit with multilateral organizations were hardly used.

In 2009, monetary and exchange-rate policy continued to be directed towards price stability and migration towards a flexible exchange-rate scheme. The central bank found less need to adjust the exchange-rate band than it had in 2008, mainly because there was less turbulence and pressure in the currency market. Since the end of August, the exchange rate has eased back from the upper limit of the band, thanks to a lower current account deficit. In mid-November, the nominal exchange rate was 565 colones

COSTA RICA: GDP AND INFLATION

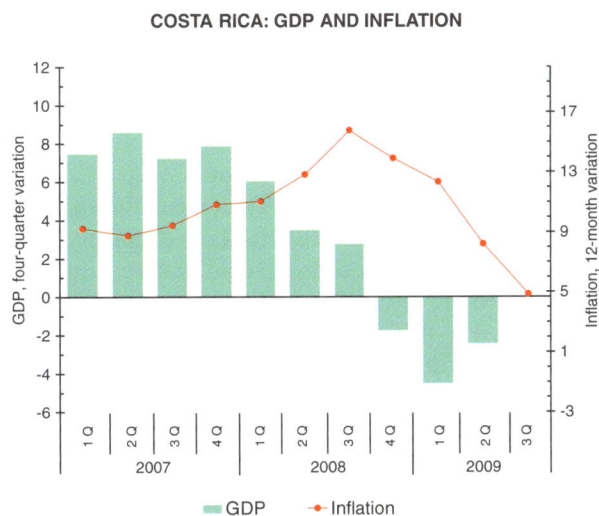

Source: Economic Commission for Latin America and the Caribbean (ECLAC), on the basis of official figures.

per dollar, which represents a depreciation of about 3% compared with the rate at the start of the year. This movement has caused a slight depreciation in the real bilateral exchange rate with the United States, following three years of movement in the opposite direction.

The central bank adopted a tight monetary policy aimed at countering potential inflationary pressures, despite the pullback in economic activity. Until the end of November, the monetary-policy rate had been reduced once, and by only a single percentage point (from 10% to 9%). The financial system's average nominal lending rate closed the year at 24.6%, which translates into a real rate of 17.8%. The average nominal deposit rate ended the year at 10.7%, returning the real rate to positive territory (3.8%) after its negative figures of 2008. Foreign-currency deposits grew by 25%, which reflects the increasing dollarization of the economy.

During 2009, several rounds of talks were held with a view to a free trade agreement with China. Negotiations on the proposed association agreement between Central America and the European Union had to be suspended, pending resolution of the crisis in Honduras. In order to comply with commitments undertaken in the framework of the World Trade Organization (WTO), the government sent a bill to the Legislative Assembly to modify the law on free zones.

The economic downturn was sharper in the first half of 2009 and, since April, the decline in the monthly index of economic activity has eased. The plunge in gross domestic investment (-24.1%) reflected the contraction in construction and machinery purchases and heavy inventory drawdowns. Consumption grew by 1.8% (4.3% in 2008), despite deteriorating economic conditions, driven by rising real wages, increased public spending on remuneration and procurement of goods and services, and the strengthening of social programmes. By sector, manufacturing (-4.9%) and commerce, restaurants and hotels (-4.4%) felt the effect of slumping external demand, whereas agriculture and livestock (-4.7%) were also hurt by adverse weather events and pests.

Inflation, as measured by the consumer price index, dropped significantly in 2009. The year-on-year rate in December is expected to come in at 4.5% (compared with 13.9% in 2008). This decrease is attributable primarily to the economic slowdown and lower international food and fuel prices. Also, the new exchange-rate scheme has helped keep currency fluctuations from being passed through to domestic prices. The nationwide unemployment rate rose sharply (by 2.9 percentage points), following

COSTA RICA: MAIN ECONOMIC INDICATORS

	2007	2008	2009 [a]
	Annual percentage growth rates		
Gross domestic product	7.8	2.6	-1.2
Per capita gross domestic product	6.3	1.2	-2.5
Consumer prices	10.8	13.9	4.0 [b]
Average real wage [c]	1.4	-2.0	9.4 [d]
Money (M1)	22.6	1.5	0.6 [e]
Real effective exchange rate [f]	-2.5	-3.4	-1.1 [g]
Terms of trade	-1.0	-3.8	8.0
	Annual average percentages		
Urban unemployment rate	4.8	4.8	7.6
Central government overall balance/GDP	0.6	0.2	-3.8
Nominal deposit rate	7.1	5.4	8.7 [h]
Nominal lending rate	17.3	16.7	21.7 [h]
	Millions of dollars		
	12 852	13 660	12 631
Imports of goods and services	14 103	16 444	13 271
Current account balance	-1 646	-2 732	-1 195
Capital and financial account balance [i]	2 794	2 384	1 462
Overall balance	1 148	-348	267

Source: Economic Commission for Latin America and the Caribbean (ECLAC), on the basis of official figures.
[a] Preliminary estimates.
[b] Twelve-month variation to October 2009.
[c] Average wages reported by workers covered by social security.
[d] Estimate based on data from January to September.
[e] Twelve-month variation to November 2009.
[f] A negative rate indicates an appreciation of the currency in real terms.
[g] Year-on-year average variation, January to October.
[h] Average from January to November, annualized.
[i] Includes errors and omissions.

three years of decline. Real wages in the formal sector increased because of the drop in inflation.

The current account deficit narrowed significantly, mainly as a result of goods imports (which were down by around 20%). In the case of durable and capital goods, the fall in imports was due to the contraction of economic activity and, in the case of fuels and lubricants, to lower international prices as well. Exports also contracted, but at a lesser rate of some 7%. In the first half of 2009, exports from free zones fell sharply, but towards the end of the year the pace of the decline had slowed.

Exports of services decreased by about 9%, because of reduced revenues from transport and tourism. Exports of business services are thought to have continued to rise, however, thanks to the arrival of new businesses seeking to lower costs. FDI flows totalled US$ 1.4 billion, compared with US$ 2 billion in 2008, as investment in construction and tourism fell. Though the financial account surplus shrank, it still exceeded the current account deficit in absolute terms, which led to an accumulation of reserves.

El Salvador

The international financial crisis had a devastating effect on external demand in El Salvador, as well as on remittances and FDI. Uncertainty surrounding the legislative and presidential elections held at the beginning of 2009 impacted consumption and investment. Given the general slowdown in economic activity, ECLAC estimates that GDP decreased by 2.5% in 2009, with per capita GDP falling by 3%. The flooding at the end of the year had a minimal effect on economic activity.

Although 12-month inflation was negative up to October 2009, inflation for the year as a whole is expected to come in at around 0.5%. Given the worsening situation of public finances, a deficit of 5.5% of GDP is projected for the non-financial public sector (including pensions), 2.4 percentage points higher than in 2008. Owing to the sharp decline in imports, the current account deficit is expected to reach approximately 2% of GDP, down from 7.6% in 2008. For 2010, ECLAC is projecting a moderate recovery, with both GDP growth and inflation at 2%, a current account deficit of 3% of GDP and a non-financial public sector deficit (including pensions) of 4.5% of GDP.

In regard to public finances, the government faced a difficult situation. While income tax receipts grew by 2.5%, value added tax (VAT) receipts declined by 14.7% owing to the economic slowdown. As a result, the central government's current revenues fell by 12%. On the expenditures side, wage payments rose by 10%, while investment fell by nearly 5% after having increased by nearly 30% in 2008. A deficit of 5.5% is projected for the non-financial public sector, including the broader public sector and pensions.

In light of this situation, the government had to renegotiate the terms of its foreign-loan agreements, and throughout the year treasury bills were used intensively to cover current expenditures. At the end of September the government announced that it intended to sign a new precautionary loan agreement with the International Monetary Fund for US$ 800 million, with a term of 3 years. This would replace the agreement signed by the previous government in January 2009.

The total debt of the non-financial public sector in 2009, including pensions, is estimated to swell by an amount equivalent to five percentage points of GDP to reach 45% of GDP. It is then expected to continue increasing and to peak at 50% of GDP in 2011. Thus, in mid-2009, both Standard and Poor's and Fitch Ratings lowered their ratings for El Salvador's sovereign debt. Nevertheless, at the end of November, the country issued bonds in the international market for close to US$ 800 million, which will be used to pay down short-term debt.

Greater risk aversion on the part of Salvadoran commercial banks meant that loans to the private sector decreased by 5% in real terms. Banks took advantage of available liquidity to almost halve their external debt, as well as to improve the time profile of their risks.

EL SALVADOR: GROWTH AND INFLATION

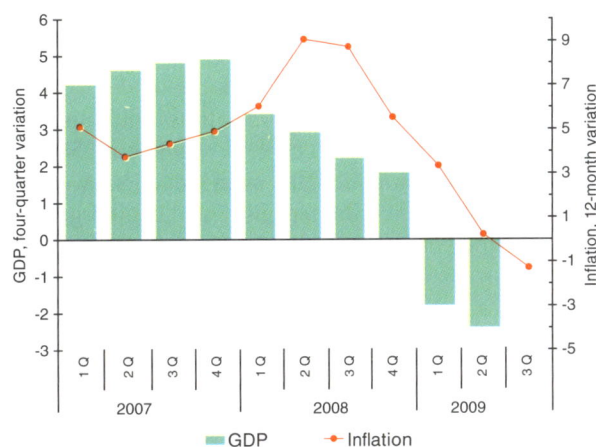

Source: Economic Commission for Latin America and the Caribbean (ECLAC), on the basis of official figures.

Economic growth slowed in practically all sectors, with the exception of government services. The slump in manufacturing and trade, triggered by the sharp drop in foreign and domestic demand, had the largest impact on overall growth. Although economic activity was low and growth remained negative, the slowdown moderated during the second half of 2009. At the beginning of November, the central part of the country was hit by floods caused by hurricane Ida. Though some municipalities suffered severe damage, the overall impact was mild. As a result, the decline in GDP in 2009 is projected by ECLAC to be 2.5%.

As far as spending is concerned, gross domestic investment dropped by 14.5% owing to the tighter credit conditions described earlier and the significant reduction in FDI flows. At the same time, private consumption fell by approximately 10% on account of the reduction in remittances and the worsening situation in the job market.

Up to August, the number of workers contributing to the Salvadoran Institute of Social Security declined by nearly 20,000 (6.7%). The worst-hit sector was construction, where nearly 30% of jobs were lost. Given the low levels of inflation, real minimum wages increased by around 9% in 2009 compared with 2008, when they rose by barely 0.2%.

Beginning in the third quarter of 2008, the drop in international prices for commodities led to a pronounced slowdown in the food and beverages and transportation components of the consumer price index. Consequently, inflation plummeted, with prices falling by 1.6% in the 12 months leading up to October and by 0.7% in relation to December 2008. Prices are expected to rise again in the final months of the year in comparison with those seen at the end of 2008. Thus, in December, the 12-month inflation rate is expected to be around 0.5%.

Exports of goods decreased by approximately 15%. Two thirds of the decline is attributable to the fall-off in exports from the maquila industry and the remaining third to declines in non-traditional exports, with traditional exports remaining at a level similar to that of 2008. As a result of the severe contraction in domestic demand, as well the approximately 50% drop in the oil bill, imports of goods are estimated to have fallen by about 25%. In terms of volumes imported, the main reductions were in imports of durable consumer goods and capital goods. Thus, for the year overall, the deficit of the balance of

EL SALVADOR: MAIN ECONOMIC INDICATORS

	2007	2008	2009 [a]
	Annual percentage growth rates		
Gross domestic product	4.7	2.5	-2.5
Per capita gross domestic product	4.2	2.1	-3.0
Consumer prices	4.9	5.5	-1.6 [b]
Real minimun wage	2.5	0.2	9.3
Money (M1)	16.5	1.6	1.7 [c]
Real effective exchange rate [d]	1.2	1.0	-4.5 [e]
Terms of trade	-0.9	-2.8	7.9
	Annual average percentages		
Urban unemployment rate	5.8	5.5	...
Central government			
overall balance/GDP	-0.2	-0.6	-2.3
Nominal deposit rate	4.7	4.2	4.7 [f]
Nominal lending rate	7.8	7.9	9.4 [f]
	Millions of dollars		
Exports of goods and services	5 169	5 652	5 334
Imports of goods and services	9 564	10 629	8 659
Current account balance	-1 221	-1 682	-524
Capital and financial account balance [g]	1 502	2 016	644
Overall balance	280	334	120

Source: Economic Commission for Latin America and the Caribbean (ECLAC), on the basis of official figures.
[a] Preliminary estimates.
[b] Twelve-month variation to October 2009.
[c] Twelve-month variation to September 2009.
[d] A negative rate indicates an appreciation of the currency in real terms.
[e] Year-on-year average variation, January to October.
[f] Average from January to October, annualized.
[g] Includes errors and omissions.

goods and services is expected to shrink by more than US$ 1.7 billion to US$ 3.325 billion (14.9% of GDP).

In contrast, the income account deficit is expected to widen slightly. Remittances, which represent 16% of GDP, declined by around US$ 400 million. Thus, the current account deficit is estimated to have contracted from more than US$ 1.2 billion to US$ 418 million (2% of GDP). FDI inflows to El Salvador in 2009 are estimated to have dropped by approximately US$ 700 million, while total remittances have amounted to barely US$ 88 million over the course of the year.

For 2010, a moderate revival is projected for both foreign and domestic demand, meaning that once again net exports will be in the negative range. Although the flow of remittances is expected to increase, this will not be sufficient to prevent a slight increase in the current account deficit, which is estimated to reach 3% of GDP.

Guatemala

In 2009, the Guatemalan authorities faced major challenges in their efforts to offset the impact of the international financial crisis and, in particular, the recession in the United States, on the country's economy. The crisis was transmitted through slumps in exports, remittances, foreign direct investment (FDI) and tourism. According to estimates, the Guatemalan economy contracted by 1% in 2009, as compared with 4% growth in 2008. The inflation rate fell from 9.4% to 2% and the fiscal deficit was 3.4% of GDP. Although the trade deficit reached 11% of GDP, the inflow of remittances, albeit at a reduced rate, kept the balance-of-payments current account deficit at 2.2% of GDP.

According to forecasts economic growth of 2% in 2010 with inflation at around 3%, due to the economic revival occurring in the United States and increased foreign capital inflows. Authorities are projecting the central government deficit at approximately 3.4% of GDP.

The fiscal deficit in 2009, as a proportion of GDP, is estimated to have doubled compared with 2008. In May 2009, given the downturn in economic activity and the real reduction in tax revenues of around 2.6% of GDP, the budget was adjusted to reduce the resulting gap (approximately 4 billion quetzales over the amount budgeted). In addition, the National Congress authorized an increase in the issuance of domestic currency bonds for a total of 3 billion quetzales, and approved a World Bank loan of US$ 350 million (41.5% to be disbursed in 2009 and the remainder in 2010) and another loan of US$ 38 million from the Inter-American Development Bank (IDB). Thus, it is estimated that the public debt will be 22% of GDP, compared with 20% of GDP in 2008.

Total real government revenues were down by 9.4% compared with 2008, while total expenditures grew by 5.5%, primarily as a result of increased current expenditures (10.5%), with capital expenditures dropping 4.6% in real terms. The tax burden was 9.9% of GDP, 1.5 percentage points lower than in 2008, settling well below the regional average and below the figure stipulated in the Peace Accords.

One year after the submission of a proposal for fiscal modernization and expanded tax collections (amounting to just over 1% of GDP), negotiations between the executive branch, the Congress and business leaders broke down. Although this initiative was withdrawn on 27 August 2009, it is vital that the country reach a fiscal agreement and that efforts to improve tax administration proceed, in order to stem tax evasion and smuggling and boost revenues.

In January 2009, an ambitious plan was announced to deal with the crisis, and the National Emergency and Economic Recovery Programme was implemented to increase countercyclical public spending, provide social protection to vulnerable segments of the population, make

GUATEMALA: MONTHLY INDEX OF ECONOMIC ACTIVITY (MIEA) AND INFLATION

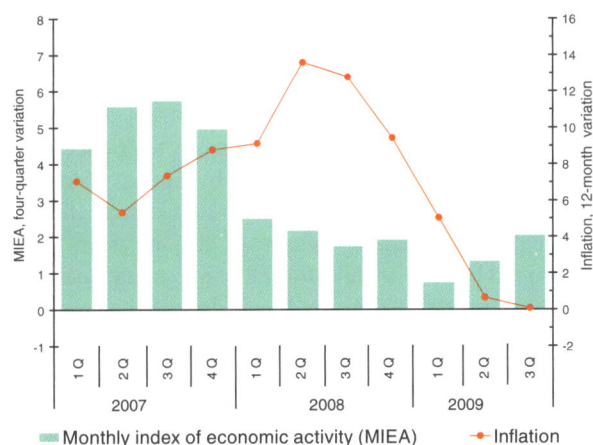

Source: Economic Commission for Latin America and the Caribbean (ECLAC), on the basis of official figures.

the budget fiscally sustainable and promote competitiveness. However, the results of this countercyclical policy were compromised by lack of funding. As a result, only marginal progress was made on reduction of poverty, inequality and insecurity, and this was compounded by a serious food crisis caused by drought in the country. Given this situation, the government was forced to intervene, and declared a "state of public calamity" in September 2009. International assistance was also sought and has been coming in gradually.

Between January and November of 2009, the main monetary policy interest rate dropped by 275 basis points. A year-end rate of around 4.5% (2.5% in real terms) is therefore being projected. In February 2009, the Monetary Board changed the rule on exchange-rate intervention in order to afford the Bank of Guatemala greater discretion to counteract volatility. The Board also authorized the central bank to supply liquidity to the financial system up to a maximum of US$ 290 million through 31 May 2009. In addition, the band of fluctuation for the daily moving average within the flexible exchange-rate system was expanded from 0.50% to 0.75%. Up to November 2009, the Bank of Guatemala intervened in the currency market on 20 occasions. It is estimated that the bilateral nominal exchange rate with respect to the United States dollar depreciated 7% (3% in real terms). At the same time, international reserves reached levels similar to those of 2008, equivalent to four months' imports of goods and services.

Real monetary aggregates increased slightly in 2009 (by between 3% and 4%) in response to the significant slowdown in economic activity. Real interest rates on loans and deposits averaged 11.1% and 2.9%, respectively, compared with the low rates recorded in 2008 (1.7% and -5.6%, respectively). Loans to the private sector increased in real terms by 4.6%, while loans to the public sector fell 19.9%. The main banking indicators, above all those relating to non-performing loans, deteriorated slightly. Accordingly, there was a rise in the number of individuals and businesses renegotiating their liabilities with banks in order to avoid default.

With the 1% drop in GDP, 20 years of continued expansion came to an end. Construction experienced the greatest contraction (-9.1%), followed by mining, which fell by 2.6%. Services, agriculture and manufacturing, on the other hand, remained flat. In terms of demand, gross fixed investment fell 14%, while domestic investment declined 32% as a result of the significant drop in inventories. Private investment saw a 15% reduction, while public investment fell by 10%. Total consumption grew by barely 1.5%. In 2009, results of surveys on economic and employment prospects, as well as consumer confidence indices, were negative. By 2010, however, a moderate recovery is expected.

GUATEMALA: MAIN ECONOMIC INDICATORS

	2007	2008	2009 [a]
Annual percentage growth rates			
Gross domestic product	6.3	4.0	-1.0
Per capita gross domestic product	3.7	1.5	-3.4
Consumer prices	8.7	9.4	-0.7 [b]
Average real wage	-1.7	-10.2	4.8
Money (M1)	14.1	3.4	7.4 [b]
Real effective exchange rate [c]	-0.8	-5.4	1.9 [d]
Terms of trade	-1.9	-2.7	7.9
Annual average percentages			
Central administration overall balance/GDP	-1.4	-1.6	-3.4
Nominal deposit rate	4.9	5.2	5.6 [e]
Nominal lending rate	12.8	13.4	13.9 [e]
Millions of dollars			
Exports of goods and services	8 714	9 637	8 894
Imports of goods and services	14 511	15 581	13 219
Current account balance	-1 786	-1 863	-628
Capital and financial account balance [f]	2 002	2 195	514
Overall balance	216	333	-114

Source: Economic Commission for Latin America and the Caribbean (ECLAC), on the basis of official figures.
[a] Preliminary estimates.
[b] Twelve-month variation to October 2009.
[c] A negative rate indicates an appreciation of the currency in real terms.
[d] Year-on-year average variation, January to October.
[e] Average from January to October, annualized.
[f] Includes errors and omissions.

Inflation slowed in 2009, reaching barely 2%, owing to the drop in economic activity and reduced prices for fuel, food and non-alcoholic beverages. In early 2009, the minimum wage rose 10.6% for farm workers and 7.2% for non-farm workers, except in the maquila industry, leading to positive real-wage figures. The unemployment rate for 2009 is expected to be around 7%, compared with 5.5% in 2008. Up to October 2009, job applications increased by approximately 50% compared with the same period in 2008.

In 2009, as a result of the global economic crisis, exports of goods fell by 8.5% as compared with 2008, due to the decline in non-traditional exports (-14%). In terms of traditional products, exports of cardamom, bananas and sugar rose, while earnings from coffee exports fell 4.4% mostly as a result of reductions in export volumes. Imports of goods dropped by 16.7%, primarily due to reductions in imports of intermediate goods (-16%), consumer goods (-17.6%) and capital goods (-18.2%). By the end of the year, revenue from family remittances will have declined by 11%. At the same time, foreign-exchange earnings from tourism decreased by approximately 10% as a result of the outbreak of influenza A (H1N1), a worsening of security problems and the effects of the global economic recession. Revenue from FDI inflows were equivalent to 2% of GDP, despite a 9.5% decline compared with 2008.

Honduras

In 2009 the Honduran economy experienced its first recession since 1999. GDP is estimated to have contracted by 3%, with a 5% decline in per capita GDP, owing to effects of the international financial crisis and the political crisis in the country. Inflation fell significantly, closing the year at 3.5%. The slowdown in economic activity led to a sharp reduction in the current account deficit, which dropped from 14% in 2008 to 7.9% in 2009. By contrast, the central government deficit expanded from the equivalent of 2.4% of GDP, to 4.5% of GDP.

The impact of the international crisis was transmitted to the Honduran economy through external demand, FDI, remittances and tourism revenues, which all contracted. These effects were magnified by the domestic political crisis that followed the removal from office of President Zelaya in June. The rupture of democratic order for first time in 30 years produced deep polarization within Honduran society. The international community, meanwhile, imposed restrictions on external financing and international cooperation.

The new government due to take office in January 2010 will face an extraordinarily difficult situation. The country is now profoundly divided politically and its economic growth is being severely limited by the aftermath of the events of 2009, combined with more deep-rooted structural factors. The latter include a high level of inequality, a poverty rate of over 60%, scant opportunities for formal employment for the vast majority, and even undernutrition, particularly among children. Macroeconomic policy faces additional challenges posed by, on the one hand, the complicated footing of public finances and, on the other, a real exchange rate that is around 20% overvalued, in comparison with the average for the last 20 years. At this juncture, broad consensus —at present, a seemingly difficult proposition— is needed to overcome these problems.

As a consequence of the crisis, fiscal revenues fell by approximately 13% in real terms, while revenues from foreign trade taxes plunged by 25% as a result of the major contraction in imports. Direct taxes slipped by 13%, with sales taxes the category least affected. Grants were down by 10%.

Overall public spending decreased slightly, by around 2% in real terms. Current expenditures grew by 2%, owing largely to wage increases (4%). The adjustment variable was capital spending, which contracted by more than 15%. Public finances are being weighed down —and could even find their sustainability threatened, if current patterns continue— by certain expenditures, such as benefits mandated by union by-laws, which are in need of overhaul. The former government had implemented a number of positive measures, which remain in force, such as free school enrolment and snacks during school hours, but no financing sources had yet been identified.

As a result of the drop in revenues and the inability to access external financing, floating debt and domestic indebtedness increased. Domestic debt grew by nearly 80%, from 3.5% of GDP in 2008 to 5.9% in 2009. External debt continued to decline as a proportion of GDP, owing to the country's participation in various debt forgiveness initiatives for highly indebted poor countries and limited access to new financing.

Monetary policy passed through two distinct stages during the year. In the first semester it was expansionary, aimed at bolstering economic activity against the effects of the international financial crisis. The monetary policy rate was reduced, from 7.75% in December 2008 to 3.5% in June 2009. The reserve requirement was lowered to 0% and the open market operations that had been used to absorb excess liquidity were suspended.

As of July, the focus has been on shoring up net international reserves and ensuring exchange rate stability. The monetary policy rate increased to 4.5%, the reserve requirement rose to 6% and the mandatory investments of financial institutions in government bonds, rose from 9% to 12%. These measures slowed the decline in reserves and secured the funds to finance the fiscal gap. The nominal interest rate on deposits rose from 6.0% to 7.2%, with nominal lending rates increasing from 17.4%, on average, between January and September 2008, to 19.6% in the same period of 2009. Due to the sharp slowdown in inflation, real interest rates rose significantly. In the financial system, indicators for non-performing, overdue and other troubled loans deteriorated, but did not reach alarming levels.

The excess liquidity seen during the first part of the year was drawn into covering the fiscal deficit through the sale of government bonds, and went into purchases of dollars that drained international reserves, which declined 11% between December 2008 and September 2009. The nominal exchange rate remained unchanged, signalling a slight real appreciation with respect to the dollar.

Economic activity contracted by around 3% after having expanded 4% in 2008 —a contraction that would have been even greater but for the creation of a fund controlled by the Honduran Bank for Production and Housing (BANHPROVI). The fund's loan portfolio grew by approximately 80% in 2009. Gross domestic investment slumped 29%. Consumption shrank slightly (by 2.1%), with the private component declining by 5% and the public by 2.5%.

The sectors worst affected by the crisis were construction and manufacturing, which contracted by 6.0% and 5%, respectively. The agricultural sector —highly important, particularly as a source of employment— contracted by more than 3%, in spite of some positive factors such as very good harvests for a number of grain crops. By contrast, the services sector performed well, with the highest growth rates in public administration and defence.

The consumer price index showed the effects of the economic slowdown combined with falling international prices for food and petroleum. The year-on-year rate to December fell from 10.8% in 2008 to 3.5% in 2009. Urban unemployment rose from 4.1% in 2008 to 4.9% in May 2009. In January 2009 there was an increase (unprecedented in the country's recent past) in the minimum wage —by as much as 96%, depending on the kind of activity— which made up some of the lag in wages from prior years and helped sustain consumption among the lower-income population.

The current account deficit declined by a significant 6 percentage points of GDP owing to the contraction in

HONDURAS: MAIN ECONOMIC INDICATORS

	2007	2008	2009 [a]
	Annual balance growth rates		
Gross domestic product	6.3	4.0	-3.0
Per capita gross domestic product	4.2	1.9	-4.9
Consumer prices	8.9	10.8	2.7 [b]
Real minimun wage	2.8	0.2	70.3
Money (M1)	16.3	1.8	2.1 [c]
Real effective exchange rate [d]	-0.3	-3.5	-8.7 [e]
Terms of trade	-1.9	-6.1	9.2
	Annual average percentages		
Urban unemployment rate	4.0	4.1	4.9 [f]
Central government overall balance/GDP	-2.9	-2.3	-4.2
Nominal deposit rate	7.8	9.5	10.9 [g]
Nominal lending rate	16.6	17.9	19.6 [g]
	Millions of dollars		
Exports of goods and services	6 344	6 956	6 117
Imports of goods and services	9 594	11 603	9 204
Current account balance	-1 225	-1 977	-1 129
Capital and financial account balance [h]	1 063	1 912	374
Overall balance	-162	-65	-755

Source: Economic Commission for Latin America and the Caribbean (ECLAC), on the basis of official figures.
[a] Preliminary estimates.
[b] Twelve-month variation to October 2009.
[c] Twelve-month variation to September 2009.
[d] A negative rate indicates an appreciation of the currency in real terms.
[e] Year-on-year average variation, January to October.
[f] Figure for May.
[g] Average from January to October, annualized.
[h] Includes errors and omissions.

imports of goods and services (19% and 17%, respectively). Exports of goods and services saw a less severe drop (12% and 15%, respectively). Traditional exports were the hardest hit, declining by 17.4%, followed by maquila exports, which were down by 12.1%. Imports of capital goods suffered a sharp 28.1% drop as a result of the economic slowdown, while most of the decline in the value of commodity and intermediate goods imports (25.4%) was due to the drop in international prices. After 12 consecutive years of deterioration, terms of trade improved, thanks to steep falls in international food and petroleum prices. Family remittances, one of the pillars of consumption and exchange-rate stability, slipped by 11%, while FDI flows fell by nearly 40%.

Mexico

The Mexican economy shrank by 6.7% in 2009, owing to across-the-board weakness in aggregate demand caused by the global recession. The economic slump led to a reduction in the wage bill and credit, which, in turn, triggered a fall in consumption. As the year moved forward, the recessive trends deepened and investment contracted —according to estimates, by more than 10%. The main channels of transmission of the global crisis have been dwindling global trade, alongside, to a lesser extent, declining foreign investment, tourism and remittances from workers abroad.

Decreasing economic activity led to a reduction in public revenue. However, total public spending —which was mainly focused on meeting social needs— is projected to have declined by a smaller proportion than has public revenue. The low tax burden made it difficult to implement large-scale fiscal measures to address the crisis. Moreover, by preferring the nominal stability of the economy over real stability, the authorities did not take advantage of the healthy public debt position in order to obtain loans with which to implement a countercyclical policy that would have provided a stronger boost to aggregate demand.

Annual inflation is projected to come in at 4% in 2009 as a result of falling prices for raw materials and energy, sluggish demand and the easing of pressure on the exchange rate. Public-sector borrowing requirements are estimated at 3.0% of GDP (up from 2.1% in 2008). In light of weak external demand, especially from the United States, and the consequent decline in imports due to lower consumption, the trade balance and balance-of-payments current account deficits are expected to be lower than in 2008.

The Mexican economy should enter a period of recovery in 2010 (with 3.5% growth), spearheaded by the expected upturn in the United States economy. However, not until 2011 is the economy expected to return to the level of activity seen in 2008. Inflation is projected to rise to 5%, partly because of the increase in value added tax (VAT) and the other taxes slated to be introduced in 2010 in a context of moderately higher consumption.

Real public-sector revenue fell by 8.7% between January and September 2009 because of the decline both in oil revenue and in non-oil tax receipts (down 24.4% and 12.8%, respectively). The drop in oil revenue stemmed from falling prices on world markets, production levels and exports. Tax receipts fell as collections of VAT dropped by 19.5%, income tax by 12.0% and the flat-rate business tax (IETU) by 7.5%. In response to the revenue shortfall, the authorities cut projected spending by the equivalent of 0.9% of GDP for the year. However, social programmes were left untouched by the budget cuts. The rest of the budget shortfall was offset with an operating surplus of Banco de México (for 95 billion pesos) and with oil price hedges and other non-recurring revenue (totalling 247.9 billion pesos).

MEXICO: GDP, INFLATION AND UNEMPLOYMENT

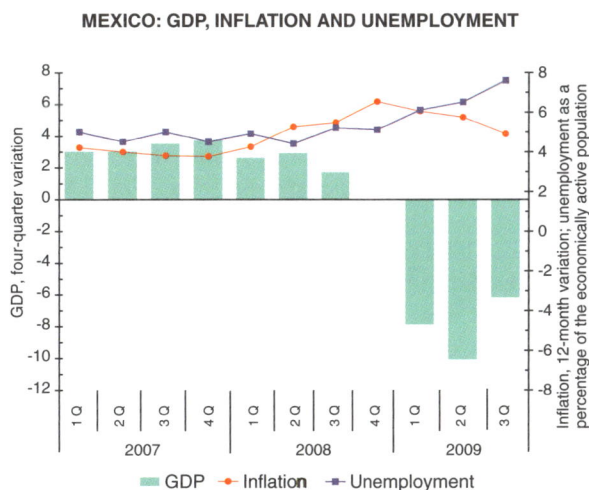

Source: Economic Commission for Latin America and the Caribbean (ECLAC), on the basis of official figures.

Real public-sector budget spending rose by 4.2%
from January to September 2009 as a result of a 36.8%
increase in capital spending and a 1.0% drop in current
expenditures. For the year overall, real spending is expected
to rise slightly. Together with declining revenue, this should
lead to an increase in the traditionally calculated deficit,
from 0.1% of GDP in 2008 to 2.1% according to official
estimates in 2009. The balance of the external public
debt in September was 9.6% of GDP, compared with
21.1% for domestic debt. Starting in 2009, both figures
include debt on Projects with a Deferred Impact on Public
Expenditure Recording (PIDIREGAS), which raised the
debt-to-GDP ratio from 21% to 31%. In late November
2009, the government secured a one-year credit line of
approximately US$ 1.504 billion with the World Bank to
mitigate the impact of the financial crisis and improve the
conditions for growth to resume in the medium term.

In 2010, new taxes will be introduced while others will be
raised. A new 3% tax will be charged on telecommunications;
temporarily the maximum individual and corporate income
tax rate will rise from 28% to 30%; VAT will increase
from 15% to 16%; and the tax on gaming and lotteries
will jump from 20% to 30%. Levies on tobacco, beer and
other alcoholic beverages will also go up.

The benchmark interest rate was lowered as a
consequence of the global recession, falling international
prices for raw materials and the freeze on certain domestic
energy prices. In the first seven months of 2009, the central
bank lowered the benchmark rate by 375 basis points, to
a slightly negative real rate of 4.5%. The average market
deposit rate was also negative in real terms, while lending
rates remained relatively high. The benchmark rate remained
stable from August to October 2009, and from January to
September the monetary base expanded by 9.1% in real
terms. The M1 and M2 monetary aggregates grew by
8.2%, while M3 and M4 increased by more than 6%.

Until September, commercial bank lending to the private
sector had fallen by 4.9%, in real terms, while consumer
lending had plummeted by 21.7%. The rate of growth of
lending to non-financial companies and self-employed
individuals slowed to only 3.9%, from 17.6% in 2008.

After appreciating in real terms from 2005 to August
2008, the peso depreciated abruptly (16% in real terms)
in October 2008 and continued falling until March 2009.
It stabilized in subsequent months. The real value of the
peso declined by an average of 19% in the first 10 months
of the 2009, on a year-on-year basis. Banco de México
intervened in the exchange market throughout the year.
In response to speculative pressure, in February the
central bank injected dollars into the currency market
and the following month it began holding daily auctions
for US$ 100 million. The central bank also left open the
possibility of conducting special sales of hard currency if

market conditions necessitated doing so. In April, a one-
year, US$ 47 billion contingent line of financing from
the International Monetary Fund (IMF) was announced.
Although the credit has not been used, it has helped relieve
pressure on the peso.

In May, the gradual easing of pressure in the foreign-
exchange market led the authorities to reduce the amount of
the daily auction from US$ 100 million to US$ 50 million.
In addition, the amount of the daily auction offered in the
event of a peso slide of more than 2% from one business
day to the next was reduced from US$ 300 million to
US$ 250 million, although the possibility of conducting
special sales of foreign currency remained. In October, the
US$ 50 million daily auctions were suspended. Fluctuations
in the country's international reserves reflected conditions
in the currency market. Up to July, the country's reserves
generally trended downwards; from August they recovered
and reached nearly US$ 82 billion, that is, to US$ 1 billion
below their level at the beginning of the year.

The Mexican economy entered into recession in the
last quarter of 2008. The global crisis exposed its structural
deficiencies and its vulnerability to external shocks as well
as the weakness and lack of resilience of its productive base
and the limited manoeuvring room there was for public
policy to counteract the effects of those shocks.

MEXICO: MAIN ECONOMIC INDICATORS

	2007	2008	2009 ª
Annual percentage growth rates			
Gross domestic product	3.4	1.3	-6.7
Per capita gross domestic product	2.3	0.3	-7.7
Consumer prices	3.8	6.5	4.5 ᵇ
Average real wage ᶜ	1.0	2.2	0.6 ᵈ
Money (M1)	11.7	9.0	12.7 ᵇ
Real effective exchange rate ᵉ	1.1	2.2	17.6 ᶠ
Terms of trade	0.9	0.8	-1.1
Annual average percentages			
Urban unemployment rate	4.8	4.9	6.8 ᵍ
Public sector			
overall balance/GDP	0.0	-0.1	-2.1
Nominal deposit interest rate	6.0	6.7	5.3 ʰ
Nominal lending interest rate	7.6	8.7	7.6 ⁱ
Millions of dollars			
Exports of goods and services	289 365	309 383	243 056
Imports of goods and services	305 743	333 723	256 668
Current account balance	-8 335	-15 806	-6 074
Capital and financial account balance ʲ	18 621	23 244	-1 422
Overall balance	10 286	7 438	-7 496

Source: Economic Commission for Latin America and the Caribbean (ECLAC), on the basis of official figures.
ª Preliminary estimates.
ᵇ Twelve-month variation to October 2009.
ᶜ Manufacturing sector.
ᵈ Estimate based on data from January to September.
ᵉ A negative rate indicates an appreciation of the currency in real terms.
ᶠ Year-on-year average variation, January to October.
ᵍ Estimate based on data from January to October.
ʰ Average from January to October, annualized.
ⁱ Average from January to September, annualized.
ʲ Includes errors and omissions.

In the first half of the year, economic activity decreased by 9.2%. In the third quarter, it contracted by 6.2%, and for the year overall, the projected decline is 6.7%. Accordingly, the economy is expected to turn the corner in the fourth quarter as a prelude to a recovery in 2010. Activity declined sharply in the commerce and construction sectors, while in September industrial output fell for the fourteenth consecutive month.

In terms of spending, private consumption and investment are estimated to have decreased by 6.5% and 11%, respectively. Exports fell by 23% in the first semester, while imports were down 25%.

The A (H1N1) influenza epidemic dealt a severe blow to the economy: tourism flows dwindled, and drastic measures were taken to cope with the epidemic (suspension of activities, principally in Mexico City). ECLAC estimates that the impact was equivalent to a loss of about 0.7% of GDP. Sectors associated with tourism (commerce, restaurants and hotels) were the hardest hit.

The automobile industry was the most affected within the manufacturing sector due to its strong ties to the United States economy. The automobile industry's contribution to total GDP (3.3%) and total exports (24%), as well as its linkages with 33 branches of production (including 30 in manufacturing), was a key factor in the country's economic slowdown. Automobile output fell by 35% and auto exports by 33%, in real terms, between January and October 2009. If these figures hold true for the year overall, 1.1 percentage points of the overall decline in GDP will be the direct consequence of the automobile industry slump alone —without taking into account the concomitant multiplier effects.

The fall in output also took a toll on the labour market. The open unemployment rate continued to trend upward, rising from 3.9% in September 2007 to 4.3% a year later and to 6.4% in September 2009. Given that the informal sector absorbed 28% of the economically active population, more than one third of the workforce was either unemployed or underemployed.

The number of workers registered at the Mexican Social Security Institute (IMSS) decreased by nearly 500,000, or 3.4%, between October 2008 and October 2009. The sectors that shed the largest number of jobs were manufacturing (-7.0%), construction (-9.5%) and transportation (-4.3%).

Exports were the main channel of transmission of the international financial crisis. Given that exports account for a high proportion of GDP (35%), the repercussions of lower exports spread quickly and forcefully. The value of total exports fell by 28.7% between January and September while that of imports dropped by 29.6%. Imports of consumer goods contracted the most (36.8%), followed by capital goods and intermediate goods, owing to the sharp drop in exports and the reduction in private consumption. In addition, the dwindling volume of petroleum exports and falling international prices slashed oil revenue by 53% in the same period. The trade deficit decreased by just over US$ 4.6 billion from January to September 2009 compared with the same period the previous year, to US$ 4.329 billion (0.51% of GDP). Excluding oil, the trade deficit exceeded US$ 25 billion (3% of GDP) in the same period.

The financial crisis in the United States had a considerable impact on remittances to Mexico. Between January and October 2009, the accumulated value of remittances was US$ 18.127 billion, which represented a 16.1% year-on-year decrease. FDI continued to slide, and the estimated value of FDI inflows —between US$ 13 and US$ 15 billion in 2009— is between 33% and 42% lower than in 2008.

Nicaragua

According to ECLAC estimates, the Nicaraguan economy posted 1.5% negative GDP growth in 2009 after 15 years of uninterrupted expansion and compared with 3.2% positive growth in 2008. External demand, which has driven growth in recent years, fell by 2.5%. Gross internal investment plummeted, whereas consumption grew slightly. Inflation is expected to be significantly lower and end the year at about 2.5%. The current account deficit shrank to 15% of GDP, compared with 23.8% in 2008. In contrast, the fiscal deficit, including donations, expanded to 3.5% of GDP, from 1.2% in 2008.

In August 2009, the Ministry of Finance introduced a fiscal reform bill in order to tackle the slide in fiscal revenues triggered by the economic slowdown and the decline in donations from abroad. The bill's main objectives are to make the tax system more equitable, to generalize the levying of taxes and to modernize and simplify tax payment procedures.

According to ECLAC estimates, the economy will grow by 2% in 2010, driven by a resurgence in external demand. Inflation will remain near 5%, and the balance-of-payments current account deficit will be similar to what it was in 2009. Pressure on public financing will ease slightly, thanks to growth in economic activity and the fiscal reform.

For 2009, total revenue of the central government is expected to drop by 4.1%, in real terms. Import tax receipts have been the hardest hit and fell by 15.9% because of the slump in purchases of durable consumer and capital goods. The 3.3% reduction in indirect taxes reflects both sluggish economic activity and fuel tax credits claimed against value added tax. Total expenditures by the central government are estimated to have risen by 6% in real terms. Current expenditures increased by 8.4% owing to higher wages and direct transfers, whereas capital expenditures decreased by 0.6% because of a lack of funds and delays in the execution of projects. In January, the government introduced a package of measures to counteract the impact of the economic crisis. These measures include initiatives that address financial stability, public investment, support of production and private investment, and job creation.

However, shrinking revenues have made it difficult to implement some of these counter-cyclical measures. In fact, during 2009, the public budget had to be adjusted downwards three times.

In this context, the central Government's fiscal deficit grew considerably and was financed mostly through loans from multilateral organizations. Public external debt is thus expected to reach 58.7% of GDP by the end of 2009, compared with 55.2% in 2008.

In 2009, monetary policy continued to make use of pre-announced mini-devaluations in order to rein in inflationary expectations. The annualized devaluation rate held steady at 5%, closing out the year with the official exchange rate at 20.8 córdobas per dollar. The real bilateral exchange rate (with the United States) depreciated slightly, ending a three-year spell of appreciation. The nominal interest rate for deposits in national currency was 5.5%

NICARAGUA: GDP AND INFLATION

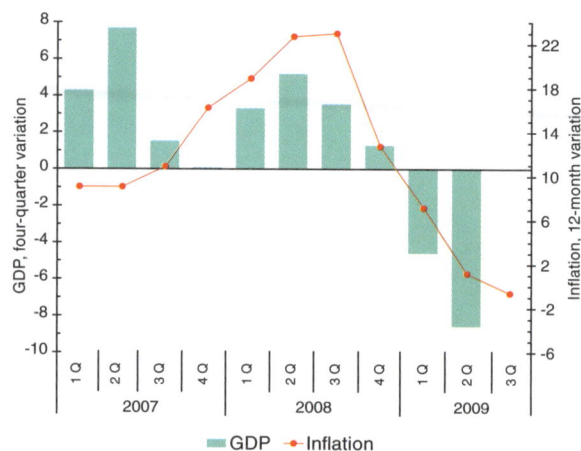

Source: Economic Commission for Latin America and the Caribbean (ECLAC), on the basis of official figures.

in September, compared with 6.3% for the same month in 2008. The nominal lending rate for loans in national currency was 14.2% in September, compared with 12.7% for the same month in 2008. Real interest rates, which were negative throughout 2008, were positive in 2009 because of lower inflation, which exacerbated the credit crunch in the private sector. International reserves are expected to increase by US$ 250 million, primarily because of the Special Drawing Rights disbursement from the International Monetary Fund (IMF), and to close the year at US$ 1.29 billion.

As far as trade policy is concerned, in 2009, the first meetings were held to negotiate a free trade agreement with Chile. Meanwhile, negotiations on an association agreement between Central America and the European Union were suspended after seven rounds of talks, pending resolution of the crisis in Honduras.

The Nicaraguan economy felt the toll of the international financial crisis and, particularly, of the recession in the United States in 2009. The primary transmission channels were weaker external demand, a decrease in the flow of remittances and shrinking foreign direct investment (FDI). The economic downturn was more acute during the first half of the year; the decline of the monthly economic activity indicator slowed in the second semester. The 15.6% plunge in gross internal investment was attributable to the shrinking of credit and FDI and to contraction in the construction sector, against a backdrop of recessive trends and uncertainty sparked by factors unrelated to the economy. Private consumption was up slightly (by 1.9%) because of the increase in real wages and public grant transfer programmes. The hardest-hit sectors were manufacturing, which shrank by 1.5%, construction (by 3.4%) and commerce, restaurants and hotels (by 1.8%).

Inflation, as measured by the consumer price index, was down significantly and is expected to end the year at 2.5%, from 13.8% in 2008. This drop is attributable to lower international prices of food and fuels and the slowdown in economic activity. Negative monthly inflation rates were recorded in three months (April, July and August). Low inflation played a major role in the marked increase in real wages.

The current account deficit shrank as a result of the sharp drop in goods imports (down by 18.5%). The oil bill was down 36%, mainly because of lower international prices,

NICARAGUA: MAIN ECONOMIC INDICATORS

	2007	2008	2009 [a]
Annual percentage growth rates			
Gross domestic product	3.2	3.2	-1.5
Per capita gross domestic product	1.8	1.9	-2.8
Consumer prices	16.2	12.7	-0.1 [b]
Average real wage	-1.8	-3.8	7.7 [c]
Money (M1)	23.6	2.8	1.9 [b]
Real effective exchange rate [d]	3.6	-4.9	-1.4 [e]
Terms of trade	-1.0	-4.4	10.5
Annual average percentages			
Urban unemployment rate	6.9	8.0	...
Central government overall balance/GDP	0.4	-1.2	-3.5
Nominal deposit rate	6.1	6.6	6.1 [f]
Nominal lending rate	13.0	13.2	14.1 [f]
Millions of dollars			
Exports of goods and services	2 709	2 937	2 826
Imports of goods and services	4 649	5 357	4 460
Current account balance	-1 001	-1 513	-818
Capital and financial account balance [g]	1 093	1 499	1 024
Overall balance	92	-14	207

Source: Economic Commission for Latin America and the Caribbean (ECLAC), on the basis of official figures.
[a] Preliminary estimates.
[b] Twelve-month variation to October 2009.
[c] Estimate based on data from January to September.
[d] A negative rate indicates an appreciation of the currency in real terms.
[e] Year-on-year average variation, January to October.
[f] Average from January to September, annualized.
[g] Includes errors and omissions.

whereas the 42% fall in imports of durable consumer goods and the 19.3% decline in capital goods were attributable primarily to reduced economic activity.

Goods exports were down by 9.4%. Reduced external demand had a huge negative impact on exports from free trade zones, which shrank by 7.2%. Traditional exports were down by 11.2%, a result that was compounded by weather issues, such as altered rainfall patterns due to El Niño, and by the timing of the low-point in the two-year coffee cycle. The international crisis also choked FDI flows, which are expected to reach US$ 420 million in 2009, compared with US$ 626 million in 2008. Remittances from family members were down by 5.7%. As is often the case, remittances proved to be more resilient than other foreign currency flows (such as exports and FDI) when the countries in which they are generated face economic downturns.

Panama

In 2009, Panama's economy slowed sharply and grew only 2.5%, compared to the 9% average annual rate registered over the previous five years. This performance reflected the fact that, though some domestic market sectors performed well, they were unable to offset the contraction in activities related to the external sector. Inflation, as measured by the consumer price index, came down and is estimated to end up at 2% year-on-year for December (it was 6.8% in 2008). Also, for the first time in three years the fiscal balance is expected to be in deficit (by 1.8% of GDP). The balance-of-payments current account deficit is expected to shrink to 9.2% of GDP because of the significant decrease in the trade deficit. In November 2009, Standard & Poor's upgraded Panama's long-term sovereign rating from stable to positive, stating that the country could shortly attain investment grade.

In 2010, GDP is expected to grow 4.5%, helped along by an upswing in world trade and the execution of infrastructure projects begun some time back, including the construction of the third set of locks in the Panama Canal and widening of the coastal beltway. Growth could be even greater if some of the large investments announced by President Martinelli come to fruition, such as the construction of a subway in the capital, another international airport in the southern part of the country and social housing. Inflation is expected to remain low. Estimates point to a smaller fiscal deficit (1.4% of GDP), thanks to the economic upturn and to implementation of new fiscal reforms, some of which were approved in September 2009.

A new fiscal and social responsibility law, which caps the fiscal deficit at 1% of GDP, went into effect in January 2009. In June, the government obtained authorization to raise the ceiling to 2.5%. In 2009, following three years of surpluses, the non-financial public sector (NFPS) posted a deficit. During the first half of 2009 this deficit was 0.8% of GDP and is expected to climb an additional percentage point by year's end, owing to the countercyclical fiscal policy deployed. For the period January to August 2009, the central government revenues fell off by 7.9%. Non-tax revenue slid by 35%, while tax income was up 11%. Expenditures increased 15%. Panama placed a bond issue on the international market for US$ 323 million in March and another, for US$ 1 billion, in November.

President Martinelli, who took office in July 2009, underscored that one of the goals of his administration is to modernize infrastructure projects and institute fiscal reform. In September, the Chamber passed a bill that, in addition to eliminating several exemptions and raising some taxes, for the first time will begin to consider activities of the Colón Free Zone (FTZ) as taxable transactions, subject to income tax. The next phase of the reform, expected to

PANAMA: GDP AND INFLATION

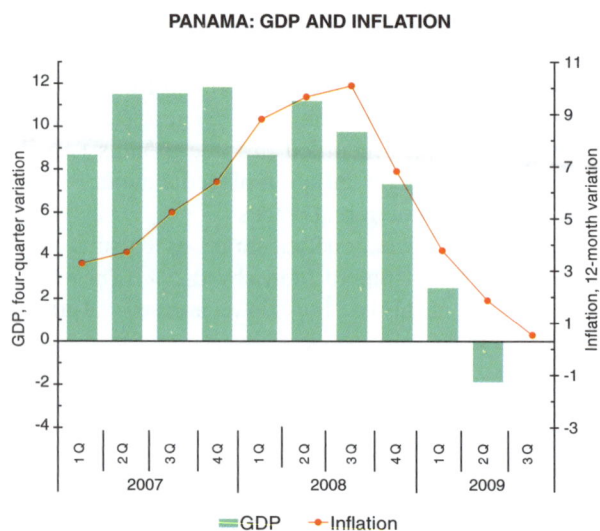

Source: Economic Commission for Latin America and the Caribbean (ECLAC), on the basis of official figures.

be introduced in 2010, will seek to replace the current income tax with a single-rate tax.

Because of the international financial crisis, the country's banking system —foreign-owned and local banks alike— adopted a more precautionary stance. As the preference for liquidity increased, lending to most sectors began to fall from February 2009 onwards. In response, in March the government introduced a financial stimulus programme valued at 1.1 billion balboas, with resources from the Inter-American Development Bank (IDB), the Andean Development Corporation (CAF) and the National Bank of Panama, to encourage banks to resume local lending. By June, the programme had narrowed to 600 million balboas, as IDB funding was excluded. The Panama Banking Association has expressed disagreement with the requirements for access to the stimulus fund since it was first set up. Since then, the programme resources have been practically unused and, though bank deposits have increased, lending continues to be sluggish. In September 2009, the nominal balance of bank lending to the private sector was 1.4% higher than 12 months earlier and only 0.5% higher than that of private banks, principally reflecting the 30% decline in new loans.

In 2009, the six-month deposit rate reversed the downward trend begun in 2008 and, by September, reached 3.06%, which was 240 basis points above the London Inter-Bank Offered Rate (LIBOR). This contrasted the previous year in which the six-month deposit rate remained below LIBOR. Lending rates hovered close to their 2008 closing levels. In September, the rate for credit cards was 15.37% and for personal loans, 11.69%. In real terms this meant an increase in rates, given the lower inflation. An overly precautionary stance does reduce risks to the banking system, but it also restricts the countercyclical scope of some aspects of economic policy.

In the second half of 2008 it became evident that Panama's economy was slowing down. Nevertheless, between January and June 2009, real GDP growth was 2.4% up on the year-earlier period, driven primarily by growth in construction, transport, storage and communications. Growth in mining and construction reflected mainly works already under way, since new construction fell off significantly. Building work seems to have shifted away from multifamily luxury skyscrapers in the capital and towards lower-cost single family homes in the provinces. Expansion in the telecommunications sector was mainly the result of growth in cellular telephony. Manufacturing grew slightly, while agriculture, livestock and forestry declined, owing to adverse weather effects related to El Niño. Commerce also contracted. The monthly economic activity index showed an annualized decline of more than 3% between July and August. The global recession acted as a drag on activity in the Panama Canal. The number of

PANAMA: MAIN ECONOMIC INDICATORS

	2007	2008	2009 [a]
	Annual growth rates		
Gross domestic product	12.1	10.7	2.5
Per capita gross domestic product	10.2	8.9	0.9
Consumer prices	6.4	6.8	0.7 [b]
Average real wage	1.3	-0.6	...
Real effective exchange rate [c]	1.4	-1.8	-5.8 [d]
Terms of trade	-1.0	-4.5	4.2
	Annual average percentages		
Urban unemployment rate [e]	7.8	6.5	7.9
Central government			
overall balance/GDP	1.2	0.3	-1.8
Nominal deposit rate [f]	4.8	3.5	3.5 [g]
Nominal lending rate [h]	8.3	8.2	8.3 [g]
	Millions of dollars		
Exports of goods and services	14 263	16 153	16 209
Imports of goods and services	14 627	17 604	16 715
Current account balance	-1 422	-2 792	-1 974
Capital and financial account balance [i]	2 044	3 377	2 124
Overall balance	622	584	150

Source: Economic Commission for Latin America and the Caribbean (ECLAC), on the basis of official figures.
[a] Preliminary estimates.
[b] Twelve-month variation to October 2009.
[c] A negative rate indicates an appreciation of the currency in real terms.
[d] Year-on-year average variation, January to October 2009.
[e] Includes hidden unemployment.
[f] Six-month deposits.
[g] Average from January to September, annualized.
[h] On one-year loans for commercial activities.
[i] Includes errors and omissions.

transits through the canal is estimated to have dropped by 2.4% in 2009, with cargo volume down 3.4%. Revenue was up, however, thanks to a toll hike, which translated into some improvement in the canal's cargo services and logistical support.

Inflation, as measured by the consumer price index, was down in 2009 because of lower prices for energy products and some foods. Year-on-year, the inflation rate dropped from 6.8% in December 2008 to 0.7% in October 2009, with a cumulative rate of 1.7% for January to October. The prices of electricity, gas and water (-10%) and transport (-1.9%) came down significantly. Furniture and household appliances posted the highest price increases (3.8%). Food and beverage inflation dropped off even more sharply, from 15.1% in December 2008 to 2.7% in October 2009. Estimates are that by the end of December 2009, inflation for the year will be about 2%.

Despite a shortage of data on the evolution of average wages, slowing inflation lessened erosion of real minimum wages, with nominal minimum pay remaining stable through November. The Minimum Wage Commission was formed in August 2009 and is expected to review wages in 2010. In August 2009 the unemployment rate was 6.6%, one percentage point higher than a year earlier. Unemployment rose faster in urban areas (7.9%) than in rural areas (3.9%), compared with 2008 when it was at 6.5% and 3.7%, respectively.

Between January and August 2009, the trade deficit was reduced by 52% because of a reduction in the goods trade deficit (39%) and an expansion in services trade surplus (4.8%). Imports of goods fell off by 8.9%, whereas exports climbed 5.8%, driven by activities in the Colón Free Zone (12.2%). Imports of services were down 18.8%, with exports up 2.4% due to higher receipts from tourism (1.5%) and Panama Canal transit tolls (8.2%). In September 2009, Canada and Panama signed a free trade agreement aiming to expand trade between the two countries. In 2008, the value of imports from Canada was 128 million balboas; exports to Canada amounted to a mere 3.4 million balboas. Also, during the first half of 2009, foreign direct investment was down 39% compared with the previous year.

The Caribbean

Bahamas

The recession in the Bahamian economy deepened in 2009 with growth estimated to contract by 3.9%, as the recession in its major market, the United States, led to a sharp fall in tourism and foreign direct investment and to less dynamic offshore financial services. The government implemented a series of fiscal stimulus measures to counter the downturn in demand and bolster economic activity. With reduced private-sector demand, monetary developments were marked by a slowdown in credit and a build-up in liquidity. The current account deficit decreased reflecting the weakness in import demand and lower fuel prices. Services exports fell owing mainly to the decline in tourism receipts. An upturn is expected in 2010 (2%), as growth returns following a recovery in the United States; inflation will then be fuelled by increased demand and higher commodity prices and the fiscal deficit will remain stable.

Economic policy in 2009 sought to provide an effective response to the recession in major markets and its repercussions on growth and employment in the Bahamas. The government's stimulus programme has involved fast-tracking infrastructure projects and providing unemployment benefits to cushion the fall-out in terms of unemployment.

Shrinking revenues (-6.1%) and growth in expenditure (4.5%) led to an increase in the fiscal deficit from 2.0% of GDP in fiscal year 2007/08 to 3.0% of GDP in fiscal year 2008/09.[1] Tax receipts were undermined by domestic recessionary conditions, which reduced the take from both domestic and border taxes. Taxes on international trade and transactions fell by 13% owing to reduced imports, and a 15% contraction in the proceeds of the departure tax. On the other hand, total expenditure increased by 4.5%, boosted by higher current spending and outlays on the capital formation component of capital expenditure. Growth in current spending resulted from a 4.2% increase in outlays on wages and salaries, aimed partly at maintaining consumption during the downturn. Capital expenditure contracted by 6.7% owing partly to reduced acquisition of assets. Nevertheless, expenditure on capital formation, an important part of capital spending, rose by 8.8% and was associated with government building projects and

road works undertaken in order to stimulate activity. The deficit was financed through domestic borrowing and external loans and public-sector debt climbed to nearly 50% of GDP, well above the medium-term objective of 30% to 35% of GDP. Domestic debt accounted for 86% of the total. A fiscal deficit of 3.3% of GDP is projected for fiscal year 2009/10 with demand remaining weak at least into the early months of 2010 and some fiscal stimulus being maintained to spur growth.

Monetary policy continued to target the build-up of reserves in order to maintain the pegged exchange rate, which has been a source of stability. The Bahamas received US$ 186.8 million in special drawing rights (SDRs) from IMF under the general allocation programme to help countries affected by the crisis. The central bank's benchmark discount rate and prime lending rate remained unchanged and therefore did nothing to facilitate economic recovery. Dampened consumer confidence and business uncertainty led to a deceleration in credit growth to 5.9% year-on-year in June 2009 compared with 8.4% in June 2008. The bulk of the credit allocated went to personal loans with little directed at stimulating productive activity. Credit quality worsened with consumer loan delinquencies rising by 7.2% to 33% during the second quarter of the year.

Real output dropped by 3.9% in 2009, deepening the decline in 2008 (-1.7%). In the wake of the recession, the

---

[1]   In the Bahamas, the fiscal year runs from 1 July to 30 June.

mainstay of the economy —tourism— which accounts for around 50% of GDP, was badly weakened by the slump in demand from the United States. Real value added in tourism contracted during the year as growth in the cruise component was largely counterbalanced by a decline in the heavy-spending stay-over segment. The hosting of the Miss Universe event in August provided only a temporary boost to the tourism sector. The other key sector, financial services, also experienced a fall-off in activity. Construction slowed as the global financial crisis stifled foreign investment in the sector.

Inflationary pressures moderated to 3.5% (September-September) with the slowdown in demand and the slackening of international prices of commodities, especially fuel. Of particular concern is the rise in unemployment, notably in tourism, from 12.1% in 2008 to 14.2% in May of 2009, the highest level in recent decades. A recovery in activity in 2010 is expected to lead to improved labour demand and lower unemployment.

A sharp fall in merchandise imports (more than 20%) more than compensated for the reduction in the services and income surpluses, leading to a marked narrowing of the current account deficit from 13.3% of GDP in the first half of 2008 to 8.6% in the first half of 2009. Imports plummeted owing to stalled private-sector demand and lower prices for some commodities; fuel imports, in particular, plunged by some 40% following a sharp fall in both price and volumes. The services surplus declined by around 5% as tourism receipts were down by around 6%. Foreign

BAHAMAS: MAIN ECONOMIC INDICATORS

	2007	2008	2009 [a]
Annual percentage growth rates			
Gross domestic product	0.7	-1.7	-3.9
Per capita gross domestic product	-0.5	-2.9	-5.0
Consumer prices	2.4	4.8	0.8 [b]
Money (M1)	3.4	-1.7	-3.4 [b]
Annual average percentages			
Unemployment rate [c]	7.9	8.7	12.4
Central government overall balance/GDP [d]	-2.4	-2.0	-3.0
Nominal deposit rate [e]	3.7	3.9	3.8 [f]
Nominal lending rate [g]	10.6	11.0	10.6 [f]
Millions of dollars			
Exports of goods and services	3 401	3 499	703 [h]
Imports of goods and services	4 536	4 559	2 468 [h]
Current account balance	-1 315	-1 118	-544
Capital and financial account balance [i]	1 269	1 228	919
Overall balance	-46	109	375

Source: Economic Commission for Latin America and the Caribbean (ECLAC), on the basis of official figures.
[a] Preliminary estimates.
[b] Twelve-month variation to September 2009.
[c] Includes hidden unemployment.
[d] Fiscal year.
[e] Deposit rate, weighted average.
[f] Average from January to September, annualized.
[g] Lending and overdraft rate, weighted average.
[h] In 2009, refers to goods only.
[i] Includes errors and omissions.

direct investment contracted, partly reflecting reduced land purchases. As a result, the capital and financial account surplus shrank by 5.1% and international reserves amounted to US$ 651 million, covering 12 weeks of imports.

Barbados

The slowdown in the Barbados economy, which began in 2008, intensified with an estimated contraction of 3.6%, as the tourism, international business, and non-trade sectors declined significantly in the first half of 2009. The slide in international prices for commodities resulted in reduced inflation rates, lower total import values, and, consequently, an improved external current account. However, the sluggish pace of credit growth, the widening fiscal deficit and continuing pressure to sustain fiscal stimulation and debt levels suggest that the rate of recovery of the Barbados economy will be slow in 2010.

In terms of public finance, the accumulated fiscal deficit increased during the first half of 2009 to 5.7% of GDP, representing a worsening of the fiscal position from the end of 2008, when the deficit was equivalent to 3.5% of GDP. By mid 2009, total revenues declined by 1.2%, following an 11% reduction in indirect taxes, due to the economic slowdown. At the same time, current and capital expenditure increased by 10% and 2.8% respectively, over the previous year, as the government implemented fiscal stimulus measures in response to the global economic crisis. The increased deficit was financed by domestic borrowings. Central government debt thus increased from 88% of GDP at the end of 2008 to over 100% in June 2009, while non-financial public-sector debt reached 110% of GDP that month. Domestic debt stood at 71% of total central government debt in June 2009.

Although an expansionary monetary policy was applied, credit to the non-financial institutions was sluggish with only 0.3% growth in the first half of 2009, compared with 2.7% in the corresponding half of 2008. Deposit growth also slowed to 1.0% relative to 6% in the same period in 2008, while the liquid assets ratio increased from 9.0% in 2008 to 10.4% in June 2009. In August, the Central Bank of Barbados lowered the benchmark deposit rate to 2.5%, which represents a further reduction from the 2008 level of 4.5%. Minor adjustments were also made to the prime lending rate, which ranged between 8.15% and 9.20% at the end of July, 2009, compared with 9.0% - 9.8% one year earlier. The three-month treasury bill rate also fell from 4.81% at

the end of 2008 to 3.56% by September 2009. Although these actions were considered successful, the prevailing international climate weakened domestic loan demand, which in turn tempered the impact of reduced interest rates on domestic credit.

The global economic downturn also moderated inflationary trends in Barbados since the last quarter of 2008. From 8.9% in June 2008, inflation fell to 1.8% in June 2009. Unemployment also increased from 8.6% in June 2008 to 9.9% in June 2009 with female unemployment being slightly higher at 10.1%. The higher unemployment figure is attributable to job losses in tourism, construction, quarrying, transportation and communication and general services.

The two key sectors, tourism and international business and finance, declined significantly, as stay-over arrivals fell by 10.4%, while the registration of new international businesses fell by 37% during the first half of the calendar year. Further real-sector declines were observed for construction (-18.4%), and mining and quarrying (-35.6%) in that period. Marginal declines were also observed for the non-traded sectors, where wholesale and retail activity and transportation, storage and communications both contracted by 2.8%. At the same time, however, the agricultural sector grew slightly, led by non-sugar agriculture and fishing with 1.5%, while the sugar industry showed 1.2% growth. In sum, the economy is expected to contract by 3.6% in 2009.

Another outcome of the global economic contraction was an improvement in the current account situation (from a deficit of 10% of GDP in 2008 to a projected deficit of approximately 5% in 2009), as imports fell by 27.9% between January and June 2009. Exports also declined by 17%, while travel credits from services fell by 10%. The capital and financial account surplus also suffered a 20% reduction when compared with the first three quarters of 2008, because of a substantial decline in private capital inflows. However, significant public sector borrowings on the regional market bolstered long-term capital inflows. Net international reserves were further boosted by a government bond issue in the third quarter of 2009, and additional special drawing rights issued by the International Monetary Fund.

The overall outlook for the Barbados economy remains weak, with real GDP growth projected to contract by 3.6% in 2009 and modest recovery of 2% forecast for 2010. This is based on the performance expected in the tourism sector, which is not likely to rebound until the global economy regains significant growth momentum. The capital and financial account is also unlikely to recover over the short term, and could face increasing pressure as the government grapples with mounting public debt. Lastly, the need to sustain fiscal stimulation with stagnating government revenues suggests a worsening of the fiscal deficit for 2009/2010.

BARBADOS: MAIN ECONOMIC INDICATORS

	2007	2008	2009 [a]
Annual percentage growth rates			
Gross domestic product	3.4	0.2	-3.6
Per capita gross domestic product	3.0	0.2	-4.0
Consumer prices	4.7	7.3	1.4 [b]
Money (M1)	20.5	-3.4	-4.6 [c]
Annual average percentages			
Open unemployment rate [d]	7.4	8.1	10.0 [e]
Non-financial public-sector overall balance/GDP [f]	-1.8	-5.9	-3.2
Nominal deposit rate [g]	5.5	4.9	3.6 [h]
Nominal lending rate [i]	10.4	9.7	8.8 [h]
Millions of dollars			
Exports of goods and services	2 117	2 050	380 [j]
Imports of goods and services	2 344	2 429	1 303 [j]
Current account balance	-182	-363	-187
Capital and financial account balance [k]	461	142	...
Overall balance	278	-221	...

Source: Economic Commission for Latin America and the Caribbean (ECLAC), on the basis of official figures.
[a] Preliminary estimates.
[b] Twelve-month variation to July 2009.
[c] Twelve-month variation to August 2009.
[d] Includes hidden unemployment.
[e] January-June average.
[f] Fiscal year.
[g] Interest rate on savings.
[h] Average from January to August, annualized.
[i] Prime lending rate.
[j] In 2009, refers to goods only.
[k] Includes errors and omissions.

Belize

The year 2009 saw a reversal of the robust growth achieved in 2008 (3.8%) with the economy expected to contract by 0.5% owing mainly to declines in agriculture and tourism. Falling international prices led to a fall in year-on-year inflation to -3.5% in August, compared with a positive rate of 4.4% in November 2008. Fiscal policy remained strained given the level of public-sector indebtedness; however, the government was able to achieve a primary and overall surplus in the first quarter of fiscal year 2009/2010.[1] Monetary policy focused on maintaining the stability of the peg. Reflecting slackening domestic demand, the current account deficit narrowed to around 4% of GDP in June 2009. Economic performance is expected to recover in 2010 with growth forecast to reach 2%.

The economic downturn and the fall-out on the employment situation were such that some fiscal stimulus was needed to cushion the impact, but high public debt limited the scope for countercyclical measures. The government brought forward spending on roads and other infrastructure projects. Moreover, it nationalized the major telecommunications provider, Belize Telemedia Limited, amid concern over the agreement negotiated with the previous administration. The intention, however, is that the corporation should soon return to private hands.

Government revenues fell in the first quarter of fiscal year 2009/2010, but, at the same time, the authorities curbed expenditure, thus achieving an overall fiscal surplus of 1.2% of GDP, and a primary surplus of 1.6% of GDP (up from an overall surplus 0.3% of GDP in fiscal year 2008/2009). This surplus enabled the government to pay off a commercial bank loan. Nevertheless, public-sector debt edged up from 82.7% of GDP at the end of 2008 to 86.8% of GDP in September 2009, thanks mainly to loans from the Inter-American Development Bank and the Caribbean Development Bank. Belize also benefited from a US$ 13.9 million tranche under the IMF emergency assistance for natural disasters. Lower international interest rates facilitated a reduction in debt service payments. However, sharp falls in tax and non-tax receipts and a marginal decline in expenditure are expected to result in a smaller surplus at the end of the current fiscal year.

Monetary policy was neutral and did not provide the impetus for credit expansion. The central bank maintained its reserve requirement and widened interest spreads despite the weak demand for credit. Sluggish demand slowed broad money growth by 5.0% in the first half of 2009 to roughly half of the level recorded in the corresponding period of 2008. Commercial banks repaid foreign debt obligations, thus succeeding in improving their net foreign asset position. Therefore, growth in credit to the private sector was weak (1.4%), providing very little stimulus to the economy. The central bank eliminated the fixed rate on treasury bills during the year to allow banks to bid competitively, as part of a monetary policy reform.

Real output is expected to contract by 0.5% in 2009 as the pass-through effects of the global downturn constrained domestic activity, especially in the tradable sectors. Agriculture, the main productive sector, declined by 10.9% in the first half of the year as a result of falling output of citrus and bananas. Tourism, the third-ranking productive activity, contracted by 10% mainly as a result of the decline in stay-over visitors (down by 5.2% for the first eight months of the year), as demand from the United States market softened. Manufacturing was vibrant thanks to a 40.8% increase in petroleum production, boosted by the addition of two new wells.

Inflation fell to -3.5% (year-on-year in August) owing to a sharp decline in fuel prices and food prices. With the recession reducing employment in the construction and other sectors, it was only to be expected that unemployment would increase in 2009.

[1]   In Belize, the fiscal year runs from 1 April to 31 March.

A sharp contraction in merchandise imports (-21% in the first half of 2009), which more than offset the 18% fall in goods exports, tourism and remittances, resulted in a narrowing of the current account deficit from 8% of GDP in the first half of 2008 to 4% of GDP in the first half of 2009. Imports plummeted following the winding down of large investment projects, a significant drop in oil prices and a contraction in imports into the Commercial Free Zone, due to weaker demand. Over the first eight months of 2009, petroleum exports plunged by almost 60% following the steep fall in oil prices and in spite of higher export volumes. Uncertainty due to the global crisis has led to a slowdown in foreign direct investment in the oil sector and tourism and a reduction in loan repayments by domestic commercial banks. This has resulted in a 59% decline in the financial and capital account surplus. The reserves position swelled by US$ 10.6 million to stand at US$ 177.1 million (a sum bolstered by the one-off special drawing rights allocation received in August). Thus, the country's reserves represent 3.3 months of import cover.

The outlook for the economy suggests a slow recovery of 2% in 2010 in line with an upturn in the situation of its major trading partners. The current account is expected to worsen, however, as imports are likely to pick up with a stronger economy.

BELIZE: MAIN ECONOMIC INDICATORS

	2007	2008	2009 [a]
Annual percentage growth rates			
Gross domestic product	1.2	3.8	-0.5
Per capita gross domestic product	-1.2	1.7	-2.4
Consumer prices	4.1	4.4	-3.5 [b]
Money (M1)	14.0	0.3	-1.6 [c]
Annual average percentages			
Unemployment rate [d]	8.5	8.2	...
Central government overall balance/GDP [e]	0.0	0.3	1.2
Nominal deposit rate [f]	5.9	6.2	6.3 [g]
Nominal lending rate [h]	14.3	14.2	14.1 [g]
Millions of dollars			
Exports of goods and services	880	853	396 [i]
Imports of goods and services	806	958	616 [i]
Current account balance	-52	-150	-80
Capital and financial account balance [j]	75	208	130
Overall balance	23	58	50

Source: Economic Commission for Latin America and the Caribbean (ECLAC), on the basis of official figures.
[a] Preliminary estimates.
[b] Twelve-month variation to September 2009.
[c] Twelve-month variation to October 2009.
[d] Includes hidden unemployment.
[e] Fiscal year.
[f] Deposit rate, weighted average.
[g] Figure for March.
[h] Lending rate, weighted average.
[i] In 2009, refers to goods only.
[j] Includes errors and omissions.

Cuba

The global economic crisis has had a profound effect on Cuba's economy in 2009. The official growth target set for 2009 was reduced, first from 6% to 2.5%, then to 1.7%. The economy expanded by only 0.8% in the first half of the year. ECLAC estimates that growth through year-end will be 1%, much lower than in 2008, when it was 4.1%. Once again, the balance of payments posted a deficit equivalent to several percentage points of GDP which, given the scant possibilities of external borrowing, represented the main hindrance to growth. Inflation was negative, at -3.3%, while unemployment remained similar to its 2008 rate, at 1.6%. The fiscal deficit narrowed slightly from 6.9% of GDP in 2008 to 5% in 2009.

The Cuban economy encountered turbulence coming from three major external channels. First, the food bill rose because of higher prices and the loss of crops damaged by hurricanes that pummelled the country in 2008. Though international food prices dropped in 2009, they are still 60% higher than they were in 2000. Second, the value of exports fell significantly. The international price of nickel, Cuba's leading export, was down about 40% in 2009 following a similar decline in 2008. Third, the conditions for external financing tightened, as did access to credit from suppliers. Debt to suppliers is estimated to be between US$ 600 million and US$ 1 billion.

Fiscal revenues decreased as a result of the crisis. Meanwhile, expenditures increased, especially in the first half of 2009, as a result of damage from the hurricanes that struck in 2008, causing losses worth 20% of GDP. In response, the government tightened its policy stance and in April conducted a thoroughgoing revision of budget expenditures and revenues, in order to identify additional savings and implement a leaner budget.

Other measures were taken, such as the rationing of electricity, which further stunted economic growth because it encompassed both the people and businesses. In July, the government implemented a second round of budget cuts, which meant a new and even more stringent electricity-rationing plan and a reduction in the food products delivered to families. In both rounds of budget cuts the government sought to avoid negative impacts on investments that drive exports or promote import substitution.

In 2009, the government continued to restructure the Cabinet and State apparatus, seeking to streamline bureaucracy and make it more efficient, avoid duplication and reduce the number of State institutions. Furthermore, a new agency, the Comptroller General of the Republic, was created to oversee the proper functioning of all of Cuba's political, administrative and economic institutions. Subsidies and bonuses (including those for culture, sports and food) are under review so as to narrow their focus and lower costs to the State. Also under review is the list of products included on the ration card Cubans receive each month. Lastly, during the second half of the year, workplace lunches began to be replaced by a small wage increase.

In 2009, Cuba had difficulty not only in borrowing new money, but also in servicing its existing debt. Therefore, the government has tried to renegotiate the external debt, postpone payments and seek extensions from creditors. The financial situation improved somewhat, thanks to a loan of approximately US$ 600 million from the People's Republic of China.

Monetary and exchange-rate policy was aimed at maintaining domestic equilibrium in the context of severe external disequilibrium. This goal was met, insofar as inflation was very low and the exchange rate remained steady. A new system for controlling foreign-currency expenditures was announced, to be administered in a decentralized fashion through ministries, rather than through the Currency Approval Committee. In the second half of 2009, the central bank authorized payment of arrears to about 600 of Cuba's supplier accounts, but only those that agreed to keep doing business with the country.

After almost 50 years, Costa Rica and El Salvador re-established diplomatic ties with Cuba, leaving the United

States as the only country in the hemisphere that still does not have diplomatic relations with the country. However, the Government of the United States softened some measures of its economic embargo that had been toughened by the previous administration. Restrictions were eased for travel by Cuban-Americans to the island and for sending family remittances and some items for personal use.

Government consumption increased 3.4% and was the main driver of the positive growth rate. On the other hand, gross investment plunged by almost 25%. Exports were up 7.7%, while imports were down by 9.7%. By sector, goods declined by 3.6% and services registered positive growth.

Agriculture was the only sector whose growth figures matched those of initial estimates by authorities, up 7% during the first half of the year. Short-cycle crops posted positive, and in some cases, high output growth, whereas longer-cycle crops, such as bananas, oranges, lemons, and pineapples —which are Cuba's main exports— declined. Additionally, over 100,000 people were given rights to use some of the State's land, which should lead to higher agricultural production in 2010.

Growth in manufacturing fell owing to a drop in imports of inputs. The production of nickel, which generates as much foreign-currency revenue as tourism, also declined. Construction was down because of a shortage of workers and the suspension of most investment projects, but this was partially offset by reconstruction projects in hurricane-damaged areas. On the other hand, communications performed well because restrictions were lifted on cellular telephone purchases. The public sector's renovated fleet of vehicles spurred growth in the transport sector.

The number of tourists was up slightly, though revenues dropped because of lower average spending by tourists. Government services continued to grow, though at a slower rate than in prior years.

CUBA: MAIN ECONOMIC INDICATORS

	2007	2008	2009 [a]
Annual percentage growth rates			
Gross domestic product	7.3	4.1	1.0
Per capita gross domestic product	7.2	4.1	1.0
Consumer prices [b]	10.6	-0.1	-1.7 [c]
Average real wage	-0.9	-1.8	...
Money (M1)	3.9	9.9	...
Real effective exchange rate [d]	2.5	9.4	...
Terms of trade	5.2	...	...
Annual average percentages			
Urban unemployment rate	1.8	1.6	...
Central government overall balance/GDP	-3.2	-6.7	...
Nominal lending interest rate [e]	9.1	9.0	...

Source: Economic Commission for Latin America and the Caribbean (ECLAC), on the basis of figures from the National Statistics Office.
[a] Preliminary estimates.
[b] Local-currency markets.
[c] Twelve-month variation to October 2009.
[d] A negative rate indicates an appreciation of the currency in real terms.
[e] Average of minimum and maximum rates on loans to enterprises.

The government announced an increase in the monthly wages of Cuba's 545,000 teachers and education employees, to begin in September. This increase of between 93 and 166 pesos (or between US$ 4 and US$ 7.20) will cost the government 820 million pesos (or US$ 35.4 million) annually. Inflation was negative in markets that use domestic currency (the Cuban peso), while the unemployment rate remained low.

Imports fell by more than one third, owing to slacker economic activity and the policy of doing away with non-essential imports. The contraction in exports was somewhat smaller and largely reflected the drop in value of nickel and citrus fruit exports. The rise in international sugar prices did not benefit the country because of its low production levels. For the second year in a row, the terms of trade suffered a significant deterioration.

Dominican Republic

Despite the recession in the United States and the credit difficulties that characterized the year, the Dominican economy managed to grow in 2009, at about 2.5%. Although this growth was significantly lower than the 8.4% average rate recorded in 2004-2008, it still represented a 1.1% increase in per capita GDP. Annualized inflation was about 6%, slightly higher than in 2008. Estimates put the deficits of the central government and current account at 3% and 5.2% of GDP, respectively. ECLAC projects growth to exceed 3% in 2010 and inflation and the current account deficit to be similar to those of 2009. The central government's deficit, meanwhile, is expected to decrease to 2.5%.

Throughout 2009, public policy decisions were driven by the unfolding international financial crisis. The government's crisis response plan, announced at the start of the year, included, as pertains to fiscal policy, tax exemptions for the agricultural sector, incentives for the construction of low-cost housing, support for small- and medium-sized enterprises and the expansion of public investment, which experienced significant delays because of major problems securing financing. Monetary policy adopted an expansionist stance. As for social policy, the government announced that a number of programmes aimed at protecting the most vulnerable sectors would be broadened.

The slowdown in economic activity significantly reduced government revenues. During the first half of 2009, current income fell by 14% in real terms. Although during the same period current spending declined slightly (by 5.6%), capital expenditures were hit the hardest, shrinking by 30% in real terms.

In light of the difficulties in obtaining external financing, for much of the year the government turned to the local market, a move that changed the composition of public debt and led to a slight deterioration in the short-term debt profile. In November 2009, the government signed a stand-by agreement with the International Monetary Fund (IMF) for US$ 1.7 billion.

The consolidated public sector deficit rose from 3.2% of GDP in 2008 to 4.5% in 2009. According to the targets agreed to with IMF, public debt would increase to 35% of GDP in 2009 and up to 40% by 2011, before gradually returning to 2009 levels towards 2014. The main elements of the fiscal consolidation strategy that the government negotiated with IMF are: reducing current expenditures on wages and salaries, restructuring of subsidies (particularly those that go to the electrical power industry) and a number of administrative measures to reduce tax evasion and improve the efficiency of tax collection. There are no plans for a tax increase.

DOMINICAN REPUBLIC: GDP AND INFLATION

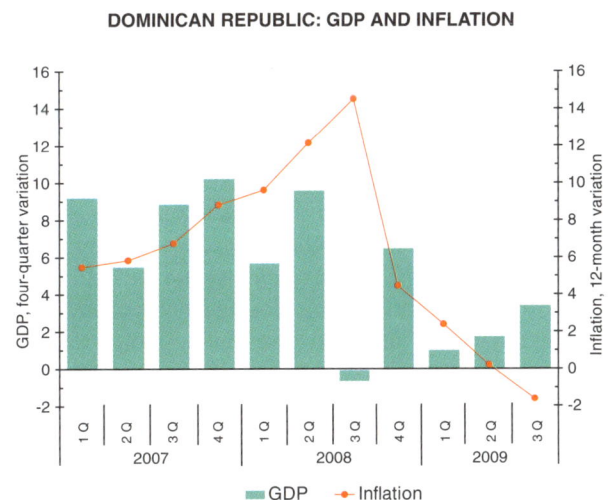

Source: Economic Commission for Latin America and the Caribbean (ECLAC), on the basis of official figures.

In order to inject liquidity into the financial system and to ease credit for both the productive sector and the housing market, during the first half of 2009, the reserve requirement for the banking sector and interest rates on central bank bonds were lowered. Debt repurchases were also approved as a short-term liquidity solution.

Between January and August, the central bank lowered its benchmark rate from 9.5% to 4%. However, given the low inflation rate in 2009, real bank lending rates remained high, at an average of 18% through October 2009, compared with 7.5% for the same period in 2008. Consequently, in real terms, lending to the private sector was negative, a trend that only turned around in the fourth quarter of 2009. Annual growth of lending to the private sector is expected to remain modest compared with lending to the public sector, which grew by almost 19%.

The central bank participated actively in the foreign-exchange market throughout the year, which allowed the Dominican peso to hold steady and depreciate by only 3%. For 2010, given the low international reserves and the low benchmark interest rate, not much leeway is expected for monetary policy. However, no major inflationary pressures are anticipated in a scenario of slow global recovery and, therefore, no changes are expected in monetary policy.

Through the third quarter of 2009, cumulative GDP growth was 2.1%. The performance of agriculture, communications, banking and housing rentals offset downturns in the manufacturing and services sectors.

Regarding expenditures, government consumption decreased significantly, whereas private consumption fell off only slightly. Some of this is attributable to the 2% drop in remittances from abroad and worsening conditions in the labour market. The broad unemployment rate during the first half of 2009 was 14.9% and is expected to be higher in the second half, which will have negative repercussions on social indicators. Gross capital formation declined by almost 20% during the first semester of 2009, heavily hit by the uncertainty stemming from the international crisis and by the high real interest rates that have prevailed all year.

Since the last quarter of 2008, year-on-year inflation has slowed markedly, even turning negative in the third quarter of 2009. This decline is the result of lower international prices for food and fuels. Although year-on-year inflation in October was 4.6%, it is expected to rise by December as the low rates recorded in the closing months of 2008 are no longer factored into the twelve-trailing-month rate.

DOMINICAN REPUBLIC: MAIN ECONOMIC INDICATORS

	2007	2008	2009 [a]
	Annual percentage growth rates		
Gross domestic product	8.5	5.3	2.5
Per capita gross domestic product	6.9	3.8	1.1
Consumer prices	8.9	4.5	-0.3 [b]
Real minimun wage	4.7	-6.4	7.0
Money (M1)	26.9	-7.4	-0.9 [c]
Terms of trade	3.3	-4.5	2.2
	Annual average percentages		
Urban unemployment rate [d]	15.6	14.1	14.9 [e]
Central government overall balance/GDP	0.1	-3.2	-3.0
Nominal deposit rate [f]	7.0	10.3	8.8 [g]
Nominal lending rate [h]	11.7	16.0	14.0 [g]
	Millions of dollars		
Exports of goods and services	11 927	11 860	9 968
Imports of goods and services	15 343	17 914	13 941
Current account balance	-2 096	-4 437	-2 353
Capital and financial account balance [i]	2 716	4 117	2 230
Overall balance	620	-320	-123

Source: Economic Commission for Latin America and the Caribbean (ECLAC), on the basis of official figures.
[a] Preliminary estimates.
[b] Twelve-month variation to October 2009.
[c] January-September 2009 variation.
[d] Includes hidden unemployment.
[e] Figure for April.
[f] Ninety-day certificates of deposit.
[g] Average from January to September, annualized.
[h] Prime rate.
[i] Includes errors and omissions.

During the period January-September 2009, the value of imports fell off by more than 30% owing to the significant drop in oil prices and to weaker domestic demand. It is important to point out that, during this period, imports of durable consumer goods and capital goods decreased by 35% and 26%, respectively. The drop in imports offset the 22.6% decline in exports, which was largely attributable to the suspension of iron nickel exports and a 15% drop in exports from free trade zones. The balance of services, for the first time, registered a decline in nominal tourism revenue, due to a 2% cumulative drop in the number of tourists visiting the country in 2009. For the year as a whole, it is anticipated that the current account deficit will narrow slightly, to an estimated 5.2% of GDP.

After reaching a record high of US$ 2.885 billion in 2008, foreign direct investment is expected to be about US$ 2 billion in 2009. The sectors that benefited most were mining, real estate and telecommunications.

Guyana

The economy of Guyana grew more slowly than expected in the first half of the year owing to a sharp contraction in its main economic sector —agriculture— and to a decline in mining, while construction, services and manufacturing expanded. Growth is therefore likely to reach only around 0.9% in 2009. The current account deficit is expected to narrow, reflecting declining imports due to lower prices of fuels and imported commodities. The urban inflation index stood at 1.3% for the first half of the year and should be no more than 2% at the end of the year. The outlook for 2010, based on the assumption that commodity prices will be favourable and that world demand will strengthen, is for a 3% expansion of the economy and for a rise in inflation in line with increasing fuel prices. In addition, the current account deficit should improve as remittances and exports recover.

The government's overall deficit is expected to narrow from 7.9% of GDP in 2008 to 6.5% in 2009, thanks to increasing revenues and declines in capital expenditure, while the current surplus increased by 50% in the first half of the year compared with the same period in 2008. This was due to an increase in current revenue (15%), attributable to higher collections of major taxes, especially excise duties (up by 54%), and income taxes from businesses and the self-employed, which rose by 4% and 5 % respectively. The deficit was financed by domestic loan receipts and external borrowing, thus the stock of public and public-guaranteed debt increased from 103.7% of GDP at the end of 2008 to 115% of GDP at the end of June 2009 despite some debt alleviation under the Heavily Indebted Poor Countries (HIPC) Debt Initiative. At the end of June, the external debt stood at 78% of GDP, while domestic debt stood at 37.2% of GDP.

In 2009 broad money expanded by 2.2% following a 10.4% increase in the banking system's net foreign assets and a 11.4% decline in net domestic credit. Private sector credit growth was flat, although commercial bank interest rates dipped marginally. This slowdown in private sector lending is attributed to slacker demand for external trade financing.

In terms of financial market developments, the Government of Guyana in September received US$ 15 million from the Caribbean Community (CARICOM) Petroleum

Fund, to enable it to deal with the collapse of the Colonial Life Insurance Company Guyana (CLICO Guyana). The emergency fund was used to pay CLICO Guyana policyholders since the company had been declared insolvent.

Growth in 2009 is likely to be much lower than the earlier projection of 4% presented in the budget in February. The economy grew less than expected in the first half of the year as a result of a 7.2% contraction in the agriculture sector, which accounts for approximately 20% of GDP. Adverse weather conditions and industrial unrest led to a 19.7% slump in sugar production compared with the end of June 2008 and rice production was also weak (down by 6.7%). Mining contracted, reflecting sluggish demand for bauxite and alumina on international markets, while quarrying also diminished. Conversely, services, which contribute significantly to GDP, recorded positive growth, as did construction and manufacturing.

Inflation for the period January-June 2009 stood at 1.3% compared with 5.8% in the corresponding period of 2008. As a result, inflation is expected to be below 2% in 2009. This decline is due to lower food and fuel prices on the world market.

Data for the first half of the year point to a narrowing of the current account deficit from 16.9% of GDP in 2008 to 10% in 2009, reflecting a reduction in the import bill due to lower fuel prices and a softening of domestic demand. Export earnings also fell compared with the same period in 2008 owing to weaker commodity prices and slower export growth. Workers' remittances, another major source of foreign exchange, dropped by 10 % since June 2008 to stand at 19% of GDP in June 2009. The capital and financial account surplus rose, despite smaller flows of FDI. Overall, the balance of payments posted a surplus and gross reserves expanded to US$ 405.1 million or 3.6 months' imports of goods and services.

The outlook for 2010 is positive with growth prospects (3%) barring any significant fall in sugar and rice prices. In addition, bauxite exports should rally on the back of stronger global demand and thus contribute to an improvement in the current account balance.

GUYANA: MAIN ECONOMIC INDICATORS

	2007	2008	2009 [a]
Annual percentage growth rates			
Gross domestic product	5.3	3.1	0.9
Per capita gross domestic product	5.3	3.2	1.0
Consumer prices	14.1	6.4	1.3 [b]
Money (M1)	12.8	12.5	3.2 [c]
Annual average percentages			
Central government overall balance/GDP	-7.5	-7.9	-6.5
Nominal deposit rate [d]	3.2	3.1	2.8 [e]
Nominal lending rate [f]	14.1	13.9	14.0 [e]
Millons of dollars			
Exports of goods and services	698	798	650
Imports of goods and services	1 063	1 300	1 000
Current account balance	-189	-299	-195
Capital and financial account balance [g]	188	306	428
Overall balance	-1	7	233

Source: Economic Commission for Latin America and the Caribbean (ECLAC), on the basis of official figures.
[a] Preliminary estimates.
[b] January-June 2009 variation.
[c] Twelve-month variation to September 2008.
[d] Small savings rate.
[e] Average from January to September, annualized.
[f] Prime rate.
[g] Includes errors and omissions.

Haiti [1]

Despite the global recession, the Haitian economy is estimated to have grown by 2% in 2009, owing in part to an upturn in the agricultural sector and a 14% reduction in the deficit of the balance-of-payments current account. Another positive development was fall in the inflation rate. The year-on-year price variation (-4.7% as at September 2009) and the annual average inflation rate (3.4%) were significantly lower than in 2008 (19.8% and 14.4%, respectively).

The fiscal deficit —1.7% of GDP— was financed from limited external funding. Nevertheless, having reached completion point under the Heavily Indebted Poor Countries (HIPC) debt relief programme in June 2009, Haiti had approximately US$ 900 million of its debt forgiven and its debt service will be reduced by nearly US$ 48 million annually. The country's foreign-debt-to-GDP ratio dropped from 31% in 2008 to 19% in 2009.

Despite the crisis in the United States, remittances rose slightly, to US$ 1.281 billion, which helped to sustain consumption. Public sector investments were lower than initially forecast, despite higher-than-expected growth in the agricultural and infrastructure sectors.

To lessen the impact of natural disasters in 2008 (the cost of which was equivalent to 15% of GDP), the government adopted a special spending policy, which started to be rolled out at the beginning of fiscal year 2009. Nevertheless, the results indicate that the budget continues to be considerably under-executed in several key economic sectors.

In 2009, the socio-economic setting in Haiti was marked by, among other things, legislative elections in April and June and a protracted standoff among different sectors of the executive and legislative branches and other social stakeholders on the proposal to raise the daily minimum wage from 70 to 200 gourdes (US$ 2 to US$ 5). In the end, it was set at US$ 4.

In late October 2009, with the removal from office of the prime minister —following a vote of no confidence by Congress— it appeared that a new political crisis might break out. Nevertheless, unlike in 2008, when the

vacuum in government lasted nearly five months, this time the new prime minister and his cabinet were ratified in just two weeks. The general policy criteria of the new authorities do not appear to herald major changes, and certain initiatives still under negotiation are expected to materialize, in particular, the extension for three more years of the Poverty Reduction and Growth Facility with the International Monetary Fund (IMF).

The primary and overall fiscal deficits (0.8% and 1.7% of GDP, respectively) were slightly up on 2008. Fiscal revenue (12.3% of GDP) remained relatively close to the targets agreed with IMF for 2009. Despite the lower import bill, real revenue grew by 14.6% thanks to growth in revenue from tariff collections (9.6%) and the implementation of stricter measures to control tax evasion. Indirect taxation collected by way of value added tax (VAT) rose by 7.3%, compared with a 49% increase in revenue from fees and permits. The impact of higher rates, especially for electric power (which doubled in price in July), and other payments and fees will likely be felt in fiscal year 2010.

Organically financed public sector investment expenditures decreased by 70%. Nevertheless, public investment programme outlays on infrastructure, agricultural projects, equipment purchases and other items were enough to push up public investment in April and end 2009 with a net increase over 2008.

Transfers to the electricity sector (composed of public and private cogeneration enterprises) stood at close to US$ 100 million, because of the purchase of hydrocarbons and payments for cogeneration services. These items accounted for nearly 40% of the central government's operating expenses.

In accordance with terms set forth in the programme agreed upon with IMF, the fiscal deficit (1.7% of GDP) was partially defrayed by the monetary authorities, who

---

[1]   This study refers to fiscal year 2009 (October 2008 to September 2009); however, in some cases, in order to facilitate comparison with other regional data, the reported statistics correspond to the calendar year.

sterilized the increased liquidity in the economy through net hard currency sales amounting to US$ 66 million.

It is estimated that GDP will grow by 2% in 2010, driven by more expansionary public spending aimed at stimulating the economy, as well as the electoral calendar —with legislative elections scheduled for the beginning of the year and the presidential election for year-end.

The monetary base expanded by 14%. From May 2009 onwards, the central bank began lowering its benchmark rate (from 7% to 3.9% overall), which represented a loosening of its monetary policy stance. Bank interest rates also fell, although less sharply. In the last two quarters real deposit rates increased for the first time in three years, by 2% and 5%, respectively, as a consequence of deflation. Meanwhile, lending rates rose to more than 20%, which explains why the upturn in private credit was a modest 6.1% even though overall lending was up by 16.6% on the back of the 33.9% rise in the public component.

The gourde depreciated 6.3% in nominal terms. In real terms, however, the depreciation was only 2.5%, owing to the central bank's multiple interventions sustained by international reserves, which stood at to US$ 314 million —up US$ 19 million from the close of 2008. Demand for foreign currency for payment of external suppliers and for debt servicing was lower than in 2008. Nevertheless, the reduction in remittances and foreign assistance inflows may also have had a hand in the change of direction in the real exchange rate.

GDP growth gained strength in 2009 (2%), thanks mainly to the strong performance of agriculture and growth in several other sectors, including the maquila industry, electric power (with a sharp rise in generation as three new thermal power plants came on stream), construction and commerce.

In 2009, the average annual inflation rate, at 3.4%, was far below the 14.4% rate recorded in 2008, due to the sharp fall in international food and hydrocarbon prices. Year-on-year variations at the end of the fiscal year (September 2009), both of the general index, which declined by 4.9%, and of the food index, which was down 9.9%, reflect this deflation.

For fiscal year 2010, the new daily minimum wage was set at 150 gourdes (approximately US$ 4). Fluctuations

in employment levels were associated with temporary hirings (for public works and sanitation) in the framework of the emergency programme approved in the wake of the disasters in 2008.

The current account deficit narrowed from 4.6% of GDP in 2008 to 1.0% in 2009. Exports increased by 12%, mainly because of a 16% jump in those of the maquila sector, while imports fell by 8%. Import volumes rose for some products, however, especially hydrocarbons (12%). The terms of trade improved significantly, in part owing to the higher value of exports but especially thanks to a considerably smaller import bill. The capital account showed extraordinary inflows stemming from the debt forgiveness programme, while FDI flows rose by 24% from 2008, to US$ 37 million, and could rise even further if certain recent initiatives materialize.

HAITI: MAIN ECONOMIC INDICATORS

	2007	2008	2009 [a]
Annual percentage growth rates			
Gross domestic product	3.4	1.3	2.0
Per capita gross domestic product	1.7	-0.4	0.3
Consumer prices	10.0	10.1	-3.5 [b]
Real minimun wage	-7.8	-12.9	28.0
Money (M1)	12.7	17.9	15.1 [c]
Terms of trade	-2.8	-28.1	30.8
Annual average percentages			
Central government overall balance/GDP [d]	-1.6	-1.2	-1.7
Nominal deposit rate [e]	5.2	2.4	1.7 [f]
Nominal lending rate [g]	31.2	23.3	21.7 [f]
Millions of dollars			
Exports of goods and services	779	833	896
Imports of goods and services	2 292	2 891	2 764
Current account balance	7	- 277	- 68
Capital and financial account balance [h]	148	374	64
Overall balance	154	98	- 4

Source: Economic Commission for Latin America and the Caribbean (ECLAC), on the basis of official figures.
[a] Preliminary estimates.
[b] Twelve-month variation to October 2009.
[c] Twelve-month variation to September 2009.
[d] Fiscal year.
[e] Average of minimum and maximum rates on time deposits.
[f] Average from January to October, annualized.
[g] Average of minimum and maximum lending rates.
[h] Includes errors and omissions.

Jamaica

The world economic crisis has seriously exacerbated Jamaica's already dire economic situation and the government is in negotiation with the International Monetary Fund (IMF) for an agreement in the amount of US$ 1.2 billion, or 10% of the country's GDP. Underlying these difficulties are chronic fiscal deficits, the high public debt-to-GDP ratio (110% in 2008) and difficulties in financing the 2009/2010 budget. Furthermore, reduced foreign-exchange inflows from remittances and exports of services and downward pressure on the currency have led international rating agencies to downgrade the country's sovereign rating. The economy is expected to contract by 3% in 2009 with a slow recovery in 2010, when growth is projected to reach 1%.

In September, the government presented a supplementary budget for fiscal year 2009/2010,[1] in which it revised the fiscal deficit from 5.5% to 8.7% of GDP to take into account a 1.9% decline in revenue and grants between April and September 2009 compared with the same period in 2008 and a 29% rise in recurrent expenditure over the same period. This expanding deficit also reflected an increase of 115% in domestic loan receipts. With revenue expected to fall further, the fiscal deficit will probably widen more to about 12% of GDP in fiscal year 2009/2010. The adjustments needed to address the fiscal deficit will force the government to reduce primary expenditure, and this is likely to push up the unemployment rate, which had already risen from 10.6% at the end of 2008 to 11.3% in July 2009.

Between January and September, the public debt stock increased by 2.6 % to J$1.16 billion, of which 55% was external debt. The debt service ratio had been rising from 13.5% in fiscal year 2007/2008 to 14.6% in fiscal year 2008/2009. Relatively weak import demand by mid-year, together with the receipt of US$330.8 million in special drawing rights from the IMF, helped to maintain stability in the exchange rate.

The Bank of Jamaica employed a less restrictive monetary policy stance in the September quarter as inflation declined and thus interest rates on its securities were generally reduced. For instance, the Bank cut its 80-day repurchase agreement (repo) rate by 17% in mid-September. Despite the gradual reduction in lending rates, however, private sector credit also declined by 0.7 %, reflecting a continuing fall in private consumer spending and investment.

The foreign-exchange market was relatively stable during the third quarter after a period of volatility between September 2008 and February 2009 during which the currency fell by 22 % in nominal terms. The exchange rate has now been stabilized at around 89 Jamaican dollars (J$) to the United States dollar, following intervention by the

JAMAICA: GDP, INFLATION AND UNEMPLOYMENT

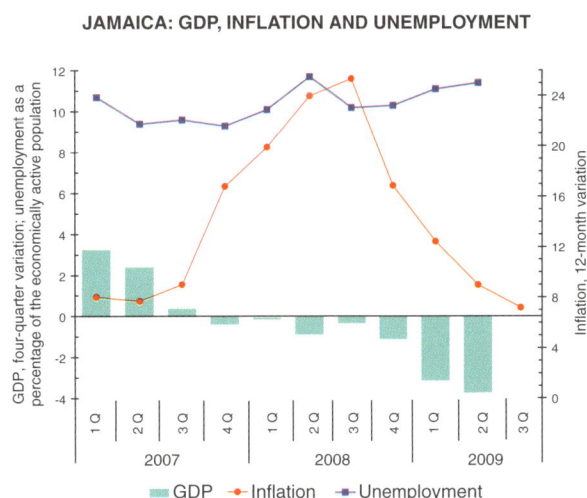

Source: Economic Commission for Latin America and the Caribbean (ECLAC), on the basis of official figures.

---

[1]   In Jamaica the fiscal year runs from 1 April to 31 March.

central bank and some improvement in the current account. In light of the impending IMF agreement, the exchange rate is likely to remain stable through to the end of the year.

In terms of growth performance, real GDP declined by 2.9% in the first quarter and by 3.7% in the second, so that the decrease for the first half of the year was 3.3%. This outcome was due to an 8.9% contraction in the goods-producing sector (made up of agriculture, mining, manufacturing and construction), which accounts for around a quarter of GDP. Mining and quarrying posted the sharpest decline (43.4%), largely due to a slump in bauxite and alumina production. The 50% cutback in production at the Alumina Partners of Jamaica (Alpart) plant has slashed foreign exchange earnings, revenues from bauxite production and the employment rate.

The contribution of services to GDP (around three quarters) declined by 1.4% in the first quarter, 0.6% in the second and an overall 1.2% for the half-year. In this sector, the steepest reduction (7.2%) was recorded in transport, storage and communication, while hotels and restaurants, which capture substantial income from tourism, recorded growth of 1.4%. This was due to a 3.4% increase in stay-over tourist arrivals in the first six months of the year. Visitors from all markets except Canada however, showed a decline. Arrivals of cruise ship passengers, the lower yield segment of tourists, were down by 14%. GDP is expected to contract by around 3% in 2009 and then start to recover to an estimated 1% in 2010.

Inflation eased during 2009, standing at 7.2% at the end of September. However, for the third quarter, it increased to 3.1%, up from 2.7% in the second. This marginal increase was due to higher fuel costs and shortages of some agricultural commodities. Overall, non-food inflation (3.7%) exceeded food inflation (2.2%). Inflation is now projected to be in the range of 10%-12% at the close of the year instead of the 14% forecast in the budget. This, however, is subject to depreciation of the Jamaican dollar, and to the extent of increases in oil and other commodity prices for the rest of the year.

The balance-of-payments current account deficit narrowed substantially thanks to a sharper decline in imports than in exports. For the first seven months of 2009, the

JAMAICA: MAIN ECONOMIC INDICATORS

	2007	2008	2009 [a]
	Annual percentage growth rates		
Gross domestic product	1.4	-0.6	-3.0
Per capita gross domestic product	0.9	-1.0	-3.4
Consumer prices	16.8	16.9	7.7 [b]
Money (M1)	14.8	2.2	5.2 [c]
Real effective exchange rate [d]	3.5	-6.2	11.1 [e]
	Annual average percentages		
Unemployment rate [f]	9.8	10.6	11.3 [g]
Central government overall balance/GDP [h]	-4.7	-7.4	-11.0
Nominal deposit rate [i]	5.0	5.1	5.9 [j]
Nominal lending rate [k]	22.0	22.3	22.8 [j]
	Millions of dollars		
Exports of goods and services	5 069	5 539	1 400 [l]
Imports of goods and services	8 486	9 914	4 200 [l]
Current account balance	-2 038	-2 794	-700
Capital and financial account balance [m]	1 598	2 689	836
Overall balance	-440	-105	136

Source: Economic Commission for Latin America and the Caribbean (ECLAC), on the basis of figures from the International Monetary Fund and national sources.
[a] Preliminary estimates.
[b] Twelve-month variation to October 2009.
[c] Twelve-month variation to September 2009.
[d] A negative rate indicates an appreciation of the currency in real terms.
[e] Year-on-year average variation, January to October.
[f] Includes hidden unemployment.
[g] Average of the figures for January, April and June.
[h] Fiscal year.
[i] Average interest rate on savings.
[j] Average from January to October, annualized.
[k] Average lending rate.
[l] In 2009, refers to goods only.
[m] Includes errors and omissions.

deficit stood at 3.8% of GDP, 83% lower than the deficit observed during the same period in 2008. The goods balance showed a deficit of 23% of GDP, 45% smaller than in 2008. Slacker domestic demand led to a fall of 39% in merchandise imports. Goods exports contracted by 54% and current transfers (which consist largely of workers' remittances) by 10%. Owing to the increase in tourism, the surplus on the services account rose by 70%. On the other hand, the capital and financial accounts deteriorated by 85% relative to the period January to July 2008. Most of this decline in the capital account was the result of a fall in private investment flows (84.3%), due to growing uncertainty about the future of the Jamaican economy.

Suriname

Despite adverse international conditions, the Suriname economy is expected to grow by 2.5% in 2009 owing to strong gold prices and a buoyant oil industry. With lending rates at their lowest for decades, credit continued to expand without causing inflation (-4.5% for September-September). The current account surplus is expected to decline for the first time since 2005, but will remain positive thanks to gold and oil exports. Faced with a crippling decline in historically important bauxite revenue, fiscal authorities are expected to post only a marginal fiscal deficit by years' end. Although the level of production capacity remains uncertain, stable growth is predicted for 2010.

A small fiscal deficit is expected for the end of the year, although half-year data showed a surplus equivalent to 4.2% of GDP. This forecast is based on an estimated drop of 50% in revenue from the bauxite sector (revenue from the two major players BHP-Billiton and Suriname Aluminium Company (Suralco) are expected to fall by 68%). Buoyed up by royalties and taxes from gold and crude oil, revenue should represent approximately 30% of GDP in 2009,, while expenditure should reach around 31% of GDP. Wages and salaries pushed up expenditure by 3% to around 16% of GDP as the government began implementing the new salary system for public servants in advance of the 2010 elections.

Suriname reinforced its reputation as a reliable debtor after settling a decades-old debt with Brazil in August 2009. The government's priority now is to pay off its last line of debt with the United States. Total public debt increased marginally, however, from 25.2% to 25.7% of GDP, with domestic debt expanding slightly from 12.5% to 14.6% of GDP and external debt falling to 11.1% of GDP from 12.7% in 2008.

Monetary policy remained loose without leading to inflation. The central bank's policy is geared towards boosting credit availability, attracting foreign direct investment and accumulating reserves to defend the currency. Notwithstanding, lending rates fell only marginally from 12% in December 2008 to 11.5% in September, probably because of increased depreciation expectations, while deposit rates increased by 0.2% to 6.5%. Credit to the public sector rose to 6% of GDP and private sector credit continued its expansion, soaring to 43% of GDP, up from 36% of GDP in 2008. Year-on-year M1 swelled by 23% to reach 28.3% of GDP in the third quarter.

The quasi-fixed regime maintained the exchange rate at approximately S$ 2.745 to US$ 1, although 2009 saw the rate go as high as S$ 2.79 to US$ 1 and as low as S$ 2.70 to US$ 1. After two unsuccessful attempts at remedying the shortage of United States dollars, which was due to imports as well as personal loans, the central bank widened the trading band for the United States dollar to S$ 2.71-S$ 2.85.

Boosted by an expansion in the gold and petroleum industries, GDP is expected to grow by 2.5% in 2009. Rosebel Gold Mines N.V. doubled its output between March and August 2009, and the value of its production for 2009 is expected to be three times as high as that of 2008. Staatsolie, the state oil company, continued refurbishment of its refinery started last year. In response to stronger demand for private housing and ongoing public infrastructure development projects, construction and commercial services continued to expand and accounts for 17% of GDP. Agriculture, which employs a sizable proportion of the workforce, and in particular the banana sector, received investments that should allow it to increase its productivity levels. Conversely, the aluminium sector's potential failure is linked to the drastic drop in inward foreign investment on which this sector has been highly dependent. If this trend continues, the results will be detrimental as mining and aluminium production are important contributors to GDP and key for export earnings. In 2010, the economy is expected to grow by around 4% on the back of increasing gold production and an expansion of the petroleum sector.

Weaker external prices brought the 12-month inflation rate down to -4.5% in September, a colossal drop from the rate of 18.1% recorded a year earlier. This negative rate is attributable to price decreases for the main items in the consumer price index basket: food and non-alcoholic beverages. Fuel prices also fell in 2009 in tandem with average oil prices. The expectation for 2010 is that inflation will increase with the global economic recovery and will close the year at 3.5%

The current account surplus is expected to reach 13% of GDP at the end of the year compared with 16% in 2008. Oil and gold prices, which had escalated by more than 40% (November-to-November), helped to offset the slump in the aluminium sector. As from June, the merchandise trade surplus worsened slightly, while the services account improved although it remained in deficit. The fall in foreign direct investment inflows, from 8% of GDP in 2008 to 0.2% of GDP in June 2009, weighed heavily upon the bauxite sector. At close of year, the capital and financial account will be in deficit, while

SURINAME: MAIN ECONOMIC INDICATORS

	2007	2008	2009 [a]
Annual percentage growth rates			
Gross domestic product	5.1	4.3	2.5
Per capita gross domestic product	4.1	3.3	1.5
Consumer prices	8.3	9.4	-5.4 [b]
Money (M1)	25.1	15.7	25.5 [b]
Annual average percentages			
Central government overall balance/GDP	7.1	2.3	-1.0
Nominal deposit rate [c]	6.4	6.3	6.5 [d]
Nominal lending rate [c]	13.8	12.2	12.0 [d]
Millions of dollars			
Exports of goods and services	1 604	1 993	1 500
Imports of goods and services	1 354	1 757	1 230
Current account balance	335	344	280
Capital and financial account balance [e]	-158	-292	-9
Overall balance	177	52	271

Source: Economic Commission for Latin America and the Caribbean (ECLAC), on the basis of official figures.
[a] Preliminary estimates.
[b] Twelve-month variation to September 2008.
[c] Rates published by the International Monetary Fund.
[d] Average from January to July, annualized.
[e] Includes errors and omissions.

the overall balance should remain positive. Strengthened by a special drawing rights allocation in August 2009, net international reserves amounted to seven months of import cover.

Trinidad and Tobago

The global economic crisis has had a profound effect on the economy of Trinidad and Tobago, bringing 15 years of uninterrupted growth to a halt. According to projections, the economy contracted by about 0.5% in 2009. Inflation fell to one-digit levels starting in June, owing to a sharp slowdown in food inflation. The central government posted a deficit equivalent to 5.3% of GDP in fiscal year 2008-2009.[1] This deficit —the first since 2002— is due to lower international energy prices and a slowdown in economic activity. The sizeable current account surplus shrank by more than 40% between 2008 and 2009 —to almost 25% of GDP— owing to a significant reduction in the trade deficit, which, in turn, was due to falling international energy prices. Economic policy will continue to be guided by the Vision 2020 national development plan and, moving forward, the key economic challenge will continue to be to reduce reliance on the energy sector, which accounts for more than 45% of GDP, more than 85% of goods exports and more than half of tax receipts. Growth of 2% is projected for 2010.

Until mid-2009 monetary policy was focused mainly on curbing inflation. Since then, however, the aim of both fiscal and monetary policy has been to boost economic activity. The new policy mix, as well as the quasi-fixed exchange rate regime, is expected to remain in place in 2010 with a view to maintain the stability of the nominal exchange rate with the United States dollar.

The central government posted a deficit equivalent to 5.3% of GDP in fiscal year 2008-2009, compared with a 7.8% surplus in the previous fiscal year. The worsening fiscal position stemmed from a 26% decline in tax receipts, only partially offset by an 18% reduction in capital expenditures from 2007-2008. Nevertheless, total spending was slightly up. Consequently, the non-energy deficit rose by more than 5 percentage points, to 18.3% of GDP, in fiscal year 2008-2009. The fiscal gap was financed largely with public savings, in particular from the Infrastructure Development Fund. Still, the country's fiscal position remains sound, with the equivalent of nearly 14% of GDP held in the Heritage Stabilization Fund and a relatively low public debt (31%

of GDP). The public budget for fiscal year 2009-2010 assumes 2% GDP growth, an average price of US$ 55 per barrel of oil and US$ 2.75 per million cubic feet of natural gas. The price of natural gas is crucial, since Trinidad

TRINIDAD AND TOBAGO: GDP, INFLATION AND UNEMPLOYMENT

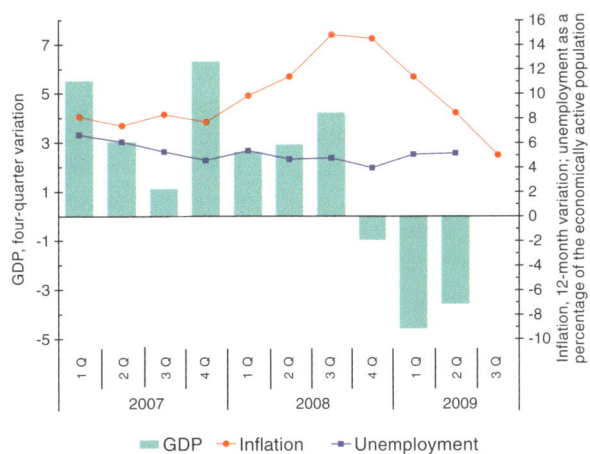

Source: Economic Commission for Latin America and the Caribbean (ECLAC), on the basis of official figures.

[1] The fiscal year runs from 1 October to 30 September in Trinidad and Tobago.

and Tobago's economy is now heavily geared towards gas production, which accounts for more than 80% of total energy production. The new budget projects a fiscal deficit of 5.4% of GDP, and is oriented towards supporting economic recovery. The new property tax regime, which enters into force in January 2010, will introduce the rental value method for property valuations and lower, uniform tax rates throughout the country.

The decline in inflation, brought about by lower global food prices and sluggish domestic demand, allowed the central bank to cut its benchmark interest rate to stimulate economic activity. The repurchase rate was cut seven times in 2009 —from 8.75% in March to 5.75% in November. In a context of high liquidity and surplus reserves in commercial banks, the repo rate cuts are mainly a signalling mechanism, since most banks rarely resort to borrowing at this rate. The rate on three-month treasury bills dropped to 1.49% in October (1.85% in September), narrowing the spread with the equivalent rate in the United States to 141 basis points (175 basis points in September and 607 basis points at the start of the year). Lending continued to grow slowly, against a backdrop of weak domestic demand: year-on-year credit growth fell from 5.3% in June 2009 to 2.1% in August —well below the 13.7% rate recorded in June 2008. Consumer lending contracted by 1.4% in the 12 months to August 2009, after having expanded by an average of 3% during the first three months of the year and 11.3% in the first quarter of 2008. Given the inflation differential, the real exchange rate continued to appreciate until the beginning of the year, given that the central bank was able to maintain the quasi-fixed nominal exchange rate nearly unchanged —thanks to the country's sound international reserve position.

The intervention by the government in CLICO Investment Bank (CIB) —which belonged to CL Financial Ltd., a major conglomerate with assets estimated to be worth 37% of the country's GDP— in January 2009 in order to prevent contagion from spreading to other financial institutions continued, for the entire year, to be a key issue for both the central bank and the Ministry of Finance. In mid-2009, the fundamentals of the country's banks remained strong, as the cash ratio reached 18% (compared with a legal minimum of 8%) and loan delinquency rates stood at about 2%.

The slight growth in the energy sector —stemming from refining activities— was insufficient to counter the impact of the economic slowdown in 2009. The non-energy sector is estimated to have contracted by nearly 5%, owing to a significant downturn in the services sector and in construction, in which both public and private projects were cancelled or put on hold.

After climbing to a 12-month rate of 11.3% in April, overall inflation began to subside, falling to 2.7% in October (compared with 14.5% in December 2008), the

TRINIDAD AND TOBAGO: MAIN ECONOMIC INDICATORS

	2007	2008	2009 [a]
	Annual percentage growth rates		
Gross domestic product	4.6	2.3	-0.5
Per capita gross domestic product	4.2	1.9	-0.9
Consumer prices	7.6	14.5	2.7 [b]
Money (M1)	12.0	10.1	24.5 [c]
Real effective exchange rate [d]	-1.8	-5.1	-9.8 [e]
	Annual average percentages		
Unemployment rate [f]	5.6	4.6	5.1 [g]
Central government overall balance / GDP [h]	1.8	7.8	-5.3
Nominal deposit rate [i]	2.4	2.4	2.1 [j]
Nominal lending rate [k]	10.5	12.3	12.6 [j]
	Millions of dollars		
Exports of goods	13 391	18 686	12 740
Imports of goods	7 670	9 622	6 628
Current account balance	5 364	8 792	5 247
Capital and financial account balance [l]	-3 824	-6 086	-7 000
Overall balance	1 541	2 706	-1 753

Source: Economic Commission for Latin America and the Caribbean (ECLAC), on the basis of official figures.
[a] Preliminary estimates.
[b] Twelve-month variation to October 2009.
[c] Twelve-month variation to August 2009.
[d] A negative rate indicates an appreciation of the currency in real terms.
[e] Year-on-year average variation, January to October.
[f] Includes hidden unemployment.
[g] Average of the figures for March and June.
[h] Fiscal year.
[i] Average of savings rates.
[j] Average from January to July, annualized.
[k] Prime lending rate.
[l] Includes errors and omissions.

lowest rate since January 2003. The easing of inflation stemmed mainly from sharply lower food inflation —the main catalyst of domestic price hikes— which fell to 6.8% in September from 10.1% in June. In the last quarter of 2008, Trinidad and Tobago recorded its lowest unemployment rate ever (3.9%). However, this decline in unemployment was reversed in the first half of 2009, reaching 5.1% in June (compared with 4.6% a year earlier). The participation rate fell from 64.1% in the first quarter of 2009 to 63.6% in the second half of the year, reflecting a contraction of the labour force.

The sharp decline in world energy prices signalled the end of Trinidad and Tobago's export boom. The country's import bill fell, as well, because of lower domestic demand along with lower international food prices. The trade surplus is expected to slide from 37% of GDP in 2008 to close to 30% in 2009. Hence, the current account surplus should decline from 34% to 24% of GDP in the same period. Together with the recurring shortfall in the capital and financial account, the smaller trade surplus is expected to reduce international reserves to some US$ 8.08 billion at the close of 2009 (down from US$ 9.83 billion one year earlier) —the equivalent of between 14 and 15 months' imports.

Eastern Caribbean Currency Union

According to estimates of the Eastern Caribbean Central Bank (ECCB), the economies of the Eastern Caribbean Currency Union (ECCU) are expected to contract by about 5.6% in 2009, a far worse result than the earlier zero-growth projections and the positive 1.9% growth reported in 2008. This expectation has been fuelled by the negative effects of the global crisis which manifested themselves through a steep decline in tourist activity, construction, and mining and quarrying. Consumer prices deflated by 0.8% in the first six months of 2009 as commodity prices on the international market fell in the last quarter of 2008. The overall fiscal balances at the end of June 2009 improved as the deficit shrank from 3.0% of GDP in June 2008 to 1.7% of GDP in 2009, although the ratio of total public debt to GDP remained unsustainable at 96%. As the impact of the global crisis intensified and began to adversely affect the balance of payments, many countries resorted to borrowing from the International Monetary Fund (IMF).

Fiscal policy in the ECCU was focused on limiting the effects of the global crisis on the economies. To this end, the governments have agreed to an eight-point stabilization programme that includes financial, fiscal, debt management and safety net programmes and aims to ensure stability and to foster economic growth and development. At the end of June 2009, the fiscal accounts posted a primary surplus equivalent to 2.0% of GDP, up from 0.9% for the corresponding period in 2008. This was the result of a 36% increase in grants along with a 19% decline in capital expenditure. Hence, the overall public-sector deficit improved to 1.7% of GDP at the end of June 2009, from 3.0% of GDP for the same period in 2008.

The total public-sector debt of ECCU swelled to 96% of GDP as at June 2009, compared to 89% of GDP in December 2008 as many countries increased their debt stock by borrowing from IMF, the Caribbean Development Bank (CDB) and the Bolivarian Alternative for Latin America and the Caribbean (ALBA), essentially the Bolivarian Republic of Venezuela, to cope with falling revenues, tourism receipts and remittances and, by extension, to ease the worsening of the balance of payments. These funds, most of which were received with less stringent conditionalities than in the past, will assist countries in the implementation of employment-generating capital projects and in maintaining an active economic environment. Total external debt expanded slightly from 44% of GDP in 2008 to 46% of GDP in 2009, while domestic debt rose more significantly, from 45% of GDP in 2008 to 51% of GDP in 2009 for comparable periods.

Monetary policy remained neutral in 2009: there were no changes in the discount rate, which remained at 6.5%, and the statutory required reserve ratio of commercial banks remained at 6%. The inter-bank market rate increased slightly, from 6% in December 2008 to 6.6% in November 2009, indicating a tighter credit market. In light of the collapse of CLICO in January 2009 and the run on the Bank of Antigua in February 2009, the Monetary Council of ECCU agreed to enhance the regulatory and supervisory framework of the financial sector by establishing a Regulatory Oversight Committee.

For the period January to August 2009, M1 shrank by approximately 8%, reflecting the decline in economic activity. Domestic credit was also down by 1.3%, with private-sector credit increasing slightly by 1.3% and net credit to the public sector declining by 37% owing to an increase in government deposits and reduced capital expenditure. The net assets of commercial banks declined in all countries except Dominica and Saint Kitts and Nevis. The level of foreign reserves in support of the fixed exchange rate nevertheless remained substantially above the statutory minimum of 60%.

The economies of the ECCU are expected to contract by 5.6% in 2009, in response to the decline in tourism (14%), construction (21%) and mining and quarrying (17%). In the mainstay tourism sector, overall tourists arrivals decreased by 9.2% in the second quarter of 2009, compared with the same period in 2008. The high-yield segment, stay-over visitors, declined by 14.6%, while cruise passengers increased by 18.4%. The drop in stay-over visitors was particularly severe in Anguilla (18%), Grenada (22%) and Saint Kitts and Nevis (27%). Activity in the construction sector and the related mining and quarrying sector shrank as some public-sector projects were completed and private-sector construction projects (mainly major tourism projects) slowed down or came to a halt owing to the difficulties in accessing finance. Economic activity is expected to slowly recover in 2010, with growth estimated at 2%.

Labour market conditions have worsened in 2009 as the tourism and construction sectors remain sluggish. In Antigua and Barbuda, the situation was exacerbated by the closure of most businesses formerly owned by Sir Allen Stanford, who is currently on trial in the United States for fraud. At least 400 persons have lost their jobs as a result. In Saint Lucia, public servants received a 3.5% wage increase in May-June 2009.

The level of inflation measured by the CPI fell in all countries in the second quarter of 2009, dipping to -0.8% compared with 3.5% for the same period in 2008, as the prices of fuel and electricity, transportation and communication, housing and utilities decreased. All countries, with the exception of Antigua and Barbuda, which already posted a low inflation rate of 0.7% in 2008,

EASTERN CARIBBEAN CURRENCY UNION: MAIN ECONOMIC INDICATORS

	2007	2008	2009 [a]
	Annual percentage growth rates		
Gross domestic product	5.4	1.4	-5.6
Consumer prices	5.5	4.8	-0.8 [b]
Money (M1)	10.4	5.9	-8.9 [c]
	Annual average percentages		
Central government overall balance/GDP	-3.9	-3.5	-1.1
Nominal deposit rate	3.3	3.3	3.3
Nominal lending rate	9.5	9.5	9.5
	Millions of dollars		
Exports of goods and services	2 135	1 903	1 833
Imports of goods and services	3 906	3 235	3 139
Current account balance	-1 861	-1 404	-1 411
Capital and financial account balance [d]	1 902	1 395	1 550
Overall balance	40	-9	141

Source: Economic Commission for Latin America and the Caribbean (ECLAC), on the basis of official figures.
[a] Preliminary estimates.
[b] January-June 2009 variation.
[c] Twelve-month variation to September 2008.
[d] Includes errors and omissions.

reported substantial drops in inflation, with rates ranging from 0% to -2.0%.

In the external sector, the current account deficit declined by 12.7% to reach 34% of GDP at the end of June 2009. This was a slight improvement from December 2008, when the current account deficit stood at almost 40% of GDP and was achieved largely on account of the near 6% increase in exports (generated by the recovery of banana exports in Dominica and Saint Lucia after the drop in output caused by Hurricane Dean) and the very miniscule 0.3% decline in imports. The services account decreased by 19%, mainly because travel receipts slumped by approximately 16% owing to the downturn in stay-over tourists. Despite the 21% decline in private capital flows and FDI, the surplus on the capital and financial account increased slightly, by 3%, mainly on account of the credit received by governments from IMF, CDB and ALBA. The Central Bank's net international reserves also increased by 13.5% to reach US$ 858 million, covering three months of imports of goods and services.

Statistical annex

Table A-1
LATIN AMERICA AND THE CARIBBEAN: MAIN ECONOMIC INDICATORS

	2000	2001	2002	2003	2004	2005	2006	2007	2008	2009 [a]
					Annual growth rates					
Gross domestic product [b]	4.0	0.4	-0.4	2.2	6.1	5.0	5.8	5.8	4.1	-1.8
Per capita gross domestic product [b]	2.5	-1.0	-1.7	0.9	4.7	3.7	4.6	4.5	3.0	-2.9
Consumer prices [c]	9.0	6.1	12.2	8.5	7.4	6.1	5.0	6.5	8.2	4.5
					Percentages					
Urban open unemployment [d]	10.4	10.2	11.1	11.0	10.3	9.1	8.6	7.9	7.4	8.3
Total gross external debt/GDP [e]	35.1	36.4	39.9	39.9	34.4	25.1	21.0	20.0	18.2 [f]	19.3 [g]
Total gross external debt/ exports of goods and services	172	181	178	169	138	101	84	82	73 [f]	75 [g]
Balance of payments [h]					**Millions of dollars**					
Current account balance	-48 394	-53 753	-15 854	8 926	21 359	34 375	44 004	9 656	-34 961	-24 343
Merchandise trade balance	-361	-7 233	20 757	41 163	56 567	76 695	91 636	63 798	36 025	36 478
Exports of goods f.o.b.	363 399	348 458	352 341	383 667	472 849	568 583	676 983	762 335	883 885	676 486
Imports of goods f.o.b.	363 760	355 691	331 583	342 504	416 282	491 888	585 348	698 538	847 860	640 009
Services trade balance	-15 031	-17 619	-12 691	-11 295	-11 690	-15 745	-17 359	-24 013	-30 472	-25 253
Income balance	-54 437	-55 165	-53 634	-58 724	-68 579	-79 609	-93 974	-96 484	-106 897	-93 238
Net current transfers	21 435	26 264	29 714	37 777	45 061	53 035	63 701	66 355	66 382	57 671
Capital and financial balance [i]	63 868	37 340	-10 089	1 538	-8 458	22 504	16 087	112 601	69 580	56 150
Net foreign direct investment	71 479	66 033	50 219	37 151	48 618	53 766	30 176	88 751	91 532	63 587
Other capital movements	-7 611	-28 693	-60 308	-35 613	-57 076	-31 262	-14 089	23 850	-21 952	-7 436
Overall balance	15 474	-16 414	-25 943	10 463	12 902	56 879	60 091	122 257	34 620	31 808
Variation in reserve assets [j]	-7 261	193	3 524	-29 102	-21 771	-35 494	-47 161	-124 554	-38 712	-32 227
Other financing	-8 213	16 221	22 419	18 639	8 869	-21 385	-12 930	2 297	4 092	419
Net transfer of resources	951	-1 567	-41 426	-39 517	-69 266	-80 723	-97 561	13 678	-40 098	-44 487
Gross international reserves	171 298	169 408	167 959	201 185	227 838	263 207	320 757	459 550	510 457	...
Fiscal sector [k]					**Percentages of GDP**					
Overall balance	-2.9	-4.2	-4.3	-3.5	-2.3	-1.1	-1.3	-0.6	-1.2	-2.6
Primary balance	0.8	-0.8	-0.8	0.1	1.1	2.2	1.8	2.1	1.5	-0.1
Total revenue	21.5	22.1	22.2	22.2	22.9	24.8	25.0	23.8	24.2	22.7
Tax revenue	17.1	17.6	17.8	17.8	18.2	19.2	19.8	18.6	18.6	...
Total expenditure	24.3	26.3	26.5	25.7	25.2	25.9	26.2	24.5	25.2	25.2
Central-government public debt [l]	42.7	45.0	58.2	57.2	50.9	42.7	35.7	29.9	27.8	28.3
Public debt of the non-financial public-sector [l]	48.0	50.2	65.0	62.6	55.8	47.6	40.4	33.4	31.4	31.7

Source: Economic Commission for Latin America and the Caribbean (ECLAC), on the basis of official figures.
[a] Preliminary figures.
[b] Based on official figures expressed in constant 2000 dollars.
[c] December-December variation.
[d] The data for Argentina and Brazil have been adjusted to allow for changes in methodology in 2003 and 2002, respectively.
[e] Estimates based on figures denominated in dollars at current prices.
[f] Does not include Bahamas and Cuba.
[g] Does not include Bahamas, Barbados, Cuba and Guyana.
[h] Does not include Barbados, Belize, Cuba, Guyana, Saint Kitts and Nevis, Suriname and Trinidad and Tobago.
[i] Includes errors and omissions.
[j] A minus sign (-) indicates an increase in reserve assets.
[k] Central government, except for Ecuador, Mexico and the Plurinational State of Bolivia, whose coverage correspond to general government, non-financial public sector and public sector, respectively. Simple averages.
[l] Includes information from 19 Latin American and Caribbean countries: Argentina, Bolivarian Republic of Venezuela, Brazil, Chile, Colombia, Costa Rica, Dominican Republic, Ecuador, El Salvador, Guatemala, Haiti, Honduras, Mexico, Nicaragua, Panama, Paraguay, Peru, Plurinational State of Bolivia and Uruguay.

Table A-2
LATIN AMERICA AND THE CARIBBEAN: GROSS DOMESTIC PRODUCT
(Annual growth rates)

	2000	2001	2002	2003	2004	2005	2006	2007	2008	2009 [a]
Latin America and the Caribbean [b]	**4.0**	**0.4**	**-0.4**	**2.2**	**6.1**	**5.0**	**5.8**	**5.8**	**4.1**	**-1.8**
Antigua and Barbuda	1.5	2.0	2.5	5.2	7.0	4.2	13.3	9.1	0.2	-6.6
Argentina	-0.8	-4.4	-10.9	8.8	9.0	9.2	8.5	8.7	6.8	0.7
Bahamas	3.7	-0.3	2.6	-0.9	-0.8	5.7	4.3	0.7	-1.7	-3.9
Barbados	2.3	-4.6	0.7	2.0	4.8	3.9	3.2	3.4	0.2	-3.6
Belize	12.3	5.0	5.1	9.3	4.6	3.0	4.7	1.2	3.8	-0.5
Bolivia (Plurinational State of)	2.5	1.7	2.5	2.7	4.2	4.4	4.8	4.6	6.1	3.5
Brazil	4.3	1.3	2.7	1.1	5.7	3.2	4.0	5.7	5.1	0.3
Chile	4.5	3.4	2.2	3.9	6.0	5.6	4.6	4.7	3.2	-1.8
Colombia	2.9	2.2	2.5	4.6	4.7	5.7	6.9	7.5	2.4	0.3
Costa Rica	1.8	1.1	2.9	6.4	4.3	5.9	8.8	7.8	2.6	-1.2
Cuba	5.9	3.2	1.4	3.8	5.8	11.2	12.1	7.3	4.1	1.0
Dominica	0.6	-3.8	-4.0	2.2	6.3	3.4	6.3	4.9	3.5	-1.5
Dominican Republic	5.7	1.8	5.8	-0.3	1.3	9.3	10.7	8.5	5.3	2.5
Ecuador	2.8	5.3	4.2	3.6	8.0	6.0	3.9	2.5	6.5	-0.4
El Salvador	2.2	1.7	2.3	2.3	1.9	3.1	4.2	4.7	2.5	-2.5
Grenada	12.0	-3.9	2.1	8.4	-6.5	12.0	-1.9	4.5	0.9	-5.0
Guatemala	3.6	2.3	3.9	2.5	3.2	3.3	5.4	6.3	4.0	-1.0
Guyana	-0.7	1.6	1.2	-0.7	1.6	-2.0	5.1	5.3	3.1	0.9
Haiti	0.9	-1.0	-0.3	0.4	-3.5	1.8	2.3	3.4	1.3	2.0
Honduras	5.7	2.7	3.8	4.5	6.2	6.1	6.6	6.3	4.0	-3.0
Jamaica	0.7	1.3	1.0	3.5	1.4	1.0	2.7	1.4	-0.6	-3.0
Mexico	6.6	-0.0	0.8	1.4	4.0	3.3	5.0	3.4	1.3	-6.7
Nicaragua	4.1	3.0	0.8	2.5	5.3	4.3	3.9	3.2	3.2	-1.5
Panama	2.7	0.6	2.2	4.2	7.5	7.2	8.5	12.1	10.7	2.5
Paraguay	-3.3	2.1	-0.0	3.8	4.1	2.9	4.3	6.8	5.8	-3.5
Peru	3.0	0.2	5.0	4.0	5.0	6.8	7.7	8.9	9.8	0.8
Saint Kitts and Nevis	4.3	2.0	1.0	0.5	7.6	5.6	5.5	2.0	4.6	-8.5
Saint Vincent and the Grenadines	1.8	2.2	3.8	3.1	6.6	2.1	9.5	8.4	1.1	-0.2
Saint Lucia	-0.2	-5.9	2.0	4.1	4.9	5.0	5.9	2.2	0.8	-3.8
Suriname	1.9	5.7	2.7	6.8	0.5	7.2	3.9	5.1	4.3	2.5
Trinidad and Tobago	6.9	4.2	7.9	14.4	8.0	5.4	14.4	4.6	2.3	-0.5
Uruguay	-1.4	-3.4	-11.0	2.2	11.8	6.6	7.0	7.6	8.9	1.2
Venezuela (Bolivarian Republic of)	3.7	3.4	-8.9	-7.8	18.3	10.3	9.9	8.2	4.8	-2.3

Source: Economic Commission for Latin America and the Caribbean (ECLAC), on the basis of official figures.
[a] Preliminary figures.
[b] Based on official figures expressed in 2000 dollars.

Table A-3
LATIN AMERICA AND THE CARIBBEAN: PER CAPITA GROSS DOMESTIC PRODUCT
(Annual growth rates)

	2000	2001	2002	2003	2004	2005	2006	2007	2008	2009 [a]
Latin America and the Caribbean [b]	**2.5**	**-1.0**	**-1.7**	**0.9**	**4.7**	**3.7**	**4.6**	**4.5**	**3.0**	**-2.9**
Antigua and Barbuda	-1.2	-0.5	1.3	3.9	5.7	1.7	11.9	7.8	-1.0	-7.7
Argentina	-1.9	-5.4	-11.8	7.8	8.0	8.1	7.4	7.6	5.7	-0.3
Bahamas	2.0	-1.6	1.3	-2.1	-2.1	4.4	2.7	-0.5	-2.9	-5.0
Barbados	2.3	-4.2	0.7	1.6	4.4	3.9	2.8	3.0	0.2	-4.0
Belize	9.2	2.5	2.7	6.9	2.3	0.8	2.5	-1.2	1.7	-2.4
Bolivia (Plurinational State of)	0.4	-0.4	0.4	0.7	2.2	2.5	2.9	2.7	4.3	1.7
Brazil	2.8	-0.1	1.2	-0.2	4.4	1.9	2.8	4.6	4.1	-0.6
Chile	3.2	2.2	1.0	2.8	4.9	4.5	3.5	3.6	2.1	-2.8
Colombia	1.2	0.5	0.8	3.0	3.0	4.1	5.3	6.0	0.9	-1.1
Costa Rica	-0.5	-1.0	0.8	4.3	2.4	4.1	7.1	6.3	1.2	-2.5
Cuba	5.6	2.9	1.2	3.6	5.6	11.1	12.0	7.2	4.1	1.0
Dominica	0.6	-3.8	-4.0	2.2	6.3	4.9	6.3	4.9	3.5	-1.5
Dominican Republic	4.0	0.2	4.2	-1.8	-0.2	7.7	9.1	6.9	3.8	1.1
Ecuador	1.4	4.0	3.0	2.4	6.8	4.8	2.8	1.4	5.4	-1.4
El Salvador	1.6	1.2	1.9	2.0	1.5	2.7	3.8	4.2	2.1	-3.0
Grenada	12.0	-3.9	1.1	8.4	-6.5	11.0	-1.9	4.5	-0.1	-5.0
Guatemala	1.2	-0.1	1.3	0.0	0.6	0.7	2.8	3.7	1.5	-3.4
Guyana	-0.7	1.5	0.9	-0.9	1.3	-2.1	5.1	5.3	3.2	1.0
Haiti	-0.9	-2.7	-1.8	-1.2	-5.0	0.2	0.7	1.7	-0.4	0.3
Honduras	3.5	0.6	1.7	2.5	4.1	3.9	4.5	4.2	1.9	-4.9
Jamaica	-0.1	0.5	0.2	2.7	0.7	0.3	2.1	0.9	-1.0	-3.4
Mexico	5.1	-1.3	-0.5	0.2	2.8	2.1	3.9	2.3	0.3	-7.7
Nicaragua	2.4	1.4	-0.6	1.2	4.0	2.9	2.5	1.8	1.9	-2.8
Panama	0.7	-1.3	0.4	2.3	5.6	5.3	6.7	10.2	8.9	0.9
Paraguay	-5.3	-0.0	-2.0	1.8	2.1	0.9	2.4	4.8	3.9	-5.2
Peru	1.4	-1.2	3.6	2.6	3.6	5.5	6.4	7.6	8.5	-0.3
Saint Kitts and Nevis	2.1	-0.1	1.0	-1.6	5.4	5.6	3.4	2.0	2.6	-10.3
Saint Vincent and the Grenadines	1.8	2.2	3.8	3.1	5.6	2.1	9.5	8.4	1.1	-0.2
Saint Lucia	-1.5	-7.1	1.4	2.8	3.7	4.4	4.6	0.9	0.3	-4.9
Suriname	0.6	4.2	1.2	5.5	-0.9	5.9	2.8	4.1	3.3	1.5
Trinidad and Tobago	6.5	3.8	7.5	14.1	7.5	5.1	14.0	4.2	1.9	-0.9
Uruguay	-1.9	-3.6	-11.0	2.2	11.9	6.6	6.8	7.3	8.6	0.9
Venezuela (Bolivarian Republic of)	1.7	1.5	-10.5	-9.4	16.2	8.4	8.0	6.3	3.0	-3.9

Source: Economic Commission for Latin America and the Caribbean (ECLAC), on the basis of official figures.
[a] Preliminary figures.
[b] Based on official figures expressed in 2000 dollars.

Table A-4
LATIN AMERICA AND THE CARIBBEAN: GROSS FIXED CAPITAL FORMATION [a]
(Percentages of GDP)

	2000	2001	2002	2003	2004	2005	2006	2007	2008	2009 [b]
Latin America and the Caribbean	**18.5**	**17.9**	**16.8**	**16.4**	**17.4**	**18.5**	**19.7**	**20.9**	**21.9**	**20.3** [c]
Argentina	16.2	14.3	10.2	12.9	15.9	17.9	19.5	20.4	20.9	18.6
Bahamas	32.1	29.9	29.7	31.0	28.7	33.8	39.5	39.1	35.3	...
Belize	28.7	25.6	23.1	18.1	16.4	17.2	16.7	17.4	16.7	...
Bolivia (Plurinational State of)	17.9	13.8	16.0	13.9	13.2	13.4	14.0	15.1	16.9	16.5
Brazil	16.8	16.6	15.4	14.5	15.0	15.0	15.7	16.9	18.3	16.3
Chile	19.8	19.9	19.8	20.2	20.9	24.5	24.0	25.7	29.8	25.3
Colombia	13.0	14.0	14.7	16.0	17.4	19.9	21.8	23.4	23.9	22.5
Costa Rica	17.8	18.0	18.7	18.8	18.0	17.7	18.0	19.7	21.5	20.0
Cuba	11.9	12.6	6.8	6.1	6.2	6.7	8.6	8.2	8.5	...
Dominican Republic	20.5	19.3	19.1	15.3	14.8	15.4	16.9	17.5	18.2	16.1
Ecuador	20.5	24.0	27.4	26.4	25.7	26.8	26.8	26.8	29.2	29.5
El Salvador	16.9	16.9	17.1	17.1	15.9	15.8	16.9	17.1	15.8	15.1
Guatemala	19.1	19.0	20.0	18.9	18.1	18.3	20.1	19.8	18.5	17.4
Haiti	27.3	27.3	28.0	28.8	28.9	28.8	28.8	28.6	28.7	28.9
Honduras	25.8	24.3	21.7	22.1	25.7	23.8	25.3	28.5	30.7	26.9
Mexico	21.4	20.2	19.9	19.7	20.5	21.3	22.3	23.1	23.9	22.8
Nicaragua	29.9	27.4	25.5	25.0	25.4	26.8	26.7	27.9	29.3	26.1
Panama	21.2	15.7	14.4	17.1	17.4	17.3	18.6	23.3	26.4	27.2
Paraguay	17.5	16.1	15.0	15.5	15.6	16.4	16.2	17.3	19.3	17.1
Peru	20.2	18.5	17.5	17.8	18.3	19.2	21.2	24.0	28.7	25.7
Uruguay	16.3	15.3	11.6	10.1	11.7	12.9	15.2	15.1	16.4	16.3
Venezuela (Bolivarian Republic of)	21.0	23.1	20.7	14.1	17.9	22.4	26.4	30.6	28.3	27.4

Source: Economic Commission for Latin America and the Caribbean (ECLAC), on the basis of official figures.
[a] Based on official figures expressed in 2000 dollars.
[b] Preliminary figures.
[c] Does not include Bahamas, Belize and Cuba.

Table A-5a
LATIN AMERICA AND THE CARIBBEAN: FINANCING OF GROSS DOMESTIC INVESTMENT
(Percentages of GDP) [a]

	2000	2001	2002	2003	2004	2005	2006	2007	2008 [c]	2009 [b c]
1. Domestic saving	20.7	18.7	19.8	20.7	22.7	22.7	23.9	23.2	23.3	20.0
2. Net factor income	-2.6	-2.7	-2.9	-3.1	-3.1	-3.0	-3.0	-2.7	-2.6	-2.3
3. Net transfers	1.0	1.3	1.6	2.0	2.0	1.9	2.0	1.8	1.6	1.4
4. Gross national saving	19.1	17.2	18.5	19.5	21.6	21.6	22.9	22.3	22.3	19.1
5. External saving	2.3	2.6	0.8	-0.6	-1.0	-1.4	-1.5	-0.4	0.7	0.4
6. Gross domestic investment	21.4	19.8	19.3	19.0	20.6	20.3	21.4	21.9	23.0	19.5

Source: Economic Commission for Latin America and the Caribbean (ECLAC), on the basis of official figures.
[a] Based on values calculated in national currency and expressed in current dollars.
[b] Preliminary figures.
[c] Does not include Cuba.

Table A-5b
LATIN AMERICA AND THE CARIBBEAN: GROSS DOMESTIC INVESTMENT, NATIONAL INCOME AND SAVING
(Annual growth rates)

	2000	2001	2002	2003	2004	2005	2006	2007	2008	2009 [a]
Gross domestic investment	7.4	-2.0	-7.7	-1.9	11.8	6.3	13.0	11.7	11.4	-15.5
Gross national disposable income	4.9	-0.3	-0.3	2.5	7.1	6.1	7.2	6.5	4.8	-3.3
National saving	10.5	-5.6	-0.1	6.6	15.3	8.2	12.4	7.2	6.2	-13.3

Source: Economic Commission for Latin America and the Caribbean (ECLAC), on the basis of official figures expressed in constant 2000 dollars.
[a] Preliminary figures.

Table A-6
LATIN AMERICA AND THE CARIBBEAN: BALANCE OF PAYMENTS
(Millions of dollars)

	Exports of goods f.o.b.			Exports of services			Imports of goods f.o.b.			Imports of services		
	2007	2008	2009 c	2007	2008	2009 c	2007	2008	2009 c	2007	2008	2009 c
Latin America and the Caribbean d	778 748	906 062	692 199	100 415	114 440	97 268	710 727	862 875	651 032	123 466	143 912	124 492
Antigua and Barbuda	76	76	80	517	520	527	649	662	686	283	290	304
Argentina	55 980	70 021	55 157	10 376	12 090	11 217	42 525	54 557	37 644	10 828	12 979	11 435
Bahamas	802	956	703	2 599	2 543	...	2 956	3 199	2 468	1 580	1 360	...
Barbados	481	461	380	1 635	1 589	...	1 528	1 685	1 303	816	744	...
Belize	426	466	396	398	386	...	642	788	616	164	170	...
Bolivia (Plurinational State of)	4 458	6 448	5 029	499	500	475	3 455	4 980	4 333	688	700	731
Brazil	160 649	197 942	154 395	23 954	30 451	27 104	120 617	173 107	128 099	37 173	47 140	43 300
Chile	67 666	66 455	51 835	8 952	10 754	8 994	44 031	57 610	39 175	9 927	11 401	9 545
Colombia	30 577	38 531	31 092	3 636	4 137	4 095	31 173	37 556	30 875	6 243	7 188	6 662
Costa Rica	9 299	9 566	8 901	3 552	4 094	3 730	12 285	14 551	11 486	1 818	1 893	1 785
Cuba	3 830	...	...	8 192	...	...	10 083	...	...	292	...	...
Dominica	39	36	36	109	116	113	172	197	193	66	71	71
Dominican Republic	7 160	6 949	5 351	4 767	4 911	4 617	13 597	16 095	12 233	1 746	1 819	1 708
Ecuador	14 870	19 147	13 321	1 200	1 313	1 263	13 047	17 776	14 551	2 572	2 954	2 844
El Salvador	4 039	4 611	3 975	1 130	1 041	1 360	8 144	9 004	6 836	1 420	1 625	1 823
Grenada	41	31	31	147	146	135	328	343	319	111	111	114
Guatemala	6 983	7 848	7 260	1 731	1 789	1 634	12 470	13 422	11 169	2 041	2 159	2 050
Guyana	698	798	650	173	...	...	1 063	1 300	1 000	272	...	...
Haiti	522	490	549	257	343	347	1 618	2 108	1 937	674	784	827
Honduras	5 594	6 046	5 326	750	910	791	8 556	10 389	8 103	1 037	1 215	1 101
Jamaica	2 363	2 744	1 400	2 707	2 795	...	6 204	7 547	4 200	2 282	2 367	...
Mexico	271 875	291 343	227 247	17 489	18 040	15 809	281 949	308 603	234 514	23 794	25 119	22 154
Nicaragua	2 336	2 538	2 422	373	399	403	4 094	4 749	3 878	555	608	582
Panama	9 338	10 289	10 495	4 924	5 864	5 714	12 521	15 003	14 103	2 107	2 601	2 612
Paraguay	5 580	7 812	5 438	962	1 081	1 035	6 093	8 948	6 325	460	595	528
Peru	27 882	31 529	24 861	3 159	3 637	3 492	19 595	28 439	20 788	4 346	5 566	4 691
Saint Kitts and Nevis	58	57	48	174	173	162	242	270	247	102	112	112
Saint Vincent and the Grenadines	51	53	54	162	143	135	288	302	287	114	110	106
Saint Lucia	101	186	176	356	368	338	542	578	520	188	189	180
Suriname	1 359	1 708	1 500	245	285	...	1 045	1 350	1 230	310	407	...
Trinidad and Tobago	13 391	18 686	12 740	...	...	...	7 670	9 622	6 628	...	...	...
Uruguay	5 043	7 100	6 274	1 807	2 158	2 111	5 598	8 654	6 811	1 124	1 414	1 360
Venezuela (Bolivarian Republic of)	69 010	95 138	55 078	1 673	1 867	1 669	46 031	49 482	38 476	8 625	10 221	7 868

Table A-6 (continued)

	Trade balance			Income balance			Current transfers balance			Current account balance		
	2007	2008	2009 [c]	2007	2008	2009 [c]	2007	2008	2009 [c]	2007	2008	2009 [c]
Latin America and the Caribbean [d]	**45 517**	**14 329**	**14 619**	**-97 742**	**-108 040**	**-94 825**	**67 050**	**67 054**	**57 715**	**14 822**	**-26 767**	**-19 429**
Antigua and Barbuda	-340	-356	-383	-64	-51	-51	24	23	22	-379	-384	-413
Argentina	13 003	14 574	17 294	-5 927	-7 651	-8 581	336	111	104	7 412	7 034	8 816
Bahamas	-1 135	-1 060	-1 765	-232	-115	...	52	56	...	-1 315	-1 118	-544
Barbados	-227	-379	-923	-101	-85	...	145	101	...	-182	-363	-187
Belize	17	-105	-220	-159	-157	...	93	112	...	-52	-150	-80
Bolivia (Plurinational State of)	815	1 267	440	-489	-536	-532	1 266	1 284	1 156	1 591	2 015	1 063
Brazil	26 813	8 146	10 100	-29 291	-40 562	-31 791	4 029	4 224	3 273	1 551	-28 192	-18 418
Chile	22 660	8 200	12 110	-18 595	-14 563	-11 834	3 123	2 924	2 631	7 189	-3 440	2 908
Colombia	-3 203	-2 075	-2 350	-7 847	-10 296	-8 487	5 231	5 514	4 590	-5 819	-6 857	-6 247
Costa Rica	-1 251	-2 784	-640	-865	-391	-950	470	442	395	-1 646	-2 732	-1 195
Cuba	1 647	...	...	-960	...	...	-199	...	...	488	...	...
Dominica	-90	-115	-116	-16	-18	-18	21	21	20	-85	-112	-114
Dominican Republic	-3 416	-6 054	-3 973	-2 081	-1 815	-1 698	3 401	3 432	3 318	-2 096	-4 437	-2 353
Ecuador	452	-270	-2 810	-2 047	-1 598	-1 426	3 246	2 989	2 633	1 650	1 120	-1 603
El Salvador	-4 395	-4 978	-3 324	-576	-536	-682	3 750	3 832	3 482	-1 221	-1 682	-524
Grenada	-251	-279	-268	-34	-36	-36	24	25	23	-261	-289	-281
Guatemala	-5 797	-5 944	-4 325	-843	-929	-904	4 854	5 010	4 601	-1 786	-1 863	-628
Guyana	-465	-502	-350	-11	-15	...	287	329	...	-189	-299	-195
Haiti	-1 513	-2 058	-1 868	2	6	6	1 517	1 776	1 793	7	-277	-68
Honduras	-3 249	-4 647	-3 087	-598	-350	-308	2 622	3 021	2 266	-1 225	-1 977	-1 129
Jamaica	-3 417	-4 375	-2 800	-662	-568	-500	2 040	2 150	1 800	-2 038	-2 794	-700
Mexico	-16 379	-24 340	-13 612	-18 371	-16 927	-14 187	26 415	25 461	21 725	-8 335	-15 806	-6 074
Nicaragua	-1 941	-2 420	-1 634	-135	-161	-173	1 075	1 068	990	-1 001	-1 513	-818
Panama	-365	-1 452	-506	-1 311	-1 579	-1 683	253	238	215	-1 422	-2 792	-1 974
Paraguay	-11	-650	-380	-162	-226	-190	373	405	364	200	-471	-205
Peru	7 099	1 161	2 873	-8 374	-8 144	-6 620	2 494	2 803	2 523	1 220	-4 180	-1 224
Saint Kitts and Nevis	-112	-153	-149	-32	-11	-33	33	33	32	-110	-131	-151
Saint Vincent and the Grenadines	-189	-216	-204	-21	-21	-23	20	20	18	-190	-217	-209
Saint Lucia	-272	-214	-186	-68	-74	-71	14	14	13	-327	-272	-244
Suriname	250	236	270	8	21	...	76	87	...	335	344	280
Trinidad and Tobago	6 268	9 679	6 788	-964	-897	-1 554	60	10	13	5 364	8 792	5 247
Uruguay	128	-811	214	-345	-454	-497	136	146	131	-80	-1 119	-152
Venezuela (Bolivarian Republic of)	16 027	37 302	10 403	2 467	698	-2 000	-431	-608	-416	18 063	37 392	7 986

Table A-6 (concluded)

	Capital and financial balance [a]			Overall balance			Reserve assets (variation) [b]			Other financing		
	2007	2008	2009 [c]	2007	2008	2009 [c]	2007	2008	2009 [c]	2007	2008	2009 [c]
Latin America and the Caribbean [d]	**109 470**	**63 993**	**49 920**	**124 282**	**37 236**	**30 679**	**-126 617**	**-41 808**	**-31 097**	**1 951**	**3 949**	**419**
Antigua and Barbuda	380	377	416	1	-7	3	-1	7	-3	0	0	0
Argentina	4 188	-10 724	-8 323	11 600	-3 690	493	-13 098	-9	-493	1 499	3 699	0
Bahamas	1 269	1 228	919	-46	109	375	46	-109	-375	0	0	0
Barbados	461	142	...	278	-221	...	-278	-221	...	...	...	...
Belize	75	208	130	23	58	50	-23	-58	-50	0	0	0
Bolivia (Plurinational State of)	361	359	-332	1 952	2 374	731	-1 952	-2 374	-731	0	0	0
Brazil	85 933	31 161	55 758	87 484	2 969	37 340	-87 484	-2 969	-37 340	0	0	0
Chile	-10 403	9 884	1 047	-3 214	6 444	3 955	3 214	-6 444	-3 955	0	0	0
Colombia	10 490	9 412	7 396	4 672	2 555	1 149	-4 672	-2 555	-1 149	0	0	0
Costa Rica	2 794	2 384	1 462	1 148	-348	267	-1 148	348	-267	0	0	0
Cuba	...	...	...	...	...	...	...	...	...	...	...	...
Dominica	84	109	133	-1	-3	19	1	3	-19	0	0	0
Dominican Republic	2 716	4 117	2 230	620	-320	-123	-679	303	123	59	17	0
Ecuador	-264	-172	1 725	1 387	948	122	-1 497	-952	-132	111	4	10
El Salvador	1 502	2 016	644	280	334	120	-280	-334	-120	0	0	0
Grenada	271	283	278	11	-6	-3	-11	6	3	0	0	0
Guatemala	2 002	2 195	514	216	333	-114	-216	-333	114	0	0	0
Guyana	188	306	428	-1	7	233	-37	-45	-233	39	38	0
Haiti	148	374	64	154	98	-4	-208	-171	-177	54	73	181
Honduras	1 063	1 912	374	-162	-65	-755	109	42	582	53	23	173
Jamaica	1 598	2 689	836	-440	-105	136	440	105	-136	0	0	0
Mexico	18 621	23 244	-1 422	10 286	7 438	-7 496	-10 286	-7 438	7 496	0	0	0
Nicaragua	1 093	1 499	1 024	92	-14	207	-173	-30	-261	80	45	54
Panama	2 044	3 377	2 124	622	584	150	-611	-579	-150	-10	-5	0
Paraguay	523	850	1 035	723	379	830	-727	-378	-830	5	-0	0
Peru	8 368	7 292	3 676	9 588	3 112	2 452	-9 654	-3 169	-2 452	67	57	0
Saint Kitts and Nevis	117	145	221	7	15	70	-7	-15	-70	0	0	0
Saint Vincent and the Grenadines	188	213	211	-2	-3	3	2	3	-3	0	0	0
Saint Lucia	345	269	292	19	-3	48	-19	3	-48	0	0	0
Suriname	-148	-302	-9	177	52	271	-177	-52	-271	0	0	0
Trinidad and Tobago	-3 824	-6 086	-7 000	1 541	2 706	-1 753	-1 541	-2 706	1 753	0	0	0
Uruguay	1 091	3 352	1 755	1 010	2 233	1 603	-1 005	-2 233	-1 603	-5	-0	0
Venezuela (Bolivarian Republic of)	-23 805	-28 117	-17 686	-5 742	9 275	-9 700	5 357	-9 456	9 700	0	0	0

Source: Economic Commission for Latin America and the Caribbean (ECLAC), on the basis of official figures from the International Monetary Fund (IMF) and national sources.
[a] Includes errors and omissions.
[b] A minus sign (-) indicates an increase in reserve assets.
[c] Preliminary figures.
[d] Does not include Cuba.

Table A-7a
LATIN AMERICA AND THE CARIBBEAN: EXPORTS OF GOODS, f.o.b.
(Indices 2000=100)

	Value			Volume			Unit value		
	2007	2008	2009 [a]	2007	2008	2009 [a]	2007	2008	2009 [a]
Latin America and the Caribbean	**210.3**	**243.7**	**186.7**	**141.5**	**142.4**	**128.8**	**148.6**	**171.2**	**145.0**
Argentina	212.5	265.8	209.4	155.6	155.8	146.5	136.6	170.6	143.0
Bolivia (Plurinational State of)	357.8	517.5	403.6	180.1	242.6	217.5	198.6	213.3	185.5
Brazil	291.6	359.3	280.3	195.0	190.2	176.6	149.6	189.0	158.7
Chile	352.2	345.9	269.8	155.3	153.8	146.3	226.9	224.9	184.5
Colombia	222.2	280.0	226.0	143.3	149.2	151.5	155.1	187.6	149.2
Costa Rica	160.0	164.6	153.1	167.3	168.7	165.2	95.6	97.5	92.7
Cuba	228.6	...	...	98.1	...	...	232.9	...	...
Dominican Republic	124.8	121.1	93.3	103.3	94.5	77.4	120.9	128.1	120.4
Ecuador	289.5	372.7	259.3	189.6	196.9	187.6	152.7	189.3	138.2
El Salvador	136.3	155.6	134.1	121.1	133.0	119.4	112.5	117.0	112.3
Guatemala	176.3	198.1	183.3	148.0	151.2	145.7	119.1	131.1	125.8
Haiti	157.4	147.8	165.5	136.7	124.0	126.2	115.2	119.2	131.1
Honduras	167.3	180.8	159.3	168.6	168.7	156.5	99.2	107.2	101.8
Mexico	163.7	175.4	136.8	126.5	126.9	108.8	129.4	138.2	125.8
Nicaragua	265.2	288.2	275.1	249.3	250.8	252.0	106.4	114.9	109.2
Panama	159.9	176.2	179.8	145.3	152.5	157.1	110.1	115.6	114.4
Paraguay	239.6	335.4	233.5	199.8	237.1	191.9	119.9	141.5	121.7
Peru	400.9	453.3	357.5	179.5	193.1	183.5	223.4	234.7	194.8
Uruguay	211.6	297.8	263.2	171.0	182.4	179.1	123.7	163.3	147.0
Venezuela (Bolivarian Republic of)	205.8	283.7	164.3	84.5	85.0	74.6	243.6	333.8	220.3

Source: Economic Commission for Latin America and the Caribbean (ECLAC), on the basis of official figures from the International Monetary Fund (IMF) and national sources.
[a] Preliminary figures.

Table A-7b
LATIN AMERICA AND THE CARIBBEAN: IMPORTS OF GOODS, f.o.b.
(Indices 2000=100)

	Value			Volume			Unit value		
	2007	2008	2009 [a]	2007	2008	2009 [a]	2007	2008	2009 [a]
Latin America and the Caribbean	**192.4**	**233.4**	**176.5**	**152.7**	**165.7**	**138.8**	**126.0**	**140.9**	**127.1**
Argentina	178.0	228.4	157.6	153.2	178.3	139.8	116.2	128.1	112.7
Bolivia (Plurinational State of)	214.6	309.3	269.1	153.5	208.7	204.0	139.8	148.2	131.9
Brazil	216.2	310.3	229.6	154.1	181.3	150.7	140.3	171.2	152.3
Chile	257.6	337.1	229.2	215.1	246.9	199.9	119.7	136.5	114.7
Colombia	281.1	338.7	278.4	225.5	249.3	220.4	124.6	135.9	126.3
Costa Rica	203.9	241.6	190.7	181.1	202.4	181.5	112.6	119.4	105.0
Cuba	210.3	...	...	155.8	...	...	135.0	...	...
Dominican Republic	143.5	169.8	129.1	116.4	124.1	102.5	123.3	136.9	125.9
Ecuador	348.6	474.9	388.8	258.0	311.0	292.7	135.1	152.7	132.8
El Salvador	173.2	191.5	145.4	145.5	150.4	128.3	119.0	127.3	113.3
Guatemala	224.3	241.4	200.9	165.5	157.7	147.4	135.5	153.1	136.3
Haiti	148.9	194.0	178.2	111.7	101.1	110.5	133.2	191.9	161.4
Honduras	214.6	260.5	203.2	176.5	186.3	167.0	121.6	139.8	121.7
Mexico	161.6	176.9	134.4	131.2	135.5	111.9	123.2	130.5	120.1
Nicaragua	227.3	263.6	215.3	168.0	172.4	163.7	135.3	152.9	131.5
Panama	179.3	214.9	202.0	146.6	159.7	158.0	122.3	134.6	127.9
Paraguay	212.6	312.2	220.7	177.4	236.9	186.0	119.8	131.8	118.6
Peru	266.0	386.1	282.2	187.7	224.8	176.7	141.7	171.8	159.8
Uruguay	169.1	261.4	205.7	121.3	150.6	141.1	139.4	173.6	145.8
Venezuela (Bolivarian Republic of)	272.9	293.4	228.1	226.4	219.3	185.3	120.5	133.8	123.1

Source: Economic Commission for Latin America and the Caribbean (ECLAC), on the basis of official figures from the International Monetary Fund (IMF) and national sources.
[a] Preliminary figures.

Table A-8
LATIN AMERICA AND THE CARIBBEAN: TERMS OF TRADE FOR GOODS f.o.b./f.o.b.
(Indices 2000=100)

	2000	2001	2002	2003	2004	2005	2006	2007	2008	2009 [a]
Latin America and the Caribbean	**100.0**	**96.3**	**96.6**	**98.6**	**103.6**	**108.7**	**115.3**	**118.0**	**121.5**	**114.1**
Argentina	100.0	99.3	98.7	107.2	109.2	106.9	113.4	117.5	133.2	126.9
Bolivia (Plurinational State of)	100.0	95.8	96.2	98.5	104.1	111.8	139.8	142.1	143.9	140.7
Brazil	100.0	99.6	98.4	97.0	97.9	99.2	104.4	106.6	110.4	104.2
Chile	100.0	93.3	97.2	102.8	124.9	139.8	183.2	189.5	164.8	160.9
Colombia	100.0	94.2	92.5	95.2	102.3	111.0	115.2	124.4	138.1	118.1
Costa Rica	100.0	98.4	96.9	95.5	91.9	88.3	85.8	84.9	81.7	88.2
Cuba	100.0	114.0	105.1	121.0	133.3	129.8	164.0	172.6	...	...
Dominican Republic	100.0	100.9	101.5	97.9	96.7	95.8	94.9	98.0	93.6	95.7
Ecuador	100.0	84.6	86.8	89.8	91.5	102.4	109.9	113.0	124.0	104.0
El Salvador	100.0	102.5	101.6	97.7	96.8	96.8	95.5	94.6	91.9	99.1
Guatemala	100.0	96.7	95.8	93.0	92.1	91.3	89.6	87.9	85.6	92.3
Haiti	100.0	101.2	100.2	98.7	96.0	92.4	88.9	86.4	62.1	81.3
Honduras	100.0	94.8	92.0	88.0	87.2	87.2	83.2	81.6	76.6	83.7
Mexico	100.0	97.4	97.9	98.8	101.6	103.6	104.1	105.1	105.9	104.7
Nicaragua	100.0	88.4	87.0	84.1	82.5	81.4	79.4	78.6	75.2	83.0
Panama	100.0	102.7	101.6	97.2	95.3	93.5	90.8	90.0	85.9	89.5
Paraguay	100.0	100.2	96.7	101.4	104.3	97.4	95.5	100.1	107.3	102.6
Peru	100.0	95.6	98.4	102.2	111.3	119.4	152.1	157.6	136.7	122.0
Uruguay	100.0	104.0	102.6	103.5	99.9	90.7	88.6	88.7	94.1	100.8
Venezuela (Bolivarian Republic of)	100.0	82.2	87.6	98.7	118.1	154.4	184.4	202.1	249.5	179.0

Source: Economic Commission for Latin America and the Caribbean (ECLAC), on the basis of official figures from the International Monetary Fund (IMF) and national sources.
[a] Preliminary figures.

Table A-9
LATIN AMERICA AND THE CARIBBEAN: NET RESOURCE TRANSFER [a]
(Millions of dollars)

	2000	2001	2002	2003	2004	2005	2006	2007	2008	2009 [b]
Latin America and the Caribbean	**951**	**-1 567**	**-41 426**	**-39 517**	**-69 266**	**-80 723**	**-97 561**	**13 678**	**-40 098**	**-44 487**
Antigua and Barbuda	16	48	49	85	56	136	260	316	326	364
Argentina	993	-16 030	-20 773	-12 535	-7 175	-3 722	-10 388	-241	-14 676	-16 905
Bahamas	240	366	175	279	213	358	1 077	1 037	1 113	919
Barbados	241	241	42	131	58	-16	149	360	57	...
Belize	161	115	91	61	8	25	-50	-84	51	130
Bolivia (Plurinational State of)	182	30	-156	-226	-565	-535	-428	-128	-177	-865
Brazil	4 077	6 778	-10 252	-14 234	-29 955	-35 633	-10 553	56 642	-9 401	23 967
Chile	-1 621	-2 022	-2 068	-4 076	-10 102	-10 220	-23 558	-28 997	-4 679	-10 786
Colombia	-2 238	-339	-1 453	-2 623	-928	-1 851	-2 923	2 644	-884	-1 091
Costa Rica	-714	-63	580	443	432	1 166	2 058	1 929	1 993	512
Dominica	31	39	36	32	23	64	49	68	91	115
Dominican Republic	-85	168	-881	-2 787	-2 324	-321	-251	694	2 319	532
Ecuador	-2 020	-817	-100	-953	-1 084	-1 580	-3 691	-2 200	-1 766	309
El Salvador	132	-293	-42	595	132	-28	324	925	1 480	-38
Grenada	61	67	109	83	30	131	170	237	247	242
Guatemala	1 494	1 618	993	1 251	1 359	995	1 096	1 160	1 266	-390
Guyana	48	-3	20	-6	-10	143	242	215	329	428
Haiti	45	129	26	5	94	-20	201	204	453	251
Honduras	348	322	86	94	743	177	149	519	1 584	240
Jamaica	517	1 168	208	-246	612	561	797	937	2 121	336
Mexico	6 491	11 161	8 502	4 315	-1 286	-2 674	-15 083	250	6 317	-15 610
Nicaragua	624	455	607	520	616	590	768	1 039	1 383	905
Panama	3	202	-39	-539	-414	418	-589	723	1 792	441
Paraguay	-30	237	-134	168	-98	72	168	365	624	845
Peru	-293	391	512	-670	-1 262	-4 596	-7 681	61	-796	-2 944
Saint Kitts and Nevis	32	84	95	71	43	23	74	85	135	188
Saint Vincent and the Grenadines	19	30	18	55	99	70	108	167	192	188
Saint Lucia	64	73	75	115	45	62	261	277	195	221
Suriname	-17	54	70	118	112	55	-72	-140	-281	-9
Trinidad and Tobago	-732	-453	-441	-1 344	-1 309	-2 461	-7 087	-4 787	-6 984	-8 554
Uruguay	672	707	-2 602	979	-137	84	-52	741	2 897	1 258
Venezuela (Bolivarian Republic of)	-7 792	-6 030	-14 783	-8 679	-17 292	-22 195	-23 103	-21 338	-27 419	-19 686

Source: Economic Commission for Latin America and the Caribbean (ECLAC), on the basis of official figures from the International Monetary Fund (IMF) and national sources.
[a] The net resource transfer is calculated as total net capital income minus the income balance (net payments of profits and interest). Total net capital income is the balance on the capital and financial accounts plus errors and omissions, plus loans and the use of IMF credit plus exceptional financing. Negative figures indicate resources transferred outside the country.
[b] Preliminary figures.

Table A-10
LATIN AMERICA AND THE CARIBBEAN: NET FOREIGN DIRECT INVESTMENT [a]
(Millions of dollars)

	2000	2001	2002	2003	2004	2005	2006	2007	2008	2009 [b]
Latin America and the Caribbean	**72 190**	**66 914**	**50 996**	**37 806**	**49 725**	**54 741**	**30 847**	**89 744**	**93 524**	**65 269**
Antigua and Barbuda	43	98	66	166	80	214	374	356	253	268
Argentina	9 517	2 005	2 776	878	3 449	3 954	3 099	4 969	7 502	3 408
Bahamas	250	192	209	247	443	563	706	746	700	945
Barbados	18	17	17	58	-16	53	0	0	133	104
Belize	23	61	25	-11	111	126	108	142	187	138
Bolivia (Plurinational State of)	734	703	674	195	63	-242	278	362	508	317
Brazil	30 498	24 715	14 108	9 894	8 339	12 550	-9 380	27 518	24 601	28 587
Chile	873	2 590	2 207	2 701	5 610	4 801	4 556	9 568	9 896	5 689
Colombia	2 111	2 526	1 277	783	2 873	5 590	5 558	8 136	8 346	3 413
Costa Rica	400	451	625	548	733	904	1 371	1 634	2 015	1 400
Dominica	18	17	20	31	26	33	27	53	52	42
Dominican Republic	953	1 079	917	613	909	1 123	1 528	1 579	2 885	2 288
Ecuador	720	1 330	1 275	872	837	493	271	194	993	689
El Salvador	178	289	496	123	366	398	268	1 408	719	98
Grenada	37	59	54	89	65	70	85	174	161	114
Guatemala	230	488	183	218	255	470	552	720	822	648
Guyana	67	56	44	26	30	77	102	110	179	108
Haiti	13	4	6	14	6	26	161	75	30	37
Honduras	375	301	269	391	553	599	669	815	875	502
Jamaica	394	525	407	604	542	582	797	800	685	670
Mexico	17 789	23 045	22 158	15 183	19 249	15 503	13 670	19 272	21 795	9 180
Nicaragua	267	150	204	201	250	241	287	382	626	481
Panama	624	467	99	818	1 019	918	2 498	1 907	2 402	1 548
Paraguay	98	78	12	22	32	47	167	177	238	245
Peru	810	1 070	2 156	1 275	1 599	2 579	3 467	5 425	4 079	4 430
Saint Kitts and Nevis	96	88	80	76	46	93	110	158	88	106
Saint Vincent and the Grenadines	38	21	34	55	66	40	109	110	121	87
Saint Lucia	54	59	52	106	77	78	234	253	105	166
Suriname	-148	-27	-74	-76	-37	28	-163	-247	-234	334
Trinidad and Tobago	654	685	684	583	973	599	513	830	1 638	892
Uruguay	274	291	180	401	315	811	1 495	1 139	2 049	1 267
Venezuela (Bolivarian Republic of)	4 180	3 479	-244	722	864	1 422	-2 666	978	-924	-2 932

Source: Economic Commission for Latin America and the Caribbean (ECLAC), on the basis of official figures from the International Monetary Fund (IMF) and national sources.
[a] Corresponds to direct investment in the reporting economy after deduction of outward direct investment by residents of that country. Includes reinvestment of profits.
[b] Preliminary figures.

Table A-11
LATIN AMERICA AND THE CARIBBEAN: TOTAL GROSS EXTERNAL DEBT [a]
(Millions of dollars)

	2000	2001	2002	2003	2004	2005	2006	2007	2008	2009 [b]
Latin America and the Caribbean	**742 889**	**749 520**	**738 310**	**767 330**	**763 459**	**673 727**	**663 891**	**734 045**	**742 715**	**766 079**
Antigua and Barbuda	456	485	528	602	662	447	529	481	436	357
Argentina	155 014	166 272	156 748	164 645	171 205	113 799	108 873	124 575	124 702	122 932
Bahamas [c]	350	328	309	363	345	338	334	326	383	436
Barbados	951	1 135	1 163	1 236	1 216	1 346	1 494	1 565	1 523	...
Belize [c]	431	495	652	806	893	971	986	973	957	969
Bolivia (Plurinational State of)	6 740	6 861	6 945	7 709	7 562	7 666	6 278	5 386	5 930	5 982
Brazil	216 921	209 935	210 711	214 929	201 373	169 451	172 589	193 219	198 340	198 996
Chile	37 177	38 527	40 504	43 067	43 515	46 211	49 497	55 671	64 768	63 868
Colombia	36 130	39 163	37 382	38 065	39 497	38 507	40 103	44 553	46 377	46 509
Costa Rica	5 307	5 265	5 310	5 575	5 710	6 485	6 994	8 341	9 082	8 405
Cuba [c d]	10 961	10 893	10 900	11 300	5 806	5 898	7 794	8 908	...	...
Dominica	154	182	209	230	224	242	249	241	234	232
Dominican Republic [c]	3 679	4 176	4 536	5 987	6 380	5 847	6 296	6 556	7 237	7 099
Ecuador	13 216	14 376	16 236	16 756	17 211	17 237	17 099	17 445	16 815	16 821
El Salvador [e]	2 831	3 148	3 987	8 603	8 870	9 420	10 259	9 808	10 691	10 144
Grenada	132	176	316	352	420	447	473	491	502	512
Guatemala [c]	2 644	2 925	3 119	3 467	3 844	3 723	3 958	4 226	4 382	4 784
Guyana [c]	1 193	1 197	1 247	1 085	1 071	1 215	1 043	718	834	...
Haiti [c]	1 170	1 189	1 229	1 316	1 376	1 335	1 484	1 628	1 917	2 017
Honduras	4 711	4 757	5 025	5 343	6 023	5 134	3 935	3 190	3 442	3 435
Jamaica [c]	3 375	4 146	4 348	4 192	5 120	5 376	5 794	6 122	6 343	6 270
Mexico	148 652	144 526	134 980	132 273	130 925	128 248	116 668	124 433	125 233	149 077
Nicaragua [c]	6 660	6 374	6 363	6 596	5 391	5 348	4 527	3 385	3 512	3 557
Panama [c]	5 604	6 263	6 349	6 504	7 219	7 580	7 788	8 276	8 477	8 907
Paraguay	2 640	2 582	2 719	2 478	2 391	2 271	2 240	2 205	2 234	2 158
Peru	27 981	27 195	27 872	29 587	31 244	28 657	28 672	33 137	34 587	34 104
Saint Kitts and Nevis	162	214	265	317	317	311	306	299	308	307
Saint Vincent and the Grenadines	163	173	172	207	243	250	255	219	232	247
Saint Lucia	178	213	260	338	368	377	393	399	364	370
Suriname [c]	291	350	371	382	384	390	391	299	316	238
Trinidad and Tobago [c]	1 680	1 666	1 549	1 553	1 382	1 361	1 295	1 392	1 456	1 432
Uruguay	8 895	8 937	10 548	11 013	11 593	11 418	10 560	12 218	12 013	12 215
Venezuela (Bolivarian Republic of)	36 437	35 398	35 460	40 456	43 679	46 427	44 735	53 361	49 087	53 699

Source: Economic Commission for Latin America and the Caribbean (ECLAC), on the basis of official figures from the International Monetary Fund (IMF) and national sources.
[a] Includes debt owed to the International Monetary Fund.
[b] Figures for the first semester.
[c] Refers to external public debt.
[d] From 2004 on refers only to active external debt; excludes other external debt, 60.2% of which is official debt owed to the Paris Club.
[e] Up to 2002 corresponds to public external debt.

Table A-12
LATIN AMERICA AND THE CARIBBEAN: GROSS INTERNATIONAL RESERVES
(Millions of dollars)

	2000	2001	2002	2003	2004	2005	2006	2007	2008	2009 I	2009 II	2009 III	2009 IV [a]
Latin America and the Caribbean	**171 298**	**169 408**	**167 959**	**201 185**	**227 838**	**263 207**	**320 757**	**459 550**	**510 457**	**482 386**	**490 066**	**519 018**	**525 698**
Antigua and Barbuda [b]	64	80	88	114	120	127	143	144	138	94	96	141 [c]	...
Argentina	32 478	15 318	10 420	13 820	19 299	27 262	31 167	45 711	46 198	46 933	46 026	45 348	47 081
Bahamas [b]	350	319	381	491	674	586	461	464	568	634	780	944	873 [d]
Barbados [b]	473	690	669	738	580	603	636	839	753	...	...	...	...
Belize [b]	123	112	115	85	48	71	114	109	166	168	177	216	215 [d]
Bolivia (Plurinational State of)	1 160	1 129	897	1 096	1 272	1 798	3 193	5 319	7 722	7 762	7 955	8 453	8 597 [d]
Brazil	33 011	35 866	37 823	49 296	52 935	53 799	85 839	180 334	193 783	190 388	201 467	221 629	236 660
Chile	15 110	14 400	15 351	15 851	16 016	16 963	19 429	16 910	23 162	23 382	23 448	26 040	26 115 [d]
Colombia	8 740	9 956	10 540	10 608	13 220	14 634	15 109	20 607	23 672	23 475	23 356	24 756	24 820 [d]
Costa Rica	1 318	1 384	1 502	1 839	1 922	2 313	3 115	4 114	3 799	4 167	3 936	4 059	4 060
Dominica	29	31	45	48	42	49	63	61	55	57	58	74 [c]	...
Dominican Republic	818	1 341	829	279	825	1 929	2 251	2 946	2 644	2 542	2 498	2 673	2 540 [d]
Ecuador	1 180	1 074	1 008	1 160	1 437	2 147	2 023	3 521	4 473	3 244	2 675	4 625	5 237
El Salvador	1 894	1 712	1 591	1 910	1 893	1 833	1 908	2 198	2 545	2 524	2 788	2 642	2 623
Grenada [b]	58	64	88	83	122	94	100	111	105	88	90	103 [c]	...
Guatemala	1 885	2 359	2 381	2 932	3 529	3 783	4 061	4 310	4 745	5 030	5 137	...	...
Guyana [b]	305	287	284	276	232	252	280	313	356	405	432	589	...
Haiti	232	191	139	112	166	187	305	494	587	602	561	...	...
Honduras	...	1 578	1 687	1 609	2 159	2 526	2 824	2 733	2 690	2 784	2 658	2 321 [c]	...
Jamaica	1 049	1 903	1 643	1 196	1 882	2 169	2 399	1 906	1 795	1 663	1 661	2 007	1 932 [d]
Mexico	35 585	44 814	50 674	59 028	64 198	74 110	76 330	87 211	95 302	85 636	81 476	87 806	88 657 [d]
Nicaragua	497	383	454	504	670	730	924	1 103	1 141	1 078	1 143	1 394	1 462
Panama [b]	723	1 092	1 183	1 011	631	1 211	1 335	1 935	...	...	...	...	...
Paraguay	714	662	603	853	1 191	1 292	1 594	2 240	2 737	2 834	2 870 [e]	...	...
Peru	8 563	8 838	9 690	10 206	12 649	14 120	17 329	27 720	31 233	30 961	30 822	32 163	33 463
Saint Kitts and Nevis [b]	45	56	66	65	78	72	89	96	110	154	185	180 [c]	...
Saint Vincent and the Grenadines [b]	55	61	53	51	75	70	79	87	84	89	74	87 [c]	...
Saint Lucia [b]	79	89	94	107	133	116	135	154	143	169	180	192 [c]	...
Suriname	63	119	106	106	129	126	215	401	433	468	612	705	...
Trinidad and Tobago	1 405	1 876	1 924	2 258	2 993	4 787	6 777	7 053	9 830	9 097	8 718	8 105 [f]	...
Uruguay	2 823	3 100	772	2 087	2 512	3 078	3 091	4 121	6 360	6 965	7 438	8 068	8 000
Venezuela (Bolivarian Republic of)	20 471	18 523	14 860	21 366	24 208	30 368	37 440	34 286	43 127	28 992	30 750	33 697	33 363

Source: Economic Commission for Latin America and the Caribbean (ECLAC), on the basis of official figures from the International Monetary Fund (IMF).
[a] Balance as of November.
[b] Does not include gold.
[c] Balance as of August.
[d] Balance as of October.
[e] Balance as of May.
[f] Balance as of July.

Table A-13

LATIN AMERICA AND THE CARIBBEAN: STOCK EXCHANGE INDICES

(National indices to end of period, 31 December 2000=100)

	2000	2001	2002	2003	2004	2005	2006	2007	2008	2009			
										I	II	III	IV[a]
Argentina	100	71	126	257	330	370	502	516	259	270	381	498	515
Brazil	100	89	74	146	172	219	291	419	246	268	337	403	439
Chile	100	109	92	137	166	181	248	281	219	229	285	311	300
Colombia	100	134	206	291	542	1 187	1 393	1 335	944	1 001	1 233	1 405	1 404
Costa Rica	100	113	117	104	88	96	169	193	177	114	116	123	117
Ecuador	100	130	195	178	216	272	353	329	349	342	302	275	300
Jamaica	100	117	157	234	390	362	348	374	277	273	280	277	288
Mexico	100	113	108	156	229	315	468	523	396	347	431	517	548
Peru	100	97	115	202	307	397	1 066	1 450	583	764	1 081	1 253	1 169
Trinidad and Tobago	100	98	124	157	243	242	220	222	191	186	176	178	176
Venezuela (Bolivarian Republic of)	100	96	117	325	439	299	765	555	514	640	653	738	782

Source: Economic Commission for Latin America and the Caribbean (ECLAC), on the basis of information from Bloomberg.
[a] Figures at 30 November.

Table A-14

LATIN AMERICA AND THE CARIBBEAN: OVERALL REAL EFFECTIVE EXCHANGE RATES [a]

(Indices 2000=100, deflacted by CPI)

	2001	2002	2003	2004	2005	2006	2007	2008[b]	2009[b c]
Latin America and the Caribbean [d]	**99.3**	**111.0**	**120.5**	**119.6**	**111.4**	**108.6**	**105.4**	**99.1**	**98.9**
Argentina	95.9	225.8	205.0	212.8	213.4	218.0	222.1	229.1	244.1
Barbados	98.3	100.0	104.3	107.4	105.8	104.0	104.9	102.9	98.7
Bolivia (Plurinational State of)	101.1	95.5	104.2	109.5	116.9	119.3	117.9	105.9	95.4
Brazil	120.4	132.6	131.2	123.8	100.4	88.9	82.5	79.2	81.9
Chile	111.7	109.4	114.7	108.5	103.2	100.9	102.5	101.7	105.9
Colombia	104.2	105.7	119.6	107.1	96.7	97.8	85.7	83.0	88.4
Costa Rica	97.5	98.6	104.4	106.0	107.3	106.1	103.5	100.0	99.8
Cuba [e]	90.5	94.1	99.8	106.1	105.4	112.3	115.1	125.9	...
Dominica	100.3	101.6	104.2	108.0	110.9	113.2	116.8	119.4	119.5
Dominican Republic [f]	96.5	98.6	131.4	125.6	87.5	95.7	95.9	98.5	102.2
Ecuador	70.7	61.8	60.3	61.6	64.7	65.3	68.1	68.7	64.4
El Salvador	99.7	99.7	100.2	98.9	101.0	101.4	102.7	103.7	99.8
Guatemala	96.3	88.6	88.7	85.8	79.3	76.9	76.3	72.2	74.3
Honduras	97.1	96.9	98.5	100.9	100.6	98.0	97.8	94.4	87.3
Jamaica	101.7	101.2	116.9	113.6	104.4	104.8	108.5	101.8	113.2
Mexico	94.4	94.0	104.5	108.3	104.6	104.7	105.8	108.1	124.2
Nicaragua	101.2	103.3	106.9	107.7	108.4	107.0	110.9	105.4	104.8
Panama	103.1	101.2	103.2	108.4	111.0	112.7	114.3	112.2	106.9
Paraguay	102.8	106.5	112.5	106.4	118.7	106.5	95.5	83.7	91.5
Peru	98.1	95.8	99.8	99.9	101.1	104.0	104.1	100.3	98.6
Trinidad and Tobago	94.6	91.1	91.9	93.6	91.0	89.1	87.6	83.1	76.4
Uruguay	101.4	118.4	150.5	152.5	134.1	128.3	127.0	116.0	115.2
Venezuela (Bolivarian Republic of)	95.3	125.1	141.1	139.5	141.0	132.4	118.6	96.6	74.2

Source: Economic Commission for Latin America and the Caribbean (ECLAC), on the basis of official figures from the International Monetary Fund (IMF).
[a] Annual averages. A country's overall real effective exchange rate index is calculated by weighting its real bilateral exchange rate indices with each of its trading partners by each partner's share in the country's total trade flows in terms of exports and imports. The extraregional real effective exchange rate index excludes trade with other Latin American and Caribbean countries. A currency depreciates in real effective terms when this index rises and appreciates when it falls.
[b] Preliminary figures, weighted by trade in 2007.
[c] January-October average.
[d] Simple average of the extraregional real effective exchange rate for 20 countries; excludes Barbados, Cuba and Dominica.
[e] Preliminary figures. Yearly calculation by ECLAC, based on consumer price data and nominal exchange rates provided by the National Statistical Office of Cuba.
[f] Owing to lack of data, the period 2002-2009 has been weighted using trade figures for 2001.

Table A-15
LATIN AMERICA AND THE CARIBBEAN: PARTICIPATION RATE
(Average annual rates)

		2000	2001	2002	2003	2004	2005	2006	2007	2008	2008	2009 [a]
											January to September average	
Argentina [b]	Urban areas	57.7	57.3	57.2	60.1	60.3	59.9	60.3	59.5	58.8	58.6	59.1
Barbados	National total	68.6	69.5	68.4	69.3	69.4	69.6	67.9	67.8	67.6	68.2	67.2 [c]
Brazil [b]	Six metropolitan areas	58.0	56.4	55.1	57.1	57.2	56.6	56.9	56.9	57.0	56.9	56.6 [d]
Chile	National total	54.4	53.9	53.7	54.4	55.0	55.6	54.8	54.9	56.0	56.0	55.9
Colombia	Thirteen metropolitan areas	63.5	64.4	64.8	65.1	63.6	63.4	62.0	61.8	62.6	62.7	64.4 [d]
Costa Rica	National total	53.6	55.8	55.4	55.5	54.4	56.8	56.6	57.0	56.7	56.7	56.5 [e]
Cuba [f]	National total	70.1	70.9	71.0	70.9	71.0	72.1	72.1	73.7	74.8	...	...
Dominican Republic	National total	55.2	54.3	55.1	54.7	56.3	55.9	56.0	56.1	55.6	55.7	53.6 [g]
Ecuador [h]	Urban total	57.3	63.1	58.3	58.2	59.1	59.5	59.1	61.2	60.1	60.7	59.4
Honduras	National total	...	52.5	51.7	50.0	50.6	50.9	50.7	50.7	51.0	50.7	53.1 [i]
Jamaica [j]	National total	63.3	63.0	63.6	64.4	64.3	64.2	64.7	64.9	65.4	65.3	63.8 [k]
Mexico	Urban areas	58.7	58.1	57.8	58.3	58.9	59.5	60.7	60.7	60.4	60.6	60.3 [d]
Panama	National total	59.9	60.5	62.6	62.8	63.5	63.5	62.6	62.7	63.9	63.9	64.1 [l]
Peru	Metropolitan Lima	64.4	66.7	68.4	67.4	68.1	67.1	67.4	68.9	68.1	68.5	67.9
Trinidad and Tobago	National total	61.2	60.7	60.9	61.6	63.0	63.7	63.9	63.5	63.5	63.0	63.3 [m]
Uruguay	Urban total	59.6	60.6	59.1	58.1	58.5	58.5	60.9	62.7	62.6	62.3	63.3 [d]
Venezuela (Bolivarian Republic of)	National total	64.6	66.5	68.7	69.2	68.5	66.3	65.4	64.9	64.7	64.9	65.1 [d]

Source: Economic Commission for Latin America and the Caribbean (ECLAC), on the basis of official figures.
[a] Preliminary figures.
[b] New measurements have been used since 2003; the data are not comparable with the previous series.
[c] The figures of the last two columns refer to the average for January-June.
[d] The figures of the last two columns refer to the average for January-October.
[e] The figures of the last two columns refer to the measurement of July.
[f] In Cuba, the working-age population is measured as follows: for males, 17 to 59 years and for females, 15 to 54 years.
[g] The figures of the last two columns refer to the data for April.
[h] New measurements have been used since 2007; the data are not comparable with the previous series.
[i] The figures of the last two columns refer to the data for May.
[j] New measurements have been used since 2002; the data are not comparable with the previous series.
[k] The figures of the last two columns refer to the average of the January, April and July data.
[l] The figures of the last two columns refer to the data for August.
[m] The figures of the last two columns refer to the average of the March and June data.

Table A-16
LATIN AMERICA AND THE CARIBBEAN: OPEN URBAN UNEMPLOYMENT
(Average annual rates)

		2000	2001	2002	2003	2004	2005	2006	2007	2008	2009 [a]
Latin America and the Caribbean [b]		**10.4**	**10.2**	**11.1**	**11.0**	**10.3**	**9.1**	**8.6**	**7.9**	**7.4**	**8.3**
Argentina [c]	Urban areas	15.1	17.4	19.7	17.3	13.6	11.6	10.2	8.5	7.9	8.8 [d]
Bahamas [e]	National total	...	6.9	9.1	10.8	10.2	10.2	7.6	7.9	8.7	12.4
Barbados [e]	National total	9.2	9.9	10.3	11.0	9.8	9.1	8.7	7.4	8.1	10.0 [f]
Belize [e]	National total	11.1	9.1	10.0	12.9	11.6	11.0	9.4	8.5	8.2	...
Bolivia (Plurinational State of)	Urban total	7.5	8.5	8.7	9.2	6.2	8.1	8.0	7.7	6.7	6.8
Brazil [g]	Six metropolitan areas	7.1	6.2	11.7	12.3	11.5	9.8	10.0	9.3	7.9	8.1 [h]
Chile	National total	9.7	9.9	9.8	9.5	10.0	9.2	7.7	7.1	7.8	9.8 [h]
Colombia [e]	Thirteen metropolitan areas	17.3	18.2	18.1	17.1	15.8	14.3	13.1	11.4	11.5	13.0 [h]
Costa Rica	Urban total	5.3	5.8	6.8	6.7	6.7	6.9	6.0	4.8	4.8	7.6
Cuba	National total	5.4	4.1	3.3	2.3	1.9	1.9	1.9	1.8	1.6	...
Dominican Republic [e]	National total	13.9	15.6	16.1	16.7	18.4	17.9	16.2	15.6	14.1	14.9 [i]
Ecuador [e] [j]	Urban total [k]	14.1	10.4	8.6	9.8	9.7	8.5	8.1	7.4	6.9	8.6 [d]
El Salvador [j]	Urban total	6.5	7.0	6.2	6.2	6.5	7.3	5.7	5.8	5.5	...
Guatemala	Urban total	...	...	5.4	5.2	4.4	...	...	...	...	...
Honduras	Urban total	...	5.9	6.1	7.6	8.0	6.5	4.9	4.0	4.1	4.9 [i]
Jamaica [e] [g]	National total	15.5	15.0	14.2	11.4	11.7	11.3	10.3	9.8	10.6	11.3 [m]
Mexico	Urban areas	3.4	3.6	3.9	4.6	5.3	4.7	4.6	4.8	4.9	6.8 [h]
Nicaragua	Urban total	7.8	11.3	11.6	10.2	9.3	7.0	7.0	6.9	8.0	...
Panama [e]	Urban total	15.2	17.0	16.5	15.9	14.1	12.1	10.4	7.8	6.5	7.9
Paraguay	Urban total	10.0	10.8	14.7	11.2	10.0	7.6	8.9	7.2	7.4	...
Peru	Metropolitan Lima	8.5	9.3	9.4	9.4	9.4	9.6	8.5	8.4	8.4	8.3 [h]
Suriname	National total	14.0	14.0	10.0	7.0	8.4	11.2	12.1	...	...	...
Trinidad and Tobago [e]	National total	12.2	10.8	10.4	10.5	8.4	8.0	6.2	5.6	4.6	5.1 [n]
Uruguay	Urban total	13.6	15.3	17.0	16.9	13.1	12.2	11.4	9.6	7.9	7.7 [h]
Venezuela (Bolivarian Republic of)	National total	13.9	13.3	15.8	18.0	15.3	12.4	10.0	8.4	7.4	8.0 [h]

Source: Economic Commission for Latin America and the Caribbean (ECLAC), on the basis of official figures.
[a] Preliminary figures.
[b] The data for Argentina and Brazil have been adjusted to reflect changes in methodology in 2003 and 2002, respectively.
[c] New measurements have been used since 2003; the data are not comparable with the previous series.
[d] Estimate based on data from January to September.
[e] Includes hidden unemployment.
[f] January-June average.
[g] New measurements have been used since 2002; the data are not comparable with the previous series.
[h] Estimate based on data from January to October.
[i] Figure for April.
[j] New measurements have been used since 2007; the data are not comparable with the previous series.
[k] Up to 2003, the figures relate to Cuenca, Guayaquil and Quito.
[l] Figure for May.
[m] Average of the January, April and July data.
[n] Average of the March and June data.

Table A-17
LATIN AMERICA AND THE CARIBBEAN: EMPLOYMENT RATE
(Employed population as a percentage of working-age population, average annual rates)

		2000	2001	2002	2003	2004	2005	2006	2007	2008	2008	2009 [a]
											January to September average	
Argentina [b]	Urban areas	49.0	47.4	45.9	49.8	52.0	52.9	54.1	54.5	54.2	53.9	53.9
Barbados	National total	62.8	62.7	61.4	61.6	62.7	63.2	61.9	62.7	62.1	62.6	60.4 [c]
Brazil [b]	Six metropolitan areas	53.8	52.9	48.7	50.1	50.6	51.0	51.2	51.6	52.5	52.4	51.9 [d]
Chile	National total	49.1	48.6	48.4	49.3	49.5	50.4	50.5	51.0	51.7	51.5	50.3 [e]
Colombia	Thirteen metropolitan areas	52.6	52.7	53.4	54.2	53.8	54.5	54.0	54.8	55.3	55.4	55.9 [d]
Costa Rica	National total	50.8	52.4	51.8	51.8	50.9	53.0	53.3	54.4	53.9	53.9	52.1 [f]
Cuba [g]	National total	66.3	68.0	68.6	69.2	69.7	70.7	70.7	72.4	73.6	...	...
Dominican Republic	National total	47.6	45.8	46.2	45.4	46.0	45.9	46.9	47.4	47.7	47.8	45.4 [h]
Ecuador [i]	Urban total	52.1	56.2	52.9	51.5	53.5	54.4	54.3	56.8	56.0	56.6	54.3
Honduras	National total	...	50.3	49.7	47.4	48.6	48.6	49.0	49.2	49.4	49.2	51.5 [j]
Jamaica [k]	National total	53.4	53.5	54.0	57.1	56.8	57.0	58.0	58.6	58.5	58.3	56.6 [l]
Mexico	Urban areas	56.8	56.0	55.5	55.6	55.8	56.7	57.9	57.8	57.5	57.7	56.2 [d]
Panama	National total	51.8	52.0	54.1	54.6	55.9	57.3	57.2	58.7	60.3	60.3	59.9 [m]
Peru	Metropolitan Lima	59.7	60.5	62.0	61.1	61.6	60.7	61.8	63.0	62.4	62.7	62.1
Trinidad and Tobago	National total	53.8	53.8	54.6	55.2	57.8	58.6	59.9	59.9	57.7	59.9	60.1 [n]
Uruguay	Urban total	51.6	51.4	49.1	48.3	50.9	51.4	53.9	56.7	57.7	57.3	58.4 [d]
Venezuela (Bolivarian Republic of)	National total	55.5	57.6	57.8	56.8	58.1	58.1	58.9	59.5	59.9	59.9	59.9 [d]

Source: Economic Commission for Latin America and the Caribbean (ECLAC), on the basis of official figures.
[a] Preliminary figures.
[b] New measurements have been used since 2003; the data are not comparable with the previous series.
[c] The figures of the last two columns refer to the period January-June.
[d] The figures of the last two columns refer to the period January-October.
[e] The figures of the last two columns refer to the measurement of September.
[f] The figures of the last two columns refer to the measurement of July.
[g] In Cuba, the working-age population is measured as follows: for males, 17 to 59 years and for females, 15 to 54 years.
[h] The figures of the last two columns refer to the measurement of April.
[i] New measurements have been used since 2007; the data are not comparable with the previous series.
[j] The figures of the last two columns refer to the measurement of May.
[k] New measurements have been used since 2002; the data are not comparable with the previous series.
[l] The figures of the last two columns refer to the average of the January, April and July data.
[m] The figures of the last two columns refer to the measurement of August.
[n] The figures of the last two columns refer to the average of the March and June data.

Table A-18
LATIN AMERICA AND THE CARIBBEAN: TRENDS IN REAL AVERAGE WAGES
(Average annual Index, 2000=100)

	2000	2001	2002	2003	2004	2005	2006	2007	2008	2009 [a]
Argentina [b]	100.0	99.2	85.4	83.9	92.2	99.0	107.8	117.6	127.9	142.8 [c]
Brazil [d]	100.0	95.1	93.1	84.9	85.5	85.2	88.2	89.5	91.4	93.3 [c]
Chile [e]	100.0	101.7	103.7	104.6	106.5	108.5	110.6	113.7	113.5	119.0 [f]
Colombia [b]	100.0	99.7	102.7	102.0	103.7	105.3	109.4	109.0	106.9	107.8 [c]
Costa Rica [g]	100.0	101.0	105.1	105.5	102.8	100.8	102.4	103.8	101.7	111.3 [c]
Cuba	100.0	96.2	105.1	107.8	114.6	129.5	144.5	143.1	140.5	...
Guatemala [g]	100.0	100.5	99.6	100.0	97.8	93.9	92.9	91.4	89.0	...
Mexico [b]	100.0	106.7	108.7	110.1	110.4	110.7	112.3	113.4	115.9	116.6 [c]
Nicaragua [g]	100.0	101.0	104.5	106.5	104.2	104.5	105.9	104.0	100.1	107.8 [c]
Panama [h]	100.0	98.8	95.8	95.3	94.5	93.4	95.3	96.5	95.9	...
Paraguay	100.0	101.4	96.3	95.6	97.2	98.2	98.8	101.1	100.4	104.7 [i]
Peru [j]	100.0	99.1	103.7	105.3	106.5	104.4	105.7	103.8	106.1	106.4 [k]
Uruguay	100.0	99.7	89.0	77.9	77.9	81.5	85.0	89.0	92.2	98.9 [f]
Venezuela (Bolivarian Republic of)	100.0	106.9	95.1	78.4	78.6	80.7	84.8	85.8	81.9	77.4 [c]

Source: Economic Commission for Latin America and the Caribbean (ECLAC), on the basis of official figures.
[a] Preliminary figures.
[b] Manufacturing. From 2005, registered private-sector workers.
[c] Estimate based on data from January to September.
[d] Workers covered by social and labour legislation. Since 2003, only the private sector.
[e] General index of hourly wages.
[f] Estimate based on data from January to October.
[g] Average wages declared by workers covered by social security.
[h] Average wages declared by workers covered by social security. The variation in wages between 2006 and 2007 refers to workers of small, medium-sized and large businesses.
[i] Figure for June.
[j] Private sector workers in the Lima metropolitan area.
[k] Estimate based on June data.

Table A-19
LATIN AMERICA AND THE CARIBBEAN: MONETARY INDICATORS
(Percentages of GDP, end-of-year balances)

	Monetary base				Money Supply (M3) [a]				Foreign-currency deposits			
	2006	2007	2008	2009 [b]	2006	2007	2008	2009 [b]	2006	2007	2008	2009 [b]
Antigua and Barbuda	14.8	13.2	12.1	...	90.7	88.3	91.8	...	7.4	9.0	8.3	...
Argentina	11.7	11.9	10.3	9.8 [c]	25.8	26.1	22.4	22.7	2.3	2.6	2.7	3.6
Bahamas	7.8	9.0	8.5	...	69.6	74.7	77.9	...	2.2	2.7	2.7	...
Barbados	13.0	16.1	16.0	...	110.8	118.6	118.9	... [d]	11.3	19.8	14.8	... [d]
Belize	13.2	13.2	13.8	... [e]	62.0	68.0	70.9	... [c]	...	...	...	...
Bolivia (Plurinational State of)	12.2	16.9	18.5	20.5 [c]	42.4	47.8	46.5	52.3 [c]	26.7	23.9	20.3	23.4 [c]
Brazil	5.1	5.6	5.1	4.8 [c]	27.9	30.1	37.1	36.6 [f]	...	...	...	...
Chile	4.5	4.3	4.8	5.1 [e]	53.2	58.2	69.6	67.1 [e]	4.7	4.8	9.1	7.7 [e]
Colombia	7.1	7.5	7.7	6.7 [c,g]	31.9	33.4	35.3	33.8 [f]	...	...	...	...
Costa Rica	6.7	7.6	7.4	7.0	44.3	43.8	47.1	50.2 [e]	20.8	18.2	22.1	25.2 [e]
Cuba	26.0	23.6	31.1	...	38.6	37.2	41.9	... [f]	...	...	...	...
Dominica	17.2	16.8	13.1	14.7	90.3	90.8	87.2	96.2	1.4	1.1	1.5	1.5
Dominican Republic	9.0	8.9	8.5	7.6 [e]	25.2	25.7	24.3	24.6	...	...	...	...
Ecuador	...	10.0	11.7	9.8	...	25.9	35.3	32.3 [f]	...	...	...	...
El Salvador	9.3	10.2	10.4	10.7	38.0	49.9	42.4	43.1 [f]	...	...	...	...
Grenada	17.2	18.4	15.7	...	97.3	99.8	95.7	...	5.0	7.3	6.9	...
Guatemala	11.1	10.9	9.7	9.9 [c]	37.8	37.1	35.4	37.3 [c]	4.2	4.7	4.8	6.2 [c]
Guyana	27.7	25.1	25.7	...	78.5	75.1	78.0	...	...	...	...	...
Haiti	20.0	19.4	18.6	19.8	37.9	35.8	33.9	36.0	15.6	15.2	14.8	16.8
Honduras	9.6	11.2	11.2	9.1	55.0	56.5	51.4	48.3	13.8	14.0	13.3	12.8
Jamaica	7.4	7.3	7.0	6.7 [c]	32.6	33.6	30.8	29.3	9.6	10.9	10.1	10.2
Mexico	4.3	4.4	4.8	4.5 [c]	49.3	50.2	54.5	57.6 [c]	1.4	1.3	1.4	1.6 [c]
Nicaragua	8.7	9.4	8.4	7.4 [d]	39.4	41.2	37.5	38.7 [c]	25.8	27.0	25.6	27.9 [c]
Panama	4.9	5.1	4.4	4.3	86.1	87.5	...	...	...	...	...	...
Paraguay	9.2	10.5	10.3	11.6	26.8	30.0	31.3	36.0	10.6	10.7	12.1	14.9
Peru	4.6	5.3	6.0	5.4 [e]	24.3	26.9	30.3	29.3 [c]	12.4	12.4	14.2	13.2 [c]
Saint Kitts and Nevis	18.3	18.7	17.8	30.8	98.7	104.2	107.2	128.7	30.9	32.0	25.9	29.7
Saint Vincent and the Grenadines	14.5	15.5	14.5	...	69.9	67.2	68.2	...	2.3	2.6	2.3	...
Saint Lucia	13.4	14.1	14.4	16.5	81.8	84.4	92.6	98.7	8.3	4.3	6.0	6.5
Suriname	17.2	19.5	17.6	22.0 [c]	61.0	68.2	61.3	71.0	29.2	32.6	28.4	31.4
Trinidad and Tobago	7.2	7.0	8.6	...	37.4	37.2	35.7	... [d]	9.1	9.0	9.9	... [d]
Uruguay	4.5	5.5	5.3	4.3 [c]	56.5	48.8	54.5	51.3 [d]	45.3	36.4	42.2	40.3 [d]

Source: Economic Commission for Latin America and the Caribbean (ECLAC), on the basis of official figures.
[a] According to the ECLAC definition, this corresponds to M1 plus savings and time deposits in national currency plus foreign currency deposits.
[b] Balance as of September.
[c] Balance as of October.
[d] Balance as of August.
[e] Balance as of November.
[f] Refers to M2.
[g] According to the country's definition, this also includes deposits of entities in liquidation and term deposit certificates of special entities and demand deposits of non-bank entities.

Table A-20
LATIN AMERICA AND THE CARIBBEAN: REPRESENTATIVE LENDING RATES
(Annual average of monthly annualized rates)

	2000	2001	2002	2003	2004	2005	2006	2007	2008	2009 [a]
Antigua and Barbuda [b]	...	...	...	...	...	11.2	10.7	10.3	10.1	9.8
Argentina [c]	11.1	26.5	53.0	19.1	6.8	6.2	8.6	11.1	19.5	21.3 [d]
Bahamas [e]	...	...	...	12.0	11.2	10.3	10.0	10.6	11.0	10.6 [f]
Barbados [c]	...	...	...	7.6	7.4	8.5	10.0	10.4	9.7	8.8 [g]
Belize [h]	16.0	15.5	14.8	14.4	13.9	14.2	14.2	14.3	14.2	14.1 [i]
Bolivia (Plurinational State of) [j]	...	13.7	10.9	9.1	8.2	8.2	7.8	8.2	8.9	8.6
Brazil [k]	41.9	41.1	44.4	49.8	41.1	43.7	40.0	34.5	38.8	41.1
Chile [l]	18.7	16.7	14.4	13.0	11.0	13.5	14.4	13.6	15.2	13.4
Colombia [m]	18.8	20.7	16.3	15.2	15.1	14.6	12.9	15.4	17.2	13.6
Costa Rica [n]	28.1	26.7	26.8	26.2	23.4	24.0	22.7	17.3	16.7	21.7
Cuba [o]	...	...	...	9.6	9.7	9.8	9.4	9.1	9.0	...
Dominica [b]	...	...	...	...	...	9.9	9.5	9.2	9.1	10.0
Dominican Republic [c]	23.6	20.0	21.3	27.8	30.3	21.4	15.7	11.7	16.0	14.0 [f]
Ecuador [p]	15.2	15.5	14.1	12.6	10.2	8.7	8.9	10.1	9.8	9.2
El Salvador [q]	10.7	9.6	7.1	6.6	6.3	6.9	7.5	7.8	7.9	9.4
Grenada [b]	...	...	...	...	...	10.0	9.8	9.7	9.4	10.8
Guatemala [b]	20.9	19.0	16.9	15.0	13.8	13.0	12.8	12.8	13.4	13.9
Guyana [c]	17.2	17.3	17.3	16.6	16.6	15.1	14.9	14.1	13.9	14.0
Haiti [r]	25.1	28.6	25.5	30.7	34.1	27.1	29.5	31.2	23.3	21.7
Honduras [b]	26.8	23.8	22.7	20.8	19.9	18.8	17.4	16.6	17.9	19.6
Jamaica [s]	32.9	29.4	26.1	25.1	25.1	23.2	22.0	22.0	22.3	22.8
Mexico [t]	16.9	12.8	8.2	6.9	7.2	9.9	7.5	7.6	8.7	7.6 [f]
Nicaragua [u]	18.1	18.6	18.3	15.5	13.5	12.1	11.6	13.0	13.2	14.1 [f]
Panama [v]	10.3	10.6	9.2	8.9	8.2	8.2	8.1	8.3	8.2	8.3 [f]
Paraguay [w]	26.8	28.3	34.3	30.5	21.2	15.3	16.6	14.6	14.6	16.2 [f]
Peru [x]	...	...	22.3	20.2	18.7	17.9	17.1	16.5	16.7	16.3
Saint Kitts and Nevis [b]	...	...	...	...	...	9.9	9.2	9.3	8.6	8.6
Saint Vincent and the Grenadines [b]	...	...	...	...	...	9.6	9.7	9.6	9.5	9.2
Saint Lucia [b]	...	...	...	...	...	10.4	10.5	9.9	9.3	9.4
Suriname [t]	29.0	25.7	22.2	21.0	20.4	18.1	15.7	13.8	12.2	12.0 [d]
Trinidad and Tobago [c]	16.5	15.6	13.4	11.0	9.4	9.1	10.2	10.5	12.3	12.6 [d]
Uruguay [y]	32.1	38.1	116.4	56.6	26.0	15.3	10.7	10.0	13.1	16.9 [f]
Venezuela (Bolivarian Republic of) [z]	24.5	24.8	38.4	25.7	17.3	15.6	14.6	16.7	22.8	21.0

Source: Economic Commission for Latin America and the Caribbean (ECLAC), on the basis of official figures.
[a] Average monthly rate from January to October.
[b] Weighted average lending rates.
[c] Prime lending rate.
[d] Average monthly rate from January to July.
[e] Interest rate on loans and overdrafts, weighted average.
[f] Average monthly rate from January to September.
[g] Average monthly rate from January to August.
[h] Rate for personal and business loans, residential and other construction loans; weighted average.
[i] Average monthly rate from January to March.
[j] Nominal dollar rate for 60-91-day banking operations.
[k] Preset lending rates for legal persons.
[l] Lending rates for periods of 90-360 days, non-adjustable operations.
[m] Total lending rate of the system. Weighted average of all lending rates.
[n] Average rate of the financial system for loans in national currency.
[o] Corporate lending rate in convertible pesos.
[p] Benchmark dollar lending rate.
[q] Basic lending rate for up to 1 year.
[r] Average of minimum and maximum lending rates.
[s] Average interest rate on loans.
[t] Lending rate published by the International Monetary Fund.
[u] Weighted average of the weekly lending rate for loans in national currency in the system.
[v] Interest rate on 1-year trade credit.
[w] Weighted average of effective lending rates in national currency, not including overdrafts or credit cards.
[x] Average lending rate, constant structure.
[y] Business credit, 30-367 days.
[z] Average rate for loan operations for the six major commercial banks.

Table A-21
LATIN AMERICA AND THE CARIBBEAN: CONSUMER PRICES
(Percentage variation December-December)

	2000	2001	2002	2003	2004	2005	2006	2007	2008	2009 [a]
Latin America and the Caribbean [b]	**9.0**	**6.1**	**12.2**	**8.5**	**7.4**	**6.1**	**5.0**	**6.5**	**8.2**	**4.5**
Antigua and Barbuda	...	...	2.5	1.8	2.8	2.5	0.0	5.2	2.3	...
Argentina	-0.7	-1.5	41.0	3.7	6.1	12.3	9.8	8.5	7.2	6.5
Bahamas	1.0	2.9	1.9	2.6	1.4	2.2	2.0	2.4	4.8	0.8 [c]
Barbados	3.8	-1.2	0.9	0.3	4.3	7.4	5.6	4.7	7.3	1.4 [d]
Belize	0.6	1.1	2.3	2.6	3.1	4.2	3.0	4.1	4.4	-3.5 [c]
Bolivia (Plurinational State of)	3.4	0.9	2.5	3.9	4.6	4.9	4.9	11.7	11.8	0.8
Brazil	6.0	7.7	12.5	9.3	7.6	5.7	3.1	4.5	5.9	4.2
Chile	4.5	2.6	2.8	1.1	2.4	3.7	2.6	7.8	7.1	-1.9
Colombia	8.8	7.6	7.0	6.5	5.5	4.9	4.5	5.7	7.7	2.7
Costa Rica	10.2	11.0	9.7	9.9	13.1	14.1	9.4	10.8	13.9	4.0
Cuba [e]	...	-1.4	7.3	-3.8	2.9	3.7	5.7	10.6	-0.1	-1.7
Dominica	1.1	1.1	0.5	2.8	0.8	2.7	1.8	6.0	2.0	...
Dominican Republic	9.0	4.4	10.5	42.7	28.7	7.5	5.0	8.9	4.5	-0.3
Ecuador	91.0	22.4	9.4	6.1	1.9	3.1	2.9	3.3	8.8	3.5
El Salvador	4.3	1.4	2.8	2.5	5.4	4.3	4.9	4.9	5.5	-1.6
Grenada	3.4	-0.7	2.3	1.2	2.5	6.2	1.7	7.4	5.2	...
Guatemala	5.1	8.9	6.3	5.9	9.2	8.6	5.8	8.7	9.4	-0.7
Guyana	5.8	1.5	6.0	...	...	8.2	4.2	14.1	6.4	1.3 [f]
Haiti	19.0	8.1	14.8	40.4	20.2	15.4	10.2	10.0	10.1	-3.5
Honduras	10.1	8.8	8.1	6.8	9.2	7.7	5.3	8.9	10.8	2.7
Jamaica	6.1	8.7	7.3	14.1	13.7	12.9	5.8	16.8	16.9	7.7
Mexico	9.0	4.4	5.7	4.0	5.2	3.3	4.1	3.8	6.5	4.5
Nicaragua	9.9	4.7	4.0	6.6	8.9	9.6	10.2	16.2	12.7	-0.1
Panama	0.7	0.0	1.8	1.5	1.5	3.4	2.2	6.4	6.8	0.7
Paraguay	8.6	8.4	14.6	9.3	2.8	9.9	12.5	6.0	7.5	2.8
Peru	3.7	-0.1	1.5	2.5	3.5	1.5	1.1	3.9	6.6	0.7
Saint Kitts and Nevis	...	...	1.7	3.1	1.7	6.0	7.9	2.1	7.6	...
Saint Vincent and the Grenadines	0.4	5.5	-0.7	0.5	1.7	3.9	4.8	8.3	8.7	...
Saint Lucia	1.4	-0.2	0.4	2.7	...	...	...	6.8	3.8	...
Suriname	76.2	...	...	13.5	9.7	15.8	4.7	8.3	9.4	-5.4 [c]
Trinidad and Tobago	5.6	3.2	4.3	3.0	5.6	7.2	9.1	7.6	14.5	2.7
Uruguay	5.1	3.6	25.9	10.2	7.6	4.9	6.4	8.5	9.2	6.5
Venezuela (Bolivarian Republic of)	13.4	12.3	31.2	27.1	19.2	14.4	17.0	22.5	31.9	28.9

Source: Economic Commission for Latin America and the Caribbean (ECLAC), on the basis of official figures.
[a] Twelve-month variation to October 2009.
[b] The only English-speaking Caribbean countries included are Barbados, Jamaica and Trinidad and Tobago.
[c] Twelve-month variation to September 2009.
[d] Twelve-month variation to July 2009.
[e] Refers to national-currency markets.
[f] Variation January-June 2009.

Table A-22
LATIN AMERICA AND THE CARIBBEAN: CENTRAL GOVERNMENT BALANCE
(Percentages of GDP)

	Primary balance					Overall balance				
	2005	2006	2007	2008	2009 [a]	2005	2006	2007	2008	2009 [a]
Latin America and the Caribbean	**2.2**	**1.8**	**2.1**	**1.5**	**-0.1**	**-1.1**	**-1.3**	**-0.6**	**-1.2**	**-2.6**
Latin America	**1.2**	**2.3**	**2.3**	**1.0**	**-1.0**	**-1.1**	**0.1**	**0.3**	**-0.6**	**-2.8**
Latin America (exc. Cuba)	**1.5**	**2.5**	**2.5**	**1.4**	**-1.0**	**-1.0**	**0.3**	**0.5**	**-0.3**	**-2.8**
Argentina [b]	2.3	2.7	2.7	2.8	1.4	0.4	1.0	0.6	0.7	-0.8
Bolivia (Plurinational State of) [c]	0.4	5.3	3.5	0.8	-1.4	-2.3	3.5	2.3	-0.0	-3.2
Brazil [d]	2.5	2.1	2.3	2.5	0.9	-3.6	-2.9	-1.9	-1.3	-2.9
Chile	5.4	8.4	9.4	5.8	-3.1	4.6	7.7	8.8	5.3	-3.6
Colombia [e]	-1.2	0.1	1.0	0.9	-0.6	-4.1	-3.5	-2.7	-2.3	-3.7
Costa Rica	2.0	2.7	3.7	2.4	-1.5	-2.1	-1.1	0.6	0.2	-3.8
Cuba	-3.3	-2.0	-1.8	-5.3	...	-4.6	-3.2	-3.2	-6.7	...
Dominican Republic [f]	0.7	0.3	1.4	-1.6	-1.4	-0.6	-1.1	0.1	-3.2	-3.0
Ecuador [g]	2.9	5.4	4.0	-0.2	-3.1	0.7	3.3	2.1	-1.5	-3.8
El Salvador	1.1	2.0	2.2	1.7	0.8	-1.0	-0.4	-0.2	-0.6	-2.3
Guatemala [h]	-0.3	-0.6	0.0	-0.3	-1.9	-1.7	-1.9	-1.4	-1.6	-3.4
Haiti	0.5	0.8	-1.2	-0.9	-1.4	-0.5	-0.0	-1.6	-1.2	-1.7
Honduras	-1.1	-0.1	-2.3	-1.7	-3.6	-2.2	-1.1	-2.9	-2.3	-4.2
Mexico [i]	1.9	2.1	1.9	1.6	0.1	-0.1	0.1	0.0	-0.1	-2.1
Nicaragua	0.1	1.8	1.9	0.0	-2.1	-1.8	0.0	0.4	-1.2	-3.5
Panama [j]	0.5	4.4	4.7	3.4	1.3	-3.9	0.2	1.2	0.3	-1.8
Paraguay [h]	2.0	1.5	1.8	3.3	-0.0	0.8	0.5	1.0	2.6	-0.7
Peru	1.1	3.2	3.5	3.6	-0.1	-0.7	1.5	1.8	2.2	-1.4
Uruguay	2.7	3.2	2.1	1.7	0.6	-1.6	-1.0	-1.6	-1.0	-2.1
Venezuela (Bolivarian Republic of)	4.6	2.1	4.5	0.1	-4.1	1.6	0.0	3.0	-1.2	-5.5
The Caribbean [k]	**3.7**	**1.2**	**1.8**	**2.3**	**1.3**	**-1.0**	**-3.5**	**-2.1**	**-2.0**	**-2.3**
Antigua and Barbuda	21.8	-4.3	-3.1	-3.6	-4.5	18.0	-7.8	-6.4	-6.7	-7.1
Bahamas	0.2	0.9	0.2	0.6	-2.7	-2.6	-1.5	-2.4	-2.0	-3.0
Barbados	0.6	3.1	2.8	-0.5	0.1	-4.3	-2.0	-1.8	-5.9	-3.2
Belize	3.5	2.8	4.3	4.1	1.6	-3.4	-4.2	0.0	0.3	1.2
Dominica	5.8	5.4	4.0	4.2	4.2	2.6	1.4	1.0	0.8	2.2
Grenada	5.6	-4.5	-4.6	-4.2	-3.6	3.7	-6.4	-6.6	-6.1	-5.8
Guyana	-9.1	-9.3	-4.6	-5.1	-4.0	-13.5	-13.1	-7.5	-7.9	-6.5
Jamaica	11.1	8.8	8.1	5.6	3.0	-3.5	-5.3	-4.7	-7.4	-11.0
Saint Kitts and Nevis	4.0	6.0	6.0	8.9	19.7	-4.1	-2.4	-2.4	0.4	10.9
Saint Vincent and the Grenadines	-1.3	-0.7	-0.6	2.1	0.7	-4.2	-3.9	-3.6	-1.3	-3.0
Saint Lucia	-3.5	-3.0	0.9	2.9	5.5	-6.5	-6.1	-2.1	-0.2	1.3
Suriname	1.7	1.7	5.7	5.8	0.8	-0.8	-0.6	7.1	2.3	-1.0
Trinidad and Tobago	7.5	8.3	3.7	9.7	-3.3	5.0	6.3	1.8	7.8	-5.3

Source: Economic Commission for Latin America and the Caribbean (ECLAC), on the basis of official figures.
[a] Preliminary figures.
[b] National public administration, on an accrual basis.
[c] General government.
[d] Central government. The figures are derived from the primary balance based on the-below- the-line criterion and nominal interest.
[e] Central national government. Does not include the cost of financial restructuring.
[f] Accrual basis. The primary balance and the overall balance includes the residue.
[g] Non-financial public sector, on an accrual basis.
[h] Central administration.
[i] Public sector. Balances include non-recurrent income from the sale of companies and the non-budgetary balance.
[j] The overall balance for 2005 includes an adjustment for compensation to bondholders amounting to 111.6 million balboas.
[k] Fiscal year.

Table A-23
LATIN AMERICA AND THE CARIBBEAN: REVENUE AND EXPENDITURES OF THE CENTRAL GOVERNMENT
(Percentages of GDP)

	Total revenue			Tax revenue			Total expenditure		
	2007	2008	2009 [a]	2007	2008	2009 [a]	2007	2008	2009 [a]
Latin America and the Caribbean	**23.8**	**24.2**	**22.7**	**18.6**	**18.6**	**...**	**24.5**	**25.2**	**25.2**
Latin America	**21.7**	**21.8**	**19.1**	**16.3**	**15.9**	**...**	**21.3**	**22.5**	**22.0**
Latin America (exc. Cuba)	**20.4**	**20.5**	**19.1**	**15.6**	**15.5**	**...**	**19.9**	**20.9**	**22.0**
Argentina	18.2	19.3	20.9	17.2	18.0	18.9	17.5	18.6	21.7
Bolivia (Plurinational State of) [b]	32.7	32.7	28.5	18.3	19.5	...	30.5	32.7	31.8
Brazil	23.8	24.7	24.4	23.8	24.7	24.4	25.7	26.0	27.3
Chile [c]	27.5	26.4	21.8	20.2	20.1	16.2	[d] 18.7	21.1	25.4
Colombia [e]	15.0	15.7	16.1	13.4	13.5	13.6	17.6	18.1	19.8
Costa Rica [f]	15.5	15.9	14.5	15.2	15.6	13.9	[g] 14.9	15.7	18.3
Cuba	46.0	45.9	...	27.7	23.6	...	49.2	52.6	...
Dominican Republic [f]	17.7	15.9	15.4	16.0	15.0	...	17.6	19.6	18.4
Ecuador [h]	29.4	37.7	33.8	20.9	21.0	23.7	27.3	39.2	37.6
El Salvador [f]	14.6	14.7	14.2	13.4	13.0	12.6	[g] 14.8	15.3	16.5
Guatemala	12.9	12.1	10.7	12.3	11.6	9.9	14.3	13.7	14.1
Haiti [f]	10.9	9.6	9.4	10.3	9.5	9.3	12.4	10.8	11.1
Honduras [f]	19.1	19.3	17.5	16.3	15.6	...	[g] 21.9	21.7	21.7
Mexico [i]	22.3	23.8	22.4	9.0	8.3	9.4	[j] 22.3	23.8	24.6
Nicaragua [f]	23.3	21.9	20.7	18.1	17.6	16.5	22.9	23.1	24.3
Panama [f]	19.5	19.7	19.2	10.7	10.6	...	18.3	19.5	21.0
Paraguay	17.6	18.3	18.9	12.6	13.7	14.2	[g] 16.7	15.7	19.6
Peru	18.2	18.3	15.9	15.6	15.6	13.8	16.4	16.1	17.3
Uruguay	20.3	19.4	20.9	17.8	17.2	17.6	21.8	20.4	23.0
Venezuela (Bolivarian Republic of)	28.9	24.7	18.4	16.1	13.5	...	[k] 25.8	25.8	23.9
The Caribbean [l]	**29.1**	**30.3**	**33.8**	**24.6**	**25.4**	**...**	**32.4**	**32.1**	**35.3**
Antigua and Barbuda	24.0	23.8	24.6	22.1	21.3	23.2	30.5	30.5	31.7
Bahamas	17.8	16.9	...	16.1	15.5	...	20.3	18.0	...
Barbados	...	...	...	...	...	...	...	...	...
Belize	...	...	...	...	...	...	...	...	...
Dominica	...	...	...	...	...	...	...	...	...
Grenada	27.2	28.2	29.3	24.4	23.7	27.0	33.8	34.3	35.1
Guyana	...	...	...	...	...	...	...	...	...
Jamaica	32.3	31.1	...	27.7	26.5	...	37.1	38.4	...
Saint Kitts and Nevis	41.9	41.7	51.2	28.8	27.0	31.0	44.3	41.2	40.3
Saint Vincent and the Grenadines	30.5	34.3	34.0	26.7	28.1	30.2	34.1	35.6	37.1
Saint Lucia	27.4	29.6	36.5	25.5	27.1	33.7	29.6	29.8	35.2
Suriname	...	...	...	...	...	...	...	...	...
Trinidad and Tobago	31.3	36.5	27.2	25.6	33.8	24.7	29.5	28.7	32.5

Source: Economic Commission for Latin America and the Caribbean (ECLAC), on the basis of official figures.
[a] Preliminary figures.
[b] General government.
[c] Total revenue corresponds to revenue plus sales of financial assets.
[d] Total expenditure refers to expenditure plus investment, capital transfers and fixed capital consumption.
[e] Total revenue includes special funds and incorporates accrued revenues.
[f] Total revenue includes grants.
[g] Total expenditure includes net lending.
[h] Non-financial public sector, on an accrual basis.
[i] Public sector.
[j] Total expenditure includes not-programable expenditure.
[k] Total expenditure includes extrabudgetary expenditure and net lending.
[l] Fiscal year.

Table A-24
LATIN AMERICA AND THE CARIBBEAN: PUBLIC DEBT
(Percentages of GDP)

		Central government					Non-financial public sector			
	2005	2006	2007	2008	2009 [a]	2005	2006	2007	2008	2009 [a]
Latin America and the Caribbean	**60.2**	**53.6**	**47.2**	**45.7**	**48.0**	**51.4**	**44.8**	**38.8**	**37.8**	**38.4**
Latin America	**42.7**	**35.7**	**29.9**	**27.8**	**28.3**	**47.6**	**40.4**	**33.4**	**31.4**	**31.7**
Argentina	[b] 72.8	63.6	55.7	48.3	52.1	87.6	76.3	66.7	56.9	60.8
Bolivia (Plurinational State of)	[c] 75.6	49.8	37.1	33.8	34.7	[d] 78.3	52.6	40.0	36.7	34.3
Brazil	[e] 30.9	31.0	31.4	25.2	29.6	[f] 38.5	47.0	46.2	39.9	44.0
Chile	[g] 7.3	5.3	4.1	5.2	4.0	[g] 13.0	10.6	9.1	12.1	9.4
Colombia	[h] 39.6	37.6	32.9	33.5	35.0	[i] 50.8	47.5	43.7	42.9	43.1
Costa Rica	37.5	33.3	27.6	24.9	24.8	42.9	38.4	31.9	29.9	29.8
Dominican Republic	22.0	20.4	18.4	20.0	23.4	[j] ...	...	19.0	20.8	24.1
Ecuador	35.9	29.4	27.5	22.7	21.2	[d] 38.6	32.0	30.0	24.8	23.2
El Salvador	[c] 37.6	37.5	34.5	33.4	33.8	[d] 39.7	39.7	36.6	35.7	36.2
Guatemala	[c] 20.8	21.7	21.4	20.2	20.8	[d] 21.5	21.9	21.6	20.5	21.1
Haiti	[k] 44.1	35.6	32.2	37.6	36.5	[k] 47.5	38.1	34.5	39.6	38.4
Honduras	44.7	28.7	17.3	16.6	16.8	44.8	30.0	18.2	18.3	18.3
Mexico	[l] 20.3	20.7	21.2	24.7	27.1	[m] 23.0	22.7	23.0	27.2	34.5
Nicaragua	92.6	68.7	42.4	38.2	34.6	92.8	69.1	43.3	39.3	35.6
Panama	[n] 65.1	60.3	53.2	44.6	43.0	66.2	61.0	53.7	45.2	44.3
Paraguay	31.4	23.8	16.9	15.3	16.1	32.8	24.8	19.9	18.3	18.7
Peru	[o] 36.9	30.1	26.2	24.4	22.3	38.2	31.3	27.2	24.8	22.6
Uruguay	64.2	57.2	48.2	46.2	48.3	67.4	60.4	51.4	49.4	51.6
Venezuela (Bolivarian Republic of)	[p] 32.7	23.9	19.3	14.0	13.3	32.7	23.9	19.3	14.0	13.3
The Caribbean	**85.8**	**79.7**	**72.6**	**71.8**	**79.3**	**74.3**	**71.5**	**72.9**	**78.3**	**102.0**
Antigua and Barbuda	107.8	94.6	82.0	82.6	90.2	...	...	...	...	...
Bahamas	32.9	32.8	35.1	36.6	...	41.8	42.6	44.7	47.9	...
Barbados	82.0	79.0	84.0	88.0	101.7	99.0	95.0	101.0	103.0	116.0
Belize	79.5	75.1	71.4	82.7	86.8	82.1	76.8	72.9	84.0	88.0
Dominica	95.9	92.6	82.0	74.1	72.3	...	...	...	...	...
Grenada	109.5	112.4	107.5	100.0	95.8	...	...	...	...	...
Guyana	188.4	155.3	98.8	103.7	115.2	...	...	...	...	...
Jamaica	119.1	117.8	110.9	109.9	118.5	...	...	...	...	...
Saint Kitts and Nevis	115.1	112.0	109.4	100.7	105.2	...	...	...	...	...
Saint Vincent and the Grenadines	70.6	66.3	56.1	54.1	57.8	...	...	...	...	...
Saint Lucia	55.8	56.8	61.7	60.7	63.2	...	...	...	...	...
Suriname	38.9	24.9	28.5	25.2	25.7	...	...	...	...	...
Trinidad and Tobago	20.1	16.8	16.8	14.5	19.0	...	...	...	...	...

Source: Economic Commission for Latin America and the Caribbean (ECLAC), on the basis of official figures.
[a] Preliminary figures to June 2009.
[b] National public administration. As from 2005, does not include debt not presented for swap.
[c] Does not include publicly guaranteed private debt.
[d] Includes external debt of the non-financial public sector and domestic debt of the central government.
[e] Net public debt. Federal government and central bank.
[f] Net public debt. Public sector.
[g] Consolidated gross public debt.
[h] Central national government.
[i] Consolidated non-financial public sector.
[j] Public sector.
[k] Does not include public sector commitments to commercial banks.
[l] Federal government.
[m] Includes external debt of the public sector and domestic debt of the federal government.
[n] Does not include domestic floating debt.
[o] Includes local and regional government debt with the Banco de la Nación.
[p] Non-financial public sector.

Publicaciones de la CEPAL / *ECLAC publications*

Comisión Económica para América Latina y el Caribe / *Economic Commission for Latin America and the Caribbean*
Casilla 179-D, Santiago de Chile. E-mail: publications@cepal.org
Véalas en: www.cepal.org/publicaciones
Publications may be accessed at: www.eclac.org

Revista CEPAL / *CEPAL Review*

La Revista se inició en 1976 como parte del Programa de Publicaciones de la Comisión Económica para América Latina y el Caribe, con el propósito de contribuir al examen de los problemas del desarrollo socioeconómico de la región. Las opiniones expresadas en los artículos firmados, incluidas las colaboraciones de los funcionarios de la Secretaría, son las de los autores y, por lo tanto, no reflejan necesariamente los puntos de vista de la Organización.

La *Revista CEPAL* se publica en español e inglés tres veces por año.

Los precios de suscripción anual vigentes para 2009 son de US$ 30 para la versión en español y de US$ 35 para la versión en inglés. El precio por ejemplar suelto es de US$ 15 para ambas versiones. Los precios de suscripción por dos años (2008-2009) son de US$ 50 para la versión en español y de US$ 60 para la versión en inglés.

CEPAL Review first appeared in 1976 as part of the Publications Programme of the Economic Commission for Latin America and the Caribbean, its aim being to make a contribution to the study of the economic and social development problems of the region. The views expressed in signed articles, including those by Secretariat staff members, are those of the authors and therefore do not necessarily reflect the point of view of the Organization.

CEPAL Review is published in Spanish and English versions three times a year.

Annual subscription costs for 2009 are US$ 30 for the Spanish version and US$ 35 for the English version. The price of single issues is US$ 15 in both cases. The cost of a two-year subscription (2008-2009) is US$ 50 for Spanish-language version and US$ 60 for English.

Informes periódicos institucionales / *Annual reports*

Todos disponibles para años anteriores / *Issues for previous years also available*

- *Balance preliminar de las economías de América Latina y el Caribe, 2009, 180 p.*
  Preliminary Overview of the Economies of Latin America and the Caribbean, 2009, *172 p.*
- *Estudio económico de América Latina y el Caribe, 2008-2009, 370 p.*
  Economic Survey of Latin America and the Caribbean, 2008-2009, *362 p.*
- *Panorama de la inserción internacional de América Latina y el Caribe, 2008. Tendencias 2009, 112 p.*
  Latin America and the Caribbean in the World Economy, 2007. 2008 Trends, *100 p.*
- *Panorama social de América Latina, 2008, 262 p.*
  Social Panorama of Latin America, 2008, *256 p.*
- *La inversión extranjera directa en América Latina y el Caribe, 2008, 160 p.*
  Foreign Direct Investment of Latin America and the Caribbean, 2008, *156 p.*
- *Anuario estadístico de América Latina y el Caribe /* **Statistical Yearbook for Latin America and the Caribbean** (bilingüe/*bilingual*), 2008, 430 p.

Libros de la CEPAL

105 ***Regulation, Worker Protection and Active Labour-Market Policies in Latin America*, Jürgen Weller (ed.)**
104 *La República Dominicana en 2030: hacia una nación cohesionada*, Víctor Godínez y Jorge Máttar (coords.), 2009, 582 p.
103 *L'Amérique latine et les Caraïbes au seuil du troisième millénaire*, 2009, 138 p.
102 *Migración interna y desarrollo en América Latina entre 1980 y 2005*, Jorge Rodríguez y Gustavo Busso, 2009, 272 p.
101 *Claves de la innovación social en América Latina y el Caribe*, Adolfo Rodríguez Herrera y Hernán Alvarado Ugarte, 2009, 236 p.
100 *Envejecimiento, derechos humanos y políticas públicas*, Sandra Huenchuan (ed.), 2009, 232 p.
99 *Economía y territorio en América Latina y el Caribe. Desigualdades y políticas*, 2009, 212 p.

98 *La sociedad de la información en América Latina y el Caribe: desarrollo de las tecnologías y tecnologías para el desarrollo,* Wilson Peres y Martin Hilbert (eds.), 2009, 388 p.

97 *América Latina y el Caribe: migración internacional, derechos humanos y desarrollo,* Jorge Martínez Pizarro (ed.), 2008, 375 p.

96 *Familias y políticas públicas en América Latina: una historia de desencuentros,* Irma Arriagada (coord.), 2007, 424 p.

95 *Centroamérica y México: políticas de competencia a principios del siglo XXI,* Eugenio Rivera y Claudia Schatan (coords.), 2008, 304 p.

94 *América Latina y el Caribe: La propiedad intelectual después de los tratados de libre comercio,* Álvaro Díaz, 2008, 248 p.

93 *Tributación en América Latina. En busca de una nueva agenda de reformas,* Oscar Cetrángolo y Juan Carlos Gómez-Sabaini (comps.), 2007, 166 p.

92 *Fernando Fajnzylber. Una visión renovadora del desarrollo en América Latina,* Miguel Torres Olivos (comp.), 2006, 422 p.

91 *Cooperación financiera regional,* José Antonio Ocampo (comp.), 2006, 274 p.

90 *Financiamiento para el desarrollo. América Latina desde una perspectiva comparada,* Barbara Stallings con la colaboración de Rogério Studart, 2006, 396 p.

89 *Políticas municipales de microcrédito. Un instrumento para la dinamización de los sistemas productivos locales. Estudios de caso en América Latina,* Paola Foschiatto y Giovanni Stumpo (comps.), 2006, 244 p.

Copublicaciones recientes / *Recent co-publications*

Gobernanza corporativa y desarrollo de mercados de capitales en América Latina, Georgina Núñez, Andrés Oneto y Germano M. de Paula (coords.), CEPAL/Mayol, Colombia, 2009.

Internacionalización y expansión de las empresas eléctricas españolas en América Latina, Patricio Rozas Balbontín, CEPAL/Lom, Chile, 2009.

El nuevo escenario laboral latinoamericano. Regulación, protección y políticas activas en los mercados de trabajo, Jürgen Weller, CEPAL/Siglo XXI, Argentina, 2009,

EnREDos. Regulación y estrategias corporativas frente a la convergencia tecnológica, Marcio Wohlers y Martha García-Murillo (eds.), CEPAL/Mayol, Colombia, 2009.

Desafíos y oportunidades de la industria del software en América Latina, Paulo Tigre y Felipe Silveira Marques (eds.), CEPAL/Mayol, Colombia, 2009.

¿Quo vadis, tecnología de la información y de las comunicaciones?, Martin Hilbert y Osvaldo Cairó (eds.), CEPAL/Mayol, Colombia, 2009.

O Estruturalismo latino-americano, Octavio Rodríguez, CEPAL/Civilização Brasileira, 2009.

L'avenir de la protection sociale en Amérique latine. Accessibilité, financement et solidarité, CEPALC/Eska, France, 2009.

Fortalecer los sistemas de pensiones latinoamericanos. Cuentas individuales por reparto, Robert Holzmann, Edward Palmer y Andras Uthoff (eds.), CEPAL/Mayol, Colombia, 2008.

Competition Policies in Emerging Economies. Lessons and Challenges from Central America and Mexico, Claudia Schatan and Eugenio Rivera Urrutia (eds.), ECLAC/Springer, USA, 2008.

Estratificación y movilidad social en América Latina. Transformaciones estructurales en un cuarto de siglo, Rolando Franco, Arturo León y Raúl Atria (coords.), CEPAL/Lom, Chile, 2007.

Economic growth with equity. Challenges for Latin America, Ricardo Ffrench-Davis and José Luis Machinea (eds.), ECLAC/Palgrave Macmillan, United Kingdom, 2007.

Mujer y empleo. La reforma de la salud y la salud de la reforma en Argentina, María Nieves Rico y Flavia Marco (coords.), CEPAL/Siglo XXI, Argentina, 2006.

El estructuralismo latinoamericano, Octavio Rodríguez, CEPAL/Siglo XXI, México, 2006.

Gobernabilidad corporativa, responsabilidad social y estrategias empresariales en América Latina, Germano M. de Paula, João Carlos Ferraz y Georgina Núñez (comps.), CEPAL/Mayol, Colombia, 2006.

Desempeño económico y política social en América Latina y el Caribe. Los retos de la equidad, el desarrollo y la ciudadanía, Ana Sojo y Andras Uthoff (comps.), CEPAL/Flacso-México/ Fontamara, México, 2006.

Política y políticas públicas en los procesos de reforma de América Latina, Rolando Franco y Jorge Lanzaro (coords.), CEPAL/Flacso-México/Miño y Dávila, México, 2006.

Finance for Development. Latin America in Comparative Perspective, Barbara Stallings with Rogério Studart, ECLAC/Brookings Institution Press, USA, 2006.

Coediciones recientes / *Recent co-editions*

Perspectivas de la agricultura y del desarrollo rural en las Américas: una mirada hacia América Latina y el Caribe 2009, CEPAL/FAO/ICCA, Chile, 2009.

El envejecimiento y las personas de edad. Indicadores sociodemográficos para América Latina y el Caribe, CEPAL/UNFPA, 2009.

Espacios iberoamericanos: la economía del conocimiento, CEPAL/SEGIB, Chile, 2008.

Hacia la revisión de los paradigmas del desarrollo en América Latina, Oscar Altimir, Enrique V. Iglesias, José Luis Machinea (eds.), CEPAL/SEGIB, Chile, 2008.

Por uma revisão dos paradigmas do desenvolvimento na América Latina, Oscar Altimir, Enrique V. Iglesias, José Luis Machinea (eds.), CEPAL/SEGIB, Chile, 2008.

Las publicaciones de la Comisión Económica para América Latina y el Caribe (CEPAL) y las del Instituto
Latinoamericano y del Caribe de Planificación Económica y Social (ILPES) se pueden adquirir a los
distribuidores locales o directamente a través de:

Publicaciones de las Naciones Unidas
2 United Nations Plaza, Room DC2-853
Nueva York, NY, 10017
Estados Unidos
Tel. (1 800)253-9646 Fax (1 212)963-3489
E-mail: publications@un.org

Publicaciones de las Naciones Unidas
Sección de Ventas
Palais des Nations
1211 Ginebra 10
Suiza
Tel. (41 22)917-2613 Fax (41 22)917-0027

Unidad de Distribución
Comisión Económica para América Latina y el Caribe (CEPAL)
Av. Dag Hammarskjöld 3477, Vitacura
7630412 Santiago
Chile
Tel. (56 2)210-2056 Fax (56 2)210-2069
E-mail: publications@cepal.org

*Publications of the Economic Commission for Latin America and the Caribbean (ECLAC) and those of the
Latin American and the Caribbean Institute for Economic and Social Planning (ILPES) can be ordered from
your local distributor or directly through:*

*United Nations Publications
2 United Nations Plaza, Room DC2-853
New York, NY, 10017*
USA
*Tel. (1 800)253-9646 Fax (1 212)963-3489
E-mail: publications@un.org*

*United Nations Publications
Sales Sections
Palais des Nations
1211 Geneva 10*
Switzerland
Tel. (41 22)917-2613 Fax (41 22)917-0027

*Distribution Unit
Economic Commission for Latin America and the Caribbean (ECLAC)
Av. Dag Hammarskjöld 3477, Vitacura
7630412 Santiago*
Chile
*Tel. (56 2)210-2056 Fax (56 2)210-2069
E-mail: publications@eclac.org*

Hacia un nuevo pacto social. Políticas económicas para un desarrollo integral en América Latina, José Luis Machinea y Narcís Serra (eds.) CEPAL/CIDOB, España, 2008.

Espacios iberoamericanos: comercio e inversión, CEPAL/SEGIB, Chile, 2007.

Espaços Ibero-Americanos: comércio e investimento, CEPAL/SEGIB, Chile, 2007.

Visiones del desarrollo en América Latina, José Luis Machinea y Narcís Serra (eds.), CEPAL/CIDOB, España, 2007.

Cohesión social: inclusión y sentido de pertenencia en América Latina y el Caribe, CEPAL/SEGIB, Chile, 2007.

Social Cohesion. Inclusion and a sense of belonging in Latin America and the Caribbean, ECLAC/SEGIB, Chile, 2007.

Cuadernos de la CEPAL

93 *Privilegiadas y discriminadas. Las trabajadoras del sector financiero*, Flavia Marco Navarro y María Nieves Rico Ibáñez (eds.), 2009, 300 p.

92 *Estadísticas para la equidad de género: magnitudes y tendencias en América Latina*, Vivian Milosavljevic, 2007, 186 pp.

91 *Elementos conceptuales para la prevención y reducción de daños originados por amenazas naturales*, Eduardo Chaparro y Matías Renard (eds.), 2005, 144 p.

90 *Los sistemas de pensiones en América Latina: un análisis de género*, Flavia Marco (coord.), 2004, 270 p.

89 *Energía y desarrollo sustentable en América Latina y el Caribe. Guía para la formulación de políticas energéticas*, 2003, 240 p.

88 *La ciudad inclusiva*, Marcello Balbo, Ricardo Jordán y Daniela Simioni (comps.), CEPAL/Cooperazione Italiana, 2003, 322 p.

87 **Traffic congestion. The problem and how to deal with it**, Alberto Bull (comp.), 2004, 198 p.

Cuadernos estadísticos de la CEPAL

36 *Clasificaciones estadísticas internacionales incorporadas en el Banco de Datos de Comercio Exterior de América Latina y el Caribe de la CEPAL (Revisión 3). Solo disponible en CD*, 2008.

35 *Resultados del Programa de Comparación Internacional para América del Sur. Solo disponible en CD*, 2007.

34 *Indicadores económicos del turismo. Solo disponible en CD*, 2006.

33 *América Latina y el Caribe. Balanza de pagos 1980-2005. Solo disponible en CD*, 2006.

32 *América Latina y el Caribe. Series regionales y oficiales de cuentas nacionales, 1950-2002. Solo disponible en CD*, 2005.

Observatorio demográfico *ex Boletín demográfico* / *Demographic Observatory* formerly *Demographic Bulletin* (bilingüe/*bilingual*)

Edición bilingüe (español e inglés) que proporciona información estadística actualizada, referente a estimaciones y proyecciones de población de los países de América Latina y el Caribe. Incluye también indicadores demográficos de interés, tales como tasas de natalidad, mortalidad, esperanza de vida al nacer, distribución de la población, etc.

El Observatorio aparece dos veces al año, en los meses de enero y julio. Suscripción anual: US$ 20.00. Valor por cada ejemplar: US$ 15.00.

Bilingual publication (Spanish and English) proving up-to-date estimates and projections of the populations of the Latin American and Caribbean countries. Also includes various demographic indicators of interest such as fertility and mortality rates, life expectancy, measures of population distribution, etc.

The Observatory appears twice a year in January and July. Annual subscription: US$ 20.00. Per issue: US$ 15.00.

Notas de población

Revista especializada que publica artículos e informes acerca de las investigaciones más recientes sobre la dinámica demográfica en la región, en español, con resúmenes en español e inglés. También incluye información sobre actividades científicas y profesionales en el campo de población.

La revista se publica desde 1973 y aparece dos veces al año, en junio y diciembre.

Suscripción anual: US$ 20.00. Valor por cada ejemplar: US$ 12.00.

Specialized journal which publishes articles and reports on recent studies of demographic dynamics in the region, in Spanish with abstracts in Spanish and English. Also includes information on scientific and professional activities in the field of population.

Published since 1973, the journal appears twice a year in June and December.

Annual subscription: US$ 20.00. Per issue: US$ 12.00.

Series de la CEPAL

Comercio internacional / *Desarrollo productivo* / *Desarrollo territorial* / *Estudios estadísticos y prospectivos* / *Estudios y perspectivas* (Bogotá, Brasilia, Buenos Aires, México, Montevideo) / **Studies and Perspectives** (The Caribbean, Washington) / *Financiamiento del desarrollo* / *Gestión pública* / *Informes y estudios especiales* / *Macroeconomía del desarrollo* / *Manuales* / *Medio ambiente y desarrollo* / *Mujer y desarrollo* / *Población y desarrollo* / *Políticas sociales* / *Recursos naturales e infraestructura* / *Seminarios y conferencias.*

Véase el listado completo en: www.cepal.org/publicaciones / *A complete listing is available at*: www.cepal.org/publicaciones